THE
OFFICIAL®
IDENTIFICATION
AND
PRICE
GUIDE TO

Silver &
Silverplate

JERI SCHWARTZ

SIXTH EDITION

HOUSE OF COLLECTIBLES • NEW YORK

© 1989 by Jeri Schwartz

All rights reserved under International and Pan-American Copyright Conventions.

Published by: The House of Collectibles
201 East 50th Street
New York, New York 10022

Distributed by Ballantine Books, a division of Random House, Inc., New York, and simultaneously in Canada by Random House of Canada Limited, Toronto.

Manufactured in the United States of America

ISBN: 0-876-37784-3

Sixth Edition: November 1989

10 9 8 7 6 5 4 3 2 1

For My Father

Table of Contents

Silver and Silverplate Listings

Acknowledgments

I gratefully acknowledge the assistance of the following people in preparing this book: Joan and Sidney Cohen; Ruth Crocker of Christie's East, New York; Helaine and Burton Fendelman; Joy Freeman; Marin Gantz; Marilyn Goldberg; Linda and Tom Grande; Harriet and Irwin Green; Alice and Derek Hamilton; Stephen Helliwell of Christie's South Kensington, London; Rochelle and Peter Kassai; Jolie Lieb of Christie's East, New York; Shirley and Jerry Sprung; Nancy and Bruce Thompson.

I am grateful to the following auction houses for their help: Richard Bourne; Butterfield & Butterfield; Christie's East, New York; Christie's Park Avenue, New York; Christie's South Kensington, London; William Doyle; Richard Oliver; Phillips, London; San Rafael Auction Gallery; Robert W. Skinner; and Wolf's Auction Gallery.

A special thanks to Jean Auslander for the photography.

Introduction

⧫⧫⧫

This book is an overview of the sterling silver and silverplate market today, with special emphasis on areas rarely appearing in earlier price guides. The field of antiques collecting, including sterling silver and silverplate, is cyclical; it fluctuates as interest in particular types of objects peaks or wanes. Museum and gallery shows and new research and publications stimulate dealers, collectors, appraisers, and the general public.

Chinese and Chicago silver, Arts and Crafts, and other specialties, including needlework tools and writing accessories, are discussed. On the rise, part of a rapidly developing market and also part of the book, are Judaica and sports collectibles.

Areas formerly devoted to the Franklin Mint have been deleted because they no longer have an impact on the marketplace. The souvenir spoon category has been reduced because this collectible is not enjoying favor at present.

Prices were gathered from auction catalogs, antiques trade publications, antiques shows, and flea markets. Dimensions are given if they are mentioned in catalogs. Unless otherwise noted, all items listed are sterling silver.

In the sterling silver and silverplate field there are a number of factors to bear in mind. For example, a Tiffany piece will be priced substantially higher than a similar piece by another, lesser-known manufacturer. Scarcity of particular forms has great impact on prices. Most vinaigrettes average $200 to $1,000 in price. However, a vinaigrette by a desirable maker, a figural, or a unique example containing a music box can command up to $5,000.

Occasionally, there is a crossover of categories within the book. A Tiffany Art Deco bowl may be listed under Art Deco, Tiffany, or American hollowware. Tiffany, Gorham, Kirk, and Georg Jensen are so collectible in America that they have also been discussed and priced in separate sections. Odd bits, such as luggage tags, are in the Miscellaneous section.

Every collector and dealer dreams of the *score*, a fantasy come true—finding a 17th-century treasure in an auction box lot, in an obscure, dusty corner of a shop, hidden at the tag sale around the corner, or in the local church's rummage sale. Here's hoping this book will help you find your score. Good luck!

Silver & Silverplate

Antique or Collectible?

~~~~~~~~~~~~~~~~

Antique is defined in the dictionary as a decorated object, piece of furniture, or other work of art created in an earlier period and valued for its beauty, workmanship, and age. Though we are often in awe of antique objects, we sometimes forget that antiques were functional, essential items made for *people*. They were used for everyday living, for cooking, sewing, or decorating. Antiques really form a record of social history.

According to the U.S. Customs Service, art objects are defined as antiques when they are over 100 years old.

Collectibles are the newest phenomenon in the collecting boom. A collectible is usually a mass-produced item of more recent manufacture. Unfortunately, today many people are enticed to buy "future collectibles" that will probably have no long-term value. One of these is the series of Franklin Mint collector plates manufactured for a willing market, made in extremely large quantities and having little art value. Heavy advertising has resulted in many unsuspecting collectors having paid extremely high prices for pieces retaining little other than scrap silver value.

Antique sterling silver and silverplate appear to be good investments because there are fewer quality pieces available. Unusual antique pieces generally increase in value, while those purchased "brand new" are simply secondhand after a few years.

Don't buy just because you think you see a good investment. Fashions change in antiques; therefore, you should really like what you buy because you may not be able to sell it quickly; and if you change your mind, you may have to live with the piece or pieces for awhile.

The Market

In the sterling silver market today, pieces are judged by age, quality, condition, and weight, though weight is not nearly as important as in prior years.

During the mad silver rush (1979–1980) stimulated by the brothers Hunt in Texas, the price of meltable scrap silver escalated to $40 to $50 per troy ounce. Everyone bought sterling silver with a scale and never looked at marks or decoration. Unfortunately, this period of inflated prices saw the melting of exquisite 17th-, 18th-, and 19th-century pieces, including those by Storr, de Lamerie, Colonial American silversmiths, and manufacturers such as Tiffany, Gorham, and Kirk. Today we are no longer scrapping early and/or fine sterling silver hollowware and flatware.

The fashions in sterling—as in other antiques and collectibles—change. Today collectors and dealers look for evidence of hand chasing and embossing, fine engraving, and full-figure and enameled objects. Craftsmanship from all periods is highly desired.

In America the Tiffany mark is charismatic, and prices continue to escalate, especially for pieces with earlier Moore or Broadway marks. Recent sales in applied metals in the Japonesque taste by Tiffany, Gorham, and Shiebler have upset prior auction records. Huge centerpieces with matching plateaus are eagerly sought, especially when surmounted by medallion heads, animals, or human figures, particularly those made by Gorham or Ball, Black & Company. The current interest in mid- and late-19th-century American pieces has brought many Gothic and Renaissance Revival sterling silver compotes, tureens, and pitchers to the auction rooms.

Kirk or other embossed Baltimore styles by Schofield, Schultz, Steiff, and Jacobi & Jenkins continue to be popular. Pieces from the early 19th century with hand-chased details command the best prices.

Prices of "name" pieces spiral upward while more mundane objects by International Sterling, Towle, and Lunt remain flat. Most machine-made early-20th-century silver is still being offered by weight. Flatware pieces have experienced the same trend, with Tiffany continuing to be the best seller; while esoteric serving pieces by Gorham, Shiebler, Unger Brothers, and Whiting are in greatest demand. Large serving pieces, punch ladles, asparagus servers, salad sets, and sandwich tongs are most desirable.

Tiffany flatware sets in desirable patterns are generally dealer-priced in the range of $50 to $75 per piece. Patterns deemed uninteresting, such as Gorham Etruscan, average $10 to $15 per piece. Monogrammed flatware pieces are usually priced a little lower.

American silverplate is generating great interest in the United States and abroad; American pieces now appear in English auction catalogs and sales. Important pieces, including centerpiece bowls, punch bowls, the Magic Castor, and huge water sets, are setting higher prices than ever before.

The market for good American silverplate began several years ago in California and has moved eastward, with more dealers exhibiting silverplate booths at major shows. The lower-priced pieces continue to be ashtrays, card holders, and small trays. Most collectors look for pieces made before 1900 and tend to avoid those with embossed Dutch figure scenes and later marks. Several interesting black figural silverplated pieces have appeared; their appeal is not only to silverplate collectors but also to those collecting black memorabilia.

Collecting Sterling Silver and Silverplate

❦

Once you have decided that sterling silver or silverplate is your forte, then prepare yourself by attending every museum and gallery exhibition and every major antique show possible. Once there, *ask questions* so that you will continue to learn. Along the way you should also be accumulating a library of magazines and books. *Read* them. *Study* them. Subscribing to specialist magazines and auction catalogs will keep you abreast of the market action and inform you of new research in the field.

Whether one is a dealer or collector, there are a number of guidelines to use when judging an object prior to purchase. When judging a piece of silver, note condition and marks. Are they genuine? Is the piece of the period—Queen Anne or Victorian—or an early-20th-century copy in the style of an earlier period? Many people have been hoodwinked by the "looks just like" syndrome. You have found a similar piece, but to be truly period—or "right," as the experts note—the piece has to be *exact*. Get out your magnifying glass and check marks. Then decide if the style corresponds to the age indicated by the hallmark. Check hollowware for bruises, dents, holes, and solder marks. Look at cast finials to see if they have been married to the piece—that is, taken from another piece and added to this one to seem as if always there. Carefully examine engraving and chasing to make sure it is crisp and original. Has the piece been overpolished or buffed to hide repairs?

Examine the best examples of the period, whether 18th-century French sterling or late-19th-century American silverplate. Keep in mind that only by handling the pieces will you be able to remember which item is authentic when you're alone at a flea market in the rain!

During your travels you may find it helpful to carry books giving world marks, English hallmarks, and American manufacturers. Having an accessible up-to-date price guide is probably a good idea too.

When items are in demand, reproductions begin to appear on the market. Currently, silverplate figural napkin rings have peaked in price, and forgeries have reappeared. About ten years ago figural napkin rings were first reproduced, and now they are again showing up at auctions and flea markets. Generally, the castings on both of these later reproductions are not as sharp as on the original items. In addition, simple silverplate napkin rings have had full-figure cats, dogs, birds, and Kate Greenaway children added to raise the price. On these one can sometimes see recent solder marks or replaced tiny screws holding the figure in place. Silverplate specialist Joy Freeman mentions that unscrupulous people are altering slow-selling silverplate card receivers: removing the top from a figural napkin ring and adding it to the remaining base, thereby creating a more desirable and higher-priced piece. The new piece is referred to in the trade as "put together" or a "monkey."

In England many sterling silver matchsafes, cigar cutters, and snuffboxes are appearing on the market. When they were originally made in the late 19th century, they were made in brass or silverplate. The sterling silver copies have greater appeal to the tourist trade. Sterling silver copies of posey holders, made in Portugal, are appearing in U.S. markets. Most are crudely cast in comparison to an original.

No matter when or what you buy, be sure to get a sales check with full information regarding the piece, its dating, marks, and maker's name, where known. For high-priced major purchases, the dealer's name and address should be on the bill. If a piece is unmarked but represented as sterling silver, it is a good idea to have this information indicated on the sales check.

Remember that no matter what you buy you should very much like, if not love, the piece. And above all, enjoy the chase!

Pricing Sterling Silver

〜〜〜

𝒫resentation or commemorative pieces, pieces with historical or political provenance, or highly unusual pieces will bring the highest prices. Items belonging to show business personalities, such as Liberace, John Lennon, or Rock Hudson, or to a member of the Rockefeller or Vanderbilt family, carry a higher monetary value—for a single object or a collection.

When buying, do not listen to the dealer who says, "I bought it from the Hearst estate" or "It came from a wealthy family." These were the key selling sentences several years ago. Be advised to use your own judgment and look at the style, decoration, size, and detailing of the item. They are the first things to look for when contemplating a purchase. If all of these factors look good, then determine the provenance.

Common pieces, such as plain teaspoons and tablespoons, remain low-priced. The same piece, with figural motifs, bright-cut engraving, and regional characteristics or bearing the name of a "good" maker, increases in price considerably. Decorated hollowware with figural Indians, animals, explorers, and elaborate cutwork medallions or engraving by such well-known American makers as Tiffany, Gorham, and Kirk bring the highest prices. Simple, machine-made, unadorned pieces, including vegetable dishes, gravy boats, and tea services—referred to as wedding present silver in the trade—are generally priced by scrap weight and do not increase in value.

Other important factors to determine are condition, completeness, and amount of restoration. Are all of the parts "of the period," or are some later additions? If the maker is unlisted in your book of marks, check city directories.

Buying . . .
Buying . . .
Buying

⌒⌒⌒◆⌒⌒⌒

If you do your homework, auction buying can be very exciting. Major auction houses offer catalogs describing the objects. Since most have disclaimers regarding condition and provenance, it is best to examine the item personally. If you are far away and wish to bid by phone, ask ahead of time for information regarding condition and marks.

Previewing the objects really is an essential step before buying at auction. Go early enough to allow time to preview the pieces; use your reference books to check marks. Discuss price estimates, bidding, and premiums with the auctioneer at this time. It is best to set a limit for yourself, or you'll be carried away in the excitement.

Don't be lulled into thinking country auctions have everything at good value. Small country, and even city, auctions can be treasure troves or places where dealers dump mistakes. Box lots may contain a sleeper, so be sure to check them out.

Don't be afraid of dealers and heavy-duty collectors at an auction. Equality rules.

Whether they are called tag sales, garage sales, or estate sales, these popular marketplaces can be excellent sources of sterling silver and silverplate. Many collectors and dealers wait all night when a sale with silver and silverplate is advertised by a reliable tag sale promoter in a good neighborhood. Quite often, the goods are priced a great deal lower than at an auction. Once again, because it bears repeating, check the item before you buy. Sometimes it is difficult to examine pieces and make rational decisions with someone literally breathing down your back. If you are lucky and buy often enough from tag sale promoters, they will generally inform you if there is something of interest for you in their next sale. Always keep in mind that auction and tag sale pieces are often sold in ''as found'' condition.

Mail order buying through trade papers can be quite reliable. Many mail order dealers specialize and keep want lists. Before mailing your check or money order and if you have any doubts, verify the reliability of the dealer with other dealers or with the newspaper. Also, make sure you are able to return the piece (within a reasonable time) if it is not as described in the advertisement. Be sure to get a detailed sales slip with your purchase.

An afternoon of popping into shops to look for something for your collection can be very social. Many collectors take excursions to the country complete with picnic basket or planned stops at charming country inns. For those who live in big cities, major shopping areas offer a variety of possible stops in one location, including antiques galleries, auction houses, and museums.

In an antiques shop, poking through old sewing boxes may reward the collector with buttons, matchsafes, needlework tools, thimbles, or other small items. Flatware trays often have sterling silver and silverplate mixed together. Don't be turned away because a dealer specializes in country items when you're seeking silver. Simple candlesticks, tea caddies, and snuffs may be in these shops.

Buying at antique shows and flea markets can also be an exciting and rewarding experience. Many shows have hundreds of dealers with a great variety of merchandise, but smaller shows can be good sources too. Many show dealers maintain want lists and make phone calls to interested customers when they buy new merchandise. Guarantees regarding authenticity are usually more readily available at the bigger, established shows, but caveat emptor still prevails.

If you are contemplating an important purchase, whether at an auction, a shop, or a show, it often pays to hire a qualified appraiser to examine the artwork regarding authenticity and pricing. After the purchase, the item should be insured, with the valuation in writing.

How to Make a Deal

A great deal of the fun of collecting can be bargaining. Remember your mother's advice: being polite gets you more! Remember also that a dealer has to make a profit. A good place to start the negotiations is to ask nicely if the dealer can possibly do a bit better. Don't *ever*, no *never*, say you'll give X amount of money. This is extremely offensive. If you're buying several items, group them together and ask if there's a better price if you buy them all. Dickering is best achieved by an open, honest discussion without finding or mentioning problems with the piece. Counteroffers in the same vein are acceptable.

Caveat Emptor

When you are in the marketplace buying the goods, you are the final judge. Relying on someone else can cause problems. Here are some pointers to help you make the right decisions.

1. Buy in daylight—check marks.

2. Are all decorative elements matching?

3. Is the piece really period or "in the style of"?

4. Is the balance correct?

5. Is the piece dented?

6. Are there solder drips inside or outside the piece?

7. Has the piece been covered with excessive dirt to cover solder or broken seams?

8. Does a hollowware piece have an indentation or dimple to indicate removal of monogram?

9. Blow gently on what appears to be a blank space on silver hollowware to see if a monogram has been removed—moisture from your breath will outline the erased mark.

10. Fill teapots or pitchers with water—are there pinholes?

11. Are pairs two *similar* pieces or truly a pair?

12. Did flatware pieces begin as a matching set or have they been assembled?

13. Are you buying a vinaigrette or a box with the addition of a grille?

14. Are you buying a brooch or a buckle with a pin added?

15. Are you buying a tiny frame or brooch with a back added?

16. Do all chatelaine pieces match?

17. If the piece is stamped Tiffany or Cartier, is the mark "right"?

18. Does the lid fit properly on boxes, teapots, tea caddies, and powder jars? Check the hinges for alignment, resoldering, or replacement.

19. Examine handles to see if they are original to the piece.

20. Have the cuff links been converted from buttons?

21. Beware: French metal is simply a term for patinated base metals that look like bronze, also called spelter in the United Kingdom; and French ivory refers to celluloid, which was used a great deal in the 1920s and 1930s and looks like ivory.

22. A casting taken from an original will reproduce the piece including the original *hallmarks*.

23. Hold silver thimbles and box lids to light to check for pinholes and solder marks.

24. Hold sterling overlay pieces to strong light to check for cracks—don't forget insides of rims.

25. Check porcelain pieces with sterling overlay under black (ultraviolet) light for repairs and restorations.

The "score" is what keeps every collector and dealer in the marketplace. Haunt shops, markets, galleries, and house sales. There are still many undiscovered pieces.

Fakes, Forgeries, Reproductions, Restorations

Castor in the style of Francis I, faked with a combination of unmatched marks, c. 1880. **Courtesy of Alice and Derek Hamilton.**

Fake—a deliberate copy made to fool the buyer (a fraud).

Forgery—same as above because both are made in a period style to look original.

In the style of—made to look as if created at an earlier time, not a period piece. Example: Cellini vase made in the 20th century in the manner of the original 17th-century piece.

Marriage—two or more parts from different pieces used to form a new one. Example: Full-figure animal added to top of simple sterling silver box to increase the value of the box.

Monkey—an object to which additional decorative features have been added so that the value of the piece increases. Example: New enameled scenes added to sterling silver compacts, matchsafes, or cigarette cases bearing earlier marks.

Period—having the style characteristics of the era within which the object was made.

Reproduction—copy of an earlier piece, often made as a decorative item and not meant to deceive the buyer. Example: Unmarked museum gift shop reproduction sometimes later offered to as an original.

Restoration—replacement of parts that have been lost through time or usage. Extensive repairs or restorations will affect value.

Right—all of the various parts of the piece, including marks, patina, and style, are correct for the time in which the object was supposed to have been made.

Before You Buy

～⌒○⌒～

1. Read—go to museums—*read*—talk with collectors—*read*.

2. Check the piece for age, marks, condition.

3. Ask for written sales slip stating age, origin, and condition, with guarantee stating the piece is as represented, signed and dated by the seller.

4. Ask if the piece has been exhibited at a gallery or museum show because this usually increases value.

5. Look for a reputable dealer. You might want to ask other dealers because most good dealers have an excellent reputation with others in the trade.

6. Although bargains exist, be wary of extremely low prices because they can be an indication of a problem piece that can become an expensive mistake.

7. Put your money on the line and buy the piece because that will teach you faster than any other method.

8. Above all, love the piece you're buying.

Care—Less
Is Better

∽◦∽◦∽

The best way to keep silver looking its best is to use it, enjoy it, wash it in warm soapy water, rinse it, and dry it. With everyday use, extensive polishing is unnecessary.

To clean your silver, use a mild, nonabrasive cream polish. After applying polish, rinse the piece thoroughly and do not allow traces of the polish to sink into the cracks or embossing because this will erode the surface. A soft toothbrush is very good for those hard-to-work areas. Use hot water for the final rinse and dry the piece thoroughly with a soft, worn towel.

The oil from your skin can cause stains on silver surfaces. Most dealers and collectors recommend wearing soft cotton gloves to avoid finger marks on silver. *Do not ever—no, never*—use a silver or chemical dip. In addition to removing a layer of silver, dipping wipes away all of the years of lovely hand-polished patina and leaves a horrible white finish. Most dipping processes are guaranteed to remove tarnish quickly. Also, do not have a piece of early silver machine-buffed because, again, you are removing the lovely "butler's finish."

Flannel Pacific cloth is best for storing silver. Do not wrap silver in plastic bags because, with extremes of heat and cold, the plastic leaves marks on the silver that have to be buffed off by machine.

Never put silver in the dishwasher. The soap will pit the silver, and hollow handles can be ruined by the heating process.

United States Markets

When you want to buy or sell antique silver or silverplate, read trade papers, auction flyers, and show giveaways for places where the dealers congregate.

My favorite place each spring, summer, and fall is Brimfield, Massachusetts, a tiny New England town where dealers and collectors—thousands of them—converge by van, car, motorcycle, and bike. Different markets open every day, with collectors scurrying from one to the next and with trading going on in the lines for admission, in motel rooms, restaurants, everywhere. Outdoor spaces with tents and tables or backs of station wagons are used to display every type of merchandise. Although I feel that May's and The Girls offer the best opportunity for collectors and dealers, sterling silver and silverplate treasures have been found in all of the markets. Make sure you're there for the opening and dress for all types of weather. Snow, monsoons, and heat waves have all been known to happen in one day. Take cash and a carryall bag. Be prepared to bargain slightly. Do not hesitate at this market, or you'll surely lose your piece. This is no market for the indecisive. From 17th-century reliquaries to Art Moderne sterling silver, it's there, somewhere. Sterling silver pocket sundials, thimbles, épergnes, flatware, and silverplate water sets can be found among quilts, wooden Indians, 18th-century period furniture, and lots of kitsch.

Also for those with stamina, twice a year the Stella New York Pier Shows boast 600 dealers exhibiting on three piers overlooking the Hudson River. This show, similar to the original mid-20th-century Madison Square Garden extravaganza, has items ranging in price from a few dollars to a million. The piers are categorized according to interest, but you will find it fascinating and probably necessary to visit all three piers because they are such great sources. Dealers and collectors fly from the West Coast, London, and Europe particularly for this event. Experienced dealers, collectors, and novices rub shoulders, and everyone seems to find something special.

Foreign Markets

For those with traveling shoes, I strongly recommend buying in England, though the flea markets in Paris, Amsterdam, and Brussels can also be good sources.

In England, the markets in Bermondsey, Portobello Road, and Camden Passage offer the best buying. Shopping Bermondsey begins by flashlight at 3:30 or 4 in the morning. Be careful here because it is extremely difficult for the novice to judge marks or repairs by flashlight. Watch the "big silver boys" and see if you can judge the next trend by their pattern of buying. Most of the serious buying is over by 9 A.M.; after that, the market is best left for the tourists.

Portobello Road on Saturday is meant for those with stamina. It requires running up and down the hill because the various arcades open at different times. Remember that much wheeling and dealing goes on in the parked cars before the stalls open. By 6 A.M. the whole street comes to life, and it is easy to find sterling silver and silverplate in great quantities.

Camden Passage has an open-air market on Wednesdays and Saturdays. Again, activity begins at dawn and continues until about 3 P.M. There are many indoor markets here as well. The more sophisticated dealers here are in the building called the Mall.

Don't forget Gray's Market and Antiquarius (both are antiques centers) for sterling silver and silverplate. Also, check the newspaper for the Sunday fairs in the hotels.

When you buy, don't forget to get a receipt! You may want to take your own carrier bag to all outdoor markets because they are not generally supplied. An umbrella is always a must in London! Flashlights are not willingly shared—be prepared!

In Paris there is a three-day-weekend, year-round, indoor-outdoor market on the outskirts of the city, easily reached by Metro. The market offers everything from old clothes to vintage and new Lalique (glass). High-style French and Continental silver can be seen and purchased there also. A knowledge of

French is usually helpful when one negotiates prices.

Brussels has year-round outdoor markets on Saturday and Sunday. One is near the railroad station, and the other is near the Grand Place, both good sources for needlework tools, corkscrews, and other small objects. There is also a weekly outdoor market in Amsterdam in the center of town that offers a wide variety.

A good way to find the newest markets wherever you are is to ask a local dealer.

Appraisers

One needs a qualified appraiser for evaluating objects prior to making an expensive purchase or for seeing that objects you own are adequately insured for current replacement costs. If you decide to offer something from your collection as a gift to your favorite charity and the value exceeds $5,000, you will need an appraiser to place a value on the item. You may want to know the value of the furnishings that your recently deceased favorite aunt left you. If so, call an appraiser.

A good way to find one is to ask your friends, your lawyer, your accountant, your bank, your insurance company, or your favorite antiques dealer.

There are a few questions you can ask to find out if the appraiser is qualified to handle what you own, such as "Do you belong to one of the three major appraisal organizations?" (See list below.) Membership shows an expertise in various areas and years of experience. Ask for a client list and sample appraisal. Remember that an appraisal should state the purpose and the date conducted, as well as the age, country of origin, condition, and size of a piece. Make sure also that the document is signed by the person doing the job. It is a good idea, if you are selling a piece, not to have the person who is buying it be the one to put a price on it. What will be the cost for the appraisal? *Never, ever,* accept charges on a percentage basis. Fees should be based on an hourly rate. An excellent starting place is a contract stating what the appraiser will do and when, how much you owe and when, and what is to be appraised.

You may call any of the groups listed below to get a recommendation for a qualified appraiser in your area:

Appraisers Association of America
60 East 42nd Street
New York, NY 10165
212-867-9775

American Society of Appraisers
P.O. Box 17265
Washington, DC 20041
703-478-2228

International Society of Appraisers
P.O. Box 726
Hoffman Estates, IL 60195
312-882-0706

History

~~~~~~~~~~~~~~~~~~~~~~~~~~

From earliest times, silver and gold have been used for precious metalwork. Many different decorative motifs were used to create beautiful objects.

During major wars, outstanding silver pieces were melted down and used to finance the battles. Church silver was generally spared this fate because of the holy attribution. Often sacred objects were buried to save them from pillaging.

The Middle Ages saw the use of a great deal of gilding of silver pieces to achieve a rich appearance. Design books illustrating patterns for the silversmith also were introduced in this period.

From the late 17th century until the middle of the 18th century, most silver designs were influenced by architects and furniture makers in England and Europe. Dutch influences were also in vogue in England at this time, soon followed by a taste for chinoiserie.

In the reign of Louis XIV in France, the Baroque style disappeared, and silver designs were often geometric and more formal. The 18th century in England began with a simple form known as Queen Anne style, and 18th-century American styles copied English designs.

Louis XV introduced the style called Regency in 1715, with decorations becoming more important than the form of the object. Influences were classical heads, pendant husks, and strapwork motifs. In England the mid-1700s brought the Rococo style, with elaborate shellwork borders and S- and C-scrolls. This was followed by neoclassical design. Based on the "Greek taste"—a result of the excitement over the excavations in Italy in the 1740s—this was referred to as Regency style. Paterae, palmettes, festoons, rams' heads, and masks, often in relief, were typical of this era. American pieces also made great use of neoclassicism.

By the mid-19th century many silversmiths had given up the craft for lack of business or had entered into industrial methods of producing silver. Gothic style, which used naturalistic motifs and engraved details, was the new interest. In America, neoclassical revivals were popular again during the 1860s and 1870s.

At the end of the century the Arts and Crafts and Art Nouveau movements began and were popular until World War I. The early 20th century produced both hand-wrought and commercial silver pieces, such as objects made by the Wiener Werkstätte and the Ashbee School of Handicrafts. This was followed by the Art Moderne style, which is now called Art Deco.

Today we enjoy silver made in England, the United States, Denmark, and other European countries, most of which has been created for the mass market.

American Coin and Pseudohallmarks

~~~~~~~~∞∞~~~~~~~~

Hallmarking, as used in England, did not exist in the United States. Therefore, the Colonial silversmiths were able to mark without supervision by a guild or assayer's office. A few did not keep to the standard of sterling silver, but no hallmarking laws were ever passed. During the 18th century, American sterling silver marks consisted of the maker's name and/or initials, stars, eagles, shields, and birds' heads.

Most of the American silversmiths worked in the coin (.900) standard, though in early American silver the fineness was sometimes well below this standard. Coin silver was truly made from old coins, which varied from .800 to .900 in quality. Most silver pieces were stamped "COIN," "PURE COIN," "DOLLAR," "PREMIUM," or "STANDARD." This indicated that the piece was at least the quality of the American silver dollar. Makers' marks and town marks were also used in conjunction with the above.

While most Americans were proud of being in a new land, they were happiest when their silver bore English hallmarks. Thus in America, silver began to appear with pseudohallmarks bearing more than a slight resemblance to English marks. The stamped marks are usually about the same size, shape, and motif as those on English wares, and it is thought that many people assumed they were purchasing English silver.

To lull us into thinking pieces were of English manufacture, letters of the alphabet, often in combination with symbols such as lions, anchors, and heads, were used by American silversmiths in the late 18th and early 19th centuries. The most popular pseudohallmarks include the following:

1. Eagle. This symbol indicated the item was made from melted U.S. coins and of coin-silver fineness (.900). In most examples the eagle was in a pose similar to that on U.S. coinage, and there is at least one mark in which it is identical.

2. Lion. Lions occurred quite often as pseudohallmarks because they were repeatedly used in the hallmarking on British silver.

3. Leopard. The leopard's head, sometimes wearing a crown, was an adaptation of an English hallmark.

4. Male portrait. This mark was in the form of a three-quarter bust profile that nearly always faced to the right. In most cases the subject was indistinct, and the small size made detailing almost impossible. It was intended to make the purchaser think the figure depicted was a British sovereign. A figure of an Indian, sometimes with a feather headdress and holding a bow, also was used.

5. Bird. Even though an eagle was sometimes clearly portrayed, these birds were not usually referred to as eagle markings. Eagle marks were only those in which the bird was shown in full figure.

6. Anchor. It may be inferred that silversmiths using an anchor pseudohallmark were attempting to imitate British Birmingham hallmarks. The fact that so many smiths were located in large port cities also must have encouraged adoption of the anchor as a marking. Sometimes a ship's wheel was used instead of an anchor.

7. Crest. Crests, intended to suggest armorial bearings, are rare. No identifiable arms ever appeared on these crests.

8. Wheat. One of the more curious symbols in pseudohallmarks was wheat, usually shown as bundled sheaves, a symbol indicating harvest in America.

9. Leaf. The leaf was used infrequently in America.

10. Arm and hammer. A hand and arm holding a hammer were occasionally used in marking. The significance of this mark related to the silversmith profession.

11. Miscellaneous plants and flowers.

12. Harp. The harp was a symbol of Hibernia (Ireland).

13. Star. Both five- and six-pointed designs were used.

When symbols were used in combination, as often occurred, there could be a series of three, four, or even five of them lined up horizontally. They appeared next to the maker's mark or beneath it. Pseudohallmarks, used in sequence, were simply a decorative device on the silversmith's part.

In researching coin silver the collector should be aware that pseudohallmarks have no relationship to the fineness or quality of the silver; and where there was such a marking, it was placed there by a maker. Approximately one half of the American silver made prior to 1850 will bear pseudohallmarks, and approximately one half of those pieces will have an indication of the silver standard.

In the first quarter of the 19th century, Maryland became the first state to enact a hallmarking law, which was based on the English style. Some silversmiths who did not want to conform to the law simply moved to other areas. The Maryland system was later repealed.

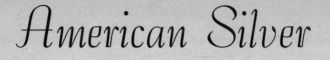

American Silver

By the late 17th century in America, silversmiths were working in New York and Boston, but Boston was considered the silversmith's capital. For the colonists, silver was the best means of saving wealth because coins, made by the silversmith until 1792, were unidentifiable and could be stolen. Spoons, belt buckles, and buttons in silver were usually available, but most early American silver was specifically made to order for a customer. It was not unusual for customers who had old silver pieces or coins to have them melted down and reworked in a new style. The buyer then paid for only the silversmith's labor. Reworking has led to the loss of many fine early pieces of silver. Silver hollowware, however, was imported for many years, design styles usually taking about ten years to wend their way to America from England.

Silversmiths often purchased their raw silver as scrap dealers do today: buying old articles from the public, placing them on a scale, and paying for them by weight and fineness. Native American silver mines were not worked for a long time, and foreign coins were used most often as raw material for the manufacture of silver objects.

Silver content of the period ranged from .800 to .958 standard, according to what had been received and then melted. Impurities were not removed, as they are in the silver produced today; and often silver held trace amounts of gold, which imparted a wonderful color to the surface of early pieces of silver.

Until the early 19th century, when America had enough wealth to support the trade, silversmiths also had to work as jewelers, clock- and watchmakers, and tinsmiths. Before 1850 most silversmiths were in the east. After the Revolutionary War, silversmiths began to work in Pennsylvania and other areas farther west. Many New England silversmiths worked their way into Maryland, Virginia, and the Carolinas.

English and Continental styles were adapted for most designs. Boston and Philadelphia were influenced by English silversmiths, whereas New York styles followed those of the Dutch, who settled in that state. Quite often regional styles were indicated on early silver by the individual preferences of a customer. These styles were then emulated by others in the town, thereby creating a local design tradition. The American style is like no other; it is a meld of regional characteristics, foreign styles, and artistic freedom.

American silver does not have date marks as do similar pieces in England. Therefore, the dating of pieces relies on makers' marks, designs, provenance, or engraved monograms. Occasionally, one can be fooled by a piece made in an earlier style or a contemporary piece engraved with a long-ago date. Marking on early American silver became easier as most smiths stamped initials or names. Initial marks are the most difficult to identify because many smiths have similar initials. The 19th century saw the addition of first and last names, addresses, city, and state marks. Unmarked pieces do exist, and occasionally they can be attributed to a particular maker, most often by style or design. It is thought that some unmarked objects were student works or teaching pieces.

Until the 1850s most silversmiths made and sold their own silver. After that time a silversmith might be working on commission for several other smiths or a retail jeweler. These pieces would most often be marked with a maker's and/or retailer's name.

There seems to be less faking of marks in silver than in other areas of collecting, but do not be lulled into complacency. Faking marks in England has always been a felony, and discovery has meant imprisonment. Most faking occurs when rare makers' marks are applied to pieces of lesser value. Paul Revere's mark, for example, has been forged more often than that of any other American silversmith. The faking of marks is often enhanced and corroborated by engraved inscriptions from the maker. It is best for the buyer to have such pieces examined for authenticity by several experts. Pieces that have been recently faked generally have a sharp, fresh look without scratch marks. Their patina is meant to indicate years of polishing. Use a strong magnifying glass to examine the mark because some fakers are now using acid to achieve a softer look. The acid tends to make the mark appear blurry or indistinct.

Important American Silversmiths

ABBOTT, JOHN

John Abbott (1790–1850) worked at Portsmouth, New Hampshire, near the Maine border. He entered business in 1817, at the age of 27, taking over the established shop of Robert Gray. At least three distinct varieties of Abbott's mark are known. In two his name appeared as J. ABBOT and in the third as J.W. ABBOTT. The lettering was raised in block characters against a lightly scalloped, rectangular frame.

ADAM, JOHN, JR.

John Adam, Jr., of Alexandria, Virginia, was the son of a silversmith. Research into his life and work has been complicated by the fact that his father was likewise named John Adam, and the son's name was not identified as "Junior." Therefore, the products of one are frequently mistaken for those of the other. The younger John Adam, born in 1780, was apprenticed to his father and probably started in business around 1800. The last dated mention of him occurred in 1846. The usual mark was I.ADAM, closely compressed, with raised lettering set in a narrow rectangle. The letter *I*, with a period following, was used to represent his first name, John (rather than *J*), to conform with classical tradition.

AITKEN, JOHN

The year of John Aitken's birth is uncertain. He was apprenticed in 1771 to a Philadelphia goldsmith. The first notice of Aitken's working independently occurs in 1785, when he was operating as a jack-of-all-trades in selling and repairing clocks, watches, and musical instruments in addition to goldsmithing and silversmithing. His last recorded notice was dated 1814, when he would have been about 56 years old. Aitken's usual mark was I. AITKEN in thin block capitals in which the serifs of the *K* and the *E* were joined.

ALEXANDER, SAMUEL

Samuel Alexander worked as a goldsmith, silversmith, and jeweler in Philadelphia from the late 18th to the early 19th century. In 1797 he was in partnership with another Philadelphia smith, a German named Christian Wiltberger. By 1800 he had gone into a new partnership, with Anthony Simmons, which lasted for several years. In 1805 or earlier he opened his own establishment and for a number of years operated as a silversmith. Thereafter, he seemed to have abandoned smithing and kept his shop strictly for the purpose of retailing wares made by others and possibly also for repairing and engraving work. The final notice of Samuel Alexander occurred in 1814. His common mark was S ALEXANDER (no period after the initial) within a plain rectangle.

ALSTYNE, JEROME

Jerome Alstyne's Christian name was Jeronimus (or in the correct European spelling, Hieronymus). Not a very prolific maker, he worked in New York City in the late 18th century and possibly the early 19th century, but no references to him dated later than 1797 were recorded. He was a goldsmith and silversmith of Dutch ancestry. The name sometimes appeared in advertisements as Allstyne (with two *l*'s), but in his mark always as Alstyne. His usual type of mark was J ALSTYNE in script letters within a wavy frame whose contour matches that of the script. The earliest reference to Jerome Alstyne as a shop proprietor occurred in 1787, so we know that his career spanned at least one full decade.

ANDREWS, JEREMIAH

Jeremiah Andrews's long career extended from at least 1774, when the first notice of him appears, until after 1800, during which time he worked in New York City; Philadelphia; Augusta, Georgia; Savannah, Georgia; and finally Norfolk, Virginia. Andrews's first recorded advertisement announced him as a jeweler from London. The final notice of his business occurs in Norfolk, Virginia, in 1803, but whether this was actually his year of retirement is doubtful. He died in 1817. Andrews used various marks, the most common of which was J ANDREWS in roughly worked block letters against a shaped rectangular frame. When working in Norfolk, he stamped the city's name on his wares, but he did not seem ever to have done this in his other places of business.

ARNOLD, THOMAS

This long-lived smith spent his entire career in Newport, Rhode Island, from the second half of the 18th century to the early 19th century. Arnold was born in 1739. When he entered the trade is not established; the first notice appears in 1760. He died at age 89 in 1828. He was still in business in 1817 (aged 78), but at that point he was probably only retailing the works of other silversmiths along with general merchandise. Arnold is known to have done work for Trinity Church in Newport. He used an unusual type of mark, which was really two marks in combination: one tool carried his initials (TA) in script; the other, his surname (ARNOLD) in bold, narrow block capitals. Although the spacing varied, he placed these together on most of his wares. On a spoon stem, the TA might occur near the terminal and ARNOLD halfway down or close to the bowl. No conclusive explanation can be given for his use of name plus initials. Possibly he started out using ARNOLD, then added the decorative initials.

AUSTIN, JOSIAH

This 18th-century Massachusetts smith was related to and associated with a number of others in the same profession. Born in 1719, he worked first in Charlestown and later in Boston, where the final printed reference to him appeared in 1770. The year of his death is not established, and it is possible he was still active during the Revolution. Austin used a number of marks, which differed considerably from one another. Among them was I. AUSTIN in Gothic lettering, in which the *S* was shown as an *F*. Sometimes Austin stamped himself as J.AUSTIN, abandoning the formal or Roman style of initial for his Christian name. Some of his pieces are marked simply I.A.

AYRES, SAMUEL

Samuel Ayres worked in Lexington and Danville, Kentucky, in the late 18th and early 19th centuries. In one form of his trademark the name appears as SAYERS (his initial and surname compressed without period or space), leading researchers to hunt for a silversmith called Sayers. He was born in 1767 and is known to have been in business in Lexington by 1790. At that time he was operating as a silversmith and jeweler. It is established that he remained in Lexington a considerable length of time because his shop is listed in both the 1806 and 1818 directories of that town. At some point, perhaps around 1810, he went into partnership with John Hiter. He left Lexington sometime in the period from 1818 to 1823 and set up in Danville, Kentucky. There he ran a smithing business with his son,

T. R. J. Ayers. He died in 1824. His most frequent mark was S AYERS in raised script lettering within a shaped rectangle.

BAKER, ELEAZER

Eleazer Baker lived to the age of 85 and had a long silversmithing career in rural Connecticut. For most of his years in business he also worked as a clock- and watchmaker and as a goldsmith. He was born in 1764 and probably was in business by the mid-1780s, but the first notice of him does not appear until 1793. He died in 1849, apparently having spent all of his years in Ashford, Connecticut. Eleazer Baker's mark normally consisted of EBAKER (no space between the initial and surname) in block letters within a rectangle. Sómetimes he used a simple punch with initials EB.

BALDWIN, JEDEDIAH

Jedediah Baldwin, born in 1769, worked in four states, in a career that spanned many years. After working briefly in Norwich, Connecticut, he moved to Northampton, Massachusetts, and announced his arrival with an advertisement that stated he was from London. In Northampton he went into partnership with Samuel Stiles. They worked as clockmakers, watchmakers, jewelers, goldsmiths, and silversmiths. This association lasted about one year and was followed by a partnership between Baldwin and Nathan Storrs. Papers were filed to dissolve this business on January 22, 1794. Baldwin afterward worked in Hanover, New Hampshire; Fairfield, Connecticut; Morrisville, New York; and finally Rochester, New York. He was in Morrisville around 1820, but the length of time he spent there is questionable. His residence in Rochester has been established for at least 11 years, from 1834 to 1844. He died in 1849 at age 80. His mark was distinctive, with the name BALDWIN in graceful slim block capitals against a smooth rectangular frame.

BALL, WILLIAM

A Baltimore smith, Ball worked in the late 18th and early 19th centuries. He was born in England in 1763. It is not known when he arrived in America, but he was in business in Baltimore by 1785. A partnership with a smith named Johnson (first name not established) ended in 1790. Ball sometimes worked alone but was for a time engaged in another partnership, with J. S. Heald. He died at age 52 in 1815. His common mark was

WBALL (no spacing) in block letters within a shaped rectangular frame.

BANCKER, ADRIAN

Adrian Bancker worked as a silversmith and goldsmith in Colonial New York City. He was born in 1703 and apprenticed at around age 15 to a Dutch goldsmith named Boelen. The association with Boelen is thought to have lasted until about 1731. Thereafter, he went into business independently. He was in business as late as 1766 and died in 1772 at the age of 69. Bancker never spelled out his name in his mark but used the initials AB. These normally were framed in a circle or oval. The AB mark within a heart-shaped punch has been recorded on wares dating from the period in which Bancker was active, but it has not yet been positively identified as his.

BARTHOLOMEW, ROSWELL

Roswell Bartholomew, born in 1781, worked in Hartford, Connecticut. He was sent at age 16 to be an apprentice smith with the shop of Beach and Ward in Hartford. By 1802 Ward, one of his masters, was in partnership with Bartholomew along with another individual known only by the initial *T*. This mysterious figure later quit the partnership, and by 1804 the firm had become simply Ward and Bartholomew. In 1809 the partners took Charles Brainard into association with them, and the three worked together until Bartholomew's death in 1830. Presumably Bartholomew was the only one of the partners who actually engaged in silversmithing because the wares bear a mark consisting of his initials only: RB on a rectangular punch.

BARTON, JOSEPH

This late-18th/early-19th-century smith, who produced great quantities of flatware, worked in Utica, New York, and Stockbridge, Massachusetts. Born in 1764, Barton had gone into business by 1791 as a clockmaker, goldsmith, and silversmith. His first location was in Stockbridge, where he remained for a number of years. By 1804 he had moved to the central New York town of Utica and continued in business there until the time of his death in 1832. In Utica he also engaged in the jewelry business. Barton was involved in several partnerships while in Utica, trading under the firm names of Barton and Smith, then Barton and Butler. Joseph Barton's mark was distinctive.

It comprised his surname preceded by initial, without space or period, contained within a sawtooth rectangular frame. Instead of a raised marking, Barton's was stamped in incuse where the lettering was sunk into the silver.

BAYLEY, JOHN

This early Philadelphia maker's career stretched from the Colonial era until after Independence. Bayley is the archaic spelling of Bailey; it can be presumed that he was of English descent. His first advertisement appeared in 1754, his last in 1783. His usual mark was a simple punch, I.B, in which the Christian name was Romanized to the initial *I* rather than *J*. The initials were set within a rectangle with rounded corners. Occasionally, he used another mark with the surname spelled out. It appeared as BAYLY rather than Bayley.

BEDFORD, JOHN

John Bedford, born in 1757, was one of many early Eastern smiths whose entire career was spent in the same rural village—in this case Fishkill, New York. Although he may have been active earlier, his first advertisement appeared in 1782. He survived to the age of 77 (1834), but it is not established whether he continued in business to the end of his life. There were several varieties of the John Bedford mark. In one it appeared as J.BEDFORD, with the initial slightly smaller than the surname letters. There was another interesting feature of his mark: the first three letters of the surname (BED) were somewhat thicker than the rest. Another version of this smith's mark comprised script initial letters contained within an oval.

BEECHER, CLEMENT

Clement Beecher enjoyed a lengthy career in the silversmithing business, spanning a number of eras in taste and carrying over from the "shop" age to factory production. All of his years in the business were spent in Connecticut, where he was in business by the age of 23. An advertisement appears in a Hartford newspaper of 1801. He worked not only as a silversmith but also as a jeweler, goldsmith, and brassworker. Generally, his mark was a simple punch with his initial letters separated by a period. The C.B. was enclosed in a rectangle with sawtooth border.

BENJAMIN, JOHN

The entire career of John Benjamin was confined to the Colonial era. He lived in Stratford, Connecticut, where he went into business around 1725. In the mid- to late 1740s he is believed to have formed a partnership with Robert Fairchild, another Stratford smith. He died in 1773 at the age of 74. John Benjamin never used anything but initials for his mark, a simple I.B. within either an oval or rectangular frame. The letters were in block form and highly raised.

BILLINGS, DANIEL

Daniel Billings worked in Stonington and Preston, Connecticut. He is known to have been born in 1749 and was presumably of English descent. It is established that he was active in business by 1790. The last dated mention of him occurs in 1795, but he probably lived for some years thereafter. Billings used a mark consisting of his full surname preceded by his initial written out in a flowing script. This was contained within a rectangle with slightly rounded corners.

BLOWERS, JOHN

John Blowers, born in 1810, was active in Boston in the first half of the 18th century. Blowers is established to have been working in or before 1738 because the Boston *Gazette* carried an advertisement for his wares in that year. His mark consisted of his surname only, without the initial letter. It was written in modified script characters without connections between the letters and was contained in a rectangle.

BOELEN, HENRICUS

One of the pioneer silversmiths of America, Henricus Boelen worked in New York City, then governed by the Dutch and called New Amsterdam. He was a Dutchman and had a brother, Jacob, who was also a smith. Boelen, like his contemporaries, worked almost strictly in the Old World taste, turning out wares very similar to those of Holland. Boelen was born in 1661 and died in 1691. He used a single mark, a set of linked initial letters in which the righthand portion of the *H* formed the ascender of the *B* for HB.

BONTECOU, TIMOTHY

Timothy Bontecou was one of the better-known silversmiths of the 18th century and certainly one of the most skilled and artistic among those who worked in America prior to the Revolutionary War. Born in New York City, he went to France at an early age and was apprenticed into silversmithing there. When he returned to America is not established, but he is known to have been in Stratford, Connecticut, by 1735. After a brief stay in that town he moved to New Haven, Connecticut, where the remainder of his career was spent. Normally his mark consisted of his initials separated by a rising period and enclosed within a rectangular frame with lobework decoration along the top.

BOUDO, LOUIS

Louis Boudo spent his entire career in Charleston, South Carolina. He emigrated there from Santo Domingo, where he had been born in 1786. The details of his early life are not known. He was in business by 1809 and possibly earlier. At first he worked in partnership with one Maurel (first name not recorded), but this association was soon dissolved. For a number of years Buodo continued at work on his own; then, in 1818, he sold his business and retired. But in the following year he returned to the silversmith trade, opened a new shop, and carried on with it until his death in 1827. His mark consisted of his surname spelled out and arranged in a wavy rectangular frame.

BOYER, DANIEL

Daniel Boyer, born in 1725, worked in Boston before and after the Revolution. The first record of him in the business dates from 1748. We know that he worked not only as a silversmith but as a goldsmith, jeweler, and importer of jewelry and jeweler's equipment. Boyer died at the age of 54 in 1779. There were three distinct varieties of Daniel Boyer's mark: (1) The surname preceded by initial letter, (2) the surname alone and in thin block characters against a rectangular frame, and (3) initial letters only in a rectangular frame with rounded corners.

BRASHER, EPHRAIM

Ephraim Brasher, a silversmith and goldsmith of New York City, is better known to the world of numismatics than of antiques. He was the manufacturer of the great "Brasher doubloon," a rare gold piece made in 1787. As a smith he was in partnership for a time with George Alexander; the shop's name was Brasher and Alexander. This association was discontinued in 1801, and Brasher went on alone until 1807, the final year in which his name appears in the city directory. He died in 1810 at the age of 66. Brasher used a number of different marks: his name spelled out but not preceded by an initial letter, his name spelled out *and* preceded by an initial letter, and initial letters only. Brasher sometimes stamped N YORK on his products.

CAMPBELL, BENJAMIN

Born in 1749, Benjamin Campbell lived to the age of 94. He apparently entered the trade in Uniontown, Pennsylvania, shortly before the Revolution. He survived until 1843 but probably had retired from business before that time. His mark consisted of his initials, BC, on a small oval punch.

CARPENTER, JOSEPH

Joseph Carpenter worked in Norwich, Connecticut, in the years preceding and following the Revolution. He was born in 1747 and was of English descent. Joseph Carpenter's son Charles also became a silversmith, working both in Norwich alongside his father and later in Boston. Joseph's mark consisted of his initials, I.C., with the *J* of Joseph changed to an *I* in conformity with the traditional style.

CASEY, GIDEON

Gideon Casey, an early smith who worked mainly in the Colonial era, was a Rhode Islander. He occupied offices in four different towns in that state. Born in 1726, Casey had a brother Samuel who was a silversmith with whom he was in partnership for awhile. Gideon Casey appears to have started in the business in Newport, then went to Exeter, South Kingston, and finally Warwick. It was a while in Kingston in the early 1750s that the partnership with his brother occurred. Gideon Casey died in 1786 at the age of 60. His mark was G.CASEY in narrow block capitals, only slightly raised, set into a rectangular frame.

CHEAVENS, HENRY

A New York City manufacturer, Cheavens was active in the first and second quarters of the 19th century. His name is found for the first time in the New York directory of 1810 and continued appearing in that publication until 1834. Beginning in 1832 he entered into a partnership with John Hyde, a watchmaker. Perhaps at that date Cheavens turned his attentions solely to silversmithing. He was not heard of after 1834. Cheavens used a mark consisting of his surname and initial in distinctively sculptured block letters.

CHITTENDEN, EBENEZER

Ebenezer Chittenden had a long career as a silversmith beginning well before the Revolution and continuing for many years afterward. All of his life was spent in Connecticut, working first in East Guilford and later in New Haven. It is not known when Chittenden entered the business. He died in 1812 at age 86. His mark consisted of a simple initial punch without a period between or following the letters, but he sometimes used one in which his surname was spelled out, E.CHITTENDEN.

CLARK, JOSEPH

Little is known of the career of Joseph Clark, who worked in the pre-Revolutionary era. He was from Massachusetts and apparently worked for a time at Saugus, Massachusetts. Clark is believed to have entered the trade in 1737. He used at least three different marks, which may represent different business locations. One carried his surname spelled out preceded by the initial of his Christian name in very crudely modeled letters. Another, much better designed (and therefore presumably of later origin) read simply CLARK in wide block capitals. The third was an initial mark, IC, in which the *J* of Joseph was transformed to *I*.

CLEVELAND, WILLIAM

William Cleveland was an Easterner, who started in the business in Connecticut, settled later in Ohio, and ended his career in the small town of Black Rock, New York. He was in partnership in New London, Connecticut, with John Trott from 1792 until 1794. From then until 1812 he carried on his own business. In 1812 he entered into a partnership with Samuel Post. He moved from New London to Norwich, Connecticut, and spent many years there. He then worked in Massachusetts and eventually quit the East for Zanesville, Ohio. From Zanesville he moved to Putnam, Ohio, and then east again. He died in 1837 at the age of 67. William Cleveland used two marks. In one the surname was spelled out without an initial letter and stamped from an incuse punch (the letters sunk into the surface rather than raised). His other mark, presumably of an earlier date, has the initials W.C.

COBB, EPHRAIM

This maker, active in Massachusetts prior to the Revolutionary War, had a fairly lengthy career. He was born in 1708 in Barnstable, Massachusetts, and was working in Plymouth, Massachusetts, by 1735. His attractive mark consisted of his surname spelled out, preceded by his initial, in upper- and lowercase characters.

COEN, DANIEL BLOOM

Daniel Bloom Coen of New York City was one of a community of Jewish silversmiths who operated in that city during the late 18th and early 19th centuries. Coen is an early or variant spelling of the name Cohen. We know that his active career spanned at least the years from 1787 to 1804 because he appeared during those years in the New York City directory. His most common mark was D.COEN in block letters set within a rectangle. Another silversmith, named Cohen, was working in New York at a slightly later period, but there was no evidence of a relationship between them.

CONEY, JOHN

This historic maker worked in Boston in the late 17th and early 18th centuries. John Coney was born in 1656. At the age of 13 or 14 he was sent to apprentice with Hull and Sanderson, who were then engaged in striking silver coins for the colony of Massachusetts as well as in general silversmithing. Coney died in 1722, at age 66, and is known to have been at work at least as late as 1718. Though his accomplishments were many, John Coney's chief impact on history came via one of his pupils: late in his career Paul Revere the elder was apprenticed to him. Coney's mark was a simple IC in a shield-shape frame with small ornaments above and below. It was sometimes accompanied by a figure of a rabbit because the archaic word for rabbit was "coney."

CORNELL, WALTER

Walter Cornell, born in 1729 in Providence, Rhode Island, worked his whole career in that town. He died in 1801, and he seems to have been active to the end. Cornell used several marks, one of which is quite distinctive because it carried the name CORNELL in block capitals against a frame with slanting sawtooth edges. In another of his marks the initial was also given; it read W CORNELL, the *W* spaced widely apart from the surname and not followed by a period.

COWELL, WILLIAM

William Cowell, a very early silversmith, was born in 1682 and entered the business in Boston about 1700 or shortly thereafter. He is believed to have learned the trade from Jeremiah Dummer, also of Boston. William Cowell's son, William, Jr., was also a silversmith. Cowell Senior's mark was a simple initial punch, WC, within an oval.

DALLY, PHILIP

Philip Dally worked in New York City in the latter part of the 18th century. In the late 1780s he was in a partnership with Jabez Halsey in a goldsmithing and silversmithing business. This partnership was dissolved in 1789. It is not established whether Dally then worked independently. He was apparently not a very prolific maker, and no references to his death have been uncovered. Dally's mark consisted of his initials, P.D., with the *P* smaller than the *D*.

DAVENPORT, JOHN

John Davenport began work in Baltimore and then moved to Philadelphia, where the remainder of his career was spent. He died in 1801 at an undetermined age. Davenport's mark consisted of the initials I.D. with the letter *I* representing the classical form of *J*, for John.

DeRIEMER, PETER

Peter DeRiemer was a distinguished New York state smith of the 18th and 19th centuries. In the late 1760s he worked in New York City. His next place of residence and work was Poughkeepsie, New York, and finally Hyde Park, where he died in 1834. His mark consisted of the letters PDR in thick European-style capital letters in a faint rectangular frame.

DIXWELL, JOHN

John Dixwell began work in New Haven, Connecticut, then moved to Boston. He was in the smithing business at least as early as 1705. He died in 1725 at the age of 44. John Dixwell's mark was ID within an oval.

DOOLITTLE, AMOS

Amos Doolittle, born in 1754, spent his entire career as a silversmith in Connecticut. He was apprenticed to Eliakim Hitchcock of Cheshire, Connecticut, in the late 1760s and is known to have been operating his own shop by 1755. He died in 1832 at the age of 78. His mark was always a set of initials, in very narrow capitals, sometimes joined and sometimes not.

DUMMER, JEREMIAH

No book on American silverware would be complete without reference to Jeremiah Dummer. He was the first goldsmith/silversmith born on American soil. Dummer was born in Boston in 1645, 25 years after the Pilgrims' landing. At the age of 14 he was apprenticed to John Hull, who was not only a silversmith but the "mintmaster" of the Massachusetts Bay Colony (Hull was employed in striking coins to alleviate the area's coin shortage). During his long career, Dummer engaged as apprentices a number of youths who became notable silversmiths. Dummer was extremely versatile and turned out silver and gold wares of all varieties. He died in 1718 at the age of 73. His mark usually consisted of his initial letters in wide block capitals within a heart-shape frame.

DUPUY, DANIEL

Daniel Dupuy, born in 1719, founded a business dynasty in his native city of Philadelphia. A number of his descendants, beginning with his son Daniel, Jr., followed him into the silversmithing trade. Dupuy Senior was still at work as late as 1807, the year of his death, when he was 88 years old. He habitually used a set of initials, DD, as his mark, sometimes impressed once and often twice on his wares.

EDWARDS, JOHN

John Edwards, born in 1671, was the patriarch of a celebrated family of Boston goldsmiths and silversmiths. It is believed he was apprenticed to Jeremiah Dummer, the leading

Boston smith of the time. Edwards was working on his own at least by 1700. He died in 1746 at the age of 75. His mark was IE, contained in a clover- or shieldlike frame and sometimes capped by a crown.

EMBREE, EFFINGHAM

Effingham Embree worked in New York City in the late 18th century. Notice of him appeared first in the New York City directory for 1789, and he continued to be listed in succeeding editions until 1795. Embree spelled out his surname in his mark, but he did not use his first initial. The lettering was thin block capitals in a rectangular frame. The mark sometimes appeared in combination with a letter punch reading IB. These were the initials of James Byrne (the *J* changed to an *I*), a smith with whom Embree was associated for awhile. Embree also was in partnership for a time with a man named Coles.

EOFF, GARRETT

Garrett Eoff was born in 1779. A Garrett Eoff was listed as a silversmith in the New York City directory for 1789, but since the silversmith Garrett Eoff was then 10 years old, he is obviously a different person. Quite likely the 1789 Garrett Eoff was the father of this smith. The younger Garrett Eoff was in business by the year 1801 and appeared continuously in the New York City directory from that date until 1845. At first he was in partnership with Paul Howell, as Eoff & Howell, then with John Conner, as Eoff & Conner. His final partnership (of which record exists) was with John C. Moore, as Eoff & Moore. His mark, confusing to beginning collectors, consisted of the Christian name initial, *G*, compressed against the surname, EOFF. Although it seems to read "GEOFF," there was a small period following the initial letter. The mark was contained within a rectangular punch.

ERWIN, JOHN

John Erwin spent most of his life in Baltimore. The dates of his birth and death were not recorded. He appeared in the directory of that city's businessmen for the first time in 1808 and apparently continued in Baltimore at least until 1820. John Erwin's mark was quite unusual. It appeared as J.ERWIN, in block capitals without the *J* converted into an *I* as was the standard practice among silversmiths. Perhaps there was another smith active, who signed himself I. ERWIN, but no such individual has been traced.

FAIRCHILD, ROBERT

Robert Fairchild, born in 1703 in Durham, Connecticut, spent most of his career there. There is no information about when he entered business. The first record occurs in Durham in 1747. From Durham he moved to Stratford, Connecticut, and then to New Haven, where he enjoyed his greatest success. Around 1789, when he was 86 years old and still active, he left Connecticut and settled in Pawling, New York, where he died in 1794 at age 91. He generally used an initial punchmark, RF, separated by a star instead of a period. The star occurred parallel to the second crossbar on the *F*. When he used a name mark, it was R. FAIRCHILD within a rectangular frame.

FERGUSON, JOHN

John Ferguson worked in Philadelphia in the early part of the 19th century. He was in partnership with Charles Moore, operating a silversmithing and goldsmithing business. The final record of his work dates from 1810. His mark consisted of the initial *I* (Romanized from *J*) followed by his full surname in stylish block capitals. There was no record of Ferguson's having ever used a plain initial punchmark.

FISHER, THOMAS

Thomas Fisher, born in 1765, worked first in Baltimore, then in Philadelphia, and concluded his career in the town of Easton, Pennsylvania. The first reference to him appeared in 1797 and the last in 1807. Thomas Fisher's mark consisted of his surname in modified script form preceded by an initial. This was an incuse mark in which the name was sunken down into the silver, rather than raised. Incuse marks were used by few of the early smiths because they tended to get rubbed and worn smooth faster.

FOLSOM, JOHN

John Folsom was born in 1756 in Stratford, Connecticut, but he moved to Albany, New York, around 1780. He died in 1839 at the age of 83. John Folsom's mark was an initial punch, IF, in which the *J* of John was changed to an *I* in keeping with the long-standing tradition of the profession.

FORBES, GARRET

A New York City smith, Forbes was born in 1785. Notice of him appears in the New York City directory from 1808 until 1815. He remained in New York, where he died in 1851 at the age of 66. He used two similar marks, both reading G.FORBES, but in one there was no period following the initial. Both were in block capitals set within a rectangular frame.

FORMAN, BENONI

Very little is known of this 19th-century smith who worked in New York State. He was active in Albany in 1813 and continued to appear in that city's directory until 1846. Thereafter he settled in Troy, New York, where the final notice of him appeared in 1848. His mark was an initial punch in which he incorporated his middle initial, *B*, to form BBF. The letters, along with his products, were stylishly designed.

FUETER, LEWIS

Lewis Fueter, the son of a goldsmith and silversmith named Daniel C. Lewis, was active in New York City around the time of the Revolutionary War. In the early to mid-1770s he worked as a goldsmith and silversmith. No record of Lewis Fueter appeared after 1775. His mark was L. Fueter in a flowing copperplate style of script, probably modeled from his signature. The frame of his mark was a modified rectangle arching outward around the large initial letters.

GAITHER, JOHN

John Gaither, active in Alexandria, Virginia, in the early part of the 19th century, was in a partnership with G. Griffith, running a silversmithing, watchmaking, and clockmaking shop. After 1811 there was no traceable record of John Gaither. His very distinctive mark consisted of his surname in bold block capitals preceded by his initial letter: J. GAITHER. It was set against a checked background.

GARDINER, JOHN

John Gardiner, born in New London, Connecticut, in 1734, spent his apprenticeship with his uncle, a local smith named Pygan Adams. By about 1750, when he was 16, he was working on his own. John Gardiner died in 1776 at the age of 42.

He used both an initial punch and a mark in which his name was spelled out, J. GARDINER, within a rectangular frame.

GEFFROY, NICHOLAS

Nicholas Geffroy's real name was Geoffroy. He was born in 1761 and seems to have fled his native land during or shortly after the French Revolution. Nicholas Geffroy died in 1839 at the age of 78. He used a very eye-catching mark, consisting of N. GEFFROY separated not by a period but by a large multi-pointed star and set within a sawtooth frame.

GERRISH, TIMOTHY

Timothy Gerrish, who worked in the latter part of the 18th and the early 19th centuries, spent his career in Portsmouth, New Hampshire. We know that he died in 1815 at the age of 66. He used both an initial punchmark and a mark in which his surname was spelled out in attractive script letters of a modernistic style.

GIBBS, JOHN

John Gibbs was born in 1751 in Providence, Rhode Island, and spent his entire career there. Gibbs died in 1797 at the age of 48. His widow carried on the business and went into partnership with John C. Jenckes. His mark consisted of a simple J. GIBBS in swelled block capitals within a shaped rectangular frame.

GILMAN, JOHN WARD

John Ward Gilman enjoyed a long career in the business. He was born in 1741 in Exeter, New Hampshire, and spent his entire career there. He was the brother of Benjamin Gilman, also a silversmith, who was his junior by more than 20 years. He died in 1823 at the age of 84 and was apparently at work until very late in life. The mark he generally used was an initial-punch IWG, in which the letters were not separated by periods and the *I* has a small bar set across its shaft.

GOELET, PHILIP

Philip Goelet, born in 1701, worked in New York City in the first half of the 18th century. The first reference to him occurred in 1731. He died in 1748. Philip Goelet's mark was an initial-punch PG within an oval.

GRIGG, WILLIAM

The first references to William Grigg occurred in the middle 1760s, at which time he was established in New York City. During the Revolutionary War he was working in Albany, New York, and he returned to New York City around 1778. It was in 1782 that he decided to push northward and test the business climate in Halifax, Nova Scotia. He stayed in Halifax until 1789, then returned to New York City. He died in 1797. He used a mark in which his surname was spelled out in flowing, thin script letters, not preceded by an initial. The mark was set within a border that conformed to the shape of the lettering. In addition, Grigg also made use of an initial punch, reading WG in very ornamental script letters.

HALL, CHARLES

Charles Hall of Pennsylvania was born in 1742 and was already in the trade by 1759, working alongside his brother, David Hall. He began advertising in 1765, by which time he had moved to Lancaster, Pennsylvania. He died in 1783 at the age of 41. Charles Hall's mark was a simple initial punch within a rectangular frame or, on occasion, his name spelled out in a similar style of frame.

HALSTED, BENJAMIN

Benjamin Halsted began business in New York City in the early 1760s. From there he moved to Elizabeth, New Jersey, and later worked his way to Philadelphia. Following the Revolutionary War he returned to New York and was still at work in 1794. We do not know the dates of his birth or death. His usual mark consisted of the name Halsted spelled out in script letters within a shaped frame (the frame border was styled to match the contours of the letters). Halsted was briefly in partnership with Myer Myers, a well-known silversmith of New York City.

HAVERSTICK, WILLIAM

William Haverstick was born in Philadelphia in 1756 and worked both there and in Lancaster, Pennsylvania. He died in 1823 at the age of 67. The marks used by him were also used by his son, William, Jr., making it difficult to assign any particular item to one or the other. The marks were all in the form of simple initial punches. In one the letters were joined at the top and not separated by a period. In another they were not joined and have a period between them.

HENCHMAN, DANIEL

Daniel Henchman of Boston was born in 1730. He was apprenticed to Jacob Hurd, a noted Boston smith, and married Hurd's daughter in 1753. Henchman died in 1775 at the age of 55. His basic mark consisted of his name spelled out in lowercase letters within a rectangular frame. He also on occasion used an initial punch reading DH.

HITCHCOCK, ELIAKIM

This Colonial and early Federal era manufacturer was born in Cheshire, Connecticut, in 1726. He started working in that town in the 1750s or possibly earlier, then moved to New Haven. He died in 1788 at the age of 62. So far as has been determined, he never used a mark in which his name was spelled out but always an initial punch. There were two types of these initial punches: one in which the initials were in squat block capitals separated by a star and one in which the letters were tall, sleek, and not separated by either a star or a period.

HOPKINS, JOSEPH

Joseph Hopkins spent his entire career in the town of Waterbury, Connecticut, working both before and after the Revolutionary War. He was born in 1730 and died in 1801. His principal mark carried the name spelled out in modified script characters, not preceded by an initial letter. Occasionally he used an initial-punch JH set in a rectangle.

HULBEART, PHILIP

Philip Hulbeart worked in Philadelphia prior to the Revolutionary War. There is no record of the year of his birth; he died in 1764. Hulbeart always used an initial-punch P.H. in which the *P* was somewhat smaller than the *H*.

HURD, JOSEPH

Joseph Hurd (1700–1758) of Boston, Massachusetts, served as an apprentice to John Edwards. He executed church pieces, hollowware, and mourning jewelry. His sons, Benjamin and Nathaniel, served as apprentices to him. His mark was stamped HURD in cartouche and also IH in cartouche.

HUTTON, ISAAC

Isaac Hutton, born in 1767, appeared to have spent his entire career in Albany, New York. He went into the trade around the age of 20, in association with John Folsom. He died at the age of 88. He used marks in which his surname was fully spelled out but not preceded by an initial letter, sometimes in combination with a punch reading ALBANY.

JACOB, GEORGE

George Jacob, born in 1775, worked in Baltimore and Philadelphia in the first half of the 19th century. He appeared continuously in the Baltimore directory as a silversmith from 1802 to 1845 and also appeared in the Philadelphia directory beginning in 1839. His mark was habitually G.JACOB in block capitals set against a rectangular frame, sometimes accompanied by numeral punches whose meaning has not been ascertained.

JOHONNOT, WILLIAM

William Johonnot worked in Connecticut and Vermont in the late 18th and early 19th centuries. The final notice of his active engagement in business was dated 1815, but he probably worked longer than that. Johonnot died in 1838. His mark was always an initial-punch IW within a sawtooth rectangular frame.

KENDALL, JAMES

James Kendall, born in 1768, worked in Wilmington, Delaware. The first notice of him appeared in a newspaper advertisement in 1796, listing him as a silversmith and jeweler. He died in 1808 at the age of 40. James Kendall primarily used an initial punch as his mark, in which the *J* for James was switched to an *I*, reading IK. Specimens are known, however, in which KENDALL was spelled out.

LAMAR, MATTHIAS

Matthias Lamar, of French extraction, settled in Philadelphia and appeared for the first time in that city's directory in 1785, when his occupation was given as silversmith. He used a mark in which his surname was spelled out in block capitals, not preceded by an initial letter, and also initial punches. In the latter, the initials were not separated by a period and were set within a rectangular frame.

LeROUX, CHARLES

Charles LeRoux, of French ancestry, was born in 1689 and died in 1748. Details regarding his life are scant. His mark was an initial punch reading CR, omitting the *L*, within a circular frame.

LITTLE, PAUL

Paul Little worked as a silversmith, goldsmith, and operator of a food store. He was born in 1740 in Portland, Maine, and was in business there as early as 1761. In his first venture he was in a partnership, which lasted until about 1765, with John Butler, a goldsmith. From Portland he moved to Windham, Maine, and stayed there for the remainder of his life. He died in 1818. His mark was always an initial punch, sometimes containing a period between the letters. The mark was invariably enclosed in a rectangular border.

LORD, T.

Nothing is known about this manufacturer because all efforts to trace him through advertisements, directories, or other means have failed. He is known to have existed only through the wares he produced, which were impressed T.LORD in bold block capitals within a rectangular frame. He apparently worked in the early part of the 19th century.

LYING, JOHN BURT

John Burt Lying worked in New York City around the time of the Revolutionary War and was still at work in 1781. He died in 1785 at an undetermined age. Unlike most of the smiths of that era, he sometimes used a town mark, N.YORK, in addition to his own mark: LYING in block capitals, not preceded by an initial letter, or an initial punch reading IBL (the *J* changed to an *I*).

MERRIMAN, MARCUS

Marcus Merriman lived to the age of 88 and spent the whole of his career in New Haven, Connecticut. He was born in 1762, though the actual date at which he entered the business has not been established. He died in 1850. Merriman used initial punchmarks as well as a mark in which his surname was spelled out in widely spaced block capitals in a sawtooth frame.

MILNE, EDMUND

Edmund Milne, born in 1724, lived his whole life in Philadelphia and died there at age 98 in 1822. His mark was usually an initial-punch EM, in which the letters were not separated by a period. At other times he used E.MILNE within a rectangular frame.

MORSE, NATHANIEL

This historic manufacturer was engaged in engraving dies for coins for his native colony of Massachusetts. He was noted as both a goldsmith and a silversmith. Nathaniel Morse was born in Boston in 1685 and spent his entire career in that city. He learned the trade from John Coney and was in business by around 1710. He died in 1748 at the age of 63. Nathaniel Morse used a number of marks, the most familiar of which were the letters NM joined together. He also sometimes marked his pieces MORS or N MORS, leaving the *E* off his name.

MUNSON, AMOS

Amos Munson's works are among the scarcer specimens of 18th-century silver because he lived only to the age of 32. He was born in New Haven, Connecticut, in 1753 and spent his career there. He used an initial punchmark, of which there were two distinct forms. In one the letters *AM* were close together and not separated by a period. In the other a period was placed between them and the letters were far apart. In both versions of Munson's mark the frame was rectangular and featured sawtooth work.

MYERS, MYER

One of the legendary names in Colonial American silversmithing, Myer Myers belonged to the small colony of Jewish smiths who operated in New York City. He was the most active and successful among them and probably inspired many others to follow the trade. Myer Myers, born in 1723, was apprenticed in the early 1740s and set up his own shop soon thereafter. He continued working in New York City until 1776. At the outbreak of the Revolutionary War, he moved to Norwalk, Connecticut, where he carried on his trade until 1780. He then went to Philadelphia briefly; and in 1783, when the war was over, he returned to New York City. He continued his business until the time of his death in 1795 at age 72. Myers used a script-type mark, with his surname only, that had a very modern tone. Other wares of his were punched with a crest-shaped initial mark, MM.

NORTON, ANDREW

Andrew Norton of Goshen, Connecticut, was born in 1765 and in the business by 21 or 22 years of age. He died in 1838 at the age of 73, having spent his whole life in Goshen. His mark carried his surname in large, narrow block capitals preceded by an initial letter. A very large period was placed after the initial, and the frame was rectangular with wavy borders at the two vertical edges.

OLIVER, ANDREW

Andrew Oliver, of French extraction, was born in 1724 and worked in Boston as a jeweler and silversmith. He died in 1776. Oliver's mark was usually A OLIVER, without a period following the initial letter, set in a rectangular frame. Occasionally, he used an initial punchmark, which will be found on the stems of spoons.

PARKER, DANIEL

Daniel Parker worked in Boston and Salem, Massachusetts, prior to the Revolutionary War. He was born in 1726 and at work as a gold- and silversmith in Boston from around 1747. In 1775 he resettled in Salem and worked there briefly. He died in 1785. Daniel Parker used two marks, one with his surname preceded by initial letter, D.PARKER, in stout block capitals in a rectangular frame. His other mark was an initial-punch DP within an oval.

PELLETREAU, ELIAS

Elias Pelletreau worked from 1726 until 1810. He began in New York City as an apprentice to Simeon Soumaine and later worked in Southampton, New York, with his sons, John and Elias, as his apprentices. He also worked in Saybrook and Simsbury, Connecticut. His mark was EP in cartouche.

PERKINS, HOUGHTON

Houghton Perkins, born in 1735, was an apprentice of Jacob Hurd. He worked as both a goldsmith and a silversmith and died in 1778. Houghton Perkins's mark consisted of a full surname in script lettering preceded by an initial. The initial was followed by a four-pointed star instead of a period, and the mark was set within a rectangular frame.

PITMAN, SAUNDERS

Saunders Pitman, a silversmith from Providence, Rhode Island, was born in 1732. About 1793 he entered into a partnership with Seril Dodge, another smith. He died in 1804 at the age of 72. As far as can be determined, Saunders Pitman never used an initial punchmark but always a mark carrying his surname without an initial letter. This was invariably in thin block capitals either in a plain rectangular border or one highlighted with a sawtooth rim.

POTWINE, JOHN

John Potwine was born in 1698 and started working in Boston around 1715. He stayed there until the late 1730s, when he moved to Hartford, Connecticut. Thereafter, he worked in Coventry and in East Windsor, where his career ended in East Windsor. His full mark consisted of his surname in script lettering preceded by the initial *I* (changed from *J* to conform to tradition). This was enclosed in a rectangular border with shaped top. He also used an initial-punchmark IP set into a shaped frame.

QUINTARD, PETER

Peter Quintard, possibly of Dutch or Flemish extraction, worked in New York City and South Norwalk, Connecticut, in the middle part of the 18th century. He was born in 1699, served his apprenticeship in New York City, and died in 1762 at the age of 63. Peter Quintard used an initial-punchmark PQ, with the *Q* shaped like a backward *P*. Sometimes a period separated the letters and sometimes not.

REVERE, PAUL, Jr.

The most famous of all American silversmiths, Paul Revere, Jr.'s works command a higher premium on the antiques market than those of any of his contemporaries. He was extremely active and turned out a great quantity of products, but generations of active collecting mean the majority of them are in museums. Paul Revere, Jr., also known as Paul Revere II, was the son of a goldsmith and silversmith. The younger Revere, born in 1735, was apprenticed to his father and worked alongside him from the 1750s. Revere died in 1818 at the age of 83, having spent his entire career in Boston. His mark was either REVERE, in gold block lettering set within a rectangular border, or the script initials PR. These markings were different from those used by his father, so there is never any problem in attributions.

RICHARDSON, JOSEPH, Jr.

Joseph Richardson, Jr., is the most celebrated of the old Philadelphia silversmiths. The son of a noted silversmith, he was born in 1752 and died in 1831 at the age of 79. He always used an initial-punchmark JR in either a rectangular or oval frame or sometimes without a frame. This differed from the punchmark of his father, who observed the old tradition among smiths and signed himself IR (changing the *J* to an *I*).

ROGERS, DANIEL

Daniel Rogers of Ipswich, Massachusetts, worked in the late 18th and early 19th centuries. He is known for his use of many different marks. A piece marked D.ROGERS, in any style of marking, is a work of this smith. Only one D. Rogers has been traced among the American silversmiths, though the variety of markings would easily lead to the conclusion that a half dozen or more were active.

ROSS, JOHN

John Ross, born in 1756, worked in Baltimore in the latter part of the 18th century. He habitually used an initial-punchmark IR, either separated by a period or without a period but always within a rectangular frame.

SAYRE, JOEL

Joel Sayre worked in Southampton, Long Island, and New York City. He was born in 1778 and was in business by 1798. After four years in Southampton he moved to New York City, and for more than a decade he shared a shop with his brother John. In 1814 Joel began working alone and continued until his death in 1818. His mark was usually in script lettering, with the surname spelled out and preceded by the initial *J*. Sometimes he also used an initial punchmark.

SHEPHERD, ROBERT

Robert Shepherd, born in 1781, worked in Albany, New York, in the first half of the 19th century. In the earlier part of his career he was engaged in a partnership known as Shepherd & Boyd, which lasted from about 1806 to 1830. He thereafter worked on his own until he died in 1853 at the age of 72. His mark was extremely interesting: R.SHEPHERD in very well modeled script lettering in a close-fitting rectangular frame with cutouts at certain strategic points.

SIMPKINS, WILLIAM

William Simpkins, born in 1704, was in business by 1728. He died in 1780 at the age of 76. His mark occurred in three styles: a surname preceded by initial letter, a surname without an initial letter, and an initial punch with the letters not separated by a period.

STANTON, ENOCH

Enoch Stanton, born in 1745, worked in Stonington, Connecticut. He died in 1781 at the age of 36. His usual mark was E:STANTON in a rectangular frame, with the *E* followed by a colon instead of a period. Sometimes he used an initial punchmark in which the letters were likewise separated by a colon, as well as an initial mark in which a period separated the letters.

STORRS, NATHAN

Nathan Storrs, a famous and very successful silversmith of Massachusetts and New York, worked from the late 18th century well into the 19th. He was born in 1768, and about 1790 he settled in New York City. Storrs was disappointed with the city and decided to settle in Northampton, Massachusetts. He retired in 1833. Nathan Storrs's mark was usually N.STORRS in block capitals within a rectangular frame but was sometimes found simply as N.S in a punchmark.

SYNG, PHILIP

Philip Syng was one of very few native Irishmen in the American silversmithing trade during the Colonial era. He was born in Cork in 1676 and arrived in this country in 1714, already an accomplished smith. He died in 1739, having worked as a silversmith in America for about two and a half decades. Philip Syng's mark was his initials, PS, crudely cut within a heart-shaped punch. No period separated the letters.

TOWNSEND, THOMAS

Thomas Townsend of Boston worked as a gold- and silversmith in the period preceding the Revolutionary War. He was born in 1701 and entered the business around 1725. He seems to have retired around the early 1760s and lived until 1777. His mark was always in the form of an initial punch with the letters separated by a period. In one version the mark rested within a tall oval frame and was surmounted by a crown.

VAN DER SPIEGEL, JACOB

Jacob Van Der Spiegel, born in 1668, was one of the early Dutch silversmiths of New York City. He served with the Dutch army assigned to New Amsterdam (New York). He appeared to have entered the silversmithing trade about 1695 and was active for a little more than a decade. He died in 1708. His mark consisted of his initials set against a cloverleaf punch.

VERNON, SAMUEL

Samuel Vernon, born in 1683 and in business until about 1725, was one of the early silversmiths in Providence, Rhode Island. He died in 1737. His works are not too often found on the market. Usually his mark consisted of the letters *SV* in a heart-shaped punch with a tiny cross beneath them.

WALRAVEN, JOHN

John Walraven worked in Baltimore in the late 18th and early 19th centuries. He was born in 1771 and died in 1814. His mark consisted of his surname in slanting script letters preceded by an initial within a shaped rectangular frame.

YOU, THOMAS

Thomas You worked in Charleston, South Carolina, in the 18th century. He was born in 1735 and by 1756 was in the business as a gold- and silversmith. You died at the age of 51. His mark was a crude initial punch with the letters *TY* inside a rectangle with rounded sides.

Important American Silver Manufacturers

ALVIN CORPORATION
Providence, Rhode Island

Alvin Corporation made sterling silver flatware, hollowware, silver deposit ware, and silverplated flatware. Today the company is a division of the Gorham Company.

BAILEY, BANKS & BIDDLE CO.
Philadelphia, Pennsylvania

In 1878 Joseph T. Bailey II, George Banks of J. E. Caldwell & Co., and Samuel Biddle of Robbins, Clark & Biddle formed a partnership under the name of Bailey, Banks & Biddle. The business was listed as jewelers and silversmiths.

BALL, BLACK & COMPANY
New York, New York

In 1851 this company was successor to Ball, Tompkins & Black and was succeeded in 1876 by Black, Starr & Frost.

BALL, TOMPKINS, & BLACK
New York, New York

In 1839 this company was successor to Marquand & Co. and was succeeded in 1851 by Ball, Black & Co.

BIGELOW, KENNARD & COMPANY, INC.
Boston, Massachusetts

This company began in 1830. Abraham O. Bigelow, M. P. Kennard, William H. Kennard, and F. P. Bemis became members of the firm, and the name was changed to Bigelow, Kennard & Company. The firm was incorporated in 1912 and went out of business in January 1922.

BLACK, STARR & FROST, LTD.
New York, New York

The present firm does not manufacture items but uses the trademarks shown:

Marquand & Co.	*1810*
Ball, Tompkins & Black	*1839*
Ball, Black & Co.	*1851*
Black, Starr & Frost	*1876*

Black, Starr, Frost-Gorham Inc.	*1929*
Black, Starr & Gorham, Inc.	*1940*
Black Starr & Frost, Ltd.	*1962*

R. BLACKINTON & CO.
North Attleboro, Massachusetts

Founded in 1862 this firm's products have consisted mostly of sterling silver, flatware, hollowware, and novelty items.

J. E. CALDWELL
Philadelphia, Pennsylvania

J. E. Caldwell was founded in 1832. The name was changed to J. E. Caldwell & Company in 1848.

ALBERT COLES & CO.
New York, New York

Albert Coles & Co. were New York silversmiths from 1836 to 1880. Albert Coles & Co. manufactured silver flatware.

CURRIER & ROBY
New York, New York

Currier & Roby were New York silversmiths who specialized in the reproduction of English and American antique silver hollowware and flatware.

DOMINICK & HAFF
New York, New York

Dominick & Haff, established by H. Blanchard Dominick and Leroy B. Haff, produced sterling silver flatware, hollowware, and novelty items.

WM. B. DURGIN CO.
Concord, New Hampshire
Providence, Rhode Island

Founded in 1853 by William B. Durgin in Concord, New Hampshire, this firm made sterling flatware, silver and plated hollowware, and novelty items. The company was purchased by the Gorham Company but continued to operate in Concord until 1931, when it was moved to Providence, Rhode Island.

J. F. FRADLEY & CO.
New York, New York

J. F. Fradley opened a small shop and in 1870 a small factory. In 1873 he added silver novelties to his productions.

WM. GALE
New York, New York

William Gale operated in New York City from 1824 to 1850. The company was purchased by the Gorham Corporation in 1961.

GOODNOW & JENKS
Boston, Massachusetts

This company was established in 1893 to manufacture and sell sterling silver.

GORHAM CORPORATION
Providence, Rhode Island

Jabez Gorham purchased his own shop in 1815 to manufacture small items. Gorham's familiar trademark was registered (#33,902) December 19, 1899, at which time it was stated that it had been in use since January 1, 1853. The Gorham Corporation now states that this trademark was used as early as 1848 and that from 1848 to 1865 the lion faced left rather than right. Gorham's various marks include the lion, anchor, G, Martelé, Athenic, and also alphabet and date letters and symbols. Flatware weights were also indicated.

GRAFF, WASHBOURNE & DUNN
New York, New York

Graff, Washbourne & Dunn may be traced back to William Gale. He was followed by the firm of Wm. Gale & Son, then Gale, Wood & Hughes and Wood & Hughes. In 1899, Wood & Hughes sold their factory to Graff, Washbourne & Dunn. The company was purchased by the Gorham Corporation in 1961. Graff, Washbourne & Dunn were makers of sterling silver hollowware and novelty items.

JACOBI & JENKINS
Baltimore, Maryland

Founded in 1894 and succeeded by Jenkins & Jenkins from 1908 until 1915, this firm made sterling silver hollowware repoussé patterns.

WM. B. KERR & CO.
Newark, New Jersey

Established by William B. Kerr in Newark, New Jersey, in 1855, this firm made sterling silver flatware, hollowware, and jewelry. They used the fleur-de-lis trademark in 1892, were purchased by the Gorham Corporation in 1906, and moved to Providence, Rhode Island, in 1927.

KIRK STIEFF CORPORATION
Baltimore, Maryland

This company, established as Kirk & Smith in 1815, has had the following organizational titles:

Kirk & Smith	1815–1820
Samuel Kirk	1821–1846
Samuel Kirk & Son	1846–1861
Samuel Kirk & Sons	1861–1868
Samuel Kirk & Son	1868–1896
Samuel Kirk & Son Co.	1896–1924
Samuel Kirk & Son, Inc.	1924–1979
Kirk Stieff Corporation	1979–

LaPIERRE MFG. CO.
Newark, New Jersey, and New York, New York

The LaPierre Company began in New York in 1888. In 1929 the business was purchased by International Silver Company and moved to Wallingford, Connecticut. They produced small hollowware pieces, novelties, and dresser items.

DANIEL LOW & CO.
Salem, Massachusetts

Daniel Low established this company in 1867. His son, Seth F. Low, designed the first Witch souvenir spoon, made by the Durgin Division of The Gorham Mfg. Co. In 1907 the business was incorporated under the name Daniel Low & Co., Inc. They produced sterling silver novelties and spoons.

THE MAUSER MANUFACTURING COMPANY
New York, New York

Frank Mauser began the manufacture of fine sterling silver goods in North Attleboro, Massachusetts, in July 1887. In 1903 the Mauser Mfg. Co. merged with the Hayes & McFarland Company of Mount Vernon, New York, and the Roger Williams Silver Company of Providence, Rhode Island, to form the Mt. Vernon Company Silversmiths, Inc. This company, in turn, was purchased by the Gorham Corporation in 1913. They were known for sterling silver hollowware, desk articles, novelty items, and colognes.

REDLICH & CO.
New York, New York

This firm began in February 1890 as Ludwig, Redlich & Co. In 1895 Adolph Ludwig sold his interest, and the company became Redlich & Co. Products were sterling silver, hollowware, and novelty items.

REED & BARTON
Taunton, Massachusetts

In 1824 Isaac Babbitt and William W. Crossman of Taunton, Massachusetts, formed the partnership of Babbitt & Crossman, now Reed & Barton. They produced sterling silver and silverplate hollowware and flatware.

GEORGE W. SHIEBLER & CO.
New York, New York

On March 4, 1876, George W. Shiebler began business under his own name. Shiebler was noted for medallion work. They produced sterling silver novelties, jewelry, and hollowware.

SHREVE & CO.
San Francisco, California

George C. and S. S. Shreve opened a jewelry shop in 1852. In 1915 they bought the Vanderslice Company. Shreve & Co. manufactured their first flatware in 1904. They also produced hollowware and special commissions.

SHREVE, CRUMP & LOW CO., INC.
Boston, Massachusetts

The company does no manufacturing but has some designs created exclusively for them.

THEODORE B. STARR
New York, New York

In business c. 1900–1924.

TIFFANY & CO., INC.
New York, New York

Tiffany & Young	*1837*
Tiffany, Young & Ellis	*1841*
Tiffany & Company	*1853*
Tiffany & Co., Inc.	*1868*

UNGER BROS.
Newark, New Jersey

Five brothers organized Unger Bros. in 1872. They produced beautiful Art Nouveau pieces, sterling silver hollowware and flatware, jewelry, and novelties.

Continental Silver

During the 15th and 16th centuries Germans made and displayed enormous quantities of silver to show their wealth. Embossed and chased motifs, sometimes to the point of excess, were common forms of decoration. The towns of Augsberg and Nuremberg were important centers for silversmithing during this time. Augsberg's town mark was a pineapple; Nuremberg's, the letter *N*. A Roman-style capital *N* was used first and later replaced by a script capital. Date letters were used in combination with town marks. Many drinking articles were produced, especially beakers, usually with engraved biblical or Classical scenes. Traveling cups were produced in sets and tankards in many sizes, often of wood, pottery, and ivory with sterling silver mounts. Candlesticks, tea services, vases, baskets, and other serving pieces were produced for domestic customers as well as for export.

In eastern Europe, Poland and what is now Czechoslovakia boasted many silversmiths during the 15th and 16th centuries. The silversmiths used genre motifs and also were influenced by the French styles.

Little silver was produced in Denmark before the late 17th century because there was not a great demand for expensive pieces. Drinking horns, usually of whalebone with sterling silver mounts, were among the first objects produced. At least three quarters of all silver produced in Denmark in the 18th century was made for drinking vessels. Ivory tankards were made with sterling silver banding and silver standing cups. Copenhagen was the most important center of silversmithing, with a town mark of three castles in a cartouche above the date.

In the 15th and 16th centuries Italy was rich in both silver and gold work with so high a standard that royalty all over Europe ordered silver services. Though goldsmith guilds date to 1035, it was not until 1873 that laws were adopted to legalize silver production.

In the 18th century Spanish silversmiths were influenced by the French style, but the English designs were in such great demand that items such as cruets were produced. The most important silversmithing centers were Madrid and Barcelona. Elaborate filigree was first produced in Barcelona. In Portugal several cities, such as Lisbon and Oporto, were silversmithing centers. France influenced Portuguese silver, as did the English. The demand for English-style silver was so great in the 18th century that some Portuguese smiths punched their objects with English marks.

Most pieces of Continental silver found in the marketplace today were made in the 19th century in earlier styles. Check the marks for appropriate dating.

English Sterling Silver and Hallmarks

In England the craft of goldsmithing was practiced as early as 1180. Goldsmithing refers to working in gold or sterling silver.

The assaying or making of sterling silver was regulated by the year 1500, and through the years various letters and symbols have been used and enforced up to the present time. Silver in pure, or 1000, form is not used because the finished product would be too soft. The addition of copper allows the piece to be worked. Hence, the numerals 925 mean 925 parts silver and 75 parts copper.

Sterling silver is weighed in troy ounces, 12 troy ounces constituting a pound of silver. The English enforced the standard of 925, and at one point .958 sterling silver was the Britannia standard. In England all sterling silver is referred to as plate; in the United States, plate is a shortened form referring to silverplate.

The adulteration of sterling marks in England in the early 19th century included using a forged stamp and shifting marks from one piece to another or onto a piece of silverplate. Conviction for any of these changes resulted in imprisonment of the offender. During the latter part of the 19th century all sterling silver pieces imported into England from foreign countries had to be assayed and hallmarked with English marks, with the addition of a stamped letter *F*, indicating foreign origin. The only pieces without marks were those deemed too ornate to have an area for marking without detriment to the design.

Marks are referred to as touch or hallmarks. Touch means testing silver by rubbing on a touchstone to judge quality. Today we rub the piece on a stone and test with acid and compare with a rubbing of pure silver.

How to Read English Hallmarks

Every piece of English sterling silver bears a mark or series of marks indicating the quality of the metal, the assay office mark, the maker's mark, and the date letter.

In England the lion passant (a standing lion) indicates sterling silver. In Scotland sterling is represented by a thistle and in Ireland by a harp. The province or town where the silver was assayed is represented by a leopard's head for London, an anchor for Birmingham, and a crown for Sheffield. For specific information about other provinces, study a book on English hallmarks. From the beginning of silver marking in England until 1821, the London punch was a crowned leopard's head. After 1821 the crown was removed, and the leopard resembled a grinning cat. The date letter (mark) is a letter of the alphabet with a change in stylization for each cycle, with only approximately 20 letters of the alphabet used. The letter style and the shape of the punch are also changed for each cycle.

A sovereign, or duty, mark is found on sterling silver pieces made in England and Scotland from 1784 until 1890 and is a punch struck with the head of the reigning monarch.

BIRMINGHAM

1773 A	1798 a	1824 Q
1774 B	1799 b	1825 R
1775 C	1800 c	1826 S
1776 D	1801 d	1827 T
1777 E	1802 e	1828 U
1778 F	1803 f	1829 V Wm. IV.
1779 G	1804 g	1830 W
1780 H	1805 h	1831 X
1781 I	1806 i	1832 Y
1782 K	1807 j	1833 Z
1783 L	1808 k	1834 A
1784 M	1809 l	1835 B
1785 N	1810 m	1836 C
1786 O	1811 n	1837 Vict.
1787 P	1812 o	1838 D
1788 Q	1813 p	1839 E
1789 R	1814 q	1840 F
1790 S	1815 r	1841 G
1791 T	1816 s	1842 H
1792 U	1817 t	1843 I
1793 V	1818 u	1844 J
1794 W	1819 v Geo. IV.	1845 K
1795 X	1820 w	1846 L
1796 Y	1821 x	1847 M
1797 Z	1822 y	1848 N
	1823 z	

In 1797 the duty on silver was doubled, and for a short time the King's Head was duplicated

BIRMINGHAM

1849 A	1867 S	1883 i
1850 B	1868 T	1884 k
1851 C	1869 U	1885 l
1852 D	1870 V	1886 m
1853 E	1871 W	1887 n
1854 F	1872 X	1888 o
1855 G	1873 Y	1889 p
1856 H	1874 Z	1890 q
1857 I		1891 r
1858 J	1875 a	1892 s
1859 K	1876 b	1893 t
1860 L	1877 c	1894 u
1861 M	1878 d	1895 v
1862 N	1879 e	1896 w
1863 O	1880 f	1897 x
1864 P	1881 g	1898 y
1865 Q	1882 h	1899 z
1866 R		

French Silver

~~~~~~⟨⟩~~~~~~

French silver was often referred to in early records as plate. In the Middle Ages silver standards were the same as in England. In 1260 a charter was formed by the government and presented as a guideline for standards and marks.

During the first quarter of the 18th century there was a formal style. This was followed by a simpler design in the middle of the century, and the latter part saw a melding of classicism and Louis XVI wreath-and-ribbon motifs combined with simple Adamesque motifs.

After the fall of the House of Bourbon, Napoleon became emperor and ordered a profusion of silver objects decorated with laurel wreaths, urns, and Egyptian Revival motifs.

During the 19th century many distinctive styles were found in the provinces in France. In Strasbourg numerous silver-gilt objects were created for the nearby German market, where elaborately gilded designs were favored. In the northern area of France, silversmiths made pieces with Dutch stylizations, and in Toulouse very ornate pieces were made for Spanish customers.

Characteristics of Decorative Styles

1. Regency, 1710–1735—scrolls and rockwork.
2. Louis XV and Louis XVI—classical style with ovals, vases, folds of drapery, floral wreaths with bowknots, and medallions.
3. Rococo—festoons, birds, and foliate decoration.

Mexican Silver

Mexican sterling silver has been regarded as little more than scrap silver for many years. This lack of interest can be attributed to the inconsistency of Mexican assaying standards. Pieces stamped sterling were often, in fact, lower in silver than the 925 standard, and occasionally even silverplated pieces have been stamped sterling. There is a new interest in Mexican silver made during the mid-20th century, especially those pieces stamped Sanborns or Spratling. Many small boxes and pieces of jewelry were produced in silver. Other silver objects were often made to resemble Jensen, Rococo, or Georgian designs. As interest and prices continue to escalate, collectors and dealers will uncover additional information on this subject.

Russian Silver

Since the 17th century Russian silver has been marked with rigid standards. Over the years a wide variety of objects, from functional vessels to cigarette cases, snuffboxes, jars, and miniatures, as well as religious icons and medals, were produced. Most of the decoration on these objects was a unique combination of European styles with a touch of genre decoration and Oriental motifs. There were a number of examples with filigree decoration, niello work, chasing, and inlay of enamel and stones. Some styles depicted Russian genre scenes with snowy landscapes, churches with onion-shape domes, and peasant figures. Others related to fairy tale and fantasy, with swan- and throne-shaped salts and cups. Niello and enamel decoration were typically Russian in feeling, while Continental influences abound in chased and embossed techniques. Nineteenth-century decoration was influenced by the Empire style, with wreath, sphinx, German Biedermeier, and other Baroque forms used. By 1900, when Art Nouveau was in full bloom in other countries, Russia had very little success with the form. A mixture of botanical forms with old Russian design structures was tried, but it was not very popular.

New pieces made to reproduce pre-Revolutionary styles are currently being made in New York City and other places. They are often stamped with the late-19th-century marks. The enamelwork is usually crudely applied, and there is a lack of detailing. It is not uncommon for such pieces to surface at little country auctions or at antiques centers.

Silver and Silverplate Listings

Aesthetic

Aesthetic taste, applied metal fruit bowl, c. 1881, Gorham, $5,000. Courtesy of Christie's East, New York.

A particularly attractive style, Aesthetic was influenced by the Japanese in the late 19th century. Popular in America, England, and other countries, its main decorative motifs depict birds, insects, and plant forms, often enhanced with bright-cut engraving, frosted motifs, parcel-gilt areas, and the extensive use of fan motifs.

CHRISTENING SET, bright-cut with flowers, foliage, and birds in the Aesthetic taste, comprising knife, fork, spoon, and napkin ring, in a fitted case, T. & Co., Glasgow, 1888. **$275/set**
DISH, MEAT, BEADED OVAL, cover engraved in the Aesthetic taste with Chinese figures, birds, butterflies, and plants, silver-plated, Mappin and Webb. **$135**

SALAD SPOON AND FORK, bright-cut with scrolling foliage, handles with applied beaded mounts, in fitted case, Birmingham, 1877.   **$475/set**

TEASPOONS AND PAIR OF SUGAR TONGS, parcel-gilt, shaped handles struck with birds and flowers on frosted grounds and with fan terminals, in case, Frederick Elkington, Birmingham, 1879.   **$400/set**

Animals

American silverplated smoke set, c. 1885, $350. Photo by J. Auslander.

During the past year there has been an increase in the number of collectors seeking animal-related objects in sterling silver. Trophy cups, dog collars, medals, and other dog-related objects are being sought. In addition, inkwells, humidors, paperweights, spoons, and canes with representations of animals of various kinds have increased in price. It is not unusual for many of these objects to have presentation inscriptions. From compacts to children's cups, most collectors can find many objects for their own menagerie.

Georgian dog collars with engraved plaques indicating the owner's name and address and the name of the dog are found in many sizes, from lapdog to St. Bernard. Antiques collectors look for sterling cat collars with original bells, lock, and key, again varying in size and date. Sterling pepperettes, salt and pepper shakers, pitchers, and inkstands, all in animal form, were made in England and on the Continent during the 19th century. Snuffboxes were engraved with depictions of cats, often including dates and legend. Many matchsafes portray full-figure cats and dogs, Puss in Boots, cat and mouse, or hunt scenes with a pack of dogs.

Silver and silverplate have been used, along with glass and pottery with silver mounts. Novelties have included an inkstand with double wells in the shape of cats' heads, a coral and silver-gilt dip pen with carved cat at the tip, and perfume bottles in sterling silver depicting a band of cats playing musical instruments.

Sterling silver cigarette cases and matchsafes have often been enameled with a portrait of the family pet, generally with engraved dates. Rattles, always popular collectors' pieces, were made in full-figure form, with teddy bears, ducks, cats, dogs, and pigs represented.

BUD VASE, crystal, with silverplated cat on base, English, late 19th century.   **$325**

COMPACT, cat form with garnet eyes, small size.   **$750**

DOG COLLAR, large, Victorian, paneled, mount engraved "Lord Charles Beresford's Alec, HMS Ramillies," W.T., London, 1877.   **$250**

DOG COLLAR, silverplated, wirework with 14 bells.   **$40**

DOG COLLAR, sterling silver, with two rows of studs, complete with padlock, by Henry William Dee, 1877.   **$675**

FOX TERRIER, wire-haired, cast model, applied to an Art Deco variegated-marble oblong paperweight, Sheffield, 1927. **$550**

FRAME, full-figure cat at base, patinated silverplate, c. 1880.
                                                                        $350

HUMIDOR, figural dog on lid, engraved decoration, American, late 19th century, silverplated.   **$350**

HUNTER with bridle and reins and cropped tail, cast model, length, 6 in.   **$800**

INKWELL in bulldog form, English, silverplated, late 19th century.   **$350**

INKWELL, wooden base with two figural glass wells that have silverplated cats' heads with glass eyes.   **$750**

LETTER KNIFE, ivory with silver dog's head at handle. **$350**

MEDAL, first-prize collie, 1899.   **$150**

NAPKIN RING, boy and dog on flat base, American, late 19th century, silverplated.   **$175**

PLACE CARD HOLDERS, set of 6, cut out in terrier form, American, early 20th century.   **$450/set**

SALT AND PEPPER SHAKERS, figural amber glass with silver-plated cats' heads, American, late 19th century.   **$275/pr**

SALT AND PEPPER SHAKERS, figural cats, silverplated, American, late 19th century.   **$250/pr**

SPANIEL, 19th-century, Continental silver, realistically modeled with bushy tail, floppy ears, and detachable head, height, 8¼ in.   **$4,000**

SPIRITED HORSE with arched neck and flowing tail, cast model, length, 7½ in.   **$1,200**

STIRRUP CUP, English, hound's head form, silverplated.

$175

TRINKET BOX, circular, lid enameled with a kitten on an ivory guilloche-enameled background, Russian, diameter, 2 in.

$525

WHISTLE in the form of a dog's head.   **$225**

WHISTLE in the form of a horse's head.   **$275**

Applied and Mixed Metal

Left. *Whiting hand-hammered applied dish*, $2,400. Right. *Mixed metal leaf-form dish, Shiebler*, $1,900. Courtesy of Christie's East, New York.

In the late 19th century a number of silversmiths, inspired by the Arts and Crafts movement, used a copper ground with a lacquered finish or a hand-hammered silver ground with applied gold, silver, copper, or bronze decoration. Gorham, Tiffany, Whiting, and Shiebler, among others, were design innovators in these mediums. The Japanese had used this combination of textures since at least the 17th century because using flowers, birds, insects, fish, and grapes as decoration gave a three-dimensional effect to a flattened piece of silver. Both hollowware and flatware were produced with Islamic- or

Japonesque-style applied work at this time.

Vases, tête-à-tête sets, pitchers, perfume bottles, bells, tea caddies, sporting trophies, porringers, and ladles were among the kinds of pieces produced with this technique.

BOWL, "Japanese style," square with bowed sides, the sides of the gilded interior applied in silver and copper with a spray of blackberries, a flying bird, a heron, and a salamander surrounded by sprays of various Oriental plants, Gorham Mfg. Co., 1880, width, 8 3/8 in.   **$4,200**

BOWL, "Japanese style," with in-curved neck, applied with a jumping fish, a snail crawling on a branch with copper berries, and a crab with copper body, with hammered surface, Whiting Mfg. Co., Providence, RI, c. 1880–90, diameter, 8 in. **$1,700**

BOWL, "Japanese style," circular, on 3 supports, hammered surface applied in copper and silver-gilt with strawberries, dogwood blossoms, two butterflies, and a bird, spoon with handle with round terminal applied in copper with strawberries, Gorham Mfg. Co., 1881.   **$4,500/2**

BOWL, fruit, body hammered and applied with wide die-rolled band of geometric designs in Persian taste, surmounted by applied cherry sprig with hummingbird, fly, and beetle, Gorham, 1881.   **$5,000**

DEMITASSE POT, "Japanese style," tapered cylindrical form applied in copper and silver with two flies above a flowering prunus spray, other side applied with a large bug above a bright-cut branch, Whiting Mfg. Co., c. 1880–90, height, 7 1/4 in.   **$1,900**

DISH, leaf-form, rectangular with curving rim, chased to simulate leaf veins and applied with copper beetles, Shiebler, length, 7 1/2 in.   **$1,900**

DISH, rectangular demi-lune form applied with crab, trailing water flowers, and shell on engraved marine plants, overall hammered surface, Whiting, length, 8 in.   **$2,400**

KNIVES, fruit, set of 6, Gorham, cast-bronze handles with Japanese motifs, sterling blades, bright-cut engraved.   **$425/set**

LIGHTER, "Japanese Style," pumpkin shape, hammered surface applied with a seated Chinaman smoking a pipe, butterfly, bird, and bee, spray of bamboo, fluted domed cover with attached extinguisher, dragon handle, Gorham Mfg. Co., 1882.
                                                       $1,400

PITCHER, Gorham, 1880, Japanese taste, squared vase form with cast handle formed as elephant's head and trunk, the hammered body applied with copper dragonfly, rose sprig, butterfly, and dogwood branches, 7 in.   **$8,500**

PITCHER, water, "Japanese Style," baluster form with hammered surface applied on one side with a lily spray, surrounded by two copper fish and a silver and copper turtle, Whiting Mfg. Co., Providence, RI, c. 1880–90, height, 7¼ in.   **$16,000**

TEA CADDY, silver and mixed metal, "Japanese Style," in the form of a quadrangular basket, one angle applied with a trailing flower spray in silver, opposite angle applied with a grapevine rising with a bunch of copper grapes, slip-on cover applied with a silver and copper fly, Whiting Mfg. Co., 1880–90.   **$2,900**

TRAY, "Japanese Style," small, rectangular, surface engraved with a furnace and applied with a seated figure blowing a pipe at the furnace mouth, a tree and a bird in flight, Gorham Mfg. Co., 1881, length, 6 in.   **$1,100**

TUREEN, "Japanese Style," rectangular form on 4 pad feet, rustic handles with laurel leaf and berry joins, body applied with crawfish, floral sprays, lily pads, and turtle, the domed cover with crab applied with copper beads, overall hammered finish.   **$19,000**

Art Deco

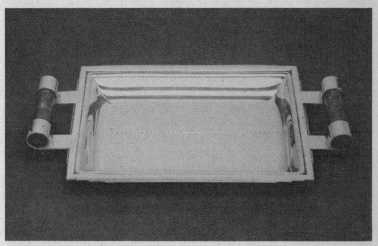

Art Deco sterling dish by Puiforcat, 20½" length, estimate, $15,000–$20,000. **Courtesy of Christie's Park Ave., New York.**

In the last few years prices for good Art Deco silver have, in many instances, outstripped Georgian sterling silver prices.

The Art Moderne style began shortly after the 1925 Paris Art Decoratif exhibition, which encompassed the entire field of decorative arts. A revival of interest in the 1960s resulted in a new name for the period, Art Deco.

The style is characterized by bold, often blocky and angular shapes, sometimes geometric in form and lacking excessive ornamentation; vivid enamel coloration; the use of engine-turned motifs, bright lacquers, inlays, and bold red, blue, or violet colors often mixed with the silver. Bakelite was sometimes used for handles and finials. Designs were often taken from nature and featured stylized palm trees and leaves, sunburst motifs, stylized flowers, and bold zigzag forms.

Jean Puiforcat is considered the founder of French Art Deco silver production. He combined silver with ivory, wood, jade, and crystal in elegant, restrained forms. Among the large

French firms working during this period, Christofle was a leader, often employing artists from other countries.

ASHTRAY, circular, on hexagonal foot, body formed as a Chinese mother-of-pearl inlaid lacquer bowl, set with carnelian square bosses, applied with 2 black-jet cigarette holders, Cartier, Paris, c. 1925, length, 5³⁄₈ in.   **$2,500**

ASHTRAY, French silver and Lac Burgauté, the body formed as a Chinese mother-of-pearl inlaid lacquer bowl, set with carnelian square bosses, applied with 2 black-jet cigarette holders, Cartier, Paris, c. 1925.   **$3,500**

BOWL, in the Cartier style, rectangular with curving edges extending over the width at each side to create rolled handles, the base resting on 2 cylindrical rolls, Reed & Barton, Taunton, MA, 1935.   **$325**

BOWL of hemispherical form applied with 5 vertical bands of overlapping fruits, Tiffany & Co., New York, c. 1930, diameter, 9¹⁄₄ in.   **$1,000**

BOWL, centerpiece, silver, circular with hammered surface on circular serrated foot, strapwork rim, applied with beaded curling strapwork handles, Hans Hansen, Copenhagen, 1931, length, 11³⁄₈ in.   **$2,200**

BOWL, fruit, circular, on a spreading foot, with molded rim and 2 ribbed split handles, London, 1933.   **$600**

BOX, cigarette, oblong, cedar-lined, decorated with ribbing, Goldsmiths and Silversmiths Co., Ltd., London, 1933.   **$800**

BOX, silver, jade, and sapphire. John Chattellier, Newark, NJ, applied with a gilt cash motif, lid applied with a rectangular carved openwork jade plaque exposing lapis lazuli below, set with cabochon sapphires, retailed by Cartier, c. 1925, length, 7¹⁄₄ in.   **$6,000**

COCKTAIL SHAKER, sterling silver, plain, tapering, Elkington and Company.   **$250**

CUP, inverted pear shape, decorated with a geometric frieze, the bowl chased with naturalistic forms, Danish, Michelsen, 1900.   **$325**

JUG, claret, glass, rib-cut oblong with star-cut base, plain sterling mount, scroll handle, and domed hinged cover, Hukin & Heath, Birmingham, 1922.   **$700**

JUG, hot water, tapering on a fluted-rim foot, with a reeded rim, shaped wood handle, and flat hinged cover. **$550**

SALVER, circular, on stylized hoof feet with molded rim and plain ground, Mappin and Webb, diameter, 10 in. **$500**

SAUCE BOAT, sterling silver, on rising oblong base with an everted rim and bracket handle. **$150**

TEA AND COFFEE SERVICE, 20th century, 4 pieces, comprising coffeepot, teapot, creamer, and 2-handled covered sugar bowl, each of navette outline on rectangular base with glass handles and arched finials, Jean E. Puiforcat, Paris. **$15,000/set**

TEA AND COFFEE SERVICE, 4 pieces, shaped rectangular form with fluted corners and squared handles, wood knop finials, Birmingham, 1921. **$800/set**

TEA SERVICE, 4 pieces, shaped oblong, teapot and hot water jug with ebonized wood handles, Sheffield, 1930. **$950/set**

TEA SERVICE, 4 pieces, oblong with gadrooned and sunburst rims, angular ebonized wood handles, and shaped oval wood finials. **$1,200/set**

TEA SERVICE, 3 pieces, compressed, with angular handles, each on a rim foot, Birmingham, 1938. **$600/set**

TEA SERVICE, 3 pieces, sterling silver, circular, with composition handle and finial, London, 1935. **$475/set**

TUREEN, soup, 20th century, silver, covered, shaped rectangular section with faceted shoulders, ivory handles and finial, Tetard Freres, Paris, height, 10¾ in. **$8,500**

VASE, parcel-gilt of oval section with flared sides, the lower body applied with 2 bands of scalloping with detachable silverplated liner, Jean E. Puiforcat, Paris, c. 1940, height, 6¼ in. **$6,500**

Art Nouveau

Pair of Art Nouveau silverplated candlesticks, $750/pair. **Photo by J. Auslander.**

The term Art Nouveau did not come into vogue nor was it used by those in the decorative arts field until the 1895 opening of L'Art Nouveau, a Parisian shop owned by Samuel Bing specializing in the modern design. By 1900, however, the term was in universal use. The popularity of this new style was short-lived, from about 1890 to 1910.

Art Nouveau has often been confused with English Arts and Crafts or Jugendstil movements because they have similar characteristics. Basic design elements of pure Art Nouveau include a blending of Japanese design and the French Rococo style and are characterized by asymmetrical, flowing, sensuous, always curving lines, often combining plant leaves, blossoms, and insect forms. When used, the female form is idealized with long flowing hair and curving folds of clothing. Floral designs, depicting roses, irises, violets, waterlilies, and poppies, were also used, especially as borders for compacts, bowls, and trays.

Art Nouveau trinket tray with nude female in swirled foliage. **Courtesy of Nancy and Bruce Thompson. Photo by J. Auslander.**

Another major influence on the Art Nouveau style was the American painter James McNeil Whistler, who was strongly influenced by Japanese art in his painting style. He used soft, subtle colors and alternating lines, as shown in his famous Peacock Room design. Many artists copied him and used the peacock as a decorative symbol at this time.

In the United States some of the best sterling silver pieces of the Art Nouveau period were created in the latter part of the 19th century by the Unger Brothers firm. They specialized in ladies' dressing table articles, with endless variations of hand mirrors, brushes, jars, and trinket trays. Many of their designs, including "Love's Dream," "Evangeline," and "Bride of the Waves," are eagerly sought today. Tiffany, Gorham, and Kerr were also known for their Art Nouveau designs.

Although famous as an architect, the Englishman Charles Robert Ashbee produced some of the finest Art Nouveau silver. It was executed by the Guild of Handicraft, founded in 1888.

Other popular small items were matchsafes, tea balls, flasks, desk sets, sewing items, and even tiny luggage tags, bookmarks, and garters. All made use of the curving, tendril-like Art Nouveau form with women's heads and full-figure human motifs.

Left. *German cut glass, Art Nouveau, claret jug with silver mounts, $1,400.*
Right. *Continental cut glass jug with silver mount, with lions' heads, $600.*
Courtesy of Christie's East, New York.

BASKET, cake, pierced oval stamped with trailing flowers and foliage, Walker and Hall, Sheffield, 1908.　　　**$350**

BASKET, cake, sterling silver, square, swing-handled with crimped rim, the wirework handle applied with two flowerheads, German, 8½ in.　　　**$150**

BEAKER, tapering, with applied frieze of lozenges, bright-cut, with an iris and scrolling foliage in Art Nouveau style, Russian.
　　　$225

BELT, paneled, buckle and 7 circular panels pierced and stamped with maidens sitting amid flowers and foliage, Birmingham, 1902.　　　**$325**

Group of American sterling bowls in Art Nouveau motifs. Courtesy of Christie's East, New York.

BISCUIT BARREL, cut and frosted tapering glass with sterling foliate-decorated mount, body cut with flowers and foliage, signed "Daum, Nancy," 5¼ in. **$550**

BOWL, centerpiece, American silver chased with irises, length, 13 in. **$500**

BOWL, everted rim applied with grapevine, hammered surface, Gorham Mfg. Co., 1905. **$1,100**

BOWL, rose, gadrooned and decorated with stylized flowers and foliage with a shell, floral, and foliate rim and 2 harp-shaped handles. **$275**

BOWL, rose, sterling silver, body chased with stylized irises, ebonized wood plinth, Sheffield, 1901, diameter, 9 in. **$1,100**

BOXES, trinket, pair, small, oblong, hobnail-pattern cut glass, sterling covers stamped with Art Nouveau–style flowers, Birmingham, 1913. **$175/pr**

CAKE STAND, circular, pedestal, pierced and stamped with floral and foliage decoration, waved rim, Continental. **$325**

CANDELABRA, pair, silverplated, 5 lights, probably American, each composed of 2 maidens with undulating robes supporting a detachable branch with 4 openwork scroll arms, with leaf-form sconces, height, 19¾ in.   **$5,200/pr**

CENTERPIECE, on rising circular foot, with a central trumpet-shape vase with 3 detachable smaller vases, Birmingham, 1905.
                                                      $750

CENTERPIECE, 2-handled oval on scroll and grapevine supports, applied with grapevine, with vine-form handles, hammered surface, Gorham Mfg. Co., Providence, RI, 1906, length over handles, 15¼ in.   **$1,400**

CHOCOLATE CUP AND SAUCER, each decorated with trailing flowers and foliage, the cup with split scroll handle with shell thumbpiece.   **$65**

COFFEE SET with matching silver tray, comprising coffeepot, creamer, and 2-handled covered sugar bowl, each of pear form, repoussé and chased with berried foliage, bud finials, tray oval with molded rim and conforming decoration, Tiffany & Co., New York, 1902–1907, length of tray, 14 in.   **$3,700/set**

CUP, large, 3-handled, of campana form with wavy rim, repoussé and chased with undulating flowers, Reed & Barton, Taunton, MA, c. 1900, height, 9½ in.   **$2,500**

DRESSER SET, comprising hand mirror, hairbrush, clothes brush, cut-glass powder jar with silver cover, shoehorn, comb, buttonhook, nail file and buff, chased in high relief with maiden's head with flowing hair within sinuously scrolling water-lilies, William B. Kerr & Co., c. 1900.   **$1,500/set**

DRESSING TABLE SET, lady's, decorated in high relief with a woman's bust with long flowing hair and open flowers with long sinuous stems, comprising hand mirror, hairbrush, 2 clothes brushes, hat brush, nail buffer, shoehorn, 2 comb frames, nail file, nail scissors, William B. Kerr & Co., Newark, NJ, c. 1901.   **$1,100/set**

DRESSING TABLE SET, 6 pieces, stamped with flowers and scrolling foliage, comprising shaped oval trinket tray, hand mirror, 2 hairbrushes, and 2 clothes brushes, William Hutton & Sons Ltd., London.   **$800/set**

DRESSING TABLE SET, 6 pieces, sterling silver stamped with flowers and with vacant cartouches, comprising hand mirror, hairbrushes, 2 clothes brushes, shoehorn, and buttonhook.
$275/set

ELECTRIC TABLE LAMP, silverplated, shaft supported by an openwork, spreading, shaped pentagonal base worked in a vintage pattern of sinuously curving canes and vines with grape leaves and berry clusters, a conforming shade above supporting a series of crystal drops at the rim, Meriden Britannia Co., Rogers Bros. Div., 1900–17.
$3,000

EVENING BAG, crocodile, with chain, applied with a sterling silver mount stamped and pierced with flowers and foliage.
$125

FORKS, pastry, set of 6, handles decorated with stylized foliage, in fitted case, Liberty & Co., Birmingham, 1934.
$225/set

INKSTAND, small, 2-handled oval on beaded scroll legs, molded with scrolls and with 2 silver-topped oval glass inkwells, W.A., Birmingham, 1906.
$400

JARDINIÈRES, pair, each on pad feet with a shaped rim, chased with stylized foliage, R., Glasgow, 1901.
$950/pr

MUG, cylindrical body chased with a continuous scene of water with jumping fish, frogs on lily pads, and a spray of bulrushes, rim formed of applied shells and applied with a lizard, the front engraved with initials.
$2,100

PLATTER, oval, with molded border of sinuous scrolls and stylized flowers, Gorham, 1906.
$650

SERVERS, salad, pair, sterling silver, handles heavily chased with the figures of Venus and Cupid, the stems with pears and leaves, reverse with leaves and vine, unmarked, probably American.
$350/pr

SPOONS, set of 6, reverses of the gilt-lined ovoid bowls engraved with irises in the Art Nouveau style, baluster finial, Russian.
$275/6

TAZZAS, figural, pair, each cast in the form of an Art Nouveau maiden on a blossom-molded, shaped base, supporting a lotus blossom on elongated tendril, the open blossom forming a wide circular bowl, Continental, c. 1900.
$2,500/pr

TEA AND COFFEE SERVICE, comprising coffeepot, teapot, creamer, and sugar bowl, globular with cylindrical neck and foot, applied with molded waistband, covers with mounted button finials, Liberty & Co., Birmingham, 1933.   **$600/set**

TEA AND COFFEE SERVICE in Water Lily pattern, inverted pyriform shape, applied with chased blossoms and leaves, comprising hot water kettle (lacking stand), coffeepot, teapot, covered sugar and waste bowls (lacking creamer), together with matching circular mahogany tray with pierced silver border, Shreve & Co., San Francisco.   **$2,500/set**

TEA AND COFFEE SERVICE with matching silver-mounted wood tray, Orvit, German, early 20th century, comprising coffeepot, teapot, creamer, and 2-handled covered sugar bowl, each embossed and chased with swirling waves and bubbles.

$3,000/set

TEA AND COFFEE SERVICE, 4-pieces with matching tray, silverplated, comprising coffeepot, teapot, creamer, and 2-handled covered sugar bowl, swollen baluster form cast with geometric devices and scrollwork angular loop handles, the oval tray with 2 handles and conforming decoration, length of tray over handles, 24 in.   **$2,700/set**

TEA AND COFFEE SERVICE, silverplated, German, c. 1900, comprising coffeepot, teapot, creamer, and 2-handled covered sugar bowl, each of swirling paneled trumpet form on bracket feet, embossed and chased with berried leaves, tray of irregular outline with 2 handles and conforming decoration, length of tray over handles, 25¼ in.   **$2,700/set**

TEAPOT, compressed pear shape, slightly domed hinged cover with tendril finial applied with 2 ivory balls, Continental.

$475

TEAPOT, frosted and parcel-gilt, barrel-shaped, domed hinged cover with baluster finial, engraved with stylized flowers and foliage and gilt-lined, Russian.   **$425**

TEAPOT, tapering oval afternoon, chased with rising stylized foliage, Sheffield, 1902.   **$225**

TEA SERVICE, 3 pieces, with applied scroll rims, each chased with flowers and foliage and a dragonfly, German.   **$750/set**

TEA SERVICE, 3 pieces, spot-hammered, compressed on scroll legs, applied split tendril handles with foliate terminals.

$750/set

TRAY, design of flowers, grapes, and foliage, Birmingham, 1901, length, 11½ in. **$300**

TRAY, oval, English silver with Art Nouveau decoration, length, 15 in. **$750**

TRAY, tea, silverplate, rounded oblong, 2 handles, ground engraved with stylized irises and scrolling foliage, Christofle, 25 in. **$475**

TRAY, tea, sterling silver, 2-handled oval, scrolling border chased with irises, handles with rushes, engraved with scrolling irises, Austrian, length, 26½ in. **$1,900**

TRAY, trinket, gadrooned quatrefoil stamped with herons in a pond, W.A., Birmingham, 1905. **$300**

TRAY, trinket, oval, stamped with flowers and foliage, center stamped with 2 peacocks amid stylized foliage, H.M., Birmingham, 1901. **$400**

TRAY, trinket, oval, with chased foliate border, German.

$135

VASE, late 19th century, tapering, pierced and chased with flowers and scrolling foliage, with a blue glass liner, Daniel Low & Co., height, 11½ in. **$450**

VASE, silver and enamel, undulating outline with bulbous neck, lower part deeply engraved with stylized foliage and tendrils, neck enameled with green flowers and white leaves, with ruffled rim, Reed & Barton, early 20th century, height, 10¾ in.

$1,200

VASE, waisted, cut-glass sterling mount stamped with trailing chrysanthemums in the Art Nouveau style, Tiffany and Company, height, 11 in. **$700**

VASES, pair, spot-hammered, tulip-shaped on rising circular bases, Chester. **$900/pr**

WAITER, sterling silver, beaded, circular, the ground engraved with flowers and foliage, Russian. **$200**

Arts and Crafts

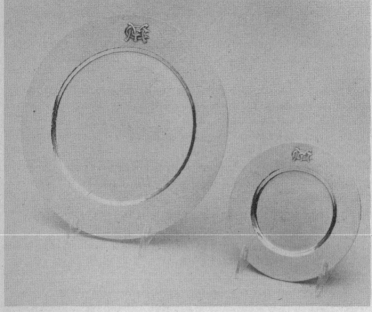

Arts & Crafts (Friedell, CA), 12 service plates, $3,575, 12 bread and butter plates, $880. **Courtesy of Butterfield & Butterfield, San Francisco.**

In contrast to the ornately exuberant machine-made Victorian pieces, in England during the late 19th century, craftsmen began to develop furniture, sterling silver, and other objects with design motifs that featured plainer surfaces, geometric decoration, and an Art Nouveau form that was more stylized than the French form. Many of the design influences reflected earlier English designs. Characteristics of the Arts and Crafts style included medieval colors, symmetrical ornamentation, stylized and rigid plant forms, and religious symbolism. Under the influence of William Morris, Charles R. Ashbee, and other skilled craftsmen, this simpler style, often using natural materials, began to emerge. John Rush and Thomas Carlyle were two other founders of the new movement. Soon hand-hammered metals, especially those with a chemically applied patina, came into use. Ashbee, considered one of the most original designers of silver in this era, founded the School and Guild of Handicraft in London in 1888. One of his favorite design details was the use of stylized flower forms for joints on leg supports and as finials. He also used peacock forms, often in combination with foliage. At the same time, Omar Ramsden and Ramsden & Alwyn Carr produced wonderful sterling silver objects with hammered grounds and inlaid enamel plaques, all in Renaissance Revival form with vivid greens and blues and strapwork detailing.

Left. *Hammered vase by the Kalo Shops (Chicago), $1,200.* Right. *Tiffany hammered fruit bowl, $1,300.* Courtesy of Christie's East, New York.

In the midst of the Arts and Crafts movement in 1875, Liberty of London was founded by Sir Arthur Lasenby Liberty. He catered to the demand for the mix of Oriental, Pre-Raphaelite, and Neoclassical styles and had a very strong influence on the movement. He produced a new line of silver, called Cymric, beginning in 1898. Hammer marks were left on Liberty silver so that the public would think that all pieces made by the firm were hand wrought, although, in fact, they were not always. Picture frames by Liberty & Company usually have machine-hammered grounds to achieve the hand-wrought look. One of the most prolific artists working for Liberty was Archibald

Knox, especially noted for producing Celtic-style ornamentation with interwoven detailing. Designs were enhanced with enamel in jewel-like colors or with semiprecious stones.

In the United States, Gorham produced an Arts and Crafts line with their hand-wrought Martelé and Athenic pieces (see Gorham Martelé). Tiffany produced some pieces in this style, and Shreve and Company of San Francisco made hand-hammered pieces with strapwork and rivet borders. In Gardiner, Massachusetts, Arthur J. Stone, who had been trained in England, reflected the influence of William Morris. His earliest designs showed light hammer marks on the surfaces and often incorporated repoussé leaves and berries into the design. His work also featured 14-karat gold inlaid into the silver.

BEAKER, footed, hammered finish, bowl chased with 3-leaf clovers and inscription, stem embossed with a double row of hearts, Omar Ramsden & Alwyn Carr, London, 1901, height, 4 in. **$800**

BISCUIT JAR, cylindrical, body lobed and chased with a girdle of wheat ears, slip-on cover with molded rim applied with 6 cherub heads, lightly hammered surface, Omar Ramsden, London, 1933, height, 5¼ in. **$2,750**

BOWL, christening, spot-hammered, with 2 shaped handles cast and chased with Tudor roses and foliage, Omar Ramsden, London, 1928. **$1,300**

BOWL, fruit, modeled in the Aesthetic taste as a lily pad, the wirework stand applied with leaves, flowers, and buds, Hukin & Heath. **$300**

BOWL, fruit, spot-hammered, the knop and the rim with geometric decoration in the Celtic style, Birmingham, 1917, 7½ in. **$700**

BOWL, roses, 2-handled, silver-gilt, spot-hammered, chased with sinuous dragons in the Celtic style, London, 1910.
$1,000

BOWL, 3 gourd-shape handles, capped by cabochon agates, hammered surface, Ramsden & Carr, London, 1906. **$1,500**

BOX, cigarette, rectangular, hinged lid decorated with a pierced scene of a ship in full sail against a blue, white, and green enamel background within a ropework rectangular frame, Omar Ramsden, 1938. **$2,400**

BOX, circular, Cymric, gilt-lined with circular disk decorated with scrolls and guilloche-enameled in bright blue, green, and red, Liberty & Co., Birmingham, 1904. **$350**

BOX, circular, Cymric, gilt-lined, molded, applied with circular boss and guilloche-enameled in bright blue, red, and green, Liberty & Co., Birmingham, 1904, diameter, 2 in. **$185**

BOX, jewelry, rectangular form with bombé sides, flat-chased to simulate wood panels within raised strapwork borders, drop loop handles, W. Comyns & Sons, London, 1900, length, 7 in. **$1,300**

CANDLESTICKS, pair, each with trumpet-form base, with 3 tendrils supporting the bullet-form sconce, with fixed broad nozzle, J. Wakley & F.C. Wheeler, London, 1908, height, 4³/4 in. **$900/pr**

CANDLESTICKS, pair, Gorham, 1910–20, hammered cut-card decoration, weighted bases. **$400/pr**

CHILD'S CUP, by Arthur Stone (Carlson), American, 1915. **$950**

CLOCK CASE, hammered, shaped, with stylized foliage, Birmingham, 1902. **$475**

COCKTAIL SHAKER, hammered and applied with strapwork at base, neck, and finial, American, Shreve & Co. **$600**

CONDIMENT SET, 3 pieces, set on flaring bases, each applied with a frieze of foliage enameled in blue and green, Liberty & Co., Birmingham, 1908. **$650/set**

CRUMB SCOOP, silverplated, triangular, with waved decoration, William Hutton & Sons. Ltd., 9 in. **$20**

CUP, in the style of Liberty & Co., shallow bowl chased with a row of buds on shaped matted ground, with leafy strap handles and slender trumpet-shaped stem, Mappin and Webb, Sheffield, 1902, height, 11¹/4 in. **$1,700**

CUP, standing, hammered finish, chased with a frieze of maenads dancing, festoons above band of theatrical masks suspended from linked ribbons, Omar Ramsden, London, 1923. **$1,600**

CUP, standing, small, hammered bowl, supported by scroll brackets above a knop chased with flowerheads set with ruby glass cabochons, molded foot chased with trefoils above a border of dolphins entwined with reeds, domed cover chased to match and with a "Tudor Rose" finial, Omar Ramsden, London, 1930, height overall, 9¹/4 in. **$1,500**

CUPS, trophy, pair, each with circular bowl on trumpet-shaped base, strapwork handles, trefoil terminals, Mappin & Webb, Sheffield, 1927–28.   **$1,000/pr**

DESSERT SET, 6 forks, 6 spoons, stylized tulip bud decoration on a background of blue and green shaded enamel, Liberty & Co. of London, Birmingham, 1922–34.   **$650/set**

DISH, bonbon, double, wicker-covered scroll handle and in-turned lips, Hukin and Heath, London, 1891.   **$575**

DISH, hammered, circular, applied with a thistle motif in center, Omar Ramsden.   **$600**

DISH, hammered, circular, flared rim applied with 6 disks, 3 chased with roses, the other 3 with fleur-de-lis, on 3 stump feet, Ramsden & Carr.   **$500**

DISH, serving, silver, trilobed, Lebolt, Chicago, diameter, 12 in.   **$1,000**

DISH, small, circular, plain spot-hammered, centers with raised, pierced, and enameled Tudor Rose boss, cast raised edges, on collet bases, inscribed Omar Ramsden Me Fecit, 1937.
                                                        $375

DRESSING TABLE SET, 9 pieces, comprising hand mirror, 2 hairbrushes, 2 clothes brushes, shoehorn, buttonhook, cylindrical box, and tray, decorated with strapwork, a maiden and tulips, the tray with copper rivets, Goldsmiths & Silversmiths Co. Ltd., London, 1900.   **$3,200/set**

FLATWARE SERVICE, silver, comprising 6 each: dinner forks, cocktail forks, dinner knives, soup spoons, teaspoons, demitasse spoons, butter spreaders; 1 serving fork, 2 serving spoons with hammered pointed handles, applied with gilt monogram, together with 6 matching butter plates with hammered surface and gilt monogram, LeBolt, Chicago, 1930.   **$1,750/set**

FORKS, pastry, set of 6, sterling silver, shaped handles decorated with stylized foliage and tendrils in the Art Nouveau taste, Liberty & Co., Birmingham, 1925.   **$200/set**

INKSTAND, silver and enamel, stand with border of blue and green leafage, detachable clear glass well with hinged cover enameled with florette, Liberty & Co., London, 1909. **$1,200**

INKWELL, capstan form with ropework borders with beads at intervals, center chased with 4 theatrical masks, mother-of-pearl bosses in corded frames, cover chased with a flaming cross, Ramsden & Carr, London, 1908.   **$1,600**

PITCHER, water, silver, simple hammered finish, American, c. 1920.   **$300**

PLATES, service, 12, circular, with hammered surface and applied strapwork monogram, Friedell, California.   **$3,250/12**

SALT CELLARS, pair, spot-hammered, pedestal, with rope-twist decoration, the bowls engraved with friezes of zigzags and with pierced rims, John Paul Cooper, London, 1914.   **$275/pr**

SALVER, circular, hammered with stylized floral motifs around the rim, raised on 8 scroll and stump feet, 1928.   **$1,200**

SALVER, lobed circular, hammered with embossed floral circular cartouche, on claw-and-ball feet, Ramsden & Carr, 1906.
$1,200

SALVER, oval, with applied reeded border, Stone, American, length, 16½ in.   **$1,200**

SERVERS, salad, pair, curved tapering handles, each engraved with a crest and motto, London, 1899.   **$125/pr**

SPOON, "wheat sheaf" with stylized rat-tail bowl, 1938.
$150

SPOON, caddy, with hammered fig-shaped bowl and stylized flower handle set at center with a carnelian boss, 1921. **$725**

SPOON, nut, Thurstone sterling, engraved and cut-out lady slipper, 4¼ in.   **$75**

SPOON, spot-hammered, pierced, shaped handle chased with a row of 5 4-petaled flowers descending in size, Ramsden and Carr, London, 1911.   **$225**

SPOON WARMER, silverplated, modeled in the Aesthetic taste as a leaf, the cover with tendril scroll handle, Hukin & Heath.
$75

TEA AND COFFEE SERVICE, 7 pieces, with tray, Stone Associates, c. 1919.   **$10,000/set**

TEAPOT, textured, tapering, split wirework handle and domed hinged cover with wirework thumbpiece, and monogram, Heath & Middleton, Birmingham, 1895.   **$650**

TEA SERVICE, 6 pieces, comprising teapot, coffeepot, cream pitcher, waste bowl, covered sugar bowl, and kettle on stand, globular form with squared handles, knop finials, on oval tray with cut-out handles, Lebolt, Chicago.   **$5,500/set**

TEA SERVICE, 3 pieces, spot-hammered applied and chased with wriggle-work bands, Birmingham, 1911.   **$650/set**

TRAY, Art Silver Shop, Chicago, length, 20 in.   **$1,000**

TUREEN, sauce, stand and ladle, oblong, with hammered surface, lightly chased with sprays of ivy leaves, Maker's Mark M in an anvil, c. 1930, length on stand, 9⅞ in.   **$800**

Left. *Gorham sterling rattle and whistle, c. 1880, $525.* Center. *English sterling and mother-of-pearl pacifier, $225.* Right. *Kerr sterling Dutch boy rattle, $275.*

Small bells or rattles were used to entertain babies in Roman times and have been popular ever since. Often they were made in conjunction with teething rings of coral or ivory or combined with a whistle mouthpiece to amuse a child.

Decorative sterling silver examples with bell and ball ornamentation became common in the 17th century in England. The decoration at this time was generally delicate bright-cut work engraved with ribbons and floral swags. By the late 18th century, rattles were larger and heavier, with elaborate repoussé detailing.

The English 18th- and 19th-century rattles should be fully hallmarked. Those without hallmarks and lacking bells should be priced considerably lower. At the end of the 19th century, in both England and the United States, figural rattles replaced the earlier silver and coral ones.

In the United States most rattles date from the late 19th and early 20th centuries and depict fairy tale or nursery rhyme characters. The handles were generally bone, ivory, or mother-of-pearl. The amusing shapes produced in great quantities in England at this time—in Chester and Birmingham—are quite collectible today. They included jesters, bears, cats, dogs, Kate Greenaway children, and moon faces. Unfortunately, many of these have been reproduced in England in the past few years and are often sold as antique. Check the hallmarks. Another novelty produced in England in the late 19th century was the baby's dummy, known in America as a pacifier. It was generally made with a sterling silver handle, a rubber nipple, and a mother-of-pearl surround and was suspended from a silver chain.

Fewer rattles were produced in the United States, but examples by Gorham, Kerr, and Unger Brothers can be found.

BABY, bulbous body engraved with foliage, with 5 bells and a turned ivory handle, English, mid-19th century. **$275**

BELLS and mother-of-pearl teething stick, Birmingham, 1880. **$495**

CHILD'S, gold, baluster form chased with bands of rococo ornament of flowers and scrolls on matted and scale grounds, hung with 8 partly fluted bells, coral teether, J.F., c. 1750–60, length, 6 in. **$5,500**

CHILD'S, with 2 tapering bells, the ivory handle carved with the man in the moon, late 19th century. **$150**

COMBINATION CHILD'S WHISTLE and coral teething stick, engraved with foliage, George III. **$200**

COMBINATION CHILD'S WHISTLE AND RATTLE, bulbous body, bright-cut, with flowers and foliage, with coral teething stick and 6 bells attached, George Knight, London, 1819. **$800**

COMBINATION RATTLE AND TEETHING RING, head of Mr. Punch with bells, London, 1898. **$350**

COMBINATION RATTLE AND WHISTLE with mother-of-pearl handle, revolving sphere engraved with flowers supported within a half moon with 4 bells, German, late 19th century.

$350

COMBINATION WHISTLE AND RATTLE, trumpet form, with 3 bells attached, French, late 19th century.   **$175**

COMBINATION WHISTLE AND RATTLE, bulbous body chased with flowers and foliage, with 5 bells attached and an amber teething stick, E.S.B., Chester, 1911.   **$225**

COMBINATION WHISTLE AND RATTLE, bulbous body chased with flowers and foliage, with 5 bells and coral teething ring attached.   **$325**

COMBINATION WHISTLE AND RATTLE, parcel-gilt, bulbous body engraved with flowers and scrollwork, with coral teething ring and 8 bells attached, maker's mark only, Ledsam, Vale & Wheeler, Birmingham.   **$400**

COMBINATION WHISTLE AND RATTLE, sterling silver, chased with flowers and foliage, with coral teething handle and 3 bells attached, George Unite, 1885.   **$200**

GEORGE III RATTLE AND WHISTLE, bright-engraved, with coral teething stick and 12 bells, 1790.   **$500**

MODELED AS A KITTEN seated on a stylized cushion, with composition teething ring, early 20th century.   **$350**

WHISTLE AND RATTLE, silver gilt, with bright-engraved decoration, 8 bells dependent and coral teething stick, by Peter, Anne & William Bateman, 1795.   **$600**

Baby Silver

Sterling baby cups, c. 1895. Left. Chased verse and drawing from Robert Louis Stevenson, $300. Center. Shiebler with 14-karat gold chrysanthemums, $1,200. Right. Kewpie motif, $350. Photo by J. Auslander.

Christening gifts in the 18th and 19th centuries almost always included a spoon and possibly a mug and porringer. They were engraved with the child's name and birth date and sometimes the names of the godparents. In England late-19th-century christening sets were sold in fitted boxes, which included a mug, spoon, fork, bowl, and sometimes a napkin ring. These were often stamped with shells or engraved with arabesques or florals. Many were gilt-lined for a richer appearance. By the turn of the 20th century, sets were substantially larger and often included an egg cup.

Ornately embossed American Victorian mugs, especially those chased and engraved with Kate Greenaway figures, nursery rhymes, Noah's Ark, Kewpies, Brownies, cats, or Humpty Dumpty figures, have "gone over the top" in price, as our British friends are fond of saying.

In the last quarter of the 19th century in America, Tiffany,

Gorham, Kerr, and Blackinton made particularly fine sets: a mug, cup, bowl, and underplate and often a matching spoon and fork. Shiebler made mixed-metal sets, including one with 14-karat gold applied chrysanthemums in Art Nouveau style on a sterling silver ground. Gorham made the most expensive children's sets, in their Martelé line, depicting nursery rhymes or wild roses on bowls and underplates, mugs, porringers, forks, and spoons. Sterling silver nursery rhyme napkin rings and fork-and-spoon sets were produced in England and America in the early 20th century.

Eighteenth-century children's mugs and beakers have become outrageously expensive due to scarcity. Late-19th-century American decorated examples are quickly following suit.

BABY SET, napkin ring, mug, bowl, and plate applied with putti holding floral garlands, Shreve & Co.   **$425/set**

BIB CLIPS, clothespin shape, pair.   **$45/pr**

BIB CLIPS, cut-out ducks, pair.   **$45**

BOWL, christening, spiral-fluted, modeled as an 18th century porringer with rope-twist body band, crimped rim, and circular cartouche, London, 1889.   **$400**

Whiting sterling bowl with underplate, with applied cherubs, $1,900.
Courtesy of Christie's East, New York.

BOWL AND UNDERPLATE, mixed metal, circular bowl applied with copper figure of Japanese lady sitting on elephant, underplate applied with Oriental mother and child on rim, hammered surface, by Dominick and Haff, 1883, bowl, 4¼ in., plate, 7½ in. **$750/2**

CEREAL SET, nursery rhyme motif, bowl and underplate, Rogers Silverplate. **$75/set**

CHILD'S SET, 3 pieces, comprising mug, bowl, and underplate, decoration of Little Bo Peep, letters of the alphabet, and plate with birds among letters and numbers, late 19th century, William Kerr & Co. **$700/set**

CHRISTENING SET, French, 4 pieces, decorated with rococo floral, foliage, and ribbon swags, tapering beaker, with napkin ring, spoon, and fork in a fitted case, 1899. **$450/set**

CHRISTENING SET, French, 4 pieces, comprising silver-gilt, foliate-decorated combination whistle and rattle with 4 bells, tapering beaker, bright-cut with flowers and foliage, spoon, and fork. **$325/set**

CHRISTENING SET, 3 pieces, bright-cut with foliate swags, egg cup, spoon with gilt bowl, and oval napkin ring, in a fitted case, Sheffield, 1914. **$200/set**

CHRISTENING SET, 3 pieces, silver-gilt, comprising knife, spoon, and fork, finely decorated all over with raised fruiting vines, in a fitted case, John Henry Lias, 1849. **$575/set**

CHRISTENING SET, 3 pieces, silver-gilt, folding knife and fork with floral and strapwork engraved mother-of-pearl handles, the spoon with scrolling foliage, Sheffield, 1869. **$400/set**

FEEDING SET, bowl, underplate, and mug with chased motifs depicting Noah's Ark, Kerr. **$650/set**

FEEDING SET, 3 pieces, set with bright-cut decoration, cased, Birmingham hallmarks. **$95/set**

KNIFE AND FORK, christening set, with carved mother-of-pearl handles, in original case with cartouche, Unite and Hilliard, Birmingham, 1832. **$150/set**

MUG, christening, gilt-lined, with loop handle, shield-shape cartouche surrounded by bright-cut ferns, Birmingham, 1915. **$110**

MUG, christening, spiral-fluted, stamped with a frieze of flowers and foliage and beaded leaf-capped scroll handle, Sheffield, 1904. **$125**

Late 19th-century sterling baby mugs, chased and embossed designs.
Courtesy of Christie's East, New York.

MUG, christening, sterling silver, with molded rim and loop handle, stamped with a 16th-century-style hunting scene, Chester, 1899.   **$275**

MUG, christening, with molded rim and scroll handle, body decorated with 2 bands of reeding, John, Henry and Charles Lias, London, 1830.   **$300**

MUG, engraved Kewpies, American, late 19th century. **$325**

NAPKIN RING, chased nursery rhymes, American.   **$125**

NAPKIN RING, cut-out duck shape, American, early 20th century.   **$75**

PORRINGER, simple tab handle, Kirk, early 20th century.
                                                             $75

PUSHER with handle depicting full-figure stork delivering baby, sterling silver.   **$52**

PUSHER, Gorham Lancaster Rose pattern.   **$35**

RATTLE with whistle, George Unite, 1890.   **$350**

SPOON with rabbit handle, Charles M. Robbins.   **$35**

SPOON with stork handle, American, early 20th century. **$35**

SPOON, curved handle, embossed roses, American, silverplate.
                                                             $15

SPOON, curved handle, chased Red Riding Hood, American, late 19th century. $75

SPOON, curved handle, man-in-the-moon motif. $75

SPOON, infant feeding, Gorham, LaScala pattern. $35

SPOON, Kirk, repoussé pattern. $50

SPOON AND PUSHER SET, Continental, 800-standard embossed cherubs and foliage. $125/set

YOUTH SET, 3 pieces, Whiting, in Pompadour pattern. $135/set

Banks

In the late 19th century banks were very popular and were used to encourage children to save their pennies. In England and on the Continent they were and still are referred to as money boxes. The most collectible ones are in figural shape, Humpty Dumpty being the most common. American firms, including Kerr, Gorham, and Tiffany, made banks with nursery rhymes that often matched their feeding sets. Full-figure pigs and teddy bears in sterling silver and silverplate remain top favorites.

English samples can be found in the forms of bobbies, mail boxes, and guard houses. Some of the finest were made by Samson Mordan.

Banks should be in good condition, without dents or bruises, preferably with the original lock and key. Today, banks in novelty shapes command the highest prices, and simple cylindrical forms are difficult to sell unless they are engraved with nursery rhymes and legends.

"ABC," silverplated, American, early 20th century. **$75**

APPLE SHAPE, sterling silver, American, early 20th century. **$250**

ART NOUVEAU, sinuous flowers and plant forms, American, late 19th century. **$300**

BARREL SHAPE, nursery rhymes, American, early 20th century. **$450**

CAT form with floppy bow collar, sterling silver, Continental, early 20th century. **$450**

EMBOSSED FLOWERS, American, early 20th century. **$150**

EMBOSSED NOAH'S ARK, English, late 19th century. **$375**

GIFT BOX form, silverplated, Continental, mid-20th century. **$75**

GINGERBREAD HOUSE, silverplated, Continental, early 20th century. **$125**

HUMPTY DUMPTY shape, American, early 20th century. **$350**

LETTER BOX, novelty, sterling silver, Birmingham, 1902. **$300**

NURSERY RHYMES, American, early 20th century. **$375**

PIG, sitting, silverplated, with lock, W.M.F., 5¼ in. **$250**

SQUIRREL, silverplated, American, early 20th century. **$29**

WINDMILL, figural, rotating blades, Continental hallmarks, height, 5½ in. **$45**

Bells

English tortoise shell and silverplated call bell, late 18th century, $750.
Photo by J. Auslander.

Bells were originally made for use on inkstands or to summon servants to the dinner table.

In the early 19th century in the United States, silver bells were chased overall with flowers, leafage, and vintage grape motifs. Design motifs changed during the century to include swags and Art Nouveau and Japonesque forms. If one could afford to order them, bells were made in patterns to match one's flatware service.

Novelty or figural bells in human and animal forms became popular in the late 19th and early 20th centuries in silver and plate. One of the most interesting subjects was the tortoise. He appeared with a real shell back and silverplated mounts and was operated by pressing the tail. He was cast completely in silverplate, as was a crouching frog. Elkington & Company featured an old woman dressed in a wide skirt, bonnet, and shawl as a bell. Her head nodded when the bell rang. Recently, brass copies of this bell have appeared in English markets.

Bells with enamel or hardstone decorations became fashionable in the 1920s and 1930s, with exquisite examples produced by Cartier in France. Georg Jensen in Denmark also made sterling silver bells in many of his popular patterns with hand-hammered grounds.

In England bells are usually marked on the outside of the lower rim or on the inside rim. In the United States the marks are generally around the lower rim. Occasionally in the United States they are made with a sterling silver handle, and the bell itself is plated.

BELL PUSH, Continental, circular, silver-mounted, enameled with green leaves with central gem-set ringing mechanism.
$250

CALL BELL, George III, by Peter, Ann and William Bateman.
$1,000

SPIRALLY LOBED SILVER BODY, fluted and chased with shells, baluster stem handle, Italian, c. 1750. **$600**

TABLE BELL, "Japanese style," body applied with partly gilt leaves and a seed pod with a bug with back inlaid with 2-color gold, the spirally twisted stork-form handle applied with a rose and yellow-gold bug, all with hammered surface. **$2,800**

TABLE BELL, cast and chased with foliage and scrolls, Mary Anne and Charles Reily, London, 1828. **$1,000**

TABLE BELL, circular, pierced, with spiral fluting, flowers, and foliage, George Unite, Birmingham, 1890. **$200**

TABLE BELL, Continental, modeled as a woman in 17th-century costume, skirt chased with shells and strapwork.
$300

TABLE BELL, Continental, modeled as a woman wearing 17th-century-style costume. **$150**

TABLE BELL, foliate-pierced, silver-mounted on an ebonized-wood base with presentation inscription, bell mount engraved with a crest, crown, and motto, Goldsmiths & Silversmiths & Co. Ltd., London, 1900. **$450**

TABLE BELL, gadrooned, handle cast in the form of a 16th century huntsman blowing a horn, London, 1935. **$425**

TABLE BELL, German, part-fluted sterling silver decorated with scrolling foliage and with baluster handle.   **$100**

TABLE BELL, International Royal Danish pattern.   **$85**

TABLE BELL, silverplated novelty formed as an old lady wearing a shawl and carrying dog beneath her arm, with nodding head, Elkington & Co., late 19th century.   **$375**

TABLE BELL, silverplated, paneled, and gadrooned with entwined dolphin handle.   **$100**

TABLE BELL, with ivory baluster handle, Edwardian, Chester, 1902.   **$200**

TABLE BELL, with putti, masks, and foliage and drunken putto handle, silverplated, Victorian, Elkington & Co.   **$200**

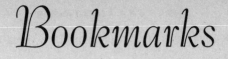

Sterling bookmarks, c. 1885. **Courtesy of Alice and Derek Hamilton, Nancy and Bruce Thompson.**

Bookmarks were produced in great quantities in the late 19th and early 20th centuries, mainly in Chester and Birmingham, England, and also in the United States. The collectible ones were generally a few inches long in figural, punch, heart, cat, owl, and trowel shapes. Others were embossed with flowers and ribbon motifs. Some made in England and Scotland were set with agate.

ART NOUVEAU FLOWER, sterling silver, Unger Brothers, 1880. **$125**
CHERUB, full figure, Kerr, 1880. **$250**

CLAW AND AGATE·BALL, silverplated clip-on, English, late 19th century.   **$150**

HEART, embossed, with ribbon, American, early 20th century.
                                                           $125

HEART shape, American, Tiffany &Co., early 20th century.
                                                            $75

INDIAN HEAD, possibly Unger Brothers, American, late 19th century.   **$150**

OWL, finely engraved, with glass eyes, Sampson Mordan & Co., London, 1894.   **$150**

PORTLY GENTLEMAN, full figure, silverplated, English, early 20th century.   **$175**

PUNCH, full figure, silverplated, English, late 19th century.
                                                           $150

SIMPLE FORM, American, Tiffany & Co., early 20th century.
                                                            $75

TROWEL SHAPE, sterling silver, with Scottish agate handle, English, late 19th century.   **$125**

Boxes

Group of 19th-century silver boxes. **Left.** *French, c. 1860, $325.* **Center.** *Continental, c. 1880, $275.* **Right.** *German, c. 1890, $275.* Photo by J. Auslander.

Sterling silver vinaigrettes and pomanders, jewel, medical, religious, sweetmeat, and snuffboxes were all hinged or had lift-off lids. Through the years the hinge treatments changed. In the 18th century hinges were most often centered, with engraved ornamentation drawing attention away from the hinge treatment. During the 19th century a less expensive type of hinged closure was used that employed a pin and rolled hinged mount.

In the late 18th and early 19th centuries English and Continental boxes used for sterling, gold, or ivory toothpicks were generally oval, lined with velvet, or had cut corners. Sometimes beautiful bright-cut engraving or allover filigree work served as decoration. Toothbrush powder boxes and boxes containing toothbrushes were also to be found. Most of the toothbrush containers have perforated ends.

From the middle of the 18th through the early 19th centuries, surgeons carried lancet or phlebotomy boxes (cases) with

Sterling ring box, c. 1910, $125. **Photo by J. Auslander.**

a variety of razor-sharp lancets inside. Many of these were engraved all over or covered with a layer of shagreen with sterling silver mounts.

Although the use of snuff dates to the time of Christopher Columbus, snuffboxes became extremely popular during the 19th century. Silver, silverplate, and gold snuffboxes and tortoise or ivory ones with sterling mounts were usually decorated with engraving, enameling, semiprecious or precious jewels, or hand-painted miniatures on ivory. Many had gilded interiors as well. Styles and shapes vary and include engraved sporting scenes, chased pastoral motifs, and highly embossed "castle tops." Boxes made in England should be fully hallmarked on lid and case. Continental examples also were usually marked.

In the late Victorian era the United States began to produce jewel, powder, glove, sachet, soap, ring, and pin boxes. Those for the dressing table were made in sterling silver or a combination of sterling silver and crystal. Heart shapes and ovals prevailed, with velvet linings and cast legs common. Gorham, Blackinton, Unger Brothers, Kerr, and Reed & Barton made small boxes in huge quantities. On the Continent and in England, boxes were often made as replicas of tables, with stamped or engraved motifs and usually with cabriole legs.

Ornamentation was a means of enriching bare surfaces, adding shading or dimension to an area, or in some cases, covering defects or imperfections. Often the design is achieved by relief methods such as embossing or engraving, the most common decorative motifs. Pique work was also employed, with tortoise-shell or mother-of-pearl boxes inlaid with sterling silver designs.

Another form of decoration begun in the early 18th century and executed freehand was bright-cut engraving. This was achieved by using a special chisel-like tool with a heavy weight on it to produce a gouged effect. Engraving was normally achieved by means of a graver, which cut away a layer of metal. Engine turning gave a feeling of texture to the surface metal and was achieved by means of a lathe. Various patterns could be formed, including basketweave. Simple straight banding and rippled and oval effects were also used with great success to decorate boxes.

For the lady, the rarest and most collectible style of box is the heart shape.

When purchasing, look for boxes in good condition with tightly closing lids and original hinges.

In England cigar smoking began to replace taking snuff in the 1840s. Many box makers started to produce cigar cases in place of snuffboxes. Generally, the early cases were quite small, corresponding to the size of the cigars at that time; late Victorian examples are substantially larger. In the mid-19th century and through the early 20th century fine sterling silver examples were made. They can also be found in crocodile skin and shagreen with sterling silver mounts.

Figural sterling silver cases were also cast, in the form of a single cigar or a bunch of cigars. Many of these were made in Birmingham, England. Later copies of these were in silverplate and chrome.

Until recently, crocodile-skin cases with silver mounts were impossible to sell. They have now peaked in price in the United States and England in a new wave of popularity.

BARREL SHAPE, chased with birds and foliate scrolls on matted background with chain attachment, Thomas Johnson, 1873.
$550

CACHOU, heart shape, lid with a vacant shaped cartouche surrounded by scrollwork and flowers and surmounted by two putti, Chester, 1896.   **$225**

CELLO FORM, stamped and chased with putti and arabesques, Continental.   **$300**

CIGAR, rectangular, with gold buttress-form supports, gold thumbpiece and gold central panel, silver body chased with panels of reeding, probably Cartier, c. 1930–40.   **$1,900**

CIGAR, tortoise-shell-mounted, cedar-lined, hinged cover, applied "Cigars," Chester, 1894.   **$325**

CIRCULAR, Continental, 800 silver, engraved with flowers and foliage, 18th century, 2 in.   **$75**

CIRCULAR, French, 19th century, waisted, gilt-lined, enameled with gold stars, lid enameled with a garland of flowers, 2 in.   **$800**

CIRCULAR, hammered surface acid-etched with sinuous scrolls, by Tiffany, 1875–91, 3 in.   **$420**

CIRCULAR, with cover engraved "Elastic Bands," Edwardian, Birmingham, 1901.   **$40**

COUNTER, Queen Anne, bone of cylindrical form with 2 silver bands, engraved with flowers, containing 25 counters. **$700**

GRAND PIANO on cabriole legs, cover die-stamped with 18th-century-style figures, Dutch, late 19th century.   **$225**

HEART shape, Austrian, silver-gilt lid enameled with figures in a rural scene, interior enameled with mill stream and dwelling, 3 in.   **$450**

HEART shape, silver-gilt filigree, probably English, 17th century.   **$550**

American Reed & Barton sterling jewel casket (box), $4,500. Courtesy of Christie's East, New York.

JEWEL, heart-shaped, embossed border, lock and key, Gorham. **$500**

JEWEL, sterling silver, heart-shaped, simple lock and key, Tiffany & Co. **$750**

MARRIAGE CASKET, heart-shaped, in the Scandinavian 18th-century taste, chased with rococo flowers and foliage, with crown surmount and 2 lion rampant supports, German, 3 in. **$225**

MINIATURE long-case clock form, hinged cover stamped and chased with 18th-century-style figures surrounded by arabesques, Continental. **$250**

OBLONG, Continental, engraved with arabesques, cover inset with a jade plaque, 4½ in. **$275**

PATCH, circular, engraved with Greek-key designs and flowerheads, John Shaw, Birmingham, 1806, 2 in. **$150**

PATCH, cover set with a miniature of a lady holding a bouquet of flowers, Joseph Taylor, Birmingham, c. 1795. **$175**

PEPPERMINT, decorated with friezes of flowers and shells, Dutch. **$120**

PEPPERMINT, Dutch, 19th century, modelled as a bow-fronted armoire, engraved with doors and drawers, 3 in. **$275**

PILL, gilt-lined, realistically formed as a brazil nut, John Marshall, London, 1896, 2 in. **$250**

PILL, spherical, chased all over with birds, flowers, and scrolls, Walter Thornhill, 1878. **$475**

PILL, sterling silver, shaped as a pencil box with slide-action cover, by Aston & Son, 1880, 2 in. **$300**

PLAYING CARDS, double, lined in silk, London, 1910. **$350**

PLAYING CARDS, oblong, stamped with flowers and scrolling foliage, Birmingham, 1899. **$225**

POWDER, circular, lid guilloche-enameled in shades of green and brown, Continental. **$400**

POWDER, sterling silver, French, c. 1900, circular, set with miniature portrait of a lady on ivory, 3 in. **$200**

POWDER, sterling silver, French, c. 1900, set with an ivory plaque painted with flags, 3 in. **$325**

RING, English, sterling silver, heart shape. **$250**

RING, English, sterling silver, scuttle shape. **$250**

RING, formed as a globe, supported by 4 silver-gilt lions on a stepped plinth, embossed with legend "The British Empire Exhibition 1924," Birmingham, 1924.   **$425**

RING, in the form of a book, spine enameled with flowers on a red ground, the covers enameled with courtship scenes within woodland landscapes.   **$400**

RING, silverplated, velvet-lined, Birks.   **$50**

RING, sterling silver, rectangular, lid embossed with scrollwork, Birmingham, 1907.   **$150**

RING, sterling silver, velvet-lined, Birks.   **$125**

SEAL, circular, with wax seal impression, Patrick Robertson, Edinburgh, c. 1788.   **$1,800**

SINGING BIRD, tortoise shell and sterling silver, rectangular, foliate engraved hinged lid, feather bird with articulated head and wings, with key.   **$800**

SNUFF, Armenian, oval, cover engraved with a bouquet of flowers, the base with inscription in Armenian script, probably early 19th century.   **$1,000**

SNUFF, Austro-Hungarian, oblong, decorated with flowers and foliage, F.S., Prague, c. 1825.   **$350**

SNUFF, bright-cut, book shape with engraved spine.   **$125**

George III regimental snuffbox, $2,000. **Courtesy of Christie's East, New York.**

SNUFF, cartouche shape, silver-gilt, enameled with Oriental scenes, German, late 19th century. **$1,000**

SNUFF, Chinese Export, oblong, chased with traditional scenes of mountains, boats, people, buildings, pagodas, and trees, Canton, c. 1850. **$1,000**

SNUFF, Continental, rectangular, silver-mounted agate. **$275**

SNUFF, Dutch, oval, silver-gilt stamped with putti and figures, scrollwork borders. **$350**

SNUFF, electroplate, modeled as fox's head with garnet eyes, 1870. **$175**

SNUFF, George III regimental, rectangular, with 3 compartments with covers, engraved with military trophies, London, 1789. **$2,000**

SNUFF, oblong, silver-gilt of basketwork design, Matthew Linwood, Birmingham, 1805. **$500**

SNUFF, curved oblong with rounded ends, engraved with an alligator on hatched background, Samuel Pemberton, Birmingham, 1805. **$225**

SNUFF, oval, lid stamped with angels' heads amid clouds, in the style of Angelica Kaufman, Birmingham, 1897. **$275**

SNUFF, pocket, oblong, engine-turned, the cover with raised cast cartouche depicting a top-hatted horseman about to mount his horse, against a wooded background, Thomas Shaw, Birmingham, 1826. **$700**

SNUFF, rectangular, gilt-lined, lid and sides cast with figures in rural landscapes, China Trade, mid-19th century. **$800**

SNUFF, rectangular, lid nielloed with birds, flowers, and foliage surrounded by scrollwork. **$200**

SNUFF, silver-mounted, enameled with birds, foliage, and flowers in green and gold on a white ground, Continental, 18th century. **$425**

SNUFF, silver-mounted hardstone oval, reeded lid with a thumbpiece, Continental, 19th century. **$75**

SNUFF, silver-mounted mother-of-pearl engraved with mythological figures, Continental, early 19th century. **$600**

SNUFF, sterling-silver-mounted cowrie shell of small oval form engraved with bird crest above monograms, John Egan, Dublin, c. 1808. **$350**

SNUFF, table size, of oblong engine-turned form with chased border of flowers, shamrocks, and thistles in high relief, cover with Masonic inscription, Francis Clark, Birmingham, 1837.
$750

SNUFF, table, nielloed with stylized flowerheads, lid nielloed with a scene depicting the painting *Rent Day* by William Powfrith, French. $700

SNUFF MULL, horn, silver-mounted, the mount engraved with a thistle, leaves, and a Masonic emblem with a presentation inscription. $600

SPICE, oval, squeeze action, engraved with flowers and scrolls, c. 1690. $650

TOBACCO, oblong, hinged cover engraved with a battle scene with buildings beyond in the mid-18th-century taste, also engraved with an armorial and coronet, Continental. $800

TOBACCO, oval, silver-mounted, with tortoise-shell cover and base, cover inlaid with a silver and mother-of-pearl figure of Punchinello, Italian, 18th century. $350

TOBACCO, sterling silver, reeded oblong, hinged cover engraved with a man in a horse-drawn cart. $275

TOILET, silver-gilt-mounted cut glass, the glass lid engraved with musical trophies and floral sprays, Continental. $250

TOILET, silver-topped cut-glass cartouche, detachable cover stamped with birds, flowers, scrolls, and a bow with a quiver of arrows, Chester, early 20th century. $250

TOILET, with cover stamped with 18th-century figures and arabesques with three putti, Dutch, late 19th century. $300

TOOTHPICK, George III, bright-cut, shaped sterling silver lined in red plush, Samuel Pemberton, Birmingham. $400

TORTOISE SHELL, silver-mounted, engraved with a putto in a woodland scene, mid-18th century, Continental. $175

TRINKET, circular, cabriole legs, lid guilloche-enameled in yellow, Birmingham, 1925. $200

TRINKET, circular, silver and tortoise shell on cabriole legs, English, early 20th century. $175

TRINKET, Continental, silver-gilt, rectangular, engraved with floral decoration, 3 in. $600

TRINKET, oval, hinged cover inset with tortoise shell inlaid with a yellow-metal vase of flowers and ribbon swags, William Comyns, London, 1910.   **$275**

TRINKET, sterling silver, octagonal on cabriole legs, with hinged cover, 2 in.   **$135**

TRINKET, sterling silver oval stamped with cherubs' heads amid clouds in the style of Angelica Kaufman, London, 1901.
$500

TRINKET, tortoise shell and silver inlaid oval on 4 curved feet, Birmingham, 1907.   **$225**

TRINKET BOX and pincushion combination, silver-mounted oblong on bracket feet, stamped with irises and scrolling foliage in Nouveau taste, Birmingham, 1903.   **$175**

TRINKET BOX and pincushion combination, 19th century, silver-gilt, circular, the mount stamped and chased with a frieze of stylized trailing vines, Tiffany & Co.   **$200**

Buckles

American sterling belt buckle with cherubs' heads, c. 1880, $200. **Photo by J. Auslander.**

In the 18th century buckles were worn on shoes and hats as well as belts. Most were made of steel with sterling silver mounts because silver was too soft to be given much hard use.

In the Victorian era buckles were cast in sterling silver and silverplate with designs of flowers, horseshoes, and cycling, yachting, and golf motifs. There were also designs using children's heads, ducks, rabbits, owls, and Art Nouveau maidens. These were replaced by stylized forms in the Art Deco period, employing enamel, semiprecious stones, or engine-turned engraving.

Belts in sterling silver from the Art Nouveau period are slow sellers; only those made by Kerr and Unger Brothers are doing better than average at this time. Today the belt links are often broken up and converted to brooches, and the buckles are sold separately for a higher profit.

Many buckles are now being reproduced from old molds, particularly those with heads of young women, semiclothed women, and Art Nouveau forms with flowing hair.

ART DECO, engine-turned, with enamel surround. **$125**

ART NOUVEAU, bulldog's head with garnet eyes, Unger Brothers, late 19th century. **$350**

ART NOUVEAU, cherubs with foliate border, Kerr, sterling, late 19th century. **$225**

ART NOUVEAU, embossed chrysanthemums and ladies' heads, stamped sterling only. **$150**

Buttonhooks

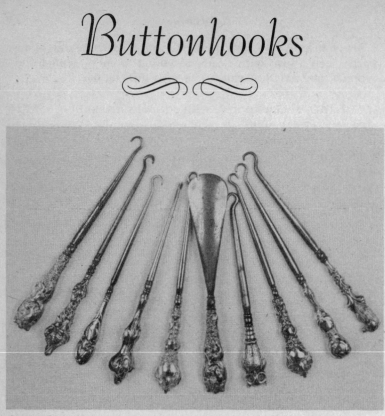

Group of late 19th- and early 20th-century English sterling buttonhooks.
Courtesy of Christie's South Kensington, London.

Since women wore unyielding corsets from the latter part of
the 19th century through the first quarter of the 20th century,
bending to button their high-topped shoes and boots was difficult. The buttonhook, ranging in size from 3 inches to approximately 12 inches in length, was helpful here and in other
areas of dressing. The largest were for boots and shoes, the
medium sizes were for dresses, and the tiniest hooks were used
to button gloves, which sometimes reached above the elbow.
Some had a ring to attach the buttonhook to a chatelaine, and
folding buttonhooks were also available. In the United States
they often matched dresser sets and are found with embossed
florals, cherubs, and beaded motifs.

Novelty English figural shapes, including owls and teddy bears with glass eyes, jesters, Punch and Judys, and semidraped female forms, command the highest prices. In America, Tiffany, Gorham, Kerr, Unger Brothers, Kirk, and Blackinton made beautiful examples with steel hooks and silver-covered handles filled with pitch for stability. Handles were also made of sterling silver with inlaid mother-of-pearl, tortoise, ivory, agate, and enamels.

ART NOUVEAU, lady's head, Kerr, late 19th century.   **$150**

ART NOUVEAU, woman with flowing hair, American, late 19th century, possibly Kerr.   **$150**

CHERUBS, Unger Brothers, American, late 19th century.
$175

DUCK IN REEDS, embossed and engraved, Birmingham, 1906.
$85

ENGRAVED, simple, Tiffany & Co., American, early 20th century.   **$125**

FOLDING, with shoehorn combination, American, Gorham, late 19th century.   **$125**

GARGOYLE, silverplated, English, late 19th century.   **$45**

GLOVE HOOK, embossed florals, Shiebler, New York, late 19th century.   **$30**

LILY OF THE VALLEY, embossed and engraved, American, late 19th century, Whiting.   **$75**

MIXED METAL, sterling silver applied bugs, Shiebler, New York, late 19th century.   **$250**

OWL figural handle, glass eyes, English, late 19th century.
$150

REPOUSSÉ FLORAL, Kirk, Baltimore, late 19th century. **$125**

ROSES, embossed, and foliage, Gorham, late 19th century.
$100

TEDDY BEAR, full figure, glass eyes, Birmingham, 1909.
$135

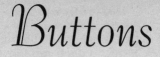

Buttons

Set of six English sterling buttons, c. 1895. Courtesy of Nancy and Bruce Thompson. Photo by J. Auslander.

Most of the buttons seen and collected today are from the 19th century. Those from earlier times were either lost or are in collections. Sterling silver buttons were made in England, France, and the United States with both engraved and pierced embossed motifs. Decorations vary from family crests and monograms to depictions of hunting dogs, sporting motifs, and classical busts. Sets are particularly prized, especially those with enamel decoration. Most were made in sets of five to eight buttons of varying sizes. Other buttons can be found with Wedgwood medallions or in polished agate, tortoise shell, or Essex crystal, all with sterling silver mounts.

At the end of the 19th century Kate Greenaway children, florals, and Gibson girls were popular motifs for buttons. Art Nouveau styles were produced in France, England, and the

United States and were characterized by fluid, curving lines, women's heads or women in flowing, draped gowns, and sinuous leafage. Some of these buttons were even irregularly shaped to conform to Art Nouveau design. Celtic designs with enamel decoration were made for Liberty & Company.

Unfortunately, over the years a great many of the best buttons were converted into earrings and cuff link sets.

ART DECO, sterling and ivory centers, set of 6.   **$350/set**

ART NOUVEAU, set of 6, shaped circles, pierced and embossed with irises.   **$120/set**

DOGS' HEADS, silverplated, set of 8.   **$175/set**

ENAMEL AND SILVER, Art Nouveau florals, set of 6.

$250/set

ENAMELED HUNT SCENE on sterling, set of 8.   **$350/set**

GEORGIAN Irish silver livery buttons, engraved with a crest, 3 large and 20 small, Henry Flavelle, Dublin, c. 1820.

$1,000/set

STAMPED "FIFE HUNT," set of 14, surrounded by a wreath of thistles and bows, unmarked, silverplated.   **$20/set**

VICTORIAN, silverplated, with owl's head center with glass eyes, set of 6.   **$225/set**

Calling Card Cases

American coin silver calling card case, c. 1860, $165. Courtesy of H & H Antiques. Photo by J. Auslander.

In the 19th century the advent of the social custom of visiting, or calling, and leaving one's card on a tray or salver instituted the use of a calling card case. Many examples were beautifully crafted from sterling silver or silverplate with stamped or chased designs depicting famous cathedrals and places of interest. Some of the finest were produced by the English silversmiths in Birmingham and Chester.

In England all card cases are referred to as visiting card cases. In the early 19th century card cases often matched snuffboxes or vinaigrettes. Subjects such as Windsor Castle, the Crystal Palace, or Brighton Pavilion were highly embossed and chased on the covers. American cases also had stamped or engraved scenes, generally set within a cartouche but most often of unidentifiable places.

Toward the end of the 19th century cases became very elaborate, with allover designs of flowers and foliage or cherubs in cartouche. During this period the Japonesque form became more popular in the United States and England. Many cases from this period are found with asymmetrical flowers, birds, and fans, sometimes with engine turning, parcel gilding, or grayed effects.

Tortoise shell and mother-of-pearl were also used for card cases, with sterling silver banding and cartouche. Coin silver cases, usually with restrained motifs, were made in the United States by Albert Coles and other manufacturers. Cases were made in several sizes and shapes, including a curved style to fit easily into a pocket. They were made with hinged or separate lids or in a book form that opened to two inner compartments. Some card cases are also found with chains and finger rings, probably for carrying to evening social events.

CHASED with Art Nouveau–style decoration, with flowers, buds, and foliage, incorporating a bone aide-memoire, Birmingham, 1913. **$275**

CHASED FRONT, with a view of Windsor Castle in high relief, Nathaniel Mills, Birmingham, 1887. **$750**

CHERUBS' HEADS, die-stamped among clouds in the style of Angelica Kauffman, Sheffield, 1898. **$250**

CHINESE GILT filigree, shaped oblong applied with dragons and flowers. **$150**

EMBOSSED with a stag at bay and 2 fawns surrounded by scrollwork, Birmingham, 1901. **$300**

ENVELOPE, with chain and finger ring, in a fitted case, engraved: "With the compliments of the Season 1913 to 1914 Hotel Metropole, London," Mappin & Webb, Birmingham, 1913. **$180**

ENVELOPE CASE, with chain and finger ring, Birmingham, 1912. **$100**

LEATHER, silver-mounted, lid applied with a church, a watch incorporated in the clock tower. **$200**

LID ENAMELED with an Arab boy and his donkey, Continental. **$1,000**

OBLONG, die-stamped with a view of St. Paul's Cathedral in high relief and with flowers and scrolling foliage, F.M., Birmingham, 1846. **$575**

PURSE FORM, with scrollwork borders, interior fitted with brown leather compartments, with chain and loop, Birmingham, 1915. **$275**

RECTANGULAR CASE, the front and back chased with scenes of Windsor Castle, surrounded by flowers, foliage, and scrollwork, Nathaniel Mills, Birmingham, 1841. **$425**

STAMPED with a church, cart and horses, flowers, foliage, and scrollwork, Birmingham, 1906. **$275**

Candlesticks

Pair of English George II silver candlesticks, $2,600/pair. Courtesy of Christie's East, New York.

In England sterling silver candlesticks date from the late 17th century. They were for practical use and indicated that the owner had a degree of wealth. At that time most candlesticks were raised from a sheet of silver in Corinthian column style. After the middle of the 18th century candlesticks were generally of the cast type, heavier and less likely to be damaged.

The Birmingham silversmiths of the 1750s offered loaded candlesticks to an eager public. Two thin sheets of silver were die-stamped, soldered together, and filled with pitch or plaster of Paris for stability. In the 19th century many silversmiths copied the Queen Anne style and also introduced candlesticks in classical or highly ornate forms.

Candlestick sizes changed over the years. Those made before 1760 ranged from 6 to 9 inches in height, and from 1760 to 1775 they were from 9½ to 11½ inches tall. After 1775 a variety of sizes were made, most with weighted bases. In the mid- to late 19th century 9- to 11-inch sizes were most common.

Very few candelabra were made prior to the middle of the 18th century. Most often the shafts were in the form of candlesticks with the addition of a branched candle arm made to fit into the candlestick base. They generally fetch three or four times more than a pair of candlesticks.

Candlesticks with weighted or loaded bases generally are of a thinner gauge of sterling silver and are easily dented. They prove almost impossible to repair with ease.

When buying, look for crisp details on cast candlesticks and bases. Make sure the sticks are not bent. Check that you are really buying a pair, not two similar sticks. Single candlesticks are very difficult to sell.

Chambersticks are candlesticks originally used to light the way from the keeping room to the bed chamber. They had a curved ring for easy carrying. Silver and pewter chambersticks were used in America until replaced by the oil lamp. In England in the 18th century the columnar taper stick or caryatid style was used. Cast reproductions of early chamber and taper sticks were made in the early and middle part of the 20th century.

A candle snuffer is a cone-shaped form with a long handle; it is used to reach across tables and extinguish candle flames. They appear with embossed motifs to match silver services or in combinations of sterling with ebonized handles.

ADAM STYLE, pair, square feet with canted corners decorated with urns, rams' heads, and stylized swags, Sheffield, 1966, weighted.   **$700/pr**

AMERICAN, banquet size, pair, early 20th century, circular weighted bases, height, 8 in.   **$40/pr**

ART NOUVEAU, pair, Dominick & Haff, 1902, Tulip pattern, weighted bases.   **$750/pr**

ARTS AND CRAFTS style, pair, on rising square bases stamped with simulated strap- and boss work, James Dixon & Sons, Sheffield, 1907, height, 9 in.   **$1000/pr**

AUSTRO-HUNGARIAN, pair, rising circular bases stamped with friezes of shell decoration and detachable nozzles, height, 8 in. **$575/pr**

BALUSTER FORM, pair, in 18th-century taste, with shell corners, William Hutton & Sons, Ltd., London, 1901. **$1,300/pr**

BALUSTER FORM, pair, on rectangular foot, engraved wreath, overall hammered finish, by LaPierre, height, 9¼ in. **$160/pr**

CANDELABRA, pair, German, cast rococo style, 7 lights with baluster stems and foliate branches richly embossed with flowers, scrolls, and foliage, J. D. Schleissner & Sons, Hanau, c. 1895. **$7,000/pr**

CARRIAGE LAMP, sterling silver, applied with a vesta case, hinged covers engraved with a crest, Thomas Johnson, London, 1864. **$2,200**

COLUMNAR FORM, set of 4, fluted stems, the capitals with rosettes connected by drapery swags, John Winter & Co., Sheffield, 1779, height, 11⅝ in. **$5,500/set**

CORINTHIAN CAPITALS, pair, each with hobnail-pattern cut-glass column, height, 6 in. **$550/pr**

CORINTHIAN COLUMN, pair, on beaded, stepped square bases, beaded, shaped square detachable nozzles, Walker and Hall, Sheffield, 1894. **$1,500/pr**

DUTCH BAROQUE style, after a pair by Nicholaas Mensma, Leeuwarden, 1670, domed bases chased with vignettes of classical scenes, spirally twisted stems chased with large flowers, wood bases, height, 10¾ in. **$1,800/pr**

DWARF (banquet size), telescopic, pair, plain circular with applied lobed gadroon borders, c. 1820. **$400/pr**

ENAMELING, guilloche, pair, pale coffee-colored with a hexagonal baluster stem and spreading circular base. **$450/pr**

FLUTED, pair, on rising shaped circular bases, Austro-Hungarian, mid-19th century, height, 10¾ in. **$650/pr**

FLUTED COLUMN, pair, on foliate-decorated stepped square bases, sockets with rising palm leaves, Sheffield, 1865, 5½ in. **$500/pr**

FRENCH, pair, various marks unidentified, 18th century, height, 3½ in. **$1,200/pr**

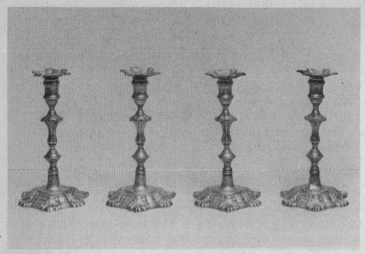

Set of four George II silver candlesticks by John Cafe, London, c. 1750,
$14,000/4. **Courtesy of William Doyle Galleries, New York.**

GEORGE II style, 4, 20th century, R. Blackinton & Co., with
slender pear-shaped stems, reeded borders, weighted bases,
height, 11½ in.   **$1,400/4**

GEORGE II, pair, sterling silver, stylized-bamboo turned standard, weighted bases, 1813, height, 6¾ in.   **$700/pr**

GEORGE III, set of 4, paneled baluster form resting on an octagonal base, John Schofield, London, 1792.   **$7,250/set**

GERMAN, 4, early 20th century, domed bases chased with water and reeds, stems formed as dolphins ridden by putti, drip
pans and sconces chased with water and flowers, height, 13¾
in.   **$3,700/4**

GERMAN, pair, foliate-decorated and fluted baluster stems on
rising shaped square bases, 11¾ in.   **$550/pr**

GERMAN, pair, on concave pedestals ending in square bases
with leafage, ropework, and beaded borders, Konigsberg, c.
1800, height, 7⅛ in.   **$900/pr**

GERMAN, pair, with detachable capitals, of tapering fluted
form on square bases, sconces with applied swags of fruit, En-
gelbert Jehle, Munich, 1796.   **$2,200/pr**

HEXAGONAL swollen columns and inverted bell-shape sockets, pair.   **$375/pr**

LOUIS XVI STYLE, pair, silver-gilt on oval bases with guilloche rims, engraved with armorials, the stems with drapery swags and headed by three female masks, urn-shape sconces, c. 1870.
$2,700/pr

OIL LAMP, classical Roman form, on 3 paw feet with a mask thumbrest, Henry William Dee, London, 1876.   **$350**

OIL LAMP, applied with shell and foliate decoration, plain tapering column and hobnail-pattern cut-glass font, fitted for electricity, height, 38 in.   **$600**

PAIR, on scrolling, shaped circular bases rising to baluster stems chased with foliate scrolls and foliage, Gorham, height, 10¾ in.   **$1,200/pr**

PAIR, silver-gilt, Black, Starr and Frost, chased with tied swags, weighted bases, early 20th century.   **$1,000/pr**

PAIR, the rising square bases, tapering columns, and molded square sockets stamped with swags and classical figures, William Comyns, London, 1899.   **$1,400/pr**

PAIR, 5 LIGHTS, silver-gilt, fluted knop stem and campana-form socket bearing detachable upper section consisting of 5 leaf- and flower-clad scrolling arms and central socket with shaped circular wax pans chased with flowers, scrolls, and gadrooning, Gorham, height, 19 in.   **$6,000/pr**

Pair of Tiffany sterling candelabra in Rococo Revival style, 1873–1891.
Courtesy of Christie's East, New York.

ROCOCO REVIVAL STYLE, pair, with fluted sides topped with urn-shape nozzle, nozzles having drip pans with an egg border, Robert Garrard, London, 1856.   **$11,000/pr**

SHAPED SQUARE BALUSTER, pair, in mid-18th-century taste, on dished bases, Sheffield, 1900.   **$400/pr**

SQUARE BASES, pair, shoulders applied with Greek key frieze decoration, each with a tapering square column, Walker & Hall, Sheffield, 1924.   **$300/pr**

SQUARE BASES, pair, with fluted frieze, baluster and fluted stems, Thomas Bradbury & Co., 1894.   **$1,400/pr**

TABLE LAMP, on a foliate- and shell-decorated rising shaped triangular base engraved with an armorial, fluted and beaded vase-shape column decorated with friezes of shells and foliage, fitted for electricity, E. and J. Barnard, London, 1866.   **$750**

TABLE LAMP, spirally fluted vase shape, on hardstone base, J.N.M., London, 1891.   **$800**

TABLE LAMPS, Corinthian capital, pair, on beaded square bases with acanthus leaf frieze decoration, fluted tapering column with laurel wreath cartouches, fitted for electricity.   **$1,700/pr**

Canes

$\mathcal{M}$any 18th-century American portraits depict gentlemen with canes, which were generally made in England or on the Continent. Their use became more popular in the 19th century as the wearing of swords by gentlemen became unfashionable.

In the mid-19th century in America canes became status symbols and were found with sterling silver or silver gilt handles. The handles were embossed or engraved with rococo scrollwork, floral or ribbon, generally with a cartouche for a monogram. The most unusual were cast in full-figure designs of animals with blown-glass eyes.

Examples were made in China in the 19th century for the American and European markets, usually with chased designs depicting animals against Oriental foliage. Collectors avidly search for Continental canes with semidraped female forms or those with risqué motifs.

In the United States, Tiffany, Gorham, Fradley, and Reed and Barton all produced figural animal cane handles with horses' heads, dogs, cats, and even seals, some with inset glass eyes.

Mechanical canes with sterling silver pop-up pencils, hidden scent bottles, and compacts were sold in the early part of the 20th century. Other examples are known to contain concealed matchsafes and snuffboxes, and a prized English cane has a sterling golf club handle with an enclosed cigarette case.

During the late 19th and early 20th centuries it was not unusual for the entrance hall of a home to have a cane stand or a hall seat with slots for canes. It also was not unusual for the fashionable gentleman to have a variety of canes for different occasions and outfits.

BATON, silver-mounted ivory, the handle and the ferrule chased with rococo scrolling foliage and flowers, in a plush-lined mahogany case. **$250**

HANDLE, "Japanese style," silver and mixed metal, of slightly serpentine outline, applied in silver, gold alloy, and copper with an iris, dragonfly, crane in flight, and spray of bulrushes on hammered ground, Tiffany & Co., New York, 1873–91, length, 3⅜ in.   **$600**

HANDLE, cane, Continental, chased with flowers and scroll-work, hinged top opening to reveal a gilt-lined compartment.
                                                              $600

HANDLE, cane, late 19th century, modeled as a parrot's head with chased plumage and green glass eyes.   **$450**

HANDLE, cane, sterling-silver-cast scene of hunting dog at-tacking a wild boar.   **$550**

HANDLE, riding crop, late Victorian, cast and chased in the form of the head of a French hunting poodle, Chester. **$450**

HANDLE, riding crop, late Victorian, cast and chased in the form of a greyhound's head.   **$550**

POLISHED STONE, clam-broth-colored tip (hairline crack) with a blue enamel border (chipped), edged with silver beading and ribbon-tied wreaths, maker's mark G.A.S., Stockholm, early 19th century, .900 standard.   **$175**

RIDING WHIP, handle cast in the form of a giraffe's head, with a woven wirework mount, London, 1827.   **$1,200**

WALKING STICK, silver-handled, knob chased with scrolling foliage and engraved with a monogram, Edinburgh, 1881.
                                                              $125

WALKING STICK, silver-topped, the handle grip modeled as a section of antler, Jonathan Howell, London, 1797. **$250**

Castors, Castor Sets, and Cruets

English sterling condiment set and castor in fitted case, Walker & Hall, Sheffield, $1,400. Courtesy of Christie's South Kensington, London.

English George III cruet. Courtesy of Christie's East, New York.

In the middle to the latter part of the 19th century in America, castor sets, always placed on the dining room table, were used for serving pickled condiments, which helped to disguise the taste of sour or rancid meats and vegetables. Lack of refrigeration caused fast deterioration of fresh foods. Often not even a block of ice could deter the rapid spoilage. Castor sets were most often made with a silverplated or sterling silver framework having a glass insert and matching tongs. The insert could

Pair of English sterling sauce boats and cruet. **Courtesy of Christie's East, New York.**

be pressed or art glass, colored or clear. Cranberry and ruby glass inserts command the highest prices.

Castors (Shakers)

Most castors (also spelled "casters"), or shakers—commonly used for powdered sugar, pepper, or other spices—found today were made in the Victorian era. Their use began in Europe in the late 17th century.

Styles vary from urn and pear shapes to octagonal and light-house forms with shaped, domed, or pierced lids. Ornamentation often included stamped or chased ribbons, floral and laurel wreaths, and beading.

In the late 19th century Dutch and German manufacturers produced castors with 18th-century rococo motifs. At the beginning of the 20th century, American sterling silver and silverplate manufacturers copied many of the 18th-century silver designs.

BALUSTER FORM, pierced bayonet top, Tyler, Boston, 1730.
$2,500

CRUET, 8-bottle oblong on scrolling foliate feet and with a wirework superstructure and scroll handle, Benjamin Preston, London, 1845. **$500**

FIVE-BOTTLE, bellflower pattern, American, silverplated. **$450**

FIVE-BOTTLE, cut glass, original stoppers, sterling silver, Tiffany. **$1,200**

FIVE-BOTTLE, original stoppers, English, silverplated, wire-wrapped decoration. **$375**

FIVE-BOTTLE, original stoppers, silverplated, Gothic-arch style. **$350**

LIGHTHOUSE FORM, engraved with reeded body bands and with a compressed finial, Pearce & Burrows, London, 1828.
$190

LIGHTHOUSE SHAPE, spirally fluted on a flaring foot, cover with fluted baluster finial and bayonet fittings, London, 1889.
$450

NOVELTY cradle-shape 6-bottle cruet mounted on wheels, with wirework superstructure, fitted with 6 glass condiment bottles.
$425

NOVELTY, modeled as a squirrel holding a nut, silverplated, grasswork base, the detachable head with glass eyes. **$175**

PICKLE, amber glass, silverplated, and tongs. **$150**

PICKLE, blue cane-pattern glass, silverplated. **$225**

PICKLE, daisy and button cranberry glass and silverplate.
$250

SUGAR, late 18th century, silver-topped cut glass on a shaped circular foot. **$110**

SUGAR, modeled as an owl with chased and engraved plumage, detachable head with shoe button eyes, G.R. and E.B., London, 1866. **$1,400**

SUGAR, octagonal baluster, William Hutton & Sons, London, 1900. **$185**

SUGAR, pear shape on dolphin feet, chased with friezes of a fox, a hound, and various birds surrounded by flowers and foliage, silverplated, Elkington and Co., London, 1909. **$575**

SUGAR, small paneled vase shape with an egg-and-dart rim and domed cover with foliate and berry finial. **$75**

SUGAR, spiral-fluted lighthouse in the Queen Anne taste, cover with bayonet fittings and fluted baluster finial, Charles Stuart Harris, London, 1900, Britannia Standard.   **$300**

SUGAR DREDGER, Edwardian, silver gilt, neoclassical vase shape with swags and ribbon festooning, domed cover with flame finial, Hasley Bros., 1910.   **$300**

THREE-BOTTLE, cane pattern and silverplated, American, late 19th century.   **$125**

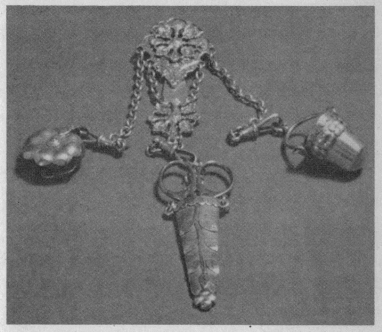

English sterling chatelaine, c. 1889, matched pieces, $750. Photo by J. Auslander.

The term *chatelaine* originated from the word *chattel*, or keeper of the keys. Chatelaines first appeared in Roman times and again in the Middle Ages, and they enjoyed a revival from the mid-18th century through the latter part of the 19th. Chatelaine referred to the clip hung at the waist, usually from a belt, with attachments such as the keys to the sugar box or the liquor cabinet, a nutmeg grater, and often a corkscrew. It was worn by the gentleman or lady of the house or the housekeeper. The mid-19th century chatelaine, usually simply engraved, was worn primarily by women. By the end of the 19th century exuberant examples with elaborately stamped mounts and paste stones became the fashion. Novelty types with horse-shoe details, animals' heads, and wheel decorations were very popular in England and America. Additional decorative motifs included flowers, birds, classical medallions, snakes, and sporting motifs. Objects suspended from the chatelaine included dance cards, pocket watches, penknives, needlework tools, and other items.

Other styles of chatelaine became important during the mid-to late 19th century. The sewing chatelaine usually held a thimble bucket, scissors and sheath, pincushion, needle case, pencil and aide-memoire (memo pad), and a scent bottle used to dry the fingertips before working on delicate fabrics. Chatelaines were also made with writing tools, corkscrews, and glove hooks, or with a cross and prayer book. In America chatelaines and chatelaine pieces were made by Whiting, Gorham, Tiffany, Unger Brothers, Kerr, and other manufacturers.

When buying, make sure all pieces on the chatelaine match. Some that appear to be right because they are so ornate may not be when they are scrutinized thoroughly.

ANCHOR SHAPE with cross and heart, English, late 19th century, silverplated.   **$75**

CLIP, cast with satyr's head surrounded by cherubs and scrollwork, various dates and makers, 5 attachments.   **$325**

CLIP, with 6 matching pieces, including whistle, stamp case, matchsafe, writing pad, pencil and box, silver gilt, turquoise studs, American, Webster, late 19th century.   **$1,200**

CLIP, applied metal, sterling silver, with insects and floral sprays, hammered ground, American, late 19th century. **$550**

CLIP, Art Nouveau, embossed with lady's head with flowing hair, unmarked, American, late 19th century.   **$325**

CLIP, belt, cast with a satyr's head, 5 attachments including a pen knife, a retractable pencil, a buttonhook, a vesta case, and a peppermint box, various dates and makers.   **$300**

CLIP, belt, cast with 2 parrots, 9 decorative appendages, South American, late 19th century.   **$500**

CLIP, gilt, with 7 appendages, including sovereign case, needle case, whistle, strawberry pomander, and cow bell, various makers, silverplated.   **$275**

CLIP, riding motifs, silver gilt, with embossed crop and 5 matching pieces: horseshoe-shape pincushion, thimble bucket, notepad, needle case, scissor case. **$1,200**

EMBOSSED, clip with 3 unmatched pieces, American, late 19th century. **$225**

EMBOSSED CHERUBS, 5 matching pieces, all marked Kerr, late 19th century. **$900**

GOLF, silverplated, with score card and pencil, English, c. 1900 **$375**

PIERCED WITH MASKS, flowers, and foliage, pendant chains supporting a crucifix and several religious medals in 18th-century style, silverplated. **$175**

SEWING, silverplated, floral clip with multicolor paste stones, 5 matching pieces, all set with stones. **$550**

SEWING, silverplated, Roman centurion clip, 5 matching pieces, allover floral-engraved. **$400**

SEWING, 3 pieces, sterling silver, matching thimble bucket, scissor case, pincushion, all with cut card work, English, 1889. **$750**

Chicago Silver

Lebolt (Chicago) tea service on tray, $5,500. Courtesy of Christie's East, New York.

The creation of Chicago sterling silver began in the early 19th century and ended with the closing of the Kalo Shop in 1970. Hand-worked pieces, inspired by the English Arts & Crafts movement, were created by silversmiths working individually or in groups. The term Chicago Silver indicates a period of hand-worked pieces made from about 1900 until after World War I, and today it is the most important area of silver collecting.

American Indian and Colonial Revival design motifs dominated, and flowers—roses, daisies, poppies, and thistles—also were used, either in repoussé work or etched onto the silver forms.

Kalo, Jarvie, Marshall Field & Co. Craft Shop, and the T.C. Shop are some of the well-known names. After World War I,

Lebolt & Co., the Randahl Shop, the Chicago Art Silver Shop, and the Frank S. Boyden Co. continued the style.

The Kalo Shop was the most prolific producer of handmade sterling silver objects in Arts and Crafts styles. These included tea sets, bowls, candlesticks, and flatware, all with hammered grounds having single-line or stylized repoussé borders. The Randahl Shop produced the same type of hammered wares, among them tea sets, vases, and candlesticks. Copper and silver art pieces were created by Carence Crafters and the Chicago Art Silver Shop, where flatware was a specialty. There is a distinctive, simple, and elegant form to pieces made at this time. In addition, the pieces are completely marked and easy to date.

From the end of World War I until 1970, a second wave of silversmiths, who had arrived in Chicago from Europe, continued to work in this style.

BOWL, centerpiece, Lebolt & Co., Chicago, engraved with foliate panels, with hammered surface.   **$500**

BOWL, centerpiece, of lobed shallow circular form on spreading foot, with applied initials and overall hammered surface, Lebolt, diameter, 15 in.   **$1,300**

BOWL, fruit, Kalo Shop, circular with lightly hammered surface, broadly fluted with scalloped rim.   **$1,200**

BOWL, salad, copper with silver servers, Kalo Shop, hand-hammered surface and silverplated interior, applied with initial B, matching silver salad spoon and fork.   **$600/set**

BOX, trinket, Kalo Shop, oval, lightly hammered finish, inset with abalone shell.   **$650**

COFFEE SERVICE, 3 pieces, hand-wrought, Lebolt, squared handle, knop finials, hammered surface, monogrammed.
                                   $1,100/set

PITCHER, water, bulbous with C-form handle and overall hammered finish, applied initials, Lebolt, height over handle, 7 in.   **$900**

PLATES, bread and butter, silver, set of 24, each circular with plain surface, The Randahl Shop, Chicago, early 20th century.
                                   $1,600/24

PLATTER, hand-wrought, woven border with fluting at intervals and lightly hammered finish, by Randahl, length, 18½ in.
$750

SERVERS, 4, hammered, comprising salad fork and spoon, pastry server, and olive spoon, each with applied initials.
$425/4

VASE, by the Kalo Shop, cylindrical with molded rim and tucked-in base, with overall hammered surface and applied initials, height, 5 in.
$1,200

Chinese Silver

Chinese tea service, $3,300. **Courtesy of Christie's East, New York.**

Chinese Export silver, also known as China Trade silver, refers to objects made in China for a foreign market.

Sterling silver pieces were often made in China to Western specifications. Therefore, there are many different designs and regional characteristics, as well as monograms and coats of arms, to be found. Objects created by Chinese silversmiths were exported to the United States and England during the 19th century. Trade with the United States continued into the early 20th century, when the quality of the work declined. Pieces from this period are often referred to as tourist sterling.

All Chinese Export silver ranges in quality from 800 fine to well over 925 sterling fine. In the late 19th century the 90 mark was also used and is thought to indicate 900 fine quality. Pseudo-American and pseudo-English hallmarks were also used but are not an indication or guarantee of sterling silver content.

Marks can be divided into three basic categories: Chinese, pseudo-American, and pseudo-English. The best source for researching hallmarks is the book *Chinese Export Silver* by Forbes, Kern, and Wilkins (refer to bibliography).

Forms include spoons, tea services, card cases, cups, mugs, beakers, posey holders, jewelry, flasks, and fans, as well as other decorative objects.

Naturalistic details derived from ancient Chinese sources abound. Bamboo and pine branches and prunus and chrysanthemum blossoms were used frequently, along with rock work, shells, and waves. The raging dragon (who represented the emperor) and the phoenix (indicating the empress) are also found. A matted or punched ground was often used in combination with beautifully detailed repoussé work. A great majority of Chinese silver hollowware, made during the mid- to late 19th century, has a grayish cast and a particularly heavy weight. Filigree wirework was at its best during this time and can be seen in beautifully executed pieces of jewelry, posey holders, fans, card cases, and baskets.

Original cases or boxes for the sterling silver objects were made of leather, brocade, ivory, and other materials, usually with silk or velvet linings. They are highly desirable, along with the silver piece, because they were often stamped with the maker's name and address and help to establish origin in the absence of hallmarks.

BOWL, Chinese Export, chased in relief with traditional scenes of processions, warriors, and entertainers, Cutshing, c. 1890.
$650

BOWL, christening, 2-handled, chased with irises on a textured ground and with a plain liner, China Trades. **$250**

BOWL, rose, chased with various flowers and insects on a textured ground with a wirework grill and carved wood stand, Woshing, Shanghai. **$550**

BOWLS, finger, set of 8, circular, spot-hammered and gilt-lined, each with a molded rim. **$400/8**

BOWLS, set of 8, spot-hammered with molded rims.
$800/set

CANDELABRA, pair, 3 lights, the shaft in trumpet form with spreading domed foot and an urn-form nozzle, each shaft with an inserting 3-branch arm (both finials missing), weighted, maker's mark in Chinese cypher, marked STERLING, height, 14 in. **$400/pr**

CANDLESTICKS, pair, China Trade, on carved-wood bases, stems chased with chrysanthemums, sinuous dragons, and characters, each with sinuous dragon support, height, 9½ in.
$800/pr

CARD CASE, China Trade, of pierced silver filigree, traditional dragons and foliage, Khecheong, Canton, c. 1870. **$450**

CARD CASE, rectangular sterling silver, stamped in high relief with a cathedral, foliate decoration on a matte ground. **$300**

CHEROOT (cigar) case, curved oblong, cover stamped and chased with two birds perched on a branch of flowering prunus. **$125**

COCKTAIL SHAKER, China Trade, chased with bamboo branches on a textured ground. **$375**

COCKTAIL SHAKER, spot-hammered, chased with elaborate sinuous dragon, and 6 beakers, each applied with a sinuous dragon. **$950/set**

COIN PURSE, silver mesh, the frame pierced with dragons, Liang, c. 1900. **$100**

CONDIMENT SET, enameled, novelty formed as a bactrian camel laden with 2 hardstone panniers, the camel and the panniers with detail decorated in guilloche enameling. **$175/set**

CUP, 19th-century China Trade, tapering on circular foot, with sinuous dragon handles, body chased with figures on a textured ground. **$850**

CUP, large, with detachable plain liner, chased and embossed with flowering prunus on a crackled ground, China Trades.
$1,200

CUP, 2 handles, Chinese Export silver, one side with figures, the other side with stylized American eagle, Sing Fat of Canton, c. 1900. **$800**

JUG, cream, pear shape, chased with a broad frieze of battling figures and sinuous dragon handle, 19th century. **$350**

MIRROR, the back cast and chased with scrolling dragon in high relief, length, 10½ in. **$450**

MUG, Chinese Export, 19th century, matte sides decorated in relief with trailing thistles, Cutshing of Canton, c. 1870.

$750

MUG, Chinese Export, 19th century, of tapering shape with dragon handle, chased with traditional scenes, Khecheong, Canton, c. 1860.   **$1,000**

MUG, Chinese Export, dragon handle chased in relief with a traditional battle scene, Leeching, c. 1875.   **$850**

SALVER, circular, on dragon's-head feet, everted rim chased with sinuous dragons with applied bamboo-style border, China Trades, diameter, 9¼ in.   **$375**

SALVER, shaped circular, spot-hammered border engraved with landscape vignettes, 12 in.   **$350**

SALVER, square, pierced border of dragons, flat-chased and hammered with a scene of courtiers, diameter, 13 in. **$1,100**

SNUFFBOX, Chinese Export, early 19th century, mother-of-pearl carved with traditional scenes, raised floral silver border.

$2,000

SNUFFBOX, Chinese Export, rectangular, basketwork decoration, Khecheong, 1860.   **$450**

SNUFFBOX, Chinese Export, silver-gilt set with bloodstone, panels of sampans, Chinamen fishing and reclining figures, "P," Canton, 1835.   **$1,000**

SNUFFBOX, pocket, China Trade, chased all over with traditional Chinese scenes, Cutshing, c. 1825.   **$900**

TEA AND COFFEE SERVICE, 5 pieces, circular, with scrolling handles, hinged covers with knop finials, on tray. **$2,000/set**

TEA AND COFFEE SERVICE, 4 pieces, comprising teapot, covered sugar bowl, cream pitcher, and waste bowl, globular shape, applied with ferocious writhing dragons, cast handles formed as dragons, covers with dragon finials, overall hammered surface.   **$3,300/set**

TEA SERVICE, Chinese, 3 pieces, comprising teapot, cream pitcher, and covered sugar bowl, with scrolling dragon motifs.

$825/set

TEA SERVICE, 3 pieces, 19th century, chased with sinuous dragons and with dragon handles, Wing Nam.   **$600/set**

TEA SET, Chinese, 3 pieces, comprising teapot, cream pitcher, and covered sugar bowl, bamboo spout, finial, and handle, all engraved with bamboo plants. **$450/set**

TEA SET, 3 pieces, comprising teapot, covered sugar, and creamer, with tree trunk sides and applied with branches of prunus blossom, angular branch handles on sides and lids, marked with Chinese characters and "SILVER" in Roman letters, 20th century. **$1,000/set**

TRAY, tea, hammered oblong, 2 handles, with applied bamboo-style border, 23 in. **$600**

TRAY, tea, oblong, wood applied with sinuous dragons and 2 vacant oval cartouches, on bracket feet, 2 dragon handles, length, 18¼ in. **$350**

TRAY, wood, 2 handles, oblong inlaid and applied with sinuous dragons amid clouds. **$400**

VASE, baluster form, engraved scene of mountains in mist, height, 8½ in. **$400**

VASES, pair, 19th century, with scrolled handles shaped as dragons, applied with gold on matte ground. **$1,500/pr**

Chinese sterling toast rack, c. 1910, $175. **Photo by J. Auslander.**

Christmas Ornaments

Contemporary Portuguese sterling Christmas ornament, $75. **Courtesy of Nancy and Bruce Thompson. Photo by J. Auslander.**

*E*ven though sterling silver and silverplate Christmas ornaments are of contemporary manufacture, they have become quite popular in the United States. They are in the form of animals, snowflakes, bells, and angels, sometimes with dates and names of makers. Hallmark, Gorham, Reed & Barton, and other manufacturers are producing ornaments for an eager public. They are also being made in Portugal for export to the United States. Collectors look for ornaments in mint condition in original boxes.

CAMPBELL KIDS (Campbell Soup).   **$18**

GORHAM, first edition, 1976, "Joys of Christmas."   **$25**

GORHAM, American Heritage, 1973, dove.   **$40**

GORHAM, Noel, 1977.   **$40**

GORHAM, snowflakes, 1970.   **$600**

GORHAM, snowflakes, 1973.   **$60**

GORHAM, snowflakes, 1986.   **$60**

GORHAM Unlimited, 1978, "Waiting for Christmas."   **$40**

HAND & HAMMER, #009, icicle, sterling.   **$25**

JOHN-JOHN reindeer, sterling.   **$48**

KIRK & SONS, 1972, Christmas angel "Tootsie."   **$40**

PORTUGUESE, holiday angel.   **$75**

R. M. TRUSH, rocking horse, sterling.   **$80**

R. M. TRUSH, teddy bear, sterling.   **$55**

R. M. TRUSH, Raggedy Andy, sterling.   **$65**

REED & BARTON, crosses, 1972, gold on sterling.   **$70**

REED & BARTON, crosses, 1984, gold on sterling.   **$40**

REED & BARTON, snowflake, 1972.   **$29**

REED & BARTON, stars, 1976.   **$25**

S. KIRK & SONS, 1972, N. Rockwell greeting card, sterling.
    $75

TOWLE, floral medallion, 1983.   **$35**

TOWLE, medallions, 1975, "Five Golden Rings."   **$45**

TOWLE, "Songs/melodies of Christmas," 1978.   **$50**

TOWLE, "Songs/melodies of Christmas," 1986.   **$50**

WALLACE, "12 Days of Christmas," 1988, "Partridge in a Pear Tree."   **$40**

WALLACE, "Peace Doves," 1972.   **$70**

Cigar Cutters

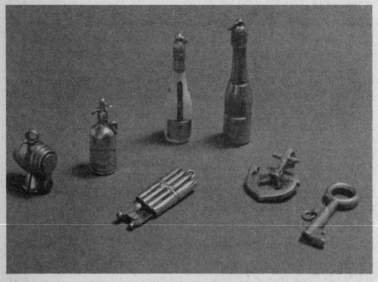

Group of Victorian figural cigar cutters. **Photo by J. Auslander.**

Cigar cutters and piercers were made in the latter part of the 19th century for use by smokers to clip or pierce the end of the cigar so that it would draw the smoke smoothly. A wide range of cutters, made of steel with sterling silver or silverplate mounts, resulted. Fob styles were made to hang from a watch chain, and they generally can still be found with the ring attached. Most examples of this type were made in novelty forms, including champagne and beer bottles, barrels, syphons, lobster claws, keys, and anchors. One of the most collectible fob cutters is in bicycle form. There is an erotic version depicting a gentleman obscenely gesturing. These were produced in sterling silver and silverplate and in combination of horn, tortoise shell, and ivory or bone with sterling silver mounts. Table- or desk-type cutters were engine-turned or engraved with a monogram or crest. Novelties, which can still be found today, included hunting dogs' heads, horses' heads, seminude or nude women and usually were large enough to serve also as a desk paperweight.

ANCHOR, silverplated, English, 1880, watch fob size. **$150**

BOAR'S TUSK, table size, Continental, mounted with cast boar's head. **$850**

BUNCH OF CIGARS, sterling silver, American, late 19th century, watch fob size. **$175**

CAT ON OVAL BASE, silverplated, watch fob size, English.

$125

CHAMPAGNE BOTTLE, silverplated, watch fob size, English.

$75

COMBINATION figure of shoe with matchsafe, silverplated.

$175

GIRL ON POTTY, sterling silver, watch fob size, English.

$175

KEY FORM, silverplated, watch fob size, English. **$125**

KEY FORM, silverplated, German, late 19th century. **$125**

SYPHON BOTTLE, silverplated, watch fob size, English.

$100

TABLE CUTTER, dog's head, silverplated, American. **$225**

TABLE CUTTER, elephant novelty, sitting upright on its haunches. **$350**

TABLE CUTTER, horse's head, silverplated, American. **$250**

TABLE CUTTER, seminude female, silverplated, Continental.

$450

Cigarette Cases

Group of late 19th- and early 20th-century English and Continental sterling and enamel cigarette cases. Courtesy of Butterfield & Butterfield, San Francisco.

Cigarette cases became popular at the turn of the 20th century and were generally made of sterling silver and later of silverplate. In the United States, Kerr and Unger Brothers produced exquisite cases with highly embossed designs depicting bulldogs with inset garnet eyes, Indians, sporting motifs, and ladies blowing smoke rings. Many had engine-turned designs. Some of the very best examples have enameled motifs with animals, flags, or seminude or risqué nude women. Check to see if the enamel is damaged or in retouched condition. It is important to make sure that you are not buying a late-19th-century case with a recently enameled design.

Art Deco examples with guilloche enameling in vivid colors are readily available. Those with geometric designs are the most salable. Cases produced in the 1920s and 1930s are generally slimmer because they were often slipped into a lady's evening bag.

The simple sterling silver cases and those with engine-turned engraved designs are slow sellers, but those with erotic scenes command huge prices today.

ARMENIAN, of oval sections, nielloed with flowers, a bird, and a checkerboard effect. **$100**

ART NOUVEAU, square case stamped with a frieze of stylized foliage, Liberty and Co., London, 1900. **$150**

ART NOUVEAU, Austrian, enameled, the cover depicting a woman with flowing brown hair and a neoclassical-style pink dress, contemplating a burning cigarette, c. 1900. **$1,300**

AUSTRIAN, enameled, cover depicting a Caucasian warrior kneeling on a rock firing a musket, his horse tied up behind him. **$1,200**

BASKETWORK with pull-off cover and applied crested cartouche, Joseph Willmore, Birmingham, 1835. **$500**

ENAMELED front with a charging horseman in a battle scene, Birmingham, 1888. **$500**

ENAMELED front with a female lute player and her admirer seated in a woodland scene surrounded by a blue enameled border, Continental. **$700**

ENAMELED front with a 4-leaf clover and ladybirds, Swedish. **$185**

ENAMELED front with a French chateau set in woodland, reverse engraved with a crest, Continental. **$800**

ENAMELED lid with "Leda and the Swan," Continental. **$1,800**

ENAMELED lid with a brown and white pointer, Continental. **$575**

ENAMELED lid with a coachhouse and a coach and horses, Continental, 1902. **$550**

ENAMELED lid with a lady in full dress carrying a bunch of flowers. **$850**

ENAMELED lid with a pair of lovers in a woodland scene, Continental. **$350**

ENAMELED lid with a reclining seminude lady, with seascape in the background. **$775**

ENAMELED lid with a scantily clad half-bust portrait of a lady with long auburn hair, silver-gilt, Birmingham, 1909. **$1,200**

ENAMELED lid with lady in a bedroom scene.   **$1,400**

ENAMELED lid with two female musicians in Oriental dress in a garden scene, Continental.   **$525**

ENAMELED with a coaching scene, Continental, 1896. **$550**

ENAMELED with a pair of lovers in a green rowboat, setting sun in the background, Continental, late 19th century. **$600**

ENAMELED with a scantily clad lady seated in an armchair, holding a bunch of roses and reading a love note, Continental.
$1,000

ENAMELED, silverplated, with an Arab slave dealer disrobing a raven-haired slave girl, Continental, German, 1900.   **$450**

ENAMELED COVER, oval cartouche with two bulldogs on a pale blue ground, dark blue geometric border, French. **$220**

ENGINE-TURNED, guilloche-enameled with two pink and two yellow roses on ivory background, matching silver-mounted Ronson lighter.   **$200/set**

ENGRAVED with turreted fortress with battlements, towers, and spires, a moat or river with swan, Russian, c. 1908.
$600

ENGRAVED LID with stylized flowers, with gem-set opening mechanism, Russian.   **$250**

FLOWER-chased exterior, scrollwork and mythological birds and animals, surrounding a vacant shaped cartouche, Austrian. **$185**

INSET LID, with an enameled plaque depicting an Indian village scene.   **$600**

NIELLO, cover depicting a dispatch carrier driven by a peasant in a horse-drawn carriage, Russian, Gustav Klingert, Moscow, 1888.   **$675**

OBLONG, with an oval cartouche enameled with two bulldogs on a pale blue ground and a dark blue border, Continental.
$375

OBLONG, guilloche-enameled in bright blue, Continental.
$150

OBLONG, quadruple panels, silver-gilt engraved with stylized flowerheads, Birmingham, 1864.   **$500**

SQUARE, stamped with a frieze of stylized foliage, Liberty & Co., London, 1900.   **$250**

TROMPE L'OEIL, modeled as a mitten with engraved bands of reeding and zigzags, Russian, by Pavel Sasikov, St. Petersburg, 1863.   **$1,850**

Clocks

English Arts & Crafts sterling clock case, c. 1902, $475. Courtesy of Christie's South Kensington, London.

The Victorian era saw the production of several types of clocks for the home and office. Boudoir clocks of sterling silver, silverplate, tortoise shell with sterling silver mounts, or enamel over sterling silver were made to match elaborate dresser sets. Floral sprays in soft colors were common decorations from the 1880s until about 1900; by the 20th century, however, clocks were brilliantly colored, with geometric motifs and guilloche enameling. The library or office often had a desk clock, usually of all sterling silver or tortoise and sterling silver, sometimes in carriage clock form. Novelty desk clocks in the style of tall-case clocks and animal forms were also popular. Timepieces in combinations with barometers and thermometers were also made for the gentleman.

Exciting Tiffany and Cartier clocks incorporating enamels, rose quartz, carnelian, and jade were made in the Art Deco era and are often found with their original silk-lined leather carrying cases.

CARRIAGE, Art Nouveau, silver and leather-mounted, swing handles, pierced and stamped with stylized flowers, Birmingham, 1900.   **$325**

CARRIAGE, gold-mounted silver *petite sonnerie*, quadrangular case with canted corners and stepped base and top decorated with panels of vertical flutes, base and mount for the angular handle decorated with gilt stripes, gold bezel, Cartier, Paris, 1935.   **$7,000**

CARRIAGE, miniature size, silver-mounted on ball feet with swing handle, marked "French movement," Chester, 1905.
                                                    $750

CARRIAGE, oblong, on bun feet with swing scroll handle and white-enameled dial, William Comyns, London, 1902.   **$550**

CARRIAGE, plain, on bun feet with swing handle and white-enameled dial, London, 1904.   **$750**

CARRIAGE, silver-gilt, swing handle, on bun feet with enameled dial with Roman numerals, London, 1897.   **$750**

CARRIAGE, small, engraved with flowers and scrollwork, looped carrying handle and French movement, Birmingham, 1898.   **$600**

CRYSTAL, sterling silver and rose quartz, Cartier.   **$3,500**

DESK, circular, arrow-form hands set with rose diamonds, case decorated with translucent blue enamel on engine-turned ground, ivory-backed with silver-gilt easel support, Cartier, Paris, 1930–40, diameter, 3 1/8 in.   **$2,900**

DESK, sterling, rectangular face with a raised niello design of a "Japanese" scene of mountains, water, clouds, birds, and various Japanese lanterns, Swiss, early 20th century.   **$300**

DRESSING TABLE, arched on bun feet with easel support, guilloche-enameled.   **$125**

DRESSING TABLE, arched, engraved with shells, flowers, and ribbon and foliate swags, Birmingham, 1915.   **$400**

DRESSING TABLE, 8-day, silver and tortoise shell-mounted, with easel support.   **$350**

DRESSING TABLE, engine-turned, applied with floral and foliate decoration on a rope-twist base, London, 1915.   **$925**

DRESSING TABLE, engraved with shells, flowers, and ribbon and foliate swags, Birmingham, 1915.   **$400**

DRESSING TABLE, shaped circular, guilloche-enameled in black and white with applied marcasite decoration, Art Deco, Birmingham, 1931. **$75**

DRESSING TABLE, silver-mounted, shaped, mount stamped with flowers and scrolling foliage, enameled dial, Birmingham, 1890. **$325**

HORSESHOE SHAPE with easel support, enameled in black and green, French, Art Deco. **$375**

MANTEL, arched, applied with ribbon, floral, and foliate swags and with a white-enameled dial, Birmingham, 1904. **$550**

MANTEL, fashioned as a miniature long-case clock with easel support, enameled dial decorated with stylized flowers and foliage, J. Grinsell and Sons, Birmingham, 1906. **$575**

MANTEL, octagonal form topped with a finial of unfolding leaves and beadwork resting on two S-scrolls with beadwork volutes, on a square stepped plinth with bud finial, slate base, Georg Jensen Silversmithy, c. 1945, numbered 333, designed by Johan Rohde, height, 12¼ in. **$15,000**

MANTEL, oval, silverplate, foliate-decorated with easel support and tortoise-shell dial. **$50**

MANTEL, with 2 applied drop handles and a ball finial, Goldsmiths & Silversmiths Co. Ltd., London, 1908. **$400**

TRAVEL, 14-karat gold, Tiffany, early 20th century. **$3,500**

TRAVEL, sterling silver, engine-turned engraving, American, early 20th century. **$250**

Compacts

Italian silver compact in hand mirror form, with concealed mirror in handle. **Reprinted by permission from "Vintage Ladies" compacts by Roslyn Gerson, Wallace-Homestead Book Co., Radmor, PA.**

One of the newest collectibles, the compact, held a lady's necessities: loose powder, a puff, and a mirror. Others contained a place for a lipstick, eye cream, and mascara. Many were encased in novelty shapes, including hands and moon faces. Most date from the 1920s and 1930s, though collectors are just beginning to ferret out 1940s and 1950s examples. Compacts were produced in both sterling silver and silver-plate, often with the addition of colorful enameling or Bakelite accents. Goldstone and silver-foil backings appear on others.

Visitors to Miami, New York, Paris, Venice, and Rome often brought back souvenir types. Others were made to commemorate world's fairs and expositions or to carry advertising legends. Design colors changed through the years; 1920s and 1930s examples had bold, geometric decorations against bright green, red, or royal blue enameled grounds on sterling silver.

Compacts were manufactured by many American companies, including Volupté, La Mode, Elgin, and Richard Hudnut. In France, Cartier produced some wonderful examples with enameled or inlaid plaques of rose quartz, jade, and carved cinnabar. Sometimes they can be found with their original cases.

Some compacts still have their original "tango-chain," originally used to display the compact while dancing.

ALLOVER ENAMEL SCENE, .800 silver, Continental, early 20th century. **$95**

ART DECO, engine turning, rectangular shape, American, early 20th century. **$75**

ART DECO, silverplated, green enamel front, circular form, American, early 20th century. **$35**

CIRCULAR, lid enameled with full-length portrait of a lady in a woodland scene, a bird perched on her hand, Continental.
$350

CIRCULAR FORM, oversize, embossed dolphin, Jensen, early 20th century. **$250**

ENAMEL and .800 silver, pastoral scene, Italian, early 20th century. **$125**

ENAMEL SILHOUETTE, depicting Kate Greenaway figure, English, early 20th century. **$150**

ENAMELED with roses on an engine-turned blue-and-white background, Continental, early 20th century. **$500**

ENAMELED, hunting scene, sterling surround, English, early 20th century. **$150**

ENAMELED GREEN, with attached lipstick and tango chain, black enamel surround, Continental, early 20th century.
$225

HEART SHAPE, floral-engraved, American, early 20th century.
$100

MUSSEL SHELL form, engraved to simulate shell, Continental, early 20th century. **$225**

OVAL, lid enameled with 3 peasant women gleaning, with a farmstead in the background, surrounded by engraved scrollwork and mottled blue/green enameling, Continental. **$125**

TORTOISE SHELL, with sterling silver mounts and marcasite thumbpiece, English, early 20th century. **$130**

Corkscrews

Left. *American sterling riding boot corkscrew, c. 1910, $125.* **Right.** *American Gorham sterling and horn corkscrew.* **Courtesy of Nancy and Bruce Thompson.**

Corkscrews are among the hottest collectible items today. Very fine examples with sterling silver handles and steel or iron screw parts for stability are readily available. They vary in size, the smallest being used to open perfume bottles.

In the late 18th century there were examples with sheathlike cases or with screws that folded up into the handle. Eighteenth-century English, French, and Dutch corkscrews were made in gold, sterling silver, and silver gilt in combination with steel. Elegant Dutch examples had mother-of-pearl medallions inset into the handles or full-figure handles with chains to attach the corkscrew to a chatelaine. Others contained pipe prickers or tampers or containers for mace or nutmegs.

During the 19th century the picnic, or folding, type became popular, with the screw hidden inside the case. Larger corkscrews with sterling silver handles or tusk or bone handles with sterling silver mounts were very popular in the last quarter of the 19th century. These were made by several American firms, including Gorham, Webster, and Tiffany.

In the late 19th century in England screw taps, called champagne taps, were patented. These were used to draw off a small amount of champagne without losing the sparkle in the remainder of the bottle. Quite often, these had unusual figural handles.

In the 1920s sterling pocket corkscrews in the form of riding boots were popular in the United States, as well as those with advertising legends.

BALUSTER SHEATH, chased with rococo foliage, ending in a pipe tamper, the handle cast in the form of cherub astride a lion, Dutch, 18th century. **$2,100**

BOTTLE SHAPE, novelty, 19th century, American, sterling silver. **$300**

EROTIC, cast handle modeled as a naked woman resting her arms on the plain T-shape handle. **$120**

FARROW AND THOMPSON type (lacking helical worm), English, Riley & Storer, 1830, engraved with boar's-head crest and monogram. **$2,800**

FOUR-PILLAR, King Screw, plated, with bone handle, "Mechi Leadenhall." **$500**

KIDNEY-SHAPE handle, Dutch, 18th century, sterling silver, Cornelis Hilberts, Amsterdam, 1749. **$750**

RIDING BOOT SHAPE, sterling silver, American, early 20th century. **$125**

SPIRALLY fluted detachable handle and mounted mother-of-pearl barrel-shape handle, English, c. 1770. **$800**

THOMASON 1802 patent corkscrew, with rare cut-out barrel applied with a Royal Coat of Arms tablet, with wire helix and bone handle with brush. **$300**

TRAVELING, peg and worm, the baluster gold terminals terminating in pierced disks, 18th century. **$750**

TRAVELING, Victorian, London, 1896. **$150**

TRAVELING, with fluted, turned ivory handle and ribbed, tapering sheath, George III, unmarked. **$250**

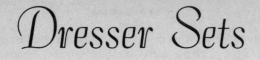

Dresser Sets

English sterling dresser pin tray, c. 1900. **Courtesy of Nancy and Bruce Thompson. Photo by J. Auslander.**

Complete dressing table sets are expensive today because they are difficult to find intact. Most 19th-century sets were composed of 12 to 24 pieces, including several types of brushes and a comb; hand and traveling mirrors; buttonhook, nail file, buffer, and tray; shoehorn; glove stretcher; powder jar; hair receiver; rouge pots; and perhaps a clock and candlesticks.

Elaborate sets date back to the 17th century, but the Victorian styles are the most readily available. Fortunately, dealers are no longer separating boxed sets, especially now that those in crocodile cases have become more collectible. In the 19th century in America, Mauser produced wonderful sets in patterns called L'Art Nouveau and Satyrs and Nymphs, both with Art Nouveau lily borders. Sets with Kerr cherubs and Unger Brothers ladies with flowing hair are eagerly sought today. The Whiting, Blackinton, and Webster companies all produced sets. The Theodore W. Foster company made an elaborate set entitled Paul and Virginia, taken from a famous painting and depicting a young boy and girl in draped clothing seated in a swing. Decorations of roses and violets, rococo scrolls, birds, ribbon swags, and trophy symbols were quite popular motifs. Masks and medallion heads were also used. English sets often featured the popular Angelica Kaufmann–style depiction of five cherubs' heads in clouds. By the early 20th century, simple, engine-turned pieces decorated with enamel and inset semiprecious stones became popular. In England, handsome sets of tortoise shell or shagreen with sterling silver mounts are more desirable. Those with clear and original beveled mirrors and in undented condition fetch the best prices.

At the end of the 19th century and into the early part of the 20th century, women used light colognes decanted into pressed- or cut-glass bottles matching the dresser sets. Sizes of jars and bottles in the dresser sets ranged from tiny rouge pots—the best in heart shapes—to large bottles used for toilet water. Some dresser sets also had matching trinket trays, jewel boxes, and ring trees.

ART NOUVEAU, silverplated, comprising brush, mirror, and comb. **$40/set**

COLOGNE BOTTLES, pair, silver-mounted cut glass, spherical, with faceted ball stoppers, mounts with stamped foliate decoration, London, 1908. **$125/pr**

DANISH, 5 pieces, comprising hand mirror, hand brush, clothes brush, pin tray, and silver-mounted comb, each with stylized blossom design, by Georg Jensen. **$650/set**

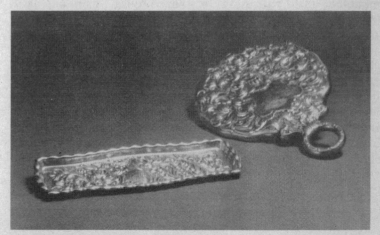

American sterling dressing table hand mirror and pin tray in Heraldic pattern, c. 1885. Mirror, $125, tray, $100. Courtesy of H & H Antiques.

DRESSING TABLE MIRROR, silver-mounted, rectangular, the everted plain rim chased with acanthus at the angles with magnifying plate, Tiffany & Co., New York, 1891–1902, height, 19¾ in. **$3,000**

DRESSING TABLE SET, comprising hand mirror, cut-glass powder jar, small jar, clothes brush, pin tray, comb, nail buffer, curling iron, nail file, buttonhook, toothbrush, embossed with Cupid and Psyche surrounded by dolphins, dragons, and scrollwork, Unger Brothers, Newark, NJ, c. 1900. **$800/set**

DRESSING TABLE SET, comprising hand mirror, hairbrush, clothes brush, hand brush, whisk, small cut-glass jar, nail buffer, shoehorn, buttonhook, nail file, high relief with a flowing-haired woman plucking daisy petals Unger Brothers, Newark, NJ, c. 1910. **$1,100/set**

DRESSING TABLE SET, 8-piece silver and shagreen-mounted, comprising hand mirror, 2 hairbrushes, 2 clothes brushes, and 3 toilet jars and bottles. **$175/set**

DRESSING TABLE SET, engine-turned, silver-mounted, engraved with butterflies, comprising hand mirror, hairbrush, clothes brush, hair receiver. **$150/set**

DRESSING TABLE SET, 5 pieces, engine-turned and foliate-stamped: hand mirror, 2 hairbrushes, and 2 clothes brushes.

$75/set

DRESSING TABLE SET, 5 pieces, silver and tortoise-shell-mounted, inlaid with swags of stylized foliage: hand mirror, 2 hairbrushes, and 2 clothes brushes. **$150/set**

DRESSING TABLE SET, 5 pieces, sterling silver, engine-turned and beaded, comprising hand mirror, 2 hairbrushes, and 2 clothes brushes, Walker & Hall. **$150/set**

DRESSING TABLE SET, 4 pieces, stamped with scrolling foliage, comprising hand mirror, 2 hair brushes, and comb, in a fitted case, London, 1889. **$225/set**

DRESSING TABLE SET, silver-mounted: hand mirror, 2 hairbrushes, 2 clothes brushes, shoehorn, buttonhook, glove stretchers, 5 silver-topped glass toilet jars, and gilt-lined circular toilet pot and cover, London, 1909. **$500/set**

DRESSING TABLE SET, silver-gilt mounts decorated with gray guilloche enameling, comprising hand mirror, 2 hairbrushes, clothes brush, and 6 toilet jars and bottles, Asprey & Co. Ltd.

$300/set

ENAMELED pink guilloche decorated and silver-gilt-mounted, 6 pieces, comprising hand mirror, 2 hairbrushes, 2 clothes brushes, and comb.

$200/set

ENAMELED silver and cut glass, 17 pieces, floral decoration on engine-turned ground.

$1,100/set

ENAMELED, 17 pieces, silver and cut glass, with engine-turned decoration, English.

$600

HAIRBRUSH, silver-mounted, and a pair of matching clothes brushes, each guilloche-enameled with lilies of the valley on shaded ivory and pale green grounds.

$75/3

HAND MIRROR, Art Nouveau, shaped circular form with curling handle, the hammered back with raised shell and marine-like decoration, Whiting Mfg. Co., c. 1900.

$600

POWDER BOWL, large, cut glass, molded circular form with silver and tortoise-shell cover with ball finial.

$250

REPOUSSÉ with flowerheads, 6 pieces, comprising hand mirror, hairbrush, and 4 clothes brushes, LaPierre Mfg. Co.

$250/set

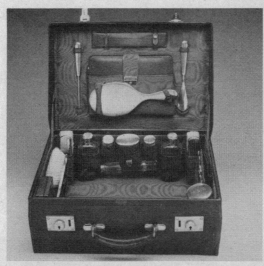

English silver-gilt traveling toilet service, London, 1910. Courtesy of Christie's East, New York.

REPOUSSÉ, Gorham, 11 pieces, decorated with floral motifs, late 19th century.   **$600/set**

STAMPED, 3-PIECE SET, with grotesque masks, flowers, and rococo scrolling foliage, comprising hand mirror, clothes brushes, and hairbrush.   **$110/set**

TOILET SET, Continental, silver and etched crystal, 4 perfume bottles and 4 powder jars.   **$650/set**

VANITY SET, 7 pieces, American silver, guilloche enamel, and jadeite, comprising 2 covered crystal boxes, mirror, clock, 2 brushes, and comb.   **$1,500/set**

Flasks

Gorham Art Nouveau flask, $800. Courtesy of Christie's East, New York.

$f$lasks were made in sterling silver, silverplate, and a combination of crystal and sterling silver. Variations include elaborately cut glass examples with screw tops or engraved versions with sporting, comic, or risqué decorations. Chased basketweave effects and allover highly embossed florals and leafage were popular motifs in the United States. Designs changed from allover repoussé florals to Japonesque examples or mixed-metal motifs in the 19th century to engine-turned examples in the early 20th century, sometimes with enamel accents.

Fine sterling silver flasks were produced in China and Japan during the 19th century, often with genre motifs. Many have extruded chrysanthemums or writhing dragon designs. A careful examination will often reveal the maker's mark in calligraphy worked within the design motifs. Flasks with sterling silver overlay were extremely popular in the late 19th century, with rococo scrollwork and Art Nouveau forms applied against the crystal base. In the 1880s Tiffany, Gorham, and Shiebler produced outstanding mixed- and applied-metal flasks incorporating insects, spiderwebs, and marine motifs in Oriental or

Moorish patterns. Comic examples were popular in the 1920s and 1930s, a common engraving being a drunk leaning on a lamp post. During the 1950s many flasks were made with engraved maps having paste stones delineating popular tourist attractions.

Sizes vary from the small, elegant ladies' flasks to those of mammoth proportions used during the Prohibition era. Flasks can have a detachable drinking cup. Those with alligator or crocodile mounts have suddenly become popular again after a decade of inactivity.

It is always wise to remove the cup on a combination glass-and-silver flask to check that the interior glass is intact.

CHINESE, plain, oblong, with screw top, late 19th century.
$300

CROCODILE-COVERED, oblong flask with sterling silver screw top and cup.   **$400**

CURVED SPIRIT FLASK, screw top and detachable gilt-lined cup, Rawlings & Summers, London, 1837.   **$550**

CUT GLASS, lady's, small, with sterling lid, LaPierre Manufacturing Company, American, late 19th century.   **$175**

CUT GLASS with gilt-lined detachable cup and screw cover, Birmingham, 1897.   **$300**

CUT GLASS OVAL, screw top and detachable gilt-lined cup, London, 1870.   **$250**

DOUBLE, International, rectangular, monogrammed, American, early 20th century, height, 9¼ in.   **$425**

ENGINE-TURNED square section, with a detachable cup, screw top applied with a yellow metal monogram.   **$575**

FACETED GLASS, silver-gilt screw top and detachable cup, London, 1870.   **$500**

GLASS, SCREW TOP and a nest of two gilt-lined beakers, Hukin & Heath, English, early 20th century.   **$110**

GLASS, SILVER-MOUNTED oblong section, the silver base etched on one side with an old-fashioned bicycle race, the other side with a bicycle accident, cover etched with bugles, flowers, and monogram, Tiffany & Co., New York, c. 1880, height, 8½ in.   **$1,900**

GLASS WITH SCREW TOP, large, partly leather-covered, detachable gilt-lined cup, James Dixon & Sons, Sheffield, 1917.

$275

JAPANESE STYLE, large, quadrangular form, hammered surface, applied and etched with a spray of reeds through which swims an exotic fish, Tiffany & Co., New York, c. 1880, height, 7⅝ in. **$2,600**

JAPANESE STYLE, large, quadrangular, hammered surface, front applied with 3 cavorting mastiffs beneath a street lamp, with the words "we won't go home till morning" above 2 bars of music, Tiffany & Co., New York, c. 1880–90. **$3,100**

OVAL, REPOUSSÉ, 2 dancing maidens, strapwork and scroll border, Gorham, late 19th century. **$800**

PEAR SHAPE, flattened, chased with shell and scrollwork and trailing flowers, chained stopper with openwork finial, Louis XV, AD, Paris, 1747. **$1,100**

TRAVELING, oblong form, detachable lid unfolds into a beaker, Thomas Johnson, 1879. **$700**

ƒlatware

Gorham sterling flatware service for 12, Versailles pattern, $4,000.
Courtesy of Robert W. Skinner Gallery, Bolton, MA.

ƒlatware includes spoons, forks, knives, and serving pieces. The spoon, one of the first utensils known to man, developed from a scoop or hollowed-out shape with a flat handle or stem. One of the earliest spoons was the French "trifid" dating from the 17th century and having a straight, flat handle in line with the bowl.

In England, this was followed by the Hanoverian and Old English styles. The Hanoverian pattern is characterized by a rounded and turned-up end. This gave way to the Old English pattern with rounded and down-turned end, which was often further decorated with bright-cut engraving, beading, or engraved feather edge. Also used was the Onslow style with scroll end, which had a revival in the late 19th century.

In America the "fiddle" handle with broad shoulder and narrow stem was popular in the late 18th and early 19th centuries. This style continued with later variations and included teaspoons, tablespoons, ladles, and dessert, mustard, and salt spoons.

Before the introduction of ladles, long spoons, also known as basting spoons, were probably used. The earliest ladle, used for tureens, had a pear-shape bowl and a curved handle with a bird's-head terminal. Smaller sizes were made for use with sauce tureens and cream pails. Marrow scoops, or marrow spoons as they were originally known, date from the late 17th century. The scoops had two grooved channels of different widths and were first used in sets with knives and forks.

In the late 16th century in many areas on the Continent and in England, forks replaced the use of fingers and spoons, and by the 17th century they had become quite popular. Sets including a knife, fork, and spoon were considered personal items and were carried by travelers.

Knives with pistol-grip handles were popular in the 18th century; later they were replaced by the straight-handle form. The late 18th century in America also saw the beginning of complete dinner services with matching designs in all pieces.

Patterns were patented as early as 1844; although by changing a minor part of the design, another silver manufacturer could use the pattern under his own patent.

Medallion, an early pattern introduced before the middle of the 19th century, featured Roman-style heads depicting famous men and women or centurions. Gorham, Reed & Barton, Shiebler, and Durgin all used variations of the Medallion pattern. At the same time, during the Classical Revival, Oval and Roman patterns began. In the late 19th century America turned to Egypt, Assyria, and Persia for design sources. This was followed by a rage for Oriental, especially Japanese, designs, including the Japanese pattern, later called Audubon by Tiffany.

Concurrently, romantic floral patterns, including Poppy, Lily, Iris, Ivy, Bridal Rose, Les Cinq Fleurs, and Les Six Fleurs, were extremely popular. During the Classical Revival era Gorham made two other fashionable patterns: Mythologique, which depicted ancient Greek myths, and Versailles, taken from designs at the Versailles Palace.

Among the popular serving pieces in the early 19th century were ice spoons, berry spoons with embossed bowls, sugar sifters, and punch ladles. By the mid- to late 19th century in America there were spoons for all types of foods from piccalilli to macaroni, as well as pea and Saratoga chip servers.

Flatware sets were specially commissioned in services of 12 to 24 settings. Patterns such as Kirk's Repoussé and the ever-popular King's (a classical style also known as Shell and Thread) were introduced in the late 19th and early 20th centuries in America. Most designs reflected the taste in architecture and furniture styles of the day.

The early 20th century saw the beginning of the Arts and Crafts and Mission styles in America. During this time flatware appeared to be hand-hammered and was often called by names such as Antique Hammered.

American

BUTTERPICK, Alvin "Orient" pattern.   **$45**

BUTTERPICK, Dominick & Haff, Charles II pattern.   **$45**

CARVING SET, roast, 2 pieces, Gorham, Lancaster pattern.
$80/set

CARVING SET, 2 pieces, International, Royal Danish pattern.
$225/set

CARVING SET, 2 pieces, Stieff, Repoussé pattern.   **$295/set**

CRUMBER, 925/1000, rope edge, Kirk, Repoussé pattern, 13½ in.   **$395**

CRUMBER, Gorham, Virginiana pattern.   **$225**

CRUMBER, Jensen, Cactus pattern.   **$925**

CRUMBER, large, with tray, Reed & Barton, Les Cinq Flowers pattern.   **$450**

DINNER SERVICE for 8, Durgin, Fairfax pattern, 66 pieces, including forks, salad forks, knives, soups, butter spreaders, double teaspoons, 10 serving pieces.   **$895/set**

DINNER SERVICE for 8, Reed & Barton, Marlborough pattern, 8-piece settings, 16 servers.   **$2,750/set**

FLATWARE SERVICE for 6, 52 pieces, Dominick & Haff, Basket of Flowers pattern.   **$2,600/set**

FLATWARE SERVICE for 12, Gorham, Buttercup pattern, 9 serving pieces, total 145 pieces.   **$3,000/set**

FLATWARE SERVICE, Tiffany, Flemish pattern, 76 pieces, consisting of luncheon forks, salad forks, teaspoons, cream soup spoons, butter knives, luncheon knives, sauce ladle, dinner knife, serving spoons, serving fork, sugar spoon. **$1,850/set**

FLATWARE SERVICE, Enchantress pattern, comprising 12 each of dinner forks, salad forks, soup spoons, and dinner knives, 10 teaspoons and 2 serving spoons, International Sterling.
$550/set

FLATWARE SERVICE, silver gilt, Tiffany & Co., New York, 20th century, in the Audubon pattern, comprising 8 each of luncheon knives, luncheon forks, teaspoons, salad forks, dessert spoons. **$2,700/set**

FLATWARE SERVICE, Stieff, Rose pattern, 120 pieces, consisting of luncheon forks, salad forks, teaspoons, citrus spoons, iced tea spoons, serving spoons, 2-piece carving set, master butter knife, cheese slice knives, butter knives, bouillon spoons, demitasse spoons, chocolate spoons, tomato server, serving spoon, sugar spoon, lemon fork. **$2,100/set**

FLATWARE SERVICE, Whiting, Lily pattern, 72 pieces, consisting of dinner forks, dessert spoons, teaspoons, dinner knives, demitasse spoons, butter knives. **$2,100/set**

FLATWARE SET, Chrysanthemum pattern, comprising 18 dinner knives, 18 tablespoons, 17 each of dessert knives, dinner forks, and teaspoons, 36 lunch forks, Tiffany & Co., New York, c. 1880–90. **$11,000/set**

FLATWARE SET, Olympian pattern, comprising 6 salad forks, 6 dinner forks, 9 ice cream spoons, 5 butter spreaders, 1 sugar spoon, 6 lunch forks, 12 coffee spoons, 6 bouillon spoons, 1 serving spoon, 1 lemon fork, Tiffany & Co., New York, c. 1900.
$2,650/set

FORK, asparagus, Gorham, Lancaster pattern. **$235**

FORK, asparagus, International, Frontenac pattern. **$450**

FORK, asparagus, Whiting, Lily pattern. **$650**

FORK, baked potato, Towle, King Richard pattern. **$95**

FORK, cocktail, Durgin, Marechal Niel pattern. **$18**

FORK, cold meat, Alvin, Bridal Bouquet pattern. **$75**

FORK, cold meat, Alvin, Bridal Rose pattern. **$80**

FORK, cold meat, Dominick & Haff, Virginiana pattern. **$85**

FORK, cold meat, large, Alvin, Old Orange Blossom pattern.
$225

FORK, cold meat, Lunt, Narcissus pattern. **$75**

FORK, cold meat, Towle, Contessina pattern. **$125**

FORK, cold meat, Towle, Georgian pattern. $125

FORK, cold meat, Wallace, Carmel pattern. $85

FORK, dinner, Alvin, Old Orange Blossom pattern. $40

FORK, dinner, Gorham, Virginiana pattern. $35

FORK, dinner, International, Frontenac pattern. $45

FORK, dinner, Wallace, Grande Baroque pattern. $40

FORK, ice cream, Durgin, Cat Tails pattern. $45

FORK, ice cream, Gorham, Buttercup pattern. $38

FORK, ice cream, Gorham, Buttercup pattern. $38

FORK, ice cream, Gorham, Buttercup pattern. $35

FORK, ice cream, Reed & Barton, Chambord pattern. $23

FORK, ice cream, Shiebler, American Beauty Rose pattern.

$75

FORK, ice cream, Wallace, Grande Baroque pattern. $45

FORK, lemon, Towle, Old Colonial pattern. $75

FORK, lettuce, Alvin, Raleigh pattern. $45

FORK, lettuce, International, in Frontenac pattern. $110

FORK, lettuce, Kirk, Repoussé pattern. $45

FORK, lunch, Frank Whiting, Lily pattern. $35

FORK, lunch, Jensen, Acorn pattern. $65

FORK, oyster, International, Queen's Lace pattern. $30

FORK, pickle, Alvin, Old Orange Blossom pattern, 6 in. $45

FORK, sardine, Towle, Canterbury pattern. $50

FORK, sardine, Whiting, King Edward pattern. $85

FORK, seafood, long, Shiebler, Rococo pattern. $35

FORK, serving, 4 prongs, Alvin, Orient pattern. $65

FORK, serving, Towle, Old English pattern. $150

FORK, serving, Whiting, Dresden pattern. $75

FORK, strawberry, Durgin, Iris pattern. $60

FORK, strawberry, International, Frontenac pattern. $85

FORK, strawberry, Wallace, Grande Baroque pattern. $25

FORK, toast, Towle, Old English pattern. $150

FORKS, cake, 12 silver-gilt, Gorham, Versailles pattern.

$350/12

FORKS, ice cream, 6, Reed & Barton, Francis I pattern.
$250/6

FORKS, luncheon, 12, Lily Pattern, by Whiting. **$150/12**

FORKS, strawberry, set of 6, Towle, Old Colonial pattern.
$165/set

FORKS, terrapin, set of 10, gilt bowls decorated with multiple shells, the handles decorated with seaweed with 2 turtles at intervals, the backs molded with shells and seaweed, Gorham Mfg. Co., c. 1875. **$1,000/set**

KNIFE, cake, Alvin, Raleigh pattern. **$45**

KNIFE, dinner, Towle, Georgian pattern. **$35**

KNIFE, fish, Whiting, Japanese pattern. **$115**

KNIFE, flat, all silver, Whiting, Arabesque pattern. **$60**

KNIFE, pie, pierced, Reed & Barton, La Parisienne pattern.
$350

KNIVES, fruit, 8, lap-over edge, etched with birds, flowers, and sinuous scrolls, Tiffany, 1875–1891 **$800/8**

KNIVES AND FORKS, fish, 8, Durgin, Louis XV pattern.
$960/8

LADLE, claret, Wallace, Lucerne pattern. **$125**

LADLE, cream, large, International, Avalon pattern. **$48**

LADLE, cream, Towle, Old Colonial pattern. **$40**

LADLE, gravy, Durgin, Chrysanthemum pattern. **$225**

LADLE, gravy, Whiting, Twist pattern. **$65**

LADLE, ice cream, Chrysanthemum pattern, gilt bowl, Tiffany.
$350

LADLE, mustard, Reed & Barton, Flora pattern. **$65**

LADLE, mustard, Reed & Barton, Six Flowers pattern. **$110**

LADLE, mustard, Whiting, Honeysuckle pattern. **$55**

LADLE, oyster, Lunt, Chateau pattern. **$125**

LADLE, oyster, Watson, Commonwealth pattern. **$120**

LADLE, punch, Durgin, Chrysanthemum pattern. **$500**

LADLE, punch, the handle embossed with calla lily design, c. 1879. **$120**

LADLE, punch, Wallace, Grande Baroque pattern. **$600**

LADLE, sauce, Durgin, Chrysanthemum pattern. **$98**

LADLE, soup, "Japanese style," Lap Over Edge pattern, applied with sycamore leaves and a bug, shaped oval bowl etched with sycamore leaf, Tiffany & Co., New York, c. 1880–90.
$1,900

LADLE, soup, "Japanese Style," with tomato-shaped bowl, stem with relief decorations of tomato vines, on granulated ground, Tiffany & Co., New York, c. 1873–91. **$1,000**

LADLE, soup, Dominick & Haff, Old Louis XIV pattern. **$145**

LADLE, soup, Frank M. Smith, Newport Shell pattern. **$275**

LADLE, soup, Honeysuckle pattern, with gilt matte bowl, Whiting Mfg. Co. **$300**

LADLE, soup, late 19th century, parcel-gilt, applied finial with a bird with outstretched wings, c. 1880. **$175**

LADLE, soup, marine fantasy of realistically modeled large and small shells, entwined with reeds and seaweed, with 2 fishes and a crab at intervals with barnacle and other encrustations, scallop-shell bowl, Gorham Mfg. Co., c. 1880, length, 14¼ in. **$2,200**

LADLE, soup, Medallion, finial with rondel of maiden's head, unmarked, 1860. **$325**

LADLE, soup, R. Wallace & Son, St. George pattern. **$125**

LADLE, soup, Reed & Barton, La Marquise pattern. **$295**

LADLE, soup, Samuel Kirk, Baltimore, mid-19th century, length, 13¾ in. **$250**

LADLE, soup, Wallace, Lucerne pattern. **$275**

LADLE, soup, Whiting, Berry pattern. **$255**

LADLE, soup, Whiting, Lily of the Valley pattern. **$550**

MASTER BUTTER, Alvin, Raphael pattern. **$135**

MASTER BUTTER, large, Whiting, Lily of the Valley pattern. **$78**

MASTER BUTTER, Wallace, Irian pattern. **$95**

MUDDLER, chocolate, International, Frontenac pattern. **$95**

SALAD SET, Alvin, Bridal Rose pattern. **$375/set**

SCOOP, almond, Towle, in the Georgian pattern. **$85**

SCOOP, cheese, large, Whiting, Louis XV pattern. **$95**

SCOOP, cracker, Durgin, Standish pattern. **$245**

SCOOP, cracker, Tiffany, Broom Corn pattern. **$495**

SERVER, asparagus, Dominick & Haff, Colonial Antique pattern. **$245**

SERVER, cucumber, Alvin, Bridal Rose pattern. **$175**

SERVER, cucumber, Whiting, Louis XV pattern. **$55**

Three Gorham Japonisme servers and Shiebler letter knife. **Courtesy of Christie's East, New York.**

SERVER, cucumber, Whiting, Empire pattern, 1892.   **$75**

SERVER, fish, Durgin, Louis XV, 11³/₄ in.   **$225**

SERVER, ice cream, by Tiffany, with openwork strawberry handle.   **$220**

SERVER, macaroni, Dominick & Haff, Louis XIV pattern.
          $195

SERVER, macaroni, Gorham, Baronial pattern.   **$350**

SERVER, macaroni, Whiting Co., Louis XV pattern.   **$275**

SERVER, pie, with ivory handle, Whiting.   **$475**

SERVER, tomato, Georg Jensen, Pyramid pattern.   **$225**

SERVER, tomato, Gorham, Cambridge pattern.   **$98**

SERVER, tomato, Gorham, Lancaster pattern.   **$100**

SERVER, tomato, Manchester, pierced handle.   **$40**

SERVER, tomato, pierced, Dominick & Haff, 1776 pattern.
          $45

SERVER, tomato, pierced, Mount Vernon, Josephine pattern.
          $150

SERVER, tomato, pierced, Towle, Candlelight pattern.   **$45**

Group of American Medallion pattern flatware serving pieces. Courtesy of Christie's East, New York.

SERVER, tomato, Shiebler, American Beauty pattern.   **$90**

SERVERS, salad, pair, large, in the Heraldic pattern, Whiting Mfg. Co., late 19th century.   **$225/pr**

SERVERS, salad, pair, Love Disarmed pattern, by Reed & Barton, gilt bowl and tines.   **$700/pr**

SERVERS, salad, pair, Vine Pattern, Tiffany, fluted bowls, grapevine decoration on stippled ground.   **$1,200/pr**

SERVING ARTICLES, mixed metal, "Japanese Style," handles decorated with copper and silver crabs, applied over sprays of rushes and engraved leaves, hammered surface, comprising pair of fish servers, serving spade, and butter knife, Whiting Mfg. Co., c. 1880.   **$1,900/4**

SERVING ARTICLES, 7, Renaissance pattern, comprising ice cream spade, pierced chip server, small pair of salad servers, cold meat fork, gravy ladle, and jelly spoon, Tiffany & Co., New York, c. 1910.   **$1,800/7**

SERVING FORK, fish, small, Wallace, Violet pattern.   **$125**

SERVING FORK, fish, Whiting, Heraldic pattern.   **$125**

SERVING SET, salad, International, Royal Danish pattern.   **$150/pr**

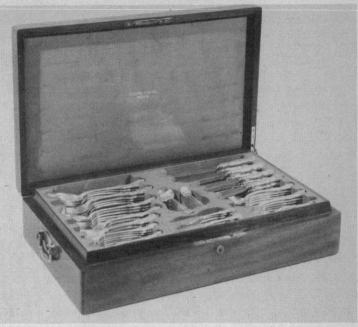

Tiffany sterling partial flatware service in King's pattern, $10,000.
Courtesy of William Doyle Galleries, New York.

SERVING SET, salad, large, engraved, Kirk, Old Maryland pattern. **$200/pr**

SERVING SET, salad, Lunt, Monticello pattern. **$200/pr**

SERVING SET, salad, Old Newbury Crafters, Old Newbury pattern. **$475/pr**

SERVING SET, salad, Reed & Barton, Love Disarmed pattern. **$750/pr**

SERVING SET, salad, Tiffany & Co., Chrysanthemum pattern, New York, 1880. **$750/pr**

SERVING SET, salad, Whiting, Heraldic pattern. **$595/pr**

SERVING SET, salad, Whiting, King Edward pattern. **$350/pr**

SLICE, fish, Gorham, Medallion pattern. **$350**

SLICE, fish, Hezekiah Silliman, New Haven, Connecticut, pre-1804, blade chased with an obelisk, shield, and tree. **$125**

SLICE, ice cream, Frank Smith, Newport Shell pattern. **$375**

SLICE, ice cream, Wood & Hughes, Angelo pattern. **$395**

SPOON, berry, Towle, Old Newbury pattern.   **$275**

SPOON, berry, Dominick & Haff, No. 10.   **$95**

SPOON, berry, Gorham, Bird's Nest pattern, 9½ in.   **$750**

SPOON, berry, Gorham, Buttercup pattern.   **$225**

SPOON, berry, large, Alvin, Bridal Rose pattern.   **$125**

SPOON, berry, large, Durgin, Chrysanthemum pattern.   **$195**

SPOON, berry, large, Durgin, Watteau pattern.   **$245**

SPOON, berry, large, Gorham, Lotus pattern.   **$195**

SPOON, berry, Reed & Barton, La Parisienne pattern.   **$225**

SPOON, berry, Shiebler, Art Nouveau pattern.   **$275**

SPOON, berry, Whiting, Lily pattern.   **$275**

SPOON, bonbon, Dominick & Haff, Grape pattern.   **$75**

SPOON, bonbon, International, Frontenac pattern.   **$55**

SPOON, bonbon, Tiffany, Holly pattern.   **$175**

SPOON, bonbon, Whiting, Lily pattern.   **$110**

SPOON, demitasse, Whiting, Lily of the Valley pattern.   **$20**

SPOON, dessert, Dominick & Haff, King pattern.   **$35**

SPOON, dessert, Reed & Barton, La Reine pattern.   **$65**

SPOON, dessert, Whiting, Violet pattern.   **$35**

SPOON, grapefruit, Durgin, Debussy pattern.   **$40**

SPOON, gumbo soup, Alvin, Majestic pattern.   **$23**

SPOON, jelly, Whiting, Lily pattern.   **$75**

SPOON, jelly, Wood & Hughes, Japanese pattern.   **$110**

SPOON, lettuce, Towle, Canterbury pattern.   **$75**

SPOON, olive, long, Towle, Paul Revere pattern.   **$45**

SPOON, olive, long, Whiting, Imperial Queen pattern.   **$60**

SPOON, olive, small, Gorham, Etruscan pattern.   **$25**

SPOON, olive, Towle, Louis XIV pattern.   **$30**

SPOON, olive, Whiting, Imperial Queen pattern.   **$60**

SPOON, preserve, Durgin, Iris pattern.   **$100**

SPOON, pudding, Reed & Barton, La Marquise pattern.   **$65**

SPOON, serving, large oval, Kirk, in Repoussé pattern.   **$80**

SPOON, serving, large, Reed & Barton, Love Disarmed pattern.
          $450

SPOON, serving, vegetable, Stieff, Rose pattern. **$90**

SPOON, stuffing, Gorham, Chantilly pattern. **$350**

SPOON, stuffing, Gorham, Strasbourg pattern. **$300**

SPOON, sugar, Easterling, American Classic pattern. **$16**

SPOONS, demitasse, set of 6, flower and fern handle with vine motifs, Wallace. **$80/set**

SUGAR SHELL, Alvin, Bridal Rose pattern. **$50**

SUGAR SHELL, Wallace, Violet pattern. **$25**

TABLESPOONS, 8, Gorham, St. Cloud pattern. **$325/8**

TEASPOON, Alvin, Old Orange Blossom pattern. **$25**

TEASPOON, Durgin, Salem Witch pattern. **$45**

TEASPOON, Gorham, Cluny pattern. **$33**

TEASPOON, Lunt, Monticello pattern. **$16**

TEASPOON, Reed & Barton, Les Six Fleurs pattern. **$32**

TEASPOON, Whiting, Dresden pattern. **$23**

TEASPOONS, 5, Lunt, Monticello pattern. **$90/5**

TONGS, ice, Gorham, Buttercup pattern. **$275**

TONGS, ice, Reed & Barton, Francis I pattern. **$350**

TONGS, ice, Shiebler, Louvre pattern. **$275**

TONGS, sardine, Whiting, Orleans pattern. **$155**

TONGS, sugar, Dominick & Haff, No. 10. **$20**

TONGS, sugar, Gorham, Chantilly pattern. **$24**

TONGS, sugar, Unger, Duvaine pattern. **$95**

Coin and Early American

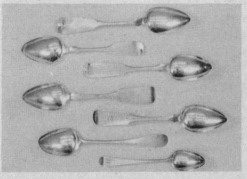

Group of coin silver spoons, late 18th and early 19th century. Courtesy of Richard A. Bourne Gallery, Hyannis, MA.

FORK, olive, long, Hotchkiss & Schreuder, Medallion pattern.
$100

LADLE, soup, fiddle pattern, R. Jordan, Richmond, Virginia, c. 1819.   **$500**

LADLE, soup, fiddle pattern, the terminal engraved with contemporary script, J. A. L'Hommedieu, Mobile, Alabama, c. 1850.   **$600**

TABLESPOON, American silver, Ephraim Brasher (New York) mid-18th century, single drop terminal.   **$225**

TABLESPOON, James Madison Barrows, Tolland, Connecticut, c. 1809.   **$30**

TABLESPOON, R & W Wilson, Philadelphia, 1825.   **$175**

TABLESPOON, raised sheaf of wheat, Jacob Sargeant, Hartford, CT, 1761–1843.   **$140**

TABLESPOON, single drop and shell, Samuel Drowne, Portsmouth, NH, 18th century.   **$25**

TABLESPOON, single drop bowl, Rufus Farnham, Boston, c. 1796.   **$25**

TABLESPOON, William S. Nicholas, Newport, RI, 19th century.   **$30**

TABLESPOONS, 3, Lincoln & Reed, Boston, c. 1835.   **$55/3**

TEASPOON, American silver, Myer Myers, New York, 1723–95.   **$225**

TEASPOON, coffin-top, Paterson & Pompton.   **$50**

TONGS, Basket of Flowers pattern, H. Porter & Co., 1830.
$175

TONGS, pair, American silver, by Matthew Petit, New York, c. 1790, engraved.   **$100**

TONGS, Sheaf of Wheat pattern, B. Benjamin, c. 1825.   **$175**

Continental

DESSERT FLATWARE, late 19th century, Odiot, Paris, silvergilt, comprising 30 forks and 30 spoons in Empire style, the handles chased with acanthus enclosing grapevine on matte reserves terminating in ivy decoration.   **$4,000/set**

FLATWARE SERVICE, Cohr, 20th century, in Modernist style with faceted handles, comprising 12 each of dinner knives, luncheon forks, teaspoons, dinner forks, salad forks, coffee spoons. **$1,000/set**

FORKS, oyster, 12, with mother-of-pearl handles, in a fitted case, French. **$250/12**

FORKS, table, set of 6, fiddle and thread pattern, French, 19th century. **$110/set**

KNIVES AND FORKS, pastry, set of 6, parcel-gilt, beaded decoration and bright-cut with foliage, Austro-Hungarian. **$300/set**

LADLE, punch, with lipped oval bowl and turned-wood handle, mount engraved with a name, Erik Ekstron, Swedish, Vaxjo, 1842. **$225**

LADLE, soup, fiddle and thread pattern, French, 19th century. **$300**

LADLE, soup, fiddle pattern engraved with a monogram. **$65**

LADLE, soup, German, handle decorated with rococo flowers, foliage, and trelliswork, 13½ in. **$250**

LADLE, toddy, with twisted whalebone handle with ivory terminal, fluted gilt-lined bowl with two lips. **$175**

SERVING IMPLEMENTS, set of 4, with parcel-gilt steel blades and prongs, handles molded with rococo scrolling foliage, Austro-Hungarian. **$100/set**

SLICE AND MATCHING SERVER, parcel-gilt with engraved curved blade, the handles decorated with arabesques. **$125/2**

SPOON, Apostle, Dutch, silver-gilt with faceted stem and fig-shaped bowl, Alkmaar, probably 1652. **$1,300**

SPOON, Norwegian, with rounded flat stem engraved with foliage, by Schweder Meyer the younger, Bergen, c. 1730. **$500**

SPOON, ornate, with sailing ship finial and foliate-pierced and chased stem, the bowl cast and chased with an armorial, 11 in. **$135**

SPOON, serving, French fiddle pattern engraved with armorials, Paris, 1773. **$450**

SPOON, sifting, with foliate-pierced circular bowl and turned wooden handle, French, 19th century.　　**$75**

SPOONS, coffee, set of 6, decorated with brightly colored guilloche enameling, in a fitted case.　　**$100/set**

SPOONS, coffee, set of 6, gilt-metal decorated with polychrome guilloche enameling, in a fitted case.　　**$50/set**

English

APPLE CORER, part-reeded, with green-stained turned ivory handle, probably Thomas Beezley.　　**$400**

BUTTER SPADE with green-stained ivory handle, blade decorated with bright-cut engraving, John Blake, London, 1788.
　　$350

CARVING SET, Victorian, 4 pieces, with steel blades and antler handles, stamped with beading, rams' masks, and ribbon swags, lined case.　　**$150/set**

CHEESE SLICE and fork combination, silver-gilt with pistol handle with shell terminal, in a fitted case, London, 1906.
　　$300/set

English assembled flatware service in Shell & Thread pattern, by William Ely and William Bell, $11,500. Courtesy of William Doyle Galleries, New York.

EGG CUTTERS, pair, Edwardian, scissor action, Birmingham, 1909. **$200/pr**

FISH SLICE, fiddle pattern, the reeded, shaped blade pierced and engraved with a fish amid scrolling foliage, Edinburgh, 1846. **$125**

FLATWARE service for 12 place settings, Queens pattern, each engraved with a crest, comprising tablespoons, table forks, dessert spoons, and dessert forks, H & I., Sheffield, 1897.
$2,600/set

FORK, toasting, with ebonized handle, the tip with suspension ring, probably by John Touliet, c. 1790. **$400**

FORK, toasting, with swiveling prongs, reeded mount, turned wood handle and swiveling hanging mount, bright-cut with a floral and foliate swag, maker's initials G.E., London, 1797.
$325

FORKS, dessert, set of 6, fiddle and thread pattern, Mary Chawner, London, 1839. **$250/set**

FORKS, dessert, set of 12, 2-pronged, silver-mounted pistol handles with shell-fluted terminals, 18th century. **$185/set**

FORKS, oyster, set of 12, feather-edged and bright-cut with spiral-twist stems, in a fitted case, 1905. **$225/set**

FORKS, table, 6, Old English pattern, each engraved with a monogram and crest, William Bateman, London, 1815.
$275/6

GRAPE SCISSORS, George IV, with vine foliage stems and handles. **$550**

KNIVES AND FORKS, dessert, 12 pairs, silver-gilt in the 18th-century taste, with pistol handles, foliate terminals, in a mahogany case, Francis Higgins, London, 1902. **$800/24**

KNIVES AND FORKS, fish, 12 pairs, with ivorine handles and floral bright-cut blades, fitted case. **$175/24**

LADLE, punch, with egg-shaped bowl, wooden handle, Wm Fordham, London, 1728. **$275**

LADLE, silver, shell bowl, Thomas Doxsey, London, 1767.
$275

LADLE, soup, bright-cut Celtic point with shell-fluted bowl, engraved with a crest, Michael Keating, Dublin, 1784. **$550**

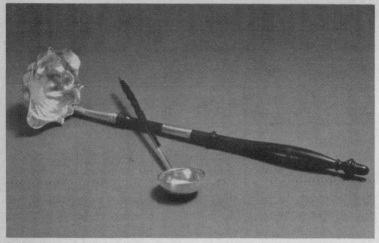

Toddy ladles, large, English, c. 1753; small, American, 18th century.
Courtesy of Alice and Derek Hamilton.

LADLE, soup, feather-edged Old English pattern, with shell-fluted bowl, London, 1770, 13¼ in. **$350**

LADLE, soup, fiddle pattern with rat-tail bowl, engraved with a monogram, Dublin, c. 1820. **$325**

LADLE, soup, fiddle pattern, Edward Thomason, Birmingham, 1817. **$200**

LADLE, soup, fiddle pattern, engraved with a crest, William Eley, London, 1818. **$225**

LADLE, soup, fiddle pattern, of typical form, by Paul Storr, London, 1816. **$600**

LADLE, soup, Old English pattern, W. Welch, Exeter, 1810. **$250**

LADLE, toddy, George III, with whalebone handle, bowl inset with a coin. **$100**

LADLE, toddy, unmarked, with twist whalebone handle, the bowl inset with a coin, c. 1780. **$90**

LADLE, toddy, with twist whalebone handle and feather-edged serpent-shaped mount, gadrooned lipped bowl with an engraved cartouche, unmarked. **$110**

LADLE, toddy, with twist whalebone handle, mount engraved with initials, probably c. 1780. **$100**

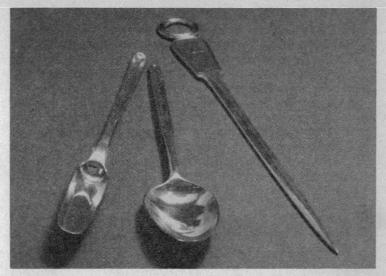

Left. *English sterling marrow scoop, c. 1817, $225.* Center. *English sterling marrow spoon, c. 1759, $375.* Right. *English sterling skewer, c. 1840, $350.* Courtesy of H & H Antiques.

LADLES, sauce, pair, Bacchanalian pattern molded with crests and mottos, Paul Storr, London, 1817. **$1,200/pr**

LADLES, sauce, pair, fiddle and thread pattern, George Adams, London, 1866. **$125/pr**

SCISSORS, grape, pair, silver-gilt vine pattern in fitted case, Francis Higgins, London, 1870. **$800**

SCOOP, marrow, George II, engraved with a crest, London, 1754. **$100**

SCOOP, marrow, George II, scratch-engraved with a monogram, Jeremiah King, London, 1727. **$200**

SCOOP, marrow, plain, engraved with a monogram, Richard Crossley, London, 1804. **$100**

SCOOP, marrow, plain, London, 1776. **$100**

SCOOP, marrow, plain, London, 1794. **$125**

SCOOP, marrow, sterling silver engraved with monogram, Newcastle, 1780. **$100**

SCOOP, Stilton, with spiral-fluted ivory handle, E.H., London, 1884. **$300**

SERVERS, salad, pair, fiddle pattern, William Eley, London, 1827.   **$300/pr**

SKEWER, meat, George III, with shaped handle, London, 1789.
                                                                 $125

SKEWER, meat, sterling silver with plain ring terminal, probably T & W Chawner, London, 1766.   **$150**

SKEWER, meat, with plain ring handle, engraved with the Prince of Wales crest and a number, Josiah and George Piercy, London, 1814.   **$185**

SKEWER, meat, with plain ring terminal, Eley, Fearn & Chawner, London, 1809.   **$150**

SKEWER, meat, with shell-and-ring handle and hammered blade, Eley and Fearn, London, 1804.   **$110**

SKEWER, meat, with shell-and-ring terminal, engraved with a crest, London, 1776.   **$375**

SKEWERS, game, pair, with plain ring terminals, Lewis Samuel of Liverpool, with London hallmarks for 1831.   **$350/pr**

SLICE, fish, fiddle pattern, engraved with a crest, shaped blade. pierced and engraved with a bird, flowers, and acorns, Houles & Co., London, 1837.   **$250**

SLICE AND FORK, fish, with foliate-pierced and engraved blade and prongs, pottery handle painted with flowers and foliage in blue and iron red, gilt decoration.   **$100/pr**

SLICE AND FORK, fish, with foliate-pierced and engraved blade and prongs, ivory handles carved with acanthus leaves, in fitted case, George Unite, Birmingham, 1881.   **$700/pr**

SLICE AND FORK, Old English pattern, the handles decorated with wriggle work, in a fitted case, London, 1911.   **$125/pr**

SPOON, basting, fiddle pattern engraved with an initial, London, 1829.   **$125**

SPOON, basting, George III, Onslow pattern, London, 1769.
                                                                 $250

SPOON, basting, Old English and thread pattern, engraved with an initial, I.B., London, 1801.   **$125**

SPOON, basting, Old English pattern, later engraved with a crest and initial, Richard Crossley, London, 1876.   **$110**

SPOON, basting, Old English pattern, Michael Keating, Dublin, 1791.   **$150**

SPOON, basting, stamped with a registration number within a garter cartouche, Onslow pattern, Sheffield, 1887. **$135**

SPOON, basting, the pointed-end stem bright-cut and engraved with a crest, the bowl of embossed scallop form, Tudor & Whitford, Dublin, 1805. **$400**

SPOON, basting, Venetian pattern, Martin Hall & Co., Sheffield, 1871. **$200**

SPOON, fruit, silver-gilt, the stem formed as bound and clustered branches and attendant vine leaves, the bowl modeled in the form of a large crinkled vine leaf, Robert Garrard, 1859, 15 oz. **$1,800**

SPOON, hash, Hanoverian pattern, scratch-engraved with initials, Adam Graham, Glasgow, c. 1765. **$550**

SPOON, mote, bowl pierced with scrolls and crosses and an embossed rocaille flowerhead and scrolls, barbed finial, c. 1745. **$200**

SPOON, mote, the bowl finely engraved and pierced with plumelike scrolls and crosses, barbed finial, William Penstone III, c. 1775. **$250**

SPOON, platter, Thomas Tookey, London, 1779. **$150**

SPOON, serving, Queen Anne, dog-nose with rat-tail bowl, William Scarlett, c. 1710. **$600**

SPOON, snuff, dog-nose, by Paul Hanet, c. 1725. **$150**

SPOON, strainer, stem bright-cut with a star and crest to pointed terminal, bowl divided by a cast pierced strainer, Michael Keating, 1787. **$600**

SPOON, stuffing, George II, Dublin, 1739, Hanoverian pattern. **$425**

SPOON, trifid-end, with rat-tail bowl, later-gilt, marks indistinct, early 18th century. **$100**

SPOONS, Apostle, set of 12, and a spoon with a figure of Christ terminal, made to commemorate the Coronation of Queen Elizabeth II in 1953, bowls struck with the special coronation hallmark. **$300/set**

SPOONS, basting, pair, bright-cut Celtic point, each engraved with a crest, Michael Keating, Dublin, 1783. **$600/pr**

SPOONS, basting, pair, Dolphin pattern, Francis Higgins, London, 1884. **$475/pr**

SPOONS, berry, pair, Old English pattern, later-chased and gilt, and a matching sifting spoon, in a fitted case, London, 1807.
$250/3

SPOONS, berry, set of 3, later-chased and gilt Old English pattern with shell-fluted bowls, in a fitted case, Eley & Fearn, London, 1798.
$350/set

SPOONS, coffee, set of 8, terminals shaped and enameled to represent the 4 suits of cards, in a fitted case.
$75/set

SPOONS, dessert, 6, feather-edged Old English pattern, each engraved with a crest, Eley & Fearn, London, 1819.
$225/6

SPOONS, fruit, 4, Dutch style, with mask finials and spiral-twist stems, Sibrey & Hall, London, 1888.
$400/4

SPOONS, fruit, 4, silver-gilt in the Dutch early-18th-century taste, 3 with figure finials, 1 with a sailing ship finial, in a fitted case, London, 1896.
$195/4

SPOONS, fruit, pair, with gadrooned shaped handles, bowls decorated with foliage and with traces of gilding, in fitted case, Mappin & Webb, Sheffield, 1900.
$125/pr

SPOONS, straining, pair, Celtic point, each engraved with a crest, Michael Keating, Dublin, 1781.
$900/pr

SUGAR NIPS, decorated with leafage, flowers, and waterlilies, the pivot modeled as a butterfly, Joseph Willmore, Birmingham, 1840.
$375

SUGAR NIPS, modeled as an outstretched monkey, by Albert William Barker, 1886.
$550

SUGAR NIPS, with scroll-decorated arms and circular floral-engraved pivot, Dublin, c. 1770.
$225

SUGAR NIPS, "fire-tong," oval grips with rat-tail decoration, c. 1725.
$180

SUGAR NIPS, the scroll and feather-edge arms with scalloped grips, Thomas Tookey, c. 1775.
$250

TABLESPOONS, 18, shell and scroll pattern, each engraved with two crests, Eley & Fern, London, 1822.
$1,700/18

TABLESPOONS, pair, plain Old English pattern, William Eley, London, 1805.
$65/pr

TEASPOONS, flower, set of 12, limited edition Royal Horticultural Society, with applied silver-gilt flower medallions, John Pinches, Sheffield, in a case with certificate.
$200/set

TEASPOONS, set of 6, Victorian Rose pattern, Houles and Co., London, 1851. **$150/set**

TEASPOONS, set of 12, silver-gilt, Onslow pattern, with shell-fluted bowls and spiral-twist stems, in case, possibly George Unite, London, 1891. **$275/set**

TEASPOONS, 12, and a pair of sugar tongs, Onslow pattern, in a fitted case, William Hutton & Sons Ltd., London, 1904.

$175/set

TONGS, asparagus, beaded fiddle pattern with ribbed blades, York, 1820. **$475**

TONGS, asparagus, fiddle pattern engraved with a monogram, Mary Chawner, London, 1839. **$350**

TONGS, asparagus, pair, fiddle pattern, the blades pierced with stylized shells and foliage, J and A Savoury, London, 1845.

$275/pr

TONGS, asparagus, plain, Samuel Neville, Dublin, 1805. **$350**

TONGS, chop, pair, in the George III taste, Thomas Wallis and Jonathon Hayne, London, 1818. **$375/pr**

TONGS, sugar, bright-engraved, by Peter & Jonathan Bateman, 1790. **$110**

Frames

Late 19th-century American sterling stamped and pierced frames and desk boxes. **Courtesy of Christie's East, New York.**

The cluttered Victorian parlor most often boasted a multitude of photograph frames in every size and shape. By the end of the 19th century, photography was inexpensive, and our ancestors recorded important family moments. In papa's study, for example, photographs of the children in appropriate frames covered his desk and bookcases. Even dollhouses of the period have minute table frames.

The frames of the Victorian period are generally of velvet or stamped leather with elaborately pierced and chased mounts.

They abound with foliage, cherubs, and hearts, often so ornate you need a good eye or magnifying glass to find the marks.

In the 1880s many frames were oblong with a cartouche at the top for engraving initials and dates, and heart shapes in desk and traveling sizes also were popular. In America, Dominick & Haff, Gorham, and Tiffany produced fine examples. In England, William Comyns seems to have made them in endless profusion.

The 1890s and 1900s brought sterling silver frames with Art Nouveau designs incorporating flower blossoms, leaves, shell and marine motifs, young women with flowing hair, and whiplash curves, often in contrast to a hammered ground. In the Art Deco period the stylized, geometric look was in fashion: simple sterling silver frames with engraved engine-turned lines and occasionally with enamel spandrels.

At auctions and flea markets there are currently many reproductions of Victorian and Art Nouveau frames, complete with old marks. The molds produce frame and marks together, giving the frames a rather soft look. Detailing is not very sharp, and buyers should be alert.

ARCHED CREST, silver, chased with pendant husks and clusters of fruits, Walker & Hall, Birmingham, 1911, height, 11½ in. **$1,000**

ARCHED OBLONG, with heart-shape aperture, mounts stamped with rococo putti, flowers, scrolling foliage, and trelliswork, English hallmarks, 7½ in. **$150**

ART NOUVEAU oblong, with easel support, stamped with stylized irises on a textured ground, Birmingham, 1904, 7 in. **$325**

ART NOUVEAU, oblong, mount stamped with lilies of the valley and stylized scrolling foliage, Birmingham, 1903. **$300**

ART NOUVEAU, shaped, mount stamped with poppies and cherubs, Walker and Hall, Sheffield, 1908. **$325**

BAROQUE NEOPOLITAN, cartouche form, centering an oval of pearls, c. 1710, height, 12 in. **$5,000**

CIRCULAR, with easel support, inset with 4 turquoise ovals, Liberty & Co., Cymric, Birmingham, 1904. **$375**

CIRCULAR, pair, with foliate and berry borders, each engraved with an armorial, 19th century, 9¼ in. **$550/pr**

DOUBLE, arched, pierced and stamped with flowers and scrolling foliage, Birmingham, 1903, 8¼ in.   **$300**

DOUBLE HEART, medium size, English, early 20th century.

$250

EASTERN SILVER, chased with palm trees, foliage, and animals, height, 9 in.   **$375**

ELONGATED CARTOUCHE SHAPE, embossed with stylized fruit and lobes, surmounted by a spray of flowers and buds, English, Birmingham, 1904, height, 13¼ in.   **$1,700**

ENAMEL decoration of geese, English, late 19th century.

$120

ENAMELED FRONT, on easel, with various-colored pansies and foliage, small, Chester, 1921.   **$300**

FILIGREE, double, with stylized foliage and berries and on ball feet, with crown surmount and applied with 2 enameled mounts, Russian, 1891.   **$750**

OBLONG, 19th-century style, stamped with birds and flowers in the Japanese taste, height 10¾ in.   **$175**

OBLONG, with scrolling simulated-bamboo mounts joined by wirework, London, 1901, height, 9 in.   **$600**

OBLONG, plain, with easel support, engine-turned engraving, height, 14¾ in.   **$175**

OBLONG, textured, applied with chrysanthemums, Japanese, late 19th century.   **$200**

OVAL, laurel wreath, silverplated, with a cast figure of a putto holding aloft a laurel wreath, Continental, height, 5 in. **$150**

PIERCED and engraved with flowers, silver-gilt, Continental, with mythological figures and applied with gems, height, 5 in.

$550

PIERCED with putti, rocaille scrolls, and trelliswork, surmounted by cartouche, Dominick and Haff, height, 8½ in.

$300

RECTANGULAR, on wooden easel back, Sanborns, Mexican.

$1,400

RECTANGULAR, borders engraved with foliate scrolls, Tiffany, late 19th century.   **$450**

RECTANGULAR, pair, engraved stylized leaves and trailing vines at corners, Grogan, length, 12½ in.   **$500/pr**

RECTANGULAR, shagreen border, silver strapwork with beaded flowerheads, English, Liberty & Co., Birmingham, 1914, height, 6¾ in. **$1,800**

RECTANGULAR FORM, embossed with butterflies and bees, sprays of roses, English, Birmingham, 1905, height, 11¾ in. **$2,000**

RECTANGULAR FORM, chased with flowers, foliage, and undulating ridges, Art Nouveau, maker's mark J A & S, Birmingham, 1908, height, 10¼ in. **$700**

RECTANGULAR FORM, chased with herons, waterlilies, cat-o'-nine-tails, and undulating tendrils, Art Nouveau, W. Aitken, Birmingham, 1905. **$2,500**

RECTANGULAR FORM, embossed and chased with flowers, foliage and undulating ridges, Art Nouveau, maker's mark J A & S, Birmingham, 1909. **$750**

RECTANGULAR FORM, repoussé and chased with a maiden picking flowers from a tree with sheep and birds at her feet, W.I. Broadway & Co, Birmingham, 1906, height, 13¾ in. **$2,100**

RECTANGULAR FORM, repoussé and chased with flowering branches, one supporting a singing bird, and a crescent moon, Birmingham, 1910, height, 9⅜ in. **$800**

RECTANGULAR FORM, repoussé and chased with flowers with undulating stems, Deakin & Francis, Birmingham, 1904, height, 8⅜ in. **$1,300**

RECTANGULAR FORM, repoussé and chased with the head of a maiden with flowing hair amid flowers and undulating tendrils, Birmingham, 1905, height, 8⅜ in. **$800**

RECTANGULAR FORM, the border and top chased with reeding and foliage, Birmingham, 1918, height, 11½ in. **$850**

RECTANGULAR FORM, with reed-and-tie rims, surmounted by crossed torches and bundles of arrows and berried foliage, J. Gloster Ltd., Birmingham, 1909, height, 9⅜ in. **$800**

ROUNDED CORNERS, oblong, with easel support, Birmingham, 1906. **$150**

SHAPED, pierced and chased with masks, flowers, and scrolling foliage, fitted with 2 hinged doors, London, 1884. **$750**

SQUARE, with Renaissance figures amid scrolls surmounted by putti, Continental, German, late 19th century. **$1,150**

Gorham

Gorham sterling tea and coffee service in Classical Revival style with silverplated tray, $1,900. **Courtesy of Robert W. Skinner Gallery, Bolton, MA.**

Rhode Island has been the home of the Gorham Company, manufacturers of silver and silverplate, since 1831. The name changed in 1863 to the Gorham Manufacturing Company. At first the company used the coin silver standard but by 1868 had changed to sterling. The lion, anchor, and *g* became the standard mark for all pieces. In addition to the mark, a series of symbols was used to indicate the year of manufacture.

Through the 19th century, many styles of sterling silver were produced, including Rococo Revival, which used C- and S-scrolls with repoussé ornaments, generally flowers and fruits with leafage. From this began the move toward the Renaissance Revival style with applied stags' heads and classical medallions, together with strapwork and naturalistic branch ornaments. The wonderful mixture of styles during this period produced some wildly esoteric pieces.

By the late 1800s the Neoclassical motif was in style again, with stamped borders depicting the Greek key motif, festoons, and friezes. About 1875 Japanese designs became another new influence. From them evolved mixed-metal objects with hammered backgrounds, along with Moorish-style pieces, also often decorated with Japanese motifs.

Some of the finest pieces came into being during the Art Nouveau period. Much of the silver was handmade at this time, with whiplash curves, flowers, and other naturalistic forms. The Martelé objects are among the finest produced in the Arts and Crafts movement, featuring exceptionally interesting pieces in combinations of ivory, bronze, copper, and iron with sterling silver. Also in the late 19th century, Gorham turned out silverplate that often matched the flatware and hollowware patterns in their sterling sets. Be aware and check the marks. Souvenir spoons, in sterling silver and silverplate in various forms, were also a large part of the Gorham production line.

BASKET, cake, George II style, in the manner of Paul de Lamerie, with applied cherubs' heads, beaded border with shells and foliage, rim applied with heads of the goddess Ceres on shells, flowers, bees, sheaves of wheat, and grape clusters, swing handles formed as caryatids and lions' masks. **$5,000**

BASKET, dessert, flared circular form, copied from a Charles I London basket of 1641, pierced and engraved with strapwork and cherub heads, c. 1910, diameter, 10⅝ in. **$750**

BASKET, sweetmeat, silver-gilt, scroll feet, repoussé scrolls, shell and husk swags, diameter, 9 in. **$350**

BOWL, centerpiece, fluted, footed oval form with 2 loop handles, beaded decoration, c. 1900, length, 15 in. **$475**

BOWL, fruit, footed, 1870, applied with lion's mask and ring handles, engraved with sprig of strawberries, butterfly, and bee, height, 8¼ in. **$925**

BOWL, fruit, shallow circular form chased with stylized geometric designs. **$250**

BOWL, Japanese style, hammered copper with silver dragonfly and a flowering plant, 1881. **$1,000**

BOWL, nut, figural, grip handles mounted with cast squirrels perched on branches, c. 1870. **$1,100**

One of a set of 12 Gorham sterling soup bowls in turtle form, with 12 terrapin spoons, $40,000/set. **Courtesy of Christie's East, New York.**

BOWL, punch, 1919, with stylized body chased with flutes, molded, reeded rim with strapwork and shells, diameter, 13 in.   **$1,200**

BOWL, seafood, and pair of servers, of lobed boat form, the ends applied with realistically modeled gilded lobsters mounted on sprays of reeds and rushes, servers and shell-fluted bowls and twig stems applied with crabs on sprays of reeds and rushes, c. 1870, length, 16 in.   **$4,200/set**

BOWL, small, Japanese style, hammered copper with ruffled rim, applied in silver and copper with a Chinaman, a rooster, and a flowering plant.   **$400**

BOWLS, soup, set of 12, oval turtle form, covered, with applied cast head, handles formed as double-scallop shells; together with 12 terrapin spoons, bowls formed as swimming turtles, cast handles formed as various shells amid seaweed.
                                                                        $40,000/set

CENTERPIECE, Neoclassical, tripod base with paw feet, scrolling handles with mask terminals with flowing hair and beard.
                                                                        $1,500

CHARGER, in Standish pattern, diameter, 14 in.   **$175**

COCKTAIL SHAKER, monogrammed on cover.   **$325**

COMPOTE, hemispherical on knopped stem, rising handles with leaf joins, die-rolled scrolling border, 1871, height, 7 in.
$800

COMPOTE, shallow frosted bowl centered with chased star, rim stamped with ivy, trumpet-shape stem and domed base wrapped with strawberry plants, partly coppered and interspersed with birds and butterflies, 1872. **$1,900**

CUP, loving, Athenic, early 20th century, tulip form on domed circular base with acanthus rim, embossed and chased with stylized foliage, height, 12⅛ in. **$2,000**

DEMITASSE SERVICE, Plymouth pattern, comprising demitasse pot, cream pitcher, and sugar basket on shaped oval tray.
$600/set

DEMITASSE SERVICE, St. Dunstan pattern, comprising coffeepot, cream pitcher, and sugar bowl, engraved with panels of foliate scrolls. **$600/set**

DESSERT SET, comprising 24 fruit knives and forks, hollow handles repoussé with twining meadow flowers. **$525/set**

DISHES, entree, pair, covered, shell and floral border, domed covers with detachable ring handles. **$1,000/pr**

American cut glass pitcher with Gorham sterling mount, c. 1901, $880.
Courtesy of Butterfield & Butterfield, San Francisco.

PITCHER, brilliant period cut glass with silver mounting, 1901, applied floral band, the glass cut in pinwheels and sheaves of grain. **$800**

PITCHER, water, helmet shape, C-scroll handle, reeded band. **$385**

PITCHER, water, Neoclassical, vase form on square foot, applied beaded borders, body part-chased with flutes, 1878. **$850**

PLATES, bread and butter, set of 12, circular, monogrammed. **$475/set**

SALTS, open, set of 8, Plymouth pattern. **$375/set**

SALTS, pair, in the form of shallow pails, handles surmounted by butterflies. **$250/pr**

SALVER, Japonisme, copper and silver, square, applied with birds and pine trees in Japanese style. **$450**

SMOKER'S SET, Art Nouveau, copper and silver, tray with lighter, cigar urn, cigarette urn, and matchstick urn, tray applied with silver scroll rims, lighter and urns applied with silver strapwork designs. **$1,200/set**

SPOON, Hizen pattern, parcel-gilt bowl formed as clamshell, engraved with seaweed, handle cast with flowers and sea life, terminating in figure of Chinaman, length, 7 in. **$385**

TANKARD, Art Nouveau, Athenic, clear-glass body cut with flowers and foliage, silver mounts chased with stylized leafage and cones. **$1,450**

TEA AND COFFEE SERVICE, 5 pieces, Plymouth pattern. **$1,200/set**

TEA AND COFFEE SET, Athenic pattern, comprising teapot, coffeepot, creamer, covered sugar bowl, waste bowl, and hot water kettle on lampstand, chased with sprays of dogwood and maple leaves, finials formed as carved-bone buds with silver calyx of leaves, c. 1905. **$5,000/set**

TEA AND COFFEE SET, Fairfax pattern, comprising teapot, coffeepot, covered sugar bowl, cream pitcher, and kettle on stand, each faceted with harp handles and knop finials. **$1,600/set**

TEA CADDY, copper and silver, Japanese style, ovoid, applied with a bird and flowering foliage, the lid applied with a mouse, 1881, height, 4½ in. **$800**

TEA SERVICE, 5 pieces, Plymouth pattern. **$875/set**

Gorham sterling soup tureen in Persian design, c. 1881, $9,000. Courtesy of Christie's East, New York.

TEA SET, comprising teapot, covered sugar bowl, creamer, and covered waste bowl, chased with a band of grapevine centered on each side of a classical medallion, Greek key borders, domed covers with putto finials, c. 1865. **$2,750/set**

TRAY, silver, modified Greek Key border, length, 25½ in. **$2,000**

TRAY, 2 handles, oval, scalloped border of scrolling foliage, length, 26 in. **$1,500**

TUREEN, soup, in Persian taste, covered, chased with spiraling scrolls, flowers and shells within bead, anthemia, oval and rocaille borders, flower-clad handles, cover chased with flutes, beads, scrolls, shells, and fringe. **$9,000/2**

VASE, squared handles applied with Indian maidens' heads with feather and jewel diadems, c. 1865. **$650**

VASE, large trumpet form engraved with floral swags, with cobalt liner, height, 22 in. **$600**

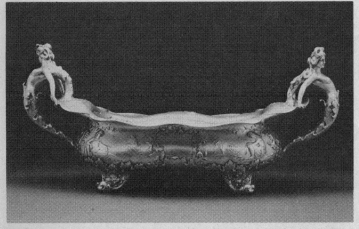

Martelé centerpiece bowl depicting the four seasons, with figural handles, $35,000. Length, 27", height, 11¼". Courtesy of Christie's Park Ave., New York.

Martelé centerpiece view of handles.

$\mathcal{A}$t the end of the 19th century the Gorham Company began a new line of hand-wrought sterling silver called Martelé, the French term for "hand-hammered." The line, created in the .925, .950, and .958 silver standards, exemplified the Arts and Crafts movement in America. No two pieces were exactly alike.

During the production of Martelé pieces, craftsmen had to be retaught to use hand methods for making silver. The objects were created from flat pieces of silver decorated with chased and embossed techniques and left with hammer marks to show their handmade origin. Each piece had to be created by two craftsmen—the silversmith to form the piece and the chaser to execute the decoration.

The designs used were all typical of the Art Nouveau movement and included whiplash lines, waves, flowers, and women's heads with flowing hair. All designs were worked against a lightly hammered ground, which gave a soft appearance to the piece. Marine themes—lobsters, crabs, sea serpents, nets, and seaweed—also were used.

Bowls, vases, tankards, tea sets, children's sets, punch bowls, candlesticks, napkin rings, inkstands, and dresser sets were made. Flatware was not produced in complete sets; however, serving pieces and fish sets were available.

BOWL, centerpiece, .950 standard, oval, the border repoussé and chased with chrysanthemums and foliage, with undulating rims, 1898–1904, length, 17⅛ in. **$6,000**

CUP, .950 standard, baluster form on 3 undulating supports, lobed sides embossed and chased with undulating flowers and foliage, the 3 ear-form handles with leaf terminals with wavy rim, c. 1900, height, 10⅛ in. **$6,300**

CUP, .958 standard, three handles, irregular campana form on tripod base, repoussé and chased with foliage, the ear-shape handles with foliate terminals with undulating rims, height, 8⅙ in. **$3,000**

INKSTAND, .958 standard, repoussé and chased with flowers and undulating foliage, 6-sided well with hinged domed cover chased with a poppy, c. 1908, length, 10 in. **$2,000**

PITCHER, .950 standard, lobed baluster form with undulating foot and rim, repoussé and chased with grapevine, 1899, height, 8⅞ in.   **$6,300**

PLATTER, .950 standard, oval, the border repoussé and chased with cones and undulating foliage, 1898–1904, length, 15⅜ in.
                                                                  $2,700

TEA AND COFFEE SERVICE and 2-handle tray, .958, comprising coffeepot, teapot, hot water kettle on stand with burner, creamer, 2-handle covered sugar bowl and 2-handle waste bowl, each of pear form, repoussé and chased with undulating flowers and foliage, domed covers with carved ivory finials, c. 1910.   **$21,000/set**

TRAY, Art Nouveau, square, with undulating border and incurved rim, chased with sprays of triangular leaves and flower-entwined joins, .950 standard, 1899, width, 9 in.   **$1,600**

VASE, with wavy rim embossed and chased with daisies and foliage, hammered surface, .950 standard, 1898–1904.
                                                                  $3,200

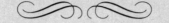

*American coin silver tea service. Anthony Rasch, Philadelphia, 1807,
$4,700. Courtesy of Richard A. Bourne Gallery, Hyannis, MA.*

Hollowware usually refers to hollow pieces such as tea sets,
pitchers, vases, punch bowls, cups, and trays.

Ornamentation and surface decoration ranges from the simple, unadorned forms of the late 17th century through various
succeeding styles such as Rococo, Neoclassicism, Empire, exuberant Victorian motifs, Art Nouveau, Arts and Crafts, and Art
Moderne. Similar decorative styles were used in England, Europe, and the United States.

American, Early and Coin

BASKETS, dessert, pair, in Dutch taste, embossed and chased
with flowers, foliage, and fruit on matte ground, A. E. Warner,
Baltimore, c. 1860, length, 12½ in.   **$2,200/pr**

BEAKER, beaded borders, J. Watts, Philadelphia, 1835. **$595**

BOWL, bright-cut sugar bowl and creamer, ovoid form on ball
feet, mid-19th century, width, 8 in.   **$200**

BOWL, dessert, boat shape, raised harp-shape handles mounted
with facing busts of John Smith and Pocahontas, the base tips
of the handles applied with classical profile medallions, Wood
and Hughes, New York, c. 1860, length, 11¾ in.   **$1,600**

BOWL, sugar, and cover, of lobed urn form with gadroon rim and angular handles, the foot and neck with a stamped band of scrolling grape and oak sprays, Charles A. Burnett, Alexandria, VA, c. 1815, height, 8¾ in.   **$1,800/2**

BOWL, sugar, and creamer, covered, .950 standard, baluster form, chased all over in a wave design, ropelike borders and covers, cornucopia handles and finials, Eoff & Shepherd, c. 1850–55.   **$1,000/set**

BOWL, sugar, egg-and-dart border and owls with outstretched wings at corners, domed cover with swan finial, unmarked.
$600/2

BUTTER DISH, Gorham, with foliate-clad tab handles, cover with medallion head in rondels, the finial formed as lion bearing shield, with removable pierced liner.   **$700**

BUTTER DISH, medallion, c. 1865, horned creatures, medallion grips, the domed cover with floral engraving and medallion finial.   **$800**

CANN, typical form, Jacob Hurd (Boston), 1740–50.   **$3,900**

COFFEEPOT, of oval vase shape with double-fluted angles, swan-neck spout, faceted urn finial, and shaped pedestal foot, Joel Sayre, New York, c. 1800.   **$2,500**

CREAMER, Federal, helmet shape with plain surface and plain loop handle, neck pinched and lip with applied threaded border, William Gethen, Philadelphia, 1798–1808.   **$135**

CREAMER, helmet form, on pedestal base, beaded borders, loop handle, John Walker, Philadelphia, c. 1790.   **$600**

CREAMER, helmet form, on pedestal foot, beaded borders, ribbon-tied drapery mantle, loop handle, Daniel Van Voorhis, New York, c. 1790.   **$900**

CUPS, julep, pair, silver, tapered cylindrial form with narrow beaded borders, maker's mark Lindner script, retailed by William Russell & Son, Bardstown, KY, c. 1860.   **$1,000/pr**

EGG CRUET, circular frame raised on leaf-chased scroll feet, with 6 vase-shape egg cups surrounding a central dome slotted for spoons, Charters, Cann & Dunn, New York, c. 1850–55.
$600

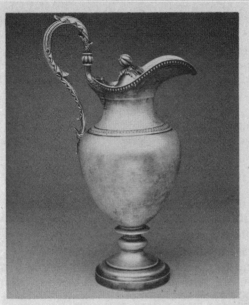

American covered ewer by Baldwin Gardiner, c. 1820, with melon finial, $1,300. Courtesy of Christie's East, New York.

EWER, oviform, chased with acanthus and flowers, foliate and shellwork decoration on matte ground, Thomas Fletcher, Philadelphia, 1825. **$4,200**

EWER, William Gale & Son, 1840, vase form with rustic border, the handle formed as curving vine, chased with grape clusters and scrolls. **$1,450**

FLAGON, covered, pear shape with circular base chased with palm leaves, girdled with engraved inscription, cover with ropework thumbpiece, Francis W. Cooper, Amity Street, New York, c. 1850. **$500**

GOBLET, hexagonal sections, each panel engraved with foliate pendants, R & W Wilson, Philadelphia, mid-19th century. **$375**

GOBLET, bright-cut work, R & W Wilson, Philadelphia, 1850. **$695**

GRAVY BOAT, Alcock & Allen, c. 1820, footed, bulbous, with embossed flowers and cartouche with monogram. **$1,200**

KETTLE on lampstand, baluster form chased with palm leaves, Obadiah Rich, Boston, c. 1840.   **$1,500**

LADLE, soup, with fluted shell-shaped bowl, the stem with feather edge, the terminal with raised vacant rococo cartouche above engraved trailing foliage, Paul Revere, Jr., Boston, c. 1770.   **$4,800**

MUG, with scrolling rustic handle, chased with chinoiserie scene of lady with bird beside fountain, castles in the background, Hyde & Goodrich, New Orleans, 19th century.   **$1,000**

PITCHER, cream, Henry J. Pepper, Philadelphia, 1844, height, 3⅝ in.   **$1,350**

PITCHER, milk, scrolling leaf-clad harp handle, chased with cattails and waterlilies, B.B. and Co., New York (Ball, Black and Company).   **$225**

PITCHER, syrup, S. Kirk & Son, 11 oz., mark.   **$175**

PITCHER, trophy, vase form with double-scroll handle, body and foot chased with oak leaves and acorns, rim of the lip chased with a swag of bunting with drops, Blynn & Baldwin, Columbus, Ohio, c. 1845.   **$350**

Nineteenth-century mug, New Orleans, Hyde & Goodrich, $1,000. **Courtesy of Christie's East, New York.**

PITCHER, water, baluster form chased with a band of rococo ornament, Conrad Bard, Philadelphia, 1845.   **$1,300**

PITCHER, water, baluster form chased with rococo ornaments, forked handle, topped with a bearded mask, William Forbes for Ball, Black and Co., New York, c. 1850, height, 11 in.   **$900**

PITCHER, water, baluster form, scrolled handle with chased floral and foliate decoration, unmarked, mid-19th century, height, 14½ in.   **$700**

PITCHER, water, baluster form chased all over with oak sprays, the angled handles formed as 2 arms shaking hands, P.L. Krider, Philadelphia, 1858, height, 12¾ in.   **$2,700**

PITCHER, water, ovoid form chased with oval panels of flower and foliate sprays, twig scroll handles, William Gale & Sons, New York, 1852, height, 13¼ in.   **$900**

PORRINGER, of typical form with keyhole handle, Jesse Churchill, Boston, c. 1800, diameter, 5⅝ in.   **$800**

PORRINGER, typical form, by Abel Moulton (Newburyport, MA), c. 1800, 5 in.   **$2,600**

SALVER, circular, with reeded borders, on bracket feet, the center engraved with wreath, Andrew Ellicott Warner, Baltimore, 1815.   **$1,000**

Pair of American silver salvers by Welles & Gelston, c. 1840, $1,400/pair.
Courtesy of Christie's East, New York.

TEA AND COFFEE SERVICE, 6 pieces, leaf-clad C-scroll handle, flower basket finials, Robert and William Wilson, Philadelphia, c. 1826. **$4,000/set**

TEA AND COFFEE SET, comprising large coffeepot, pair of teapots, covered sugar bowl, waste bowl, and creamer, pear-shape bodies chased with swags of husks pendant from rods, also chased with rococo cartouches, melon finials, together with a silverplated 2-handle tea tray, George B. Sharp, Philadelphia, c. 1850. **$3,200/set**

TEA AND COFFEE SET, comprising teapot, coffeepot, covered hot water jug, covered creamer, sugar bowl with hinged cover, waste bowl, and kettle on lampstand, pear-shape bodies chased with oak leaves and acorns, branch-form handles, Eoff & Shepherd, c. 1855. **$6,000/set**

TEA AND COFFEE SET, comprising teapot, coffeepot, covered sugar bowl, covered creamer, and waste bowl, embossed with grapevine, vine-branch handles and spouts, game bird finials, twig borders, W.I. Tenney, New York, c. 1850. **$2,300/set**

TEA AND COFFEE SET, 5 pieces, comprising teapot, coffeepot, covered sugar bowl, creamer, and waste bowl, of bombé vase shape with borders of formal foliage, flower finials and pedestal bases, Ball, Tompkins & Black, New York, c. 1835. **$2,100/set**

TEA KETTLE, pear shape with rococo ornament, swing handle, Chinaman finial, R & W Wilson, Philadelphia, c. 1850. **$800**

TEAPOT by Jones, Ball and Poor, rustic handle and spout, the finial formed as native sitting on tree stump before banana plant entwined with banana vines, clusters of bananas and leaves. **$800**

TEAPOT, allover repoussé, A. E. Warner (Baltimore), 1840. **$1,100**

TEAPOT, of partly fluted urn shape with beaded borders, detachable reel-shape cover with urn finial, James Musgrave, Philadelphia, c. 1790–1800. **$1,800**

TEAPOT, pear shape, fluted domed cover and neck, chased with a band of pendant foliage, twig handle spreading from leaves, Grosjean & Woodward, c. 1855. **$850**

TEAPOT, oviform body with initialed bud finial, pedestal foot, and corded collar, F. Masi & Co., Washington, c. 1830–40, height, 10½ in.   **$1,000**

TEAPOT, vase shape, handle formed as grapevine with tendrils twining around body of teapot, chased and repoussé with grape leaves, clusters of grapes, and scrolling tendrils, cover with grape cluster, finial, by Bailey and Co., Philadelphia, c. 1850.
$800

TEA SERVICE comprising teapot, 2-handle sugar bowl and creamer, rounded rectangular with die-rolled leaf-tip band at the rim, on ball feet, by Baldwin and Jones, Boston, c. 1815.
$1,200/set

TEA SERVICE, comprising teapot, creamer, 2-handle covered sugar bowl, and waste bowl, straight-sided oval form with bright-cut borders, shield-shape reserves, William Gale & Son, New York, 1850–60.   **$1,400/set**

TEA SERVICE, four pieces, N. Harding & Co., Boston, 1840, vase shape on pedestal foot, domed covers with urn finials.
$1,000/set

TEA SERVICE, 3-pieces, Anthony Rasch, Philadelphia, c. 1807.
$4,700/set

TEA SET, comprising teapot, creamer, 2-handle covered sugar bowl, and waste bowl, fluted vase shape with die-rolled bands of stylized leaves, bud and leaf finials, Ball, Tompkins and Black, c. 1845.   **$1,500/set**

TEA SET, five pieces, comprising 2 teapots, creamer, covered sugar urn, and waste bowl, vase shape with key-pattern borders and flower spray finials, P. L. Krider, Philadelphia.
$2,350/set

TEA SET, 4 pieces, comprising teapot, covered sugar bowl, creamer, and waste bowl, of paneled pear shape, flat-chased with rococo ornament, flower finials, openwork leafy scroll feet, grapevine-decorated handles, F.S. Cooper, New York, c. 1850.   **$1,500/set**

TEA SET, 3 pieces, comprising teapot, covered sugar bowl and creamer, partly paneled bombé form on pedestal bases, grapevine scroll handles, domed covers with grape cluster finials, Charters, Cann & Dunn, New York, c. 1850.   **$1,600/set**

TEA SET, 3 pieces, comprising teapot, covered sugar bowl, and creamer, of slightly bombé and partly fluted oval form, engraved with bands of bright-cut ornament and oval wreaths, urn finials, J. Sayre, New York, c. 1800.   **$2,200/set**

TEA SET, 3 pieces, comprising teapot, covered sugar bowl and creamer, oval, slightly bombé and fluted form, bright-cut foliate borders on shaded grounds, J. Sayre, New York, c. 1800.
                                             $3,200/set

TEA SET, 3 pieces, comprising teapot, large covered sugar, and creamer, with fluted rectangular bodies with band of alternating grape clusters and leaves, spout with an open-mouthed griffin with a scaly neck, covers with stiff leaf and berry finials, John Crawford, New York City, 1820–1830.   **$775/set**

TUREEN, soup, and cover, oval bombé form flat-chased on both sides with a rococo cartouche, foliate scroll handles and finial, John C. Moore for Ball, Tompkins and Black, New York, c. 1845, length over handles, 17½ in.   **$2,500/2**

URN, sugar, on square pedestal base, on a drapery mantle, reel-shape cover with urn finial, W.G. Forbes, New York, c. 1790–1800.   **$1,600**

American Ball, Black & Co. covered soup tureen on stand, with stag head handles, $4,000. Courtesy of Christie's East, New York.

WAITER, with shell-and-scroll rim, the surface flat-chased with rococo ornament, on 3 hoof supports, A.E. Warner, Baltimore, 1819, diameter, 7½ in. **$1,400**

WASTE BOWL, partly fluted circular form on conforming pedestal foot, bright-cut with borders of half-flowers, leaves, and arches, J. Sayre, New York, c. 1800–10, diameter, 6½ in.

$1,700

WHISTLE, bosun's, of typical form with curved tube and plane panel with pendant ring, R & W Wilson, Philadelphia, c. 1840.

$1,500

WINE COOLER, pail form, with hoops engraved with Greek key pattern between grapevine and clusters, simple raised handles, Ball, Black & Co., New York, c. 1855. **$1,900**

American Sterling

BASKETS

Baskets, with either stationary or swing handles, served many purposes. They were used to hold flowers, bread, fruit, cakes, or bonbons. In the 18th century tiny bonbon baskets were hung from the arms of a centerpiece vase or épergne. Decorations often included elaborate hand piercing, stamped or chased florals, ribbon swags, floral garlands, gadrooning, trophy symbols, rococo shellwork, and beaded borders.

Some of the loveliest examples date from the Georgian and Victorian periods. Those with Art Nouveau designs of whiplash curves, flowers, and semidraped nudes are extremely desirable. Especially coveted are the Gorham Martelé pieces. In America, Kerr, Unger, Tiffany, and Whiting made some of the most beautiful examples.

After the turn of the 20th century, mass production began in full force, and baskets were often die-stamped with decoration. At this period heart-shaped baskets also became extremely popular. In the 1920s and 1930s stylized baskets with stamped bands and pierced and ribbed borders were often given as wedding gifts.

BEAKERS

Beakers were tall handleless cups, originally used for serving ale or mulled wine. The most desirable are European in origin and date from the 17th and 18th centuries. Often they were made for christening presents, and many were produced in a small size for traveling or in graduated sizes, usually in a nest of multiples. There are also collapsible examples that fit into leather traveling cases.

Elaborately decorated Victorian examples have become collectible in the past year.

BOUILLON CUPS AND SAUCERS

Bouillon cups and saucers were extremely popular on the Victorian table and even into the early 20th century. The holder and saucer were made of sterling silver, and the inserts usually were Lenox porcelain. The bouillon cups and saucers had simple frameworks or elaborate pierced designs by Dominick & Haff, Mauser, or Unger Brothers. Most often the sets were boxed in 6 or 12 units.

BOWLS

Silver bowls were quite common in Victorian times. They were used for punch, fruit, candy, vegetables, or as centerpieces. Designs and weights vary greatly. Today the most salable pieces are those with Art Nouveau forms or applied mixed metals.

American sterling repoussé punch bowl by James Arminger, $3,200.
Courtesy of Christie's East, New York.

BUTTER DISHES

In the mid- and late 19th century, butter dishes made in sterling silver and silverplate were very popular. They held tub butter and always had a liner, usually pierced, to place over the ice in the base. Covers should be checked to be sure they are not warped and have their original finials. Butter dishes with figural medallions and full-figure animal finials are most collectible today.

CENTERPIECES

From the late 18th through the 19th centuries in England and America, the centerpiece was generally made of elegantly ornate sterling silver. It served both a decorative and functional purpose by holding fruit or flowers. Many had glass inserts or bowls for bonbons. By the end of the 19th century massive silverplated centerpieces with matching plateaus were in vogue.

DESSERT STANDS (TAZZAS)

Dessert stands, or tazzas, became popular in the 18th century in Europe and enjoyed a revival in the middle and latter part of the 19th century. They were seldom used alone. Usually several were placed on a banquet-size dining table in combination with elaborately decorated monteiths, candlesticks, and other hollowware pieces. They were made of sterling, most often with elaborate embossed and applied work or restrained and elegant gadrooning. Some can be found with weighted bases.

TEA SETS

Tea drinking was introduced to America by the British in the late 18th century, and the custom had become extremely popular by the first quarter of the 19th century. Tea sets were made in silver to replace china, which broke easily. Small pear-shaped teapots with simple decoration appeared in the 18th century, followed in 1800 by teapots on standards with matching sugars and creamers. These were decorated with chased bands of foliage and flower finials. From 1820 until 1850 tea sets became larger and taller because they were set on higher pedestals. From 1860 to 1870 urn shapes were popular, often with gadrooned or beaded rims. After 1870 pedestal bases were replaced by four legs. Decoration included chasing and ornamentation depicting birds, animals, and Egyptian and Japonesque motifs. During the 1870s the matching tray became more common. The last part of the 19th century saw an increased use of bright-cut engraving and chasing depicting naturalistic forms of birds, ferns, and insects. Other collectible forms are tête-à-tête sets and demitasse sets.

TUREENS

In the early 19th century, tureens were generally oval and set on feet; but by mid-19th century they were huge, with elaborate cast handles and finials, and were decorated to match the tea service.

VASES

Elaborate table decoration became the vogue in the mid-19th century and with it came the need for centerpieces and vases. Épergnes with sterling silver or silverplate bases, sometimes in the forms of human figures or animals, were embellished with vases in clear or colored cut glass. These were augmented with single or bud vases as individual place settings. They were also made with gadrooning, beading, embossed flowers and foliage, engraved Japonesque motifs, or allover hand hammering. Most were filled or weighted to increase their sturdiness.

BASKET, bread, marked 925/1000, oval with applied grapevine border, rustic double-loop handles with scrolling grapevines, stippled finish, length over handles, 15 in.   **$500**

BASKET, cake, in the rococo taste, scrolling foliage framing pierced cartouches of leaves, resting on 4 leafy feet, the handle pierced with leaves and bellflowers, Frank W. Smith Silver Co., Inc., 19th century.   **$1,450**

BASKET, cake, oval, on scrolling acanthus supports, pierced scrolling foliate border, lobed body engraved with scrolls and trelliswork, swing handle pierced and repoussé with scrolling acanthus leaves and bellflowers, Whiting, late 19th century.

$1,100

BASKET, cake, oval, pierced and chased with rondels of cupids amidst grape clusters and scrolls, with swing handle, Theodore B. Starr, late 19th century, length, 11 in.   **$1,200**

BASKET, die-rolled guilloche borders, swing openwork handle, Wood and Hughes, late 19th century. **$250**

BASKET, pierced, oval, with scrolling border and stylized shells, loop handles, Frank M. Whiting, late 19th century, length, 12¼ in. **$325**

BASKET, pierced, shaped oval with applied wavy border, Towle, early 20th century, length, 14 in. **$400**

BASKET, plain chased border, Dominick & Haff, late 19th century, diameter, 9 in. **$110**

BASKET, plain form with swing handle, Newport, early 20th century, diameter, 9 in. **$100**

BASKETS, sweetmeat, pair, each of bombé oval form on pierced scrolling base, chased with scrolls, Howard and Co. **$550/pr**

BOUILLON HOLDERS, 6, Watson Company, sterling with Lenox liners, early 20th century. **$180/6**

BOWL, "Japanese style," with waved rim and gilt interior, the bombé hammered body applied with a dragonfly, waterbug, fish, branch, bat, serpent, and mermaid holding a spray of rushes, George W. Shiebler & Co., New York, c. 1880–90, diameter, 4⅜ in. **$650**

BOWL, centerpiece, marked sterling only, openwork border of scrolling chrysanthemums, lobed bowl with everted rim pierced with trelliswork and applied with scrolling chrysanthemums, late 19th century, diameter, 15 in. **$1,200**

BOWL, centerpiece, circular, footed, plain body with rolled band of scrolling foliage, with raised button engraved with lotus flowers and palmettes, Schulz & Fischer, c. 1870–1890, diameter, 8 in. **$250**

BOWL, centerpiece, fluted, circular, on ring foot, the center engraved in baroque style, Redlich, late 19th century, diameter, 16 in. **$700**

BOWL, centerpiece, in vintage pattern, deep bowl of circular outline with wavy fold over lip pierced in a woven strapwork design, applied at intervals with grape cluster and leaf design, Shreve & Co., San Francisco, diameter, 14 in. **$1,100**

BOWL, centerpiece, Iris pattern, International Sterling, early 20th century. **$300**

BOWL, centerpiece, on pedestal, wide bowl with shallow proportion and hammered surface, resting on a stand with a band of shells spaced by trillium flowers, International, Meriden, CT, early 20th century, diameter, 14 in.   **$600**

BOWL, centerpiece, simple hammered lobed sides, Cartier, early 20th century, diameter, 11 1/2 in.   **$900**

BOWL, centerpiece, wide lobed everted rim, pierced with trelliswork, applied with roses and foliage, Redlich, late 19th century, diameter, 14 1/2 in.   **$2,400**

BOWL, Chrysanthemum pattern, Tiffany & Co., c. 1905.

$900

BOWL, floral repoussé, scalloped edge, Whiting, late 19th century, diameter, 11 in.   **$3,800**

BOWL, fluted form with scalloped rim, Newburyport, early 20th century, diameter, 10 in.   **$200**

BOWL, footed, shaped circular form, flat-chased with stylized foliage around the rim, Durgin Division of Gorham Mfg. Co., early 20th century.   **$250**

BOWL, fruit, chased with scrolling foliage on spreading circular foot, Gorham, diameter, 8 1/2 in.   **$420**

BOWL, fruit, cut-glass circular bowl with irises and floral sprays on shaped square silver base (base weighted), diameter, 12 in.   **$400**

BOWL, fruit, Francis I pattern, Reed & Barton, early 20th century.   **$225**

BOWL, fruit, Francis I pattern, round, repoussé with fruit and flowers with scrolling scalloped rim, Reed and Barton, diameter, 11 1/2 in.   **$450**

BOWL, fruit, Irish pattern, shaped circular, fluted bowl chased in alternating panels with scroll, shell, and diaperwork, monogrammed, by Tuttle, c. 1924, diameter, 12 in.   **$400**

BOWL, fruit, fluted circular form on domed foot, Gorham, diameter, 12 1/2 in.   **$550**

BOWL, fruit, oval, on rococo scrolling foliate ball feet, with rope-twist everted rim, the base impressed, Ball, Tompkins & Black, 11 3/4 in.   **$500**

BOWL, fruit, overall repoussé with flowerheads, scrolling foliage, and diaperwork, applied floral borders, Black, Starr & Frost, diameter, 8 in.   **$700**

BOWL, fruit, repoussé, circular, on ring foot with applied foliate scroll border, chased with flowerheads on stippled ground, Schofield Co., Baltimore, diameter, 10 in.   **$950**

BOWL, fruit, repoussé, fluted circular form, chased overall with flowerheads and ferns on stippled ground, Whiting, diameter, 9 in.   **$400**

BOWL, fruit, Wedgwood pattern, fluted, circular, on spreading foot, with border of Renaissance motifs, International Sterling, early 20th century, diameter, 11½ in.   **$325**

BOWL, oval, the center chased with a spider in an expanding web below a chased band of blackberry fruits and flowers with gilt leaves, acid-etched to simulate the web, Whiting Mfg. Co., c. 1880, length, 10 in.   **$3,800**

BOWL, punch, hemispherical, on spreading foot, embossed with shaped floral and scroll-band neck, Tiffany, diameter, 12 in.   **$1,700**

BOWL, punch, scalloped hemispherical form, applied with meandering seaweed linking oyster shells in relief, foot cast with wave and scroll ornament, Whiting Mfg. Co., c. 1880–90, diameter, 12⅛ in.   **$5,000**

Stieff sterling punch bowl, 1936, $4,700. Courtesy of Robert W. Skinner Gallery, Bolton, MA.

BOWL, punch, stylized wave borders at base and rim, Whiting, late 19th century.   **$1,250**

BOWL, repoussé floral decoration, Kirk, early 20th century, diameter, 9 in.   **$500**

BOWL, Revere reproduction, Tuttle Silversmiths, 1964–68, diameter, 8 in.   **$150**

BOWL, rose, circular, on spreading base with wide everted border, chased with foliage, pales, and laurel swags, fitted with metal frog, Gorham, diameter, 14½ in.   **$900**

BOWL, shell form, on openwork scrolling supports with flower joins and grip handle formed as leaf supporting crawfish, Gorham, 1870.   **$1,700**

BOWL, stamped sterling silver only, with reticulated edge, diameter, 10½ in.   **$165**

BUTTER DISH on stand, covered, circular, chased with rocaille and flowers, finial formed as acorn surmounting oak leaves, on circular stand with 3 openwork twig and leaf supports, Ball, Black & Co., c. 1860.   **$850**

BUTTER DISH, medallion, cover applied with medallion head in oval surrounded by engraved strapwork, finial formed as Greek helmet, Black, Ball and Co., c. 1860.   **$600/2**

CAKE STAND, circular, on ring foot with wide pierced border of trelliswork, rocaille scrolls and flowers, J. E. Caldwell and Co., diameter, 13¼ in.   **$1,000**

CANDELABRA, pair of 5-way breakdown, weighted bases, International, early 20th century.   **$200/pr**

CANDELABRA, pair, 3 lights, baluster form on circular domed base, with scrolling reeded branches, weighted bases, Gorham, height, 14½ in.   **$650/pr**

CANDLESTICKS, set of 4, each formed as Ionic column on stepped base, with beaded border and beaded bobeches, weighted bases, Gorham, 8¼ in.   **$1,500/set**

CANDLESTICKS, set of 4, lobed and fluted base shape, with oval bases, Bailey, Banks & Biddle Co., c. 1898. **$1,900/set**

CENTERPIECE, realistically formed and chased as an Indian canoe with wire-tied ends, gilt interior, Theodore B. Starr, New York, c. 1900, length, 14¾ in.   **$2,500**

CENTERPIECE, shallow circular bowl with leafy scroll handles sheltering exotic birds, supported by the raised arms and head of a classical woman, Koehler & Ritter, San Francisco, c. 1879. **$2,750**

CENTERPIECE, tripod support with openwork rosettes and beads supporting medallion rondel of maidens' heads, Wood and Hughes, 1880. **$900**

COCKTAIL SET, comprising cocktail shaker and 6 goblets, vase shape on spreading circular foot with leaf-capped loop handle, cover with pineapple finial; together with 6 bell-shape goblets, Black, Starr and Frost. **$750/set**

COCKTAIL SHAKER, typical form, Ferner. **$200**

COFFEEPOT, George III style, by Elmore after an example by F. Crump, pyriform on domed foot chased with gadrooned border, the leaf-clad scrolling spout with drop below, with ebonized handle, the hinged, domed cover with gadrooned border and spiral-fluted finial, monogrammed, height, 10½ in. **$700**

COFFEEPOT, the peened surface applied with prunus blossoms and leaves growing from a copper branch, with additional engraved leafy branches, applied with 2 copper bees, a large beetle on the reverse, and a Japanese beetle on the lid, "Japanese Movement," Whiting Mfg. Co., Providence, RI, c. 1880. **$3,500**

COFFEE SERVICE, Tiffany, comprising coffeepot, cream pitcher, and covered sugar bowl, each circular with squared handle, acid-etched at shoulder. **$1,300/set**

COFFEE SERVICE, 3 pieces, in Queen Anne style, comprising coffeepot, creamer, and 2-handle open sugar bowl, each of pear form on 3 cabriole legs. **$200/set**

COFFEE SET, 3 pieces, Poole Silver Company, early 20th century. **$250/set**

COFFEE URN on hot water stand, octagonal, on 6 scrolling supports with wood C-scroll handles, Howard and Co., 15 in. **$1,400**

COMPOTE, hemispherical, on pedestal foot, die-rolled scallop-shell border at rim, Gorham, 1873, diameter, 9 in. **$550**

COMPOTE, boat-shape bowl chased with a collar of grapevine and applied with rams' heads, handles applied with putto heads and terminating in classical medallions and beads, Ball, Black & Co., c. 1865, height, 13¾ in.　　　**$1,100**

COMPOTE, bonbon, pierced, segmented oval body on a circular stem, with threaded-ribbon-bound rim over floral pierced sides, Gorham, late 19th century, diameter, 9½ in.　　**$125**

COMPOTE, border with Georgian shell and pierced design, J. E. Caldwell, late 19th century, diameter, 9 in.　　　·**$160**

COMPOTE, bowl with raised angular handles mounted with double-sided classical medallions, trumpet-shape foot with square knop applied with 4 profile medallions, Ball, Black & Co., New York, c. 1865.　　　**$800**

COMPOTE, circular, on pedestal foot with die-rolled ivy leaf border at foot and rim, the handles with stylized leaf joins, Gorham, 1873, length over handles, 10 in.　　　**$475**

COMPOTE, in Pompeian Adam design, Towle, early 20th century, diameter, 7½ in.　　　**$90**

COMPOTE, in the form of a stylized calla lily, with a bird poised on the rim, the stem with a figure of Diana, Gorham Mfg. Co., 1869.　　　**$2,700**

COMPOTE, repoussé, flower and leaf motifs, Stieff, early 20th century, height, 3¾ in.　　　**$250**

COMPOTE, shallow frosted bowl, rim cast with exotic birds and butterflies on prunus sprays, in Japanese style, stem with petal-form knop, Starr & Marcus, New York, c. 1875. **$1,100**

CUP, loving, bombé oval form with 3 tusk handles, Meriden, CT, height, 7¼ in.　　　**$450**

CUP, loving, stamped T. Hausmann and Sons, pyriform on domed foot with 3 scrolling handles, chased with grape clusters and leaves and inset with presentation plaque, height, 12½ in.　　　**$650**

CUP, of plain form with bright-cut medallion with blank reserve framed by cattails, retailed by Braverman & Levy, San Francisco, marked "English Sterling," 1870–90.　　**$125**

CUP, 2 handles, applied with tied laurel wreath surmounted by crown with cornucopia below, Theodore Starr, late 19th century.　　　**$700**

CUPS, champagne, set of 8, Pantheon pattern, International, early 20th century.　　　**$400/set**

CUPS, cordial, set of 12, each tapering cylindrical on spreading foot with gold-washed interiors, by Black, Starr and Gorham, height, 3 in. **$400/set**

CUPS, julep, set of 10, plain, tapering, cylindrical, engraved on base, Gorham, late 19th century. **$800/set**

CUPS, julep, set of 12, cylindrical with flaring rims.

$1,100/set

CUPS, tumbler, set of 10, each a bell form on spreading foot with applied ribbing, J.E. Caldwell and Co. **$650/set**

DEMITASSE HOLDERS, saucers, and spoons, 12, repoussé with flowerheads on stippled ground, Lenox liners, Schofield Co., Inc., early 20th century. **$1,500/set**

DEMITASSE POT, ''Japanese style,'' pear shape, engine-turned in the form of a finely woven basket, tied by a cord at the top and with frilled fabric rim, applied with a flowering branch and a trailing berried vine, Whiting Mfg. Co., Providence, RI, c. 1883, height, 12½ in. **$2,700**

DEMITASSE SERVICE, bulbous with elongated neck and spout in Persian taste, Bailey, Banks and Biddle. **$800/set**

DEMITASSE SERVICE, comprising demitasse pot, sugar bowl, and cream pitcher on circular tray, each oval, with chased band of pales and pendant laurel wreaths, Gorham, 1929.

$500/set

DEMITASSE SERVICE, comprising coffeepot, cream pitcher, and sugar bowl, each tapering octagonal, with squared handle, Mauser, late 19th century. **$420/set**

DEMITASSE SERVICE, George II style, comprising coffeepot, sugar bowl, and cream pitcher, each pyriform, on 4 hoof legs, J. Wagner and Son, New York. **$325/set**

DEMITASSE SERVICE, 3 pieces with tray, Reed & Barton, 1929, Francis I pattern. **$2,500/set**

DESSERT STANDS, pair, circular, with scalloped everted rim on pedestal foot with octagonal bases, flat-chased with stylized foliage, Gorham, 1909, diameter, 9¾ in. **$950/pr**

DISH, asparagus, with liner, rectangular tray with applied threaded-ribbon-bound rim capped by scrolling acanthus leaves at the corners, pierced tray with two attached bracket handles, Ferdinand Fuchs & Bros., New York, 1884–1922. **$1,000**

DISH, asparagus, with matching liner, length, 15 in. **$350**

DISH, bonbon, swan form, glass molded with tail feathers, overlaid with sterling wings, the handle formed by the neck and head in silver, Wm. B. Durgin Co., Providence, RI, the glass by Hawkes, late 19th century.   **$800**

DISH, bread, interior repoussé floral decoration, Kirk, length, 12 in.   **$700**

DISH, butter, cover and liner, boat shape, tab handles cast with leaves, applied with 4 female masks and with displayed eagle finial, Albert Coles, New York, c. 1865.   **$1,450**

DISH, entree, marked sterling only, fluted shaped oval with gadrooned border, the domed fluted cover with ring handle, length, 12 in.   **$450/2**

DISH, grape, shallow fluted oval with foliate joins and grape cluster grips at each end, Durham, length, 15½ in.   **$600**

DISH, leaf shape, handmade Sciarrotta, early 20th century.

$125

DISH, open, vegetable, with beaded border, Whiting, late 19th century, length, 10 in.   **$80**

DISH, pickle, oval, on spreading base applied with cast pickles at each end, by J. B. McFadden and Co., Pittsburgh, c. 1870, length, 8 in.   **$950**

DISH, pickle, oval, on spreading oval foot, the scrolling handles with cucumber joins, by Whiting, late 19th century, length, 9 in.   **$275**

DISH, plain, with shaped rim, Alvin, late 19th century, diameter, 11½ in.   **$120**

DISH, rectangular, with repoussé Art Nouveau floral border, Dominick & Haff, late 19th century, length, 17 in.   **$1,500**

DISH, vegetable, and cover, pair, oval boat shape, chased with swags of drapery and flowers on matte grounds, covers applied with 4 flowerheads and with detachable lobed baluster finials surrounded by "vermicelli" pattern, Bailey & Co., Philadelphia, c. 1880.   **$3,200/pr**

DISH, vegetable, covered, oval, overall repoussé with flowerheads and leaves, detachable ring handle, Stieff, length, 11½ in.   **$1,400/2**

DISHES, serving, pair, Lord Saybrook pattern, each with plain surface, molded rim, International Silver Co., diameter, 12 in.   **$250/pr**

DISHES, serving, 2, circular, Gadroon pattern, with gadroon rims, diameter, 12½ in. **$550/2**

DISHES, vegetable, pair, 2 handles, bombé oval bodies, lobed and fluted, conforming domed covers, with borders of chrysanthemum flowers and leaves, Chrysanthemum pattern, Tiffany & Co., New York, c. 1885. **$11,000/pr**

EWER, A.G. Schultz & Co., Baltimore, pyriform vineclad rustic handle, chased with flowerheads on stippled ground, height, 14 in. **$1,700**

EWER, large, pyriform with rustic border, foot and body chased with grape bunches and vines, with rustic handle, A. G. Schultz & Co., height, 18¼ in. **$2,000**

FRAMES, ramekin, set of 11 with 9 porcelain liners, with pierced sides and threaded handles. **$100/set**

FRAMES, sherbet, set of 12 boxed, sterling silver with a pierced band of classical oil lamps and laurel wreaths, glasses etched with a floral spray, Matthews Co., early 20th century. **$225/set**

GOBLETS, cocktail, set of 12, bell form on stem with flaring foot, Ferner. **$300/set**

American Durgin silver-gilt jam jar, c. 1890, $375. Photo by J. Auslander.

GOBLETS, 8, bell form, with circular foot, early 20th century.
$600/8

GOBLETS, set of 6, plain form with monogram, Manchester Silver Co., early 20th century. **$175/set**

GOBLETS, set of 12, silver in Baltimore Rose pattern, Schofield Co., Inc. **$1,800/set**

GRAVY BOAT on stand, Windsor pattern, Reed & Barton, early 20th century. **$350/2**

JUG, claret, cut cranberry glass, body paneled and cut with branches of prunus, silver neck chased with a collar of flowers, cover chased with floral garland, spherical flower-cluster finial, Gorham Mfg. Co., 1888. **$5,500**

JUG, coffee, vase form on ring foot, chased with foliate scrolls, cover with swirling finial, Dominick and Haff, 1893. **$380**

JUG, water, vase shape, foot, collar, shoulder, and rim applied with foliate-stamped mount, with an elaborate scroll handle and with chased floral, foliate, and scale work decoration, Ball, Thompkins & Black, 1880. **$1,000**

KETTLE on stand, apple shape, bud finial, overall chased with flowerheads on stippled ground, Kirk, 1880–90. **$1,800**

KYLIX, parcel-gilt, the cast central medallion depicting Cupid restraining Cerebus with bow, surrounded by an engraved palmette and strapwork border, probably New York, c. 1865, length, 11 in. **$1,100**

NUT SET, comprising 12 nut picks, each applied with a squirrel holding a nut, and a matching serving spoon with pierced, engraved, gilt bowl applied with a cherub head and a second squirrel, George B. Sharp, Philadelphia, c. 1865. **$1,000/set**

PITCHER, cylindrical glass body with cut-glass scrolling floral design, C-scroll handle, mounted with silver collar and spout, height, 11 in. **$320**

PITCHER, small, bulbous, on ring foot, squared handle, overall chased with flowers on stippled ground, by S. Kirk and Son, height, 7 in. **$1,000**

PITCHER, water, Arts and Crafts style, bucket form, Shreve & Co. **$350**

PITCHER, water, baluster form with scrolling handle, Reed and Barton, early 20th century. **$400**

Floral chased pitcher and 12 julep cups by the Baltimore Silversmiths Co. (six shown). **Courtesy of Christie's East, New York.**

PITCHER, water, baluster form on spreading base with harp handle, chased with flowers, fishscale, and scrolls, Wallace. **$400**

PITCHER, water, baluster form on spreading circular base with multiscroll leaf-clad handle, International Sterling, early 20th century. **$375**

PITCHER, water, baluster form on spreading circular foot with multiscroll handle, repoussé with panels surrounded by rocaille and pendant bellflowers, Watson, early 20th century. **$400**

PITCHER, water, baluster shape with leaf-clad C-scroll handle with flower join, the pitcher repoussé with iris surrounded by sinuous scrolls, Mauser, late 19th century. **$1,000**

PITCHER, water, bulbous, applied ovolo band at neck, overall repoussé with flowerheads and ferns on stippled ground, height, 8 in. **$950**

PITCHER, water, bulbous, on spreading circular foot, scrolling handle, Durgin. **$300**

PITCHER, water, bulbous tapering body, flat-chased with band of strapwork centering a medallion with an inscription in reserve, W.K. Vanderslice & Co., c. 1870–74. **$1,200**

PITCHER, water, footed pear shape, early 20th century, height, 9¼ in. **$225**

PITCHER, water, helmet form on domed foot, with squared handles, chased with stylized leaf-tip bands at foot and neck, International, 9½ in. **$380**

PITCHER, water, Jensen-style, bulbous, on spreading foot with openwork band of stylized leaves and beads, height, 11 in.

$400

PITCHER, water, large, baluster form chased in Kirk style with flowers on matte ground, twig-form handle, Gorham Mfg. Co., 1895, height, 14½ in. **$1,500**

PITCHER, water, marked sterling only, bulbous form on spreading foot, with C-scroll handle and reeded rim, monogrammed. **$300**

PITCHER, water, baluster form with reeded border at base and rim, the bifurcated handle with grotesque mask, Ball, Black & Co., c. 1870, height, 10¾ in. **$950**

PITCHER, water, fluted helmet form with leaf-capped multiscroll handle, body flat-chased with panels of foliate scrolls, height, over handle, 10½ in. **$700**

PITCHER, water, helmet form on pedestal foot with beaded rim, lower body flat-chased with upright stiff leafage, the sides with paterae and laurel swags and leaf-capped ear-shaped handle, Goodnow & Jenks, early 20th century. **$750**

PITCHER, water, octagonal sections with gadroon rims, harp-shape handle, Durgin division of Gorham Mfg. Co., late 19th century. **$600**

PITCHER, water, oval cartouche form with molded rims, harp-shape handle, Reed & Barton, Taunton, MA, c. 1912. **$500**

PITCHER, water, oval, engraved with panels of diaperwork cartouches, with dentilated border at neck, Gorham, height over handle, 9 in. **$550**

PITCHER, water, pyriform on domed foot chased with scrolls and foliage, Graff, Washbourne & Dunn, New York, height, 11½ in. **$1,000**

PITCHER, water, pyriform on foliate supports, the body chased with rocaille cartouches and floral scrolls, Loring Andrews and Co., height, 9¼ in. **$650**

PITCHER, water, pyriform on spreading foot with leaf-capped multiscroll handle, Fisher, 9½ in. **$280**

PITCHER, water, Reed & Barton, Hampton Court pattern, part-fluted oval form on 4 foliate-clad scrolling supports, applied with scrolls and shells at intervals. **$420**

PITCHER, water, simple design, Shreve & Company, c. 1910.

$650

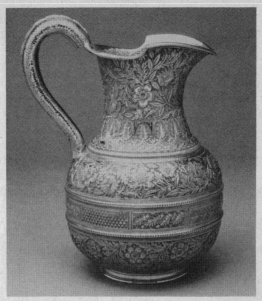

Water pitcher by Bigelow Kennard & Co., Boston, with chased body.
Courtesy of Christie's East, New York.

PITCHER, water, vase form on spreading foot with squared handle, Barbour Silver Co., early 20th century. **$350**

PLATES, bread and butter, 12, reeded border enclosing band of scrolls and flowerheads, Meriden. **$700/set**

PLATES, bread and butter, 8, each shaped circular with repoussé floral band enclosed by molded shell-and-scroll border, Stieff. **$500/8**

PLATES, bread and butter, set of 12, early 20th century. **$200/set**

PLATES, bread and butter, set of 12, octagonal, Reed & Barton, early 20th century. **$400/set**

PLATES, dinner, 8, scrolling borders pierced with floral cartouches, scrolls, and laurel swags, Bailey, Banks and Biddle. **$4,500/8**

PLATES, dinner, set of 12, plain circular with reeded border, Gorham, 1909, diameter, 10 in. **$2,600/set**

PLATES, dinner, set of 12, Edgeworth pattern, circular, with stylized leaf bands, monogrammed, Gorham, early 20th century. **$5,000/set**

PLATES, luncheon, set of 12, circular, with applied rocaille scroll border, Frank Whiting, diameter, 9½ in.   **$1,700/12**

PLATES, service, set of 12, Baltimore Rose pattern, Schofield Company, early 20th century.   **$9,000/set**

PLATES, service, set of 12, rims of ribbon-bound running laurel, borders embossed with cartouches alternating with leaf and flower-flanked shells, Graff, Washbourne & Dunn, New York, 1922.   **$6,500/set**

PLATES, service, set of 12, with ribbon-tied reeded rims, borders engraved with husk festoons, Woodside Sterling Co., c. 1920.   **$3,300/set**

PLATTER, fish, shaped oval with gadrooned border, on 4 scrolling bracket feet, Fisher, length, 18 in.   **$400**

PLATTER, meat, rectangular, with in-curved corners and molded border, Redlich, late 19th century, 20¼ in.   **$700**

PLATTER, oval, the wide border chased with scrolling acanthus and vacant cartouches within laurel border, International, length, 19¾ in.   **$700**

PLATTER, well and tree, applied shell-and-scroll border engraved with foliage sprays on each side, Howard and Company, c. 1899, length, 16 in.   **$1,400**

PLATTERS, pair, circular, with plain surfaces, molded rims, engraved with crests, diameter, 12¼ in.   **$350/pr**

PRESENTATION CUP, 3 handles, pyriform, on circular foot with fluted base, chased with factory scene and presentation inscription, Gorham, 1892, height, 8¾ in.   **$450**

SALVER, circular, on 3 bracket feet with scroll-and-bead borders, J. W. Tucker, New York, c. 1870, diameter, 12 in.
   $480

SAUCEBOAT on stand, the sauceboat marked Ball, Black and Co., oval, on spreading foot with die-rolled laurel border, stand with foliate bracket supports, length, 8 in.   **$600/2**

SAUCEBOATS, pair, George II style, bombé circular form on 3 hoof feet, with bifurcated scrolling handle, Gebelein, Boston, length, 8¼ in.   **$850/pr**

SAUCEBOATS, pair, repoussé, navette form on oval bases, rising loop floral handles, chased with flowerheads and foliage on stippled ground, Heer-Schofield Co., Baltimore, length over handle, 9⅔ in.   **$850/pr**

TEA AND COFFEE SERVICE, comprising teapot, coffeepot, covered sugar bowl, cream pitcher, waste bowl, and kettle on stand, octagonal with reeded border and squared handles, retailed by Bigelow, Kennard and Co. **$2,600/set**

TEA AND COFFEE SERVICE, comprising teapot, coffeepot, covered sugar bowl, cream pitcher, and waste bowl, each octagonal with squared handles, by Durgin. **$700/set**

TEA AND COFFEE SERVICE, comprising teapot, coffeepot, cream pitcher, covered sugar bowl, and waste bowl, each octagonal on stepped base with squared handles, Dominick and Haff, in Queen Anne pattern. **$1,300/set**

TEA AND COFFEE SERVICE, comprising teapot, coffeepot, cream pitcher, waste bowl, sugar bowl, and kettle on stand, Gorham, in Plymouth pattern. **$1,200/set**

TEA AND COFFEE SERVICE, comprising teapot, coffeepot, sugar bowl, waste bowl, and cream pitcher, each ovoid on spreading foot with squared handles and curving spouts, Reed and Barton. **$1,000/set**

TEA AND COFFEE SERVICE, 5 pieces, Georgian pattern, tray with inscription, comprising coffeepot, teapot, covered sugar, creamer, and waste with matching tray, Reed and Barton, Taunton, MA, 1941. **$3,750/set**

TEA AND COFFEE SERVICE, Queen Anne style, comprising teapot, covered sugar bowl, cream pitcher, and waste bowl, each pyriform on spreading foot with S-scroll handles, Webster. **$1,450/set**

TEA AND COFFEE SET with matching 2-handle tray, comprising teapot, coffeepot, hot water kettle on lampstand, creamer, 2-handle sugar bowl, waste bowl, of lobed bulbous form engraved around the shoulders with foliage, scrolls, shells, and diaperwork, Durgin for Gorham Mfg. Co., 20th century.
$5,000/set

TEA AND COFFEE SET with tray in Navarre pattern, comprising coffeepot, teapot, covered sugar, creamer, waste, and tray, Watson Co., Attleboro, MA, c. 1908–29. **$3,000/set**

TEA AND COFFEE SET, Iris pattern, comprising coffeepot, teapot, covered sugar, creamer, and tray, Gorham, 1873.
$3,750/set

TEA AND COFFEE SET, Adam pattern, comprising coffeepot, teapot, hot water kettle on stand, large creamer, large covered sugar, and waste bowl, unmarked, Shreve & Co.   **$2,500/set**

TEA AND COFFEE SET, 7 pieces, comprising teapot, coffeepot, hot water jug, covered sugar bowl, creamer, waste bowl, and hot water kettle on lampstand, of melon shape embossed with sprays of full-blown flowers, on leafy scroll feet, J. E. Caldwell, Philadelphia, c. 1900.   **$3,750/set**

TEA AND COFFEE SET, 6 pieces, comprising teapot, coffeepot, covered sugar bowl, creamer, waste bowl, and hot water kettle on lampstand, of partly fluted baluster form, applied borders of scrolls and flowers, loop finials, Gorham Mfg. Co.

$2,250/set

TEA AND COFFEE SET, 6 pieces, comprising teapot, coffeepot, creamer, waste bowl, covered sugar bowl, and hot water kettle on lampstand, of oval form in-curved at the angles, and chased with bands of flowers above a band of lobes, covers with patera finials, Bigelow, Kennard & Co., Boston, c. 1882. **$3,750/set**

TEA AND COFFEE SET, 6 pieces, Indian style, comprising teapot, coffeepot, creamer, covered sugar bowl, waste bowl, and kettle on lampstand, partly fluted and chased with panels of Indian-style flowers, Gorham Mfg. Co., 1881–82. **$6,000/set**

TEAPOT, individual, with repoussé floral bands, Gorham, late 19th century, height, 6 in.   **$230**

TEA SERVICE, comprising teapot, covered sugar bowl, and covered cream pitcher, vase form with beaded borders and covers with disk-and-bead finials, by Wood and Hughes.

$1,500/set

TEA SET, 5 pieces, early 20th century, enriched by chased leaves.   **$1,700/set**

TEA SET, lobed oval, footed, acanthus handles, comprising teapot, coffeepot, sugar, creamer, and waste, Dominick & Haff.

$800/set

TEA SET, Louis XIV style, comprising teapot, creamer, sugar, 12-in. tray, Towle.   **$600/set**

TEA SET, 6 pieces, allover embossed florals, inclusive of swing kettle, Gorham, late 19th century.   **$3,675/set**

Medallion tea service, Ball, Black & Co., $4,000. **Courtesy of Christie's East, New York.**

TEA SET, small, 3 pieces, Hampton Court pattern, Reed & Barton, early 20th century. **$650/set**

TEA SET, 3 pieces, plain footed pear shape, Rogers, early 20th century. **$250/set**

TRAY, Art Nouveau, Black, Starr & Frost, oval, undulating border, cast and chased with sinuously scrolling foliage and flowerheads on lightly hammered ground. **$1,700**

TRAY, bread, Gorham, Chantilly pattern, early 20th century. **$350**

TRAY, Chippendale style, plain surface with lobed circular border, reverse gadrooning on each lobe, Gorham Mfg. Co., 1953, diameter, 14¼ in. **$600**

TRAY, circular, the pierced undulating border with foliate running scrolls and scrolling foliage, Howard and Co. **$750**

TRAY, oval, repoussé with wide border of chased flowers, gadrooned, by J. E. Caldwell and Co., length, 14 in. **$550**

TRAY, oval, A.G. Schultz & Co., Baltimore, wide border repoussé with flowerheads on stippled ground, length, 20 in. **$1,700**

TRAY, oval, with gadrooned border, Gorham, 1941. **$450**

TRAY, rectangular, with molded border, engraved with laurel border, Whiting, 1911.   **$1,100**

TRAY, Rococo Revival style, border worked in repoussé and heavily chased with a scrolling foliate and arboreous blossom pattern, J.E. Caldwell & Co., Philadelphia, late 19th century.
                                                       $4,000

TRAY, tea, mahogany wood face with a pierced sterling frame and beaded edge with an openwork handle on either end, Shreve & Co., length, 22½ inches.   **$275**

TRAY, tea, rectangular, the raised and undulating border chased with berried foliage, Dominick & Haff, Newark, NJ, 1900, length, 26½ in.   **$2,600**

TRAY, tea, rectangular, the rim applied with scrolled waves, matching loop handles, Tiffany & Co., New York, c. 1895, length over handles, 19 in.   **$7,500**

TRAY, tea, 2 handles, rectangular, with ribbon-tied running leaf-tip rim, the border engraved with panels of chased foliage and swags at intervals, Black, Starr & Frost, New York, 20th century, length over handles, 34 in.   **$3,500**

TRAY, 2 handles, shaped rectangular, the handles with scroll joins, engraved with presentation inscription, length, 24 in.
                                                         $900

TROPHY, large, 2 handles, vase shape on stepped circular base with C-scroll handles, Durgin, height, 14¼ in.   **$500**

TUREEN, .950 standard, cast applied handles formed as stags' heads, domed cover engraved and surmounted by finial formed as stag, Ball, Black & Co., 1860, height, 13½ in.   **$2,750**

TUREEN, soup, on stand, covered, tureen oval on domed base with die-rolled laurel borders at foot and rim, handles formed as stags' heads, Ball, Black & Co.   **$4,000/2**

TUREEN, soup, small, chased with a variety of flowers in high relief on matte ground, gadroon loop handles, the tray-form base of conforming shape, Bigelow, Kennard & Co., Boston, c. 1881.   **$3,500/2**

TUREEN, with cover, high Renaissance Revival taste, applied with moose-head handles, Wood & Hughes, 1870. **$3,500/2**

TUREEN AND COVER, Japanese style, 2 handles, oval, the foot and domed cover chased with peapods, sides chased with a swimming turtle and a flying heron, Whiting Mfg. Co., Providence, RI, late 19th century.   **$8,000/2**

TUREENS, sauce, pair, oval with reeded band, bright-cut engraved with geometric bands, Bailey, Banks and Biddle Company, length, 9½ in. **$500/pr**

VASE, baluster form, unmarked sterling silver, weighted base, height, 12 in. **$85**

VASE, basket form, pierced rim, swing handle, Black, Starr and Frost, height, 11½ in. **$1,000**

VASE, chased with rococo motifs, Gorham, early 20th century. **$1,200**

VASE, flower, trumpet outline with wavy lip on a spreading domed circular base, plain form with a concentric triple-threaded band on weighted base, Shreve & Co., San Francisco, c. 1915, height, 17½ in. **$385**

VASE, flower, trumpet form with a swing handle and resting on a domed oval foot, the handle and flaring lip pierced and chased with an apple blossom design, Graff Washbourne & Dunn, New York, c. 1914, height with handle, 17 in. **$700**

American sterling bud vase surmounted by butterfly, c. 1865. Courtesy of Jeri Schwartz. Photo by J. Auslander.

VASE, large, trumpet form, chased and applied with sinuously scrolling irises, weighted, Shreve & Company, height, 22 in.

$2,700

VASE, medallion, body with tab handles formed as medallion roundels surmounted by beads, the body applied with medallion head in oval surrounded by engraved strapwork, William Gale, Jr., c. 1865, height, 5 in.   **$900**

VASE, 3 handles, bulbous form with 3 sinuously scrolling handles and wavy lip, Gorham, height, 5½ in.   **$240**

VASES, pair, shipboard wall, of demi-vase form with a band of embossed vertical lobes and applied rim of overlapping leaves, Graff, Washbourne & Dunn, New York, c. 1910.   **$1,500/pr**

WAITER, shaped square with repoussé foliate border engraved with diaperwork and circular wreath, Howard & Co., diameter, 9 in.   **$350**

WINE COASTERS, pair, interior with a band of anthemia, exterior with a band of elaborate scrolls, wood bases, Whiting, New York, c. 1890, diameter, 5¾ in.   **$800/pr**

WINE COASTERS, pair, large, with applied grapevine rims and bombé sides, mahogany bases inlaid with grapevine, c. 1900, diameter, 8⅜ in.   **$1,500/pr**

Continental

BASKET, flower, sterling silver, of vase form with ribbon-tied reeded border, body pierced and chased with rose swags and cornucopia, pierced swing handle with metal liner, German, height, 11¾ in.   **$750**

BASKET, bread, sterling silver, oval, pierced with scene of courtiers in landscape, border chased with floral swags, German, length, 18 in.   **$750**

BASKET, cake, oblong swing handle on a rising shaped-oblong base with shell feet, bright-cut with arabesques and with a molded rim, 1861.   **$700**

BASKET, oval, body pierced and chased with floral garlands and musical instruments, applied with rams' heads on each end, with pierced swing handle, 9½ in.   **$900**

BEAKER on fluted circular foot, applied with two wriggle-work bands and engraved with scrolling foliage and flowers, Christoffer Bauman, Swedish, Hudiksval, 1792.   **$360**

BEAKER, Dutch, 19th century, campana shape, engraved with a band of stylized foliage. **$150**

BEAKER, German, parcel-gilt with engine-turned tapering sides, probably by Johann Beckert (III), Augsburg, c. 1690. **$2,500**

BEAKER, German, silver-gilt, of tapered cylindrical form with slightly everted rim, broad matte band, Jeremias Rutter, Nuremberg, c. 1630. **$2,100**

BEAKER, late 17th century, German, parcel-gilt, matte sides simulating shagreen, Johann Jakob Petrus, Augsburg, c. 1680. **$2,200**

BEAKER, later chased with two biblical vignettes surrounded by rococo scrolling foliage, Scandinavian, 1701. **$575**

BEAKER, Norwegian, embossed around the sides with flowers and raised on 3 ball feet, Soren Joensen, Trondheim, c. 1695. **$1,400**

BEAKER, parcel-gilt, embossed with a band of scrolling leaves above 3 ball feet, German, late 17th century, height, 2³/₈ in. **$700**

BEAKER, Scandinavian, of tapered cylindrical form, the matte body inset with 3 coins, domed cover lightly engraved with festoons and inset with a coin, thumbpiece in the form of a lion wearing a red paste-set crown, early 18th century. **$650**

BEAKER, Swedish Provincial, of tapering shape with flared lip, engraved with flowers, Anders Johann Lignell, Sundsvall, 1810. **$700**

BEAKER, tapering cylindrical form with flaring rim and parcel-gilt band and interior, by Phillipp Spenglin, German, Nuremburg, c. 1690. **$1,600**

BOWL, circular, tapering, base decorated with punch-beading and chased with stylized 8-petal flower, Portuguese, 17th century. **$2,400**

BOWL, fruit, circular, with an applied shell and scroll border, with a cast cherub holding a laurel wreath, 1897, diameter, 11³/₄ in. **$875**

BOWL, fruit, pierced with overall rococo foliage, birds and rose swags, 19th century. **$1,100**

BOWL, hammered, on 3 applied dolphin feet, chased with an armorial and crest. **$300**

German silver mounted punch bowl, with 12 matching cups, chased with scrolls and foliage, $3,800/set. **Courtesy of Christie's East, New York.**

BOWL, Italian, oval fluted form, the sides with 6 applied openwork windows on spreading foot, maker's mark GP with an animal between, Venice. **$450**

BOWL, pierced, circular, scrolling supports, scroll and pendant husk handles, bottom repoussé with busts in laurel wreaths, cornucopia, urns, and foliage, length, 12¼ in. **$300**

BOWL, punch, and 12 matching cups, German, silver-mounted, glass spherical on stepped base chased with rocaille scrolls and foliage, domed cover with figure of bacchant bearing goblet, height, 23 in. **$3,800/set**

BOWL, punch, globular, on domed base with rocaille border, the body and base repoussé with rocaille scrolls and flat-chased with foliate scrolls, height, 12 in. **$1,300**

BOWL, shallow, with reed and tie border, everted rim chased with floral and foliate swags, 19th century, diameter, 11¾ in. **$500**

BOWL, silver-gilt, flat-chased inside below the molded rim with strapwork and foliage on a matte ground, spreading base with lobed rim, bearing pseudo-Augsburg hallmarks, diameter, 8¼ in. **$1,000**

Group of English and French sterling pin on poseys, 1860–1880.
Courtesy of Marion and Robert Pape.

*Pair of George III wine coolers, c. 1790,
Sheffield, estimated value $2,000–$3,000.*
Courtesy of Christie's East, New York.

Right. *American mid-19th-century unmarked
silver presentation trumpet with Royal
cypher flanked by "Stars & Stripes," c. 1850,
$4,000.* Courtesy of Phillips, London.

Left. *American
presentation covered
bowl by John Moore
for Tiffany, c. 1850.
Presented to Capt.
Wm. Symons
commanding the
Royal Mail Steamer
Medway, $18,500.*
Courtesy of
Phillips, London.

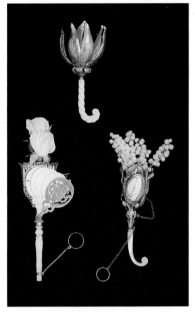

Top. *Gold mechanical posey holder.*
Courtesy of Barbara and Steve Rose.
Bottom. *Novelty posey holders.*
Courtesy of Marion and Robert Pape.

Regency épergne by Matthew Boulton,
Birmingham, estimated value
$7,000–$9,000. Courtesy of Christie's
East, New York.

Irish silver épergne, c. 1770, $16,000. Courtesy of William Doyle Galleries, New York.

Mixed metal Japonisme tureen, Whiting, c. 1880, with applied crabs, crawfish, and floral sprays, $19,000. Courtesy of Christie's East, New York.

Pair of English Sheffield plate wine coolers, c. 1775, $4,000/pair. Courtesy of Phillips, London.

Top. *One of a set of 12 Gorham sterling turtle-form soup bowls, with terrapin spoons having bowls formed as swimming turtles, $40,000/set.* Courtesy of Christie's East, New York.

Bottom. *Pair of Tiffany sterling three-light candelabra in Rococo Revival style, 1873–1891.* Courtesy of Christie's East, New York.

Top. *Set of four George II sterling candlesticks, c. 1750, $14,000/4.* Courtesy of William Doyle Galleries, New York.

Left. *George III sterling basket by Daniel Holy, Sheffield, c. 1778, ornamented with husk swags and masks of Ceres, $2,700.* Courtesy of William Doyle Galleries, New York.

Right. *French Empire-style silver-gilt tea and coffee service on tray, by Odiot, with ram's head and dragon motifs, $7,500.* Courtesy of Christie's East, New York.

German silver-gilt figure of a knight, $1,400. Courtesy of Christie's East, New York.

BOWL, sugar, oval, on 4 paw and acanthus supports, repoussé with bands of foliage, Portuguese, 19th century. **$325**

BOWL, 2 handles, fluted oval with scrolling handles, Austrian, length, 19½ in. **$1,450**

BOX, bird, body chased with scrolling strapwork, birds and grotesques in Renaissance taste. **$750**

BOX, biscuit, 1888, .900, cover chased with putti around a grape barrel, sides chased with musical instruments. **$700**

BOX, spice, multiple, in the form of a spray of 3 pears, largest with 2 compartments, smaller fruits with single compartments, engraved with scrolling foliage on reeded ground, pendant ring, unmarked, German, early 18th century. **$800**

BOX, spice, silver-gilt cartouche shape, hinged cover chased with a flower spray, the sides flat-chased with flowers, divided interior, 4 scroll feet, Peter Christian Rosen, Augsburg, 1763–65, length, 2½ in. **$1,200**

BOX, square, chased floral swags and cornucopia, finial formed as lion bearing shield, length, 5 in. **$750**

BOX, sugar, bombé-shape rounded oblong on openwork floral and scroll feet, chased with rococo flowers and scrolling foliage with a lock and scroll cartouche, Austro-Hungarian, 19th century. **$775**

BOX, sugar, 4 bun feet with hinged cover, German, 6 in.
$400

BOX, sugar, German, oval, chased with flowers, scrolls, and rocaille decoration, raised on shell and scroll feet, Reinhold Gottfried Spitta, Brunswick, 1767. **$3,500**

BOX, sugar, Polish, cocoon thumbpiece, etched with rocaille scrolls. **$850**

BOX, sugar, rectangular form, hinged bail handles, maker's mark A. Lannoyski, c. 1800. **$650**

CANDELABRA, Italian, pair, 4 lights, on scrolling triform openwork base chased with rocaille, shells, and trelliswork, surmounted by fully modeled putto bearing 4 scrolling acanthus branches, height, 17 in. **$2,800/pr**

CANDELABRA, pair, 4 lights, fluted tapered stems rising spreading leafy shoulders, foliate scroll branches, O. Pini, 1839.
$4,200/pr

CANDELABRA, pair, 2 lights, each with tiered circular foot, foliate stem, flanked at the base by 4 upward-beaded scrolls, issuing 2 curling arms, centered by grapevine finials, Copenhagen, 1933, height, 6½ in.　　　**$2,300/pr**

CANDLESTICKS, German, pair, columnar with spiral flutes, with acanthus-leaf capitals, Munich, 1831, Louis Wollenwocher, height, 9½ in.　　　**$750/pr**

CANDLESTICKS, pair, baluster form, spirally ribbed and fluted, detachable nozzles, Liege, 1772.　　　**$3,500/pr**

CANDLESTICKS, pair, baluster form, foliate bracket supports, with beaded bands.　　　**$400/pr**

CANDLESTICKS, pair, domed circular bases, columnar stems, beaded borders and detachable nozzles, Naples, late 18th century.　　　**$1,100/pr**

CANDLESTICKS, pair, Italian, on raised shaped circular bases, cast octagonal baluster stems, with lobed and fluted borders, Turin, mid-18th century.　　　**$5,000/pr**

CANDLESTICKS, pair, sterling silver, formed as Corinthian columns on stepped square bases, German, height, 13 in.　　　**$1,100/pr**

CANDLESTICKS, Polish, pair, on square bases, baluster-form stems with radiating leaves at neck, height, 9¼ in.　　　**$750/pr**

CENTERPIECE chased with laurel swags and ribbon-tied vacant cartouches, metal liner, early 20th century.　　　**$1,200**

CENTERPIECE, oval, applied with ribbon bows, pierced and chased with laurel swags and lion mask, German, late 19th century, length, 14¾ in.　　　**$3,000**

CENTERPIECE, pierced, late 19th century, oval, with rocaille scroll handles, the sides pierced with rocaille scrolls and birds amid foliage, length over handles, 19½ in.　　　**$950**

CHALICE, hammered gilt bowl, 10-sided stem with faceted, striated agate knop and spreading 5-sided base applied with a gilt stylized cross, Marcel Wolfers, Brussels, 1929, .900 standard.　　　**$1,600**

COFFEE AND TEA SERVICE of baluster form, coffeepot, teapot, and 2 handle sugar bowl with domed covers, richly chased and embossed with rocaille shells and scrolls, Italian, c. 1880.　　　**$2,000/set**

COFFEEPOT, Dutch Empire style, early 19th century, of bombé oval form on oval foot and chased foliate knop.　　　**$950**

COFFEEPOT, late 19th century, marked Moller, Trondhjem, with bud finial, body hammered and chased with flowers.

$500

COFFEEPOT, Maltese, 19th century, beaded vase shape, spout with bird's-head terminal, cover chased and embossed with rococo flowers, shells, and scrolling foliage. **$2,100**

COFFEE SET, 3 pieces, tête-à-tête, with chased repoussé panels of scrolls, flowers, and birds on a pricked ground divided by rows of bellflowers, German, post-1888, .800 standard.

$300/set

COMPOTES, pair, of silver-gilt and cut glass in Empire style, raised on swan-form stems, the scalloped glass oval bodies with scroll handles, c. 1900. **$700/pr**

COMPOTES, pair, cut glass, the bowls each supported by 3 parrots on ring perches, rising circular bases chased with acanthus leaves, the rim mounts pierced with vines and with scroll handles, 19th century. **$375/pr**

COVER, meat, circular, with crown finial, by C.C. Herman, Denmark. **$400**

Viennese silver stemmed cup, c. 1866, $1,700. **Courtesy of Robert W. Skinner Gallery, Bolton, MA.**

CUP, covered, .800 standard, trumpet-shape body with a frieze band of centaurs fighting mounted Amazons, on a bulbous stem with 4 lion masks on a pricked matte ground surmounted with a classical draped female holding a shield, German, Renaissance style, height, 16½ in.   **$900**

CUP, covered, German, mid-19th century, base chased with pineapple lobes surmounted by figure of archer with crossbow, cover with finial formed as urn of flowers, height, 17½ in.

$1,100

CUP, German, silver-gilt, double-formed as a pair of pear-shape vessels raised on domed bases, chased with scrolling flowers on matte ground, height, 16¾ in.   **$1,000**

CUPS, tumbler, set of 12, each circular with gilt interior, fitted case, Bulgari.   **$2,600/set**

DECANTER, liquor, oblong, glass cut with arabesques, the beaded openwork mount pierced and stamped with 18th-century-style figures surrounded by arabesques, finial formed as a putto.   **$400**

DECANTER, mounted cut glass with silver squared handle, collar and hinged flat cover, with ball thumbpiece, German, height, 8¼ in.   **$400**

DISH, bonbon, Dutch style, oval, on cast foliate feet, the center chased with 2 figures with buildings beyond, the border with birds, insects, and flowers, applied scroll handle with grotesque beast.   **$150**

DISH, bonbon, lobed and textured shaped oval, applied with 2 scroll handles and chased with fruit and foliage, late 19th century.   **$300**

DISH, bonbon, pierced shaped oval, decorated with bust portraits and ribbon-and-laurel swags, with reed-and-tie rim, German.   **$125**

DISH, bonbon, 2 handles, pierced, on applied ribbon-and-scroll feet, chased with 18th-century-style figures, 1901.   **$200**

DISH, circular, chased with rider in landscape, panels of flowers alternating with sheaves of wheat, Hungarian, 12½ in.

$500

DISH, German, oval, the sides pierced with trelliswork and chased fruit and rocaille scrolls, joined by pendant swags, length, 13 in.   **$450**

DISH, serving, Dutch style, Austro-Hungarian import mark for 1891–1901, rustic genre scene in repoussé and border of various fruits, diameter, 12 in. **$650**

DISH, sideboard, embossed with a Louis XVI court ballroom scene, embossed with figures supporting globes, arms of France with Victory supporters surrounded by strapwork, birds, and monsters, German. **$1,200**

DISH, sideboard, German, oval, with crimped border and wide border of strapwork and fruit enclosing scene of sea goddess and putti, length, 13½ in. **$300**

DISH, sideboard, Italian, circular, with wide, boldly chased border of foliate scrolls within crimped border, diameter, 16½ in. **$400**

DISH, sideboard, oval, German Baroque style, chased with putti and dolphins, length, 16 in. **$3,850**

DISH, sideboard, the center embossed with a portrait enclosed by mythical birds' heads and foliage, border embossed with mythical winged dogs, masks, and foliate scrolls, probably Italian, early 18th century. **$2,500**

DISH, vegetable, circular, and cover with cast rococo scroll handles with rococo scrolling foliage, Austro-Hungarian, late 19th century, 13 in. overall **$1,450**

DISHES, pair, formed and chased as shells with leaf-capped scrolled ends, one capped by a putto playing a violin, the other by a putto playing a trumpet, on 4 shell feet, German, late 19th century. **$1,800/pr**

DISHES, serving, 2, repoussé, each circular with wide, boldly chased border of foliage and rocaille scrolls, diameter, 14½ in. **$500/2**

DISH RING, Rococo style with pierced concave sides chased with large birds, scrolls, flowers, and grapes, centered at front and back with a shell-framed cartouche, pseudo-hallmarks, late 19th century, height, 3⅜ in. **$400**

EGG CUP, French, gilt-lined, applied with a frieze of baskets of flowers, with egg spoon in a fitted case. **$150/set**

ÉPERGNE FRAME, scroll wirework on 4 ball feet, fitted with 9 glass vases, 14½ in. **$275**

FIGURE OF A KNIGHT, German, on floral openwork octagonal base, the knight in medieval armor, the helmet with hinged visor, coronet and antlers, holding mace and shield with eagle, height, 9 in. **$1,400**

GLASS HOLDERS, set of 5, pierced and chased with birds, foliage and floral swags with scrolling foliate handles. **$225/set**

HOLY WATER STOUP, shaped backplate stamped with the Pietà and with crucifix finial, with a glass liner, Berthold Muller, late 19th century. **$225**

JARDINIÈRE, part-fluted molded oval, 2 handles, on mask-and-scroll feet, chased with baskets of fruit and foliage with detachable liner. **$1,200**

JARDINIÈRE, Rococo taste, late 19th century, German. **$750**

JEWELRY CASKET, chased with scenes of peasants hunting, dancing, and drinking in landscapes. **$550**

JUG, claret, cut-glass body with silver collar chased with Florentine scrolls, the scrolling handle with grotesque mask trailing foliage. **$700**

JUG, claret, German, Art Nouveau, cut-glass body, silver reeded handle, 13½ in. **$1,400**

JUG, claret, German, bulbous glass body with hammered-silver squared handle, collar, and cover, Gebruder Friedlander, height, 9 in. **$320**

JUG, cream, figural cow, in the style of John Schuppe, foliate- and floral-chased hinged cover with an applied bee. **$650**

JUG, cream, figural cow, in the style of John Schuppe, hinged cover chased with flowers and foliage with applied bee finial, Bertold Muller, 1908. **$1,000**

JUG, German, covered, baluster shape on circular foot chased and engraved with vacant rocaille cartouche, Christoph Conrad Meyer, Berlin, c. 1765. **$2,500**

JUG, hot milk, German, roses and scrolls pierced with trelliswork, rustic handle. **$875**

JUG, hot water, reeded molded oval pedestal with ebonized wood handle. **$600**

JUG, hot water, with wicker-covered scroll handle, and stylized foliate mounts. **$150**

JUG, novelty, modeled as a fish, oval base chased to simulate waves, German, 1899. **$1,200**

JUG, Portuguese, silver-mounted, glass cylindrical body mounted with scrolling spout and dolphin head join, spout with satyr's head, with flower finial, Oporto, late 19th century, height, 11 in. **$700**

JUGS, claret, pair, glass bodies cut with flowers within trellis and enclosed by Renaissance-style mounts and dolphin-and-scroll handles, late 19th century, German. **$3,500/pr**

KETTLE on stand, the spiral-fluted pyriform kettle with scrolling bail handle and removable fluted cover, the stand with 4 scrolling supports holding spirit lamp, German. **$1,200**

KOVSH AND SPOON, typical form engraved, the spoon with fig-shape bowl and rope-twist handle, Finnish, 1927. **$400/2**

LAMPS, table, pair, with mottled green onyx shafts supported by a circular silver foot on a square base, the shafts capped by a silver nozzle and rim for a shade support, electrified, Italian, height, 9¼ in. **$225/pr**

MODEL of a cock pheasant with detachable head and realistically chased plumage, 1913, 14¼ in. **$1,200**

MUG, child's, German, of tapering shape on claw feet engraved with swirling flowers and prick-dot wavy bands, Johann Alois Seethaler, Augsburg, 1808. **$325**

NEF, three-masted, with sails and rigging, on a stand with dolphin supports. **$525**

OIL AND VINEGAR STAND, 19th century, Italian, on scrolling foliate feet, central columnar handle with circular loop handle, fitted with 2 cut-glass vase-shape jugs with applied scroll handles. **$750**

OIL AND VINEGAR STAND, boat shape, with pierced Greek Key frieze decoration. **$125**

PITCHER, water, pear form, on flared circular foot, the everted lip extending to the strap handle, Kaye Fisker for A. Michelsen, Copenhagen, height, 10½ in. **$950**

PLATTER, circular, reeded shape decorated with ribbon and laurel swags, Austro-Hungarian. **$600**

PLATTER, meat, German, Bernstein, post-1888, length, 22 in. **$750**

PLATTER, meat, mid-18th century, Provincial Louis XV with shaped molded rim, the border engraved with later armorials, length, 13¾ in. **$1,000**

PLATTER, oval, applied with a rococo foliate border, Austro-Hungarian, late 19th century. **$550**

PLATTER, oval, 17th-century style, center chased with a vignette of 3 classical figures within a landscape, rim with further classical figures and rococo flowers and foliage, 14¾ in.
$275

SALVER, circular, with applied scrolling foliate border, diameter, 13 in.
$300

SALVER, circular, with applied foliate border, Austro-Hungarian.
$175

SALVER, circular, on leaf and shellcapped lion's-paw feet, border stamped with rococo shells and scrolls, Portuguese. **$275**

SAUCE BOAT, sterling, double-lipped oval form on domed foot with applied laurel band, on shaped oval stand, German.
$350/2

SUGAR BASIN, Austro-Hungarian, 19th century, swing handles pierced and stamped with flowers, shells, and scrolling foliage cartouches, with glass liner.
$325

SUGAR BASIN, beaded and foliate-pierced and chased tapering boat-shape pedestal, fitted with glass liner, German.   **$300**

SUGAR BASIN, oblong, swing-handled pedestal, shaped rim bright-cut with arabesques, Dutch, 1861.
$275

TABLE OIL LAMP, stem rising from a 2-handle vase, repeated on the cover, circular font with bacchanal mask sconces, chased with stiff leaves and hung with an extinguisher, probe, pair of snuffers and pair of tweezers, Italian, 19th century.
$4,100/set

TABLE ORNAMENT, pair of pheasants, 20th century with hinged wings and glass eyes, both stamped Sterling, lengths, 18½ in.
$1,300/pr

TABLE ORNAMENTS, figures of pheasants, 2, length, 18 in.
$1,300/2

TABLE ORNAMENTS, pair, cock form, 11½ in.   **$750/pr**

TANKARD, 18th-century style, tapering cylindrical on molded base with S-scroll handle, the domed cover with scrolling thumbpiece, Buccellati, height, 7½ in.   **$940**

TANKARD, possibly Indian, bulbous circular form with long cylindrical neck and thumbpiece formed as rampant lion bearing shield, chased with exotic animals and horsemen in landscape, height, 10½ in.
$240

Viennese silver tazza, c. 1866, with relief decoration, $3,500. Courtesy of Robert W. Skinner Gallery, Bolton, MA.

TAZZA, early 18th-century, Spanish Colonial, with slightly raised rim, the surface incised with concentric lines, screw-on molded pedestal foot, diameter, 10¾ in. **$650**

TAZZA, pair, late 19th century, German, silver-gilt, oval bases applied with lizards and winged monster supports, stems formed as caryatid scrolls with claw feet, bodies chased with masks and Gothic aprons, dish-form covers chased with reserves of fruit and flowers, with paw feet for use separately, height, 10¼ in. **$3,500/pr**

TAZZA, stem elaborately molded and applied with full-relief cherubs, swans, swags, lion's head and paws, and borders, Austria, 1866. **$3,500**

TEA AND COFFEE SERVICE, German, 4 pieces partly spiral fluted, globular, with foliate-chased frieze decoration.

$950/set

TEA AND COFFEE SET, Austrian silver, coffeepot, teapot, hot water pitcher, creamer, and 2-handle sugar bowl, lobed shape with matching oval tray. **$2,750/set**

TEA CADDY, oval, with lift-off cover stamped with putti, shells, flowers, and scrolling foliage, Berthold Muller, Dutch, 1898.   **$300**

TEA SERVICE, German, comprising teapot, coffeepot, cream pitcher, and covered sugar bowl, chased with panels of strapwork, covers with faceted knop finials, on shaped rectangular tray with molded border enclosing band of pendant foliage, length of tray, 18¼ in.   **$1,700/set**

TEA SET, Austrian, cased, in Chinese style with relief figural decoration on lobed bodies, comprising teapot, creamer, sugar, and tray, J. C. Klinkosch, Vienna, c. 1900.   **$1,700/set**

TEA SET, comprising teapot, creamer, 2-handle sugar bowl and waste bowl, with compressed circular bodies chased with flowers, scrolls, and diaper, scroll feet, Bramfeld & Gutruff, Hamburg, c. 1845.   **$1,000/set**

TRAY, Dutch, 19th century, beaded and reeded oval gallery, ground chased with vignettes of rural figures in the style of Tenniers surrounded by rococo marks and scrolling foliage, 13¼ in.   **$800**

Austrian tea tray, $1,300. Pair of German columnar candlesticks, $1,100/ pair. Austrian two-handled bowl, $1,450. **Courtesy of Christie's East, New York.**

TRAY, oval, reeded border with rocaille scrolls at intervals, leaf-clad handles with stylized shell and scrolls, Italian, length, 26 in. **$1,100**

TRAY, Portuguese, rectangular, on 4 paw-and-foliate supports, with openwork gallery of foliage and rope twist, with scrolling handles, length over handles, 20 in. **$500**

TRAY, tea, Austrian, oval, with molded laurel-leaf border and 2 laurel handles, length over handles, 26½ in. **$1,600**

TRAY, tea, 2 handles, rectangular, with reeded border, Austrian, length, 29 in. **$1,300**

TRAY, trinket, shaped, enameled with mythological figures in landscapes, Austro-Hungarian. **$2,800**

TUREEN, soup, and cover, circular, with lobed sides and ovolo rim, scroll handles and domed cover with fluted urn finial topped by a flowerhead, Swiss, Georg Adam Rehfuss, Berne, c. 1840, height, 9¾ in. **$2,700/2**

TUREEN, soup, and cover, early 20th century, boat shape, embossed with lobes and chased with flowers, harp-shape handles, finial in the form of an infant triton on swan, probably Spanish, length, 19 in. **$2,300/2**

TUREEN, soup, applied with anchor, shells, and scrolling dolphins supporting the tureen, chased with sailing scene within cartouche of sails and rocaille scrolls, the scrolling entwined rope-twist handles with shell joins, unmarked, length over handles, 18½ in. **$2,200**

URNS, pair, covered, chased with flutes, acorn finials. **$300/pr**

VASE, partly fluted, tapering, on a spreading circular foot applied with a band of waved decoration, 9¼ in. **$190**

VASES, pair, covered, baluster form, swags of flowers and spiral flutes, dolphin-form handles, winged putti finials, German, late 19th century. **$7,500/pr**

VASES, pair, modeled as double-ended cornucopia, cast figures of a putto playing a lute, the sides chased with courting couples, 1897. **$3,000/pr**

WALL SCONCES, pair, Austrian, 19th century, parcel-gilt, silver-mounted with rococo scrolling foliage, drip pans chased with shells and foliage. **$2,200/pr**

WASH BASIN, 20th century, Portuguese, shell form, deeply fluted and with ruffled edge, with a chained stopper and silverplated forked wall bracket, width, 17½ in.   **$2,000**

WICK TRIMMERS, pair, silver handles, steel on baluster supports, late 18th century.   **$90/pr**

WINE COOLER, scrolling acanthus handles, scrolling rim applied with flowers, scrolls and dentilated border, Italian.

$900

WINE COOLERS, pair, scrolled rim and handles, reverse on either side of body depicting a river, goddess, and cupid, hallmarked.   **$4,250/pr**

English

BASKET, cake, foliate-pierced, circular, swing handles, applied stylized paw feet, Henry Wilkinson & Co., Sheffield, 9¼ in.

$375

English George III sterling pierced dessert basket, $7,000. Courtesy of Phillips, London.

BASKET, cake, oval, with reeded rims and swing handle, the border engraved and pierced with bands of ribbonwork and conjoined patera, John Emes, London, 1805, length, 14⅛ in.

$1,400

BASKET, repoussé, rococo shell and flower designs, bail handle, London, 1811.

$2,300

BASKET, sugar, Edwardian reproduction of a Georgian sugar basket with swing handle, paneled over body, bright-cut frieze of interlinked leaf motifs and wriggle decorative rim, Chester, 1902.

$400

BEAKER, "hob and nob," barrel shape, McHattie & Fenwick, Edinburgh, 1799.

$1,500

BEAKER, with a molded rim and presentation inscription in Latin, Henry Archer, Sheffield, 1901.

$110

BEAKERS, pair, tapered cylindrical form engraved with crests and mottoes, Robert & Samuel Hennell, London, 1804, height, 3⅜ in.

$1,300/pr

Irish sugar basin, Dublin, 18th century. Courtesy of Alice and Derek Hamilton.

BEER JUG, covered, baluster form, lower part of the body with a frieze of acanthus leaves, cast scroll thumbpiece and floral- and foliate-ornamented silver handle, Charles Price, 1824.

$4,000

BOTTLES, oil and vinegar, in George III taste, with beaded mount, beaded scroll handle, cover with shell thumbpiece, Charles Stuart Harris, London, 1883. **$375/pr**

BOWL, circular, plain, with cast vine-and-leaf border with rope girdle, supported by 3 cast winged cherubs on a circular base, Edinburgh, 1934. **$1,800**

BOWL, fruit, foliate-pierced oval on a rising foot, the rim applied with rococo scrolling foliage, Henry Archer, Sheffield, 10 1/2 in. **$600**

BOWL, punch, wide inverted pear shape, chased spiral scrolls and flowers, Martin & Hall, Sheffield, 1899, diameter, 14 1/2 in.

$2,500

BOWL, silver-gilt, plain, circular, with bead-and-reel borders, domed foot with cast stem pierced and chased with a frieze of roses and leaves, A.E. Jones, Birmingham, 1974. **$1,000**

BOWL, small, circular, on domed foot with armorial engraving, Robert Luke, Glasgow, c. 1734, diameter, 4 1/4 in. **$450**

BOX, powder, plain, compressed circular form with lift-off cover, London, 1912, diameter, 5 1/2 in. **$250**

BOX, sandwich, hinged cover engraved with two crests and mottoes within garter cartouches, Rawlings and Summers, London, 1855. **$450**

BOX, trinket, oval, on cabriole legs, tortoise-shell cover inlaid with ribbon swags, Birmingham, 1910. **$350**

BUTTER SHELL with gadroon borders, on 3 whelk feet, Rebecca Emes & Edward Barnard, 1822. **$900**

BUTTER SHELLS, pair, on whelk feet, the tab handles applied with beaded border, rosettes, and ribbon-tied oval, Hester Bateman, London, 1778. **$1,100/pr**

CAKE STAND, contemporary, circular pedestal base with molded rim. **$325**

CANDLESTICKS, pair, baluster form on rectangular base, bright-cut engraved with flowers and tied swags, George Eaden & Co., Sheffield, 1811, height, 6 1/2 in. **$950/pr**

CANDLESTICKS, pair, cluster columns, stamped with friezes of foliage, detachable nozzles, Edward Hutton, London, 1890, height, 10 3/4 in. **$600/pr**

English George III sterling coffee biggin, c. 1802, $750. Courtesy of Christie's South Kensington, London.

CASTORS, pair, George III, urn form on foot with acorn finials, Thomas Daniel, London, 1780. **$550/pr**

CENTERPIECE, footed form, 2 loop handles with foliate ends, engraved leaf band, Maker PC, London, 1802, height, 12 in. **$3,200**

CENTERPIECE, undulating shaped-diamond base with pierced scrolling supports, surmounted by detachable upper section comprising circular bowl and trumpet-form flower holder with 2 scrolling branches supporting detachable circular dishes, Birmingham, 1919. **$2,750**

CHALICE, contemporary, with a tapering hexagonal stem and compressed ivory knop, height, 6¾ in. **$200**

CHALICE, traveling, with matching paten, George Unite, Birmingham, 1855, engraved with the holy monogram. **$50/2**

COFFEE AND TEA SERVICE, Grecian pattern, ovoid shape, the frosted sides engraved with a frieze of neoclassical figures, warriors, women, priests, and slaves between laurel leaf borders, domed covers with Greek helmet finials, Martin & Hall, 1870. **$3,200/set**

COFFEE AND TEA SERVICE, tapering octagonal bodies, matted and chased, with upper and lower panels of stylized shells, flowers, and leaves, Robert Hennell, 1867.   **$3,800/set**

COFFEEPOT, George III, pyriform, bud-finial, chased with rocaille scrolls and flowerheads, London, 1788.   **$1,800**

COFFEEPOT, pear shape, on pedestal foot, beaded borders, domed cover with urn finial, Hester Bateman, London, 1788, height, 12⅝ in.   **$3,700**

CONDIMENT STAND, the pierced oval sides on 4 claw-and-ball feet with scroll terminals, bright-cut with garlands and urns, the handle rising from the fruitwood base with a divider and terminating in a beaded loop handle, marked, height, 11½ in.   **$350**

CREAM BOAT, with bombé body and waved molded rim, rococo multiscroll handle, shellwork foot with scrolled and fluted border, Paul de Lamerie, London, 1745, length, 4¾ in.

$17,000

CRUET, William IV, rectangular, chased with foliage, fitted with 2 silver-mounted cut-glass castors, London, 1830. **$150**

CRUET FRAME, Warwick, hexafoil on shell feet rising to scrolling supports for bottle frame, central stem terminating in scroll and rocaille handle (lacking bottles), Alexander Johnson, London, 1758.   **$400**

CUP, caudle, baluster form, chased with a bold band of flowers and with scroll handles (repairs at handles), London, 1672.

$1,400

CUP, Queen Anne, with molded rim, girdle, and low domed foot, leaf-capped harp-shape handles, Robert Goble, Cork, c. 1710, height, 6⅝ in.   **$1,600**

CUP, silver-gilt, in Assyrian style, with a frieze of beaded masks and foliate-decorated scroll handle, Chester, 1905.   **$135**

CUP, stirrup, modeled as a fox's head with circular cartouche, monogrammed, Elkington & Co., Birmingham, 1897. **$1,850**

CUP, tumbler, maker's mark partially rubbed, plain form with hammered sides, Richard Gurney & Co., London, 1742. **$225**

CUP, 2 handles, baluster form with molded girdle, Hester Bateman, London, 1788, height, 5¾ in.   **$700**

CUP, 2 handles, later chased with arabesques and with later inscription, mid-18th-century Irish, height, 5 in.   **$300**

DEMITASSE SERVICE, comprising demitasse pot, cream pitcher, and sugar bowl, each of fluted circular form on reeded foot, engraved with crest and motto, by Crichton, London, 1921. **$750/set**

DESSERT STANDS, pair, square with in-curved angles, molded rims, plain surfaces, Crichton & Co., Ltd., London, 1927.
$750/pr

DISH, alms, circular, engraved with a foliate and floral frieze, center engraved with the Lamb of God surrounded by a sunburst, Elkington and Co. Ltd., Birmingham, 1898. **$185**

DISH, bacon, rectangular, beaded rim and reeded ring handles, shallow domed cover with raised urn finial, Burrage Davenport, London, 1781. **$1,750/2**

DISH, bonbon, oval, silver-gilt applied with 2 elaborate caryatid scroll handles, S.B. Thomas, London, 1874, 5¾ in. **$375**

DISH, bonbon, formed as Irish-style dish ring, pierced with scrolling foliage and chased with laurel swags, with glass liner, 4½ in. **$175**

DISH, bonbon, George III, oval, swing handles, on pedestal base, later chased with floral swags, London, 1798. **$200**

DISH, bonbon, swing handles, circular, with punched-out gadroon border, chased with foliage, festooning, and trellis piercing, Edward Aldridge, 1772. **$800**

DISH, bonbon, swing handles, oval, with rope border, pierced with intervals of chased, beaded strips, Samuel Herbert & Co., 1767. **$650**

DISH, butter, cover and base modeled as a butter churn, plain with reeded borders, Charles Fox, 1830. **$1,450/set**

DISH, cheese, George III style, with reeded rim, hinged domed cover, turned-wood handle, E.J. Greenberg, Birmingham, 1925.
$250

DISH, entrée, plain, octagonal with canted corners and cushion-dome cover, gadroon border, 1896–97. **$1,100**

DISH, fruit, Paul de Lamerie reproduction, circular, border flat-chased with shell latticework, within fluted panels below, cast scroll feet, Crichton Bros., 1914. **$775**

DISH, strawberry, fluted, circular, in 18th-century taste, contemporary Irish, 10 in. **$500**

English sterling Victorian egg frame, London, 1868, $700. **Courtesy of Christie's East, New York.**

DISH CROSS, George III, engraved with crest, London, 1771, length, 12½ in.   **$1,350**

DISH CROSS, with pear-shape lamp, swiveling arms and sliding supports, with pierced centers and thread borders, crested, Michael Plummer, London, 1796.   **$1,700**

DISHES, bonbon, pair, boat shape, pierced and stamped floral borders, Birmingham, 1896.   **$200/pr**

DISH RING, circular, pierced and chased with frolicking animals amid rocaille and floral scrolls, Dublin, 1917, diameter, 8¼ in.   **$550**

ÉPERGNE, vase-form stem, domed circular foot, with applied scrolls supporting 3 branches, each with circular detachable basket, surmounted by large circular basket, with hammered finish, James Deakin and Sons, Sheffield, 1910.   **$950**

EWER, Cellini pattern, vase form on domed-foot caryatid handle, body chased with strapwork and grotesques in Renaissance taste, Rawlins and Sumner, London, 1845, height, 12 in.
                                                      $1,500

EWER IN ETRUSCAN STYLE, vase shape, with leaf-tip engraving, applied beard borders, and scrolling reeded handle with lotus flowers, rosette, and grotesque-mask terminal, Stephen Smith, London, 1869.   **$1,100**

Irish silver épergne, c. 1770, Charles Mullin, $16,000. Courtesy of William Doyle Galleries, New York.

GOBLET, body chased in repoussé with scrolls, flowers, and foliage against a pricked ground, foot chased with a ring of flowers and foliage, probably Rebecca Emes/Edward Barnard I (lower initials rubbed), London, 1809. **$400**

GOBLETS, set of 12, each plain with circular base and bowl, James Deakin & Son, Sheffield, 1926, height, 4⅛ in.

$800/set

JARDINIÈRE, circular, plain, on spool rim, with ram's-head drop-ring handles either side, gadroon border, William Burwash, 1813. **$4,000**

JUG, cream, classical ewer body on a square base, with foliate and floral festooning, beaded decoration on the cast handle and borders, Benjamin Bickerton, 1777. **$350**

JUG, claret, "Armada" style, chased with fluting caryatids, masks, animals, birds, fruits, and foliage with caryatid scroll handle and mask spout, Hunt and Roskell, London, 1866.

$1,600

JUG, claret, body divided into vertical panels engraved with birds on fruiting branches, reeded handle capped with applied cast fruiting grapevines, William Edwards, London, 1850.

$850

JUG, claret, parcel-gilt, bulbous, on spreading circular foot, body chased with anthemia and strapwork on stippled ground and applied with putti in guise of classical figures, London, 1845, height, 11¼ in.   **$800**

JUG, cream, baluster form, on spread circular foot, scroll handle, 1973.   **$110**

JUG, cream, cast, scallop below lip with an embossed scroll cartouche depicting a goat, in the background a thatched shed, trees, and foliage, Henry Hayens, 1750.   **$1,400**

JUG, cream, helmet, with bright-cut stylistic foliate frieze, reeded rim and handle, on a raised plain square base, Peter and Ann Bateman, 1795.   **$600**

JUG, cream, pear shape, the baluster body with wavy rim, leaf-capped scroll handle and on 3 cast legs and hoof feet, possibly by David Mowdon, 1759.   **$275**

JUG, cream, reed-edge helmet shape on pedestal, square foot, bright, engraved, William Abdy, 1790.   **$800**

JUG, cream, silver-gilt, pear shape, chased above and below the body with scalloped mantle decoration, beaded scroll handle with seaweed ornamentation, Charles Fox II, 1824.   **$550**

JUG, cream, sparrow beak, body on a raised circular reeded foot, scroll handle, engraved with a crest, Thomas Parr, 1733, for family of Briggs.   **$800**

JUG, cream, the baluster body part concave, a jutting spout chased in the form of a classical head, handle of irregular shape and with flower bosses, D & C Hands, 1868.   **$375**

JUG, hot milk, spirally fluted, bulbous, with S-scroll wood handle, the hinged, domed cover with pierced thumbpiece, London, 1892, height, 7 in.   **$220**

JUG, hot water, vase shape, bead borders, the domed cover with acorn finial, engraved with armorial, Daniel Smith & Robert Sharp.   **$2,550**

JUG, hot water, plain, urn shape, on spread pedestal foot, beaded and hinged domed cover and cast urn finial, Charles Wright, 1782.   **$2,000**

JUG, milk, squat bellied circular form, plain, with a key-pattern frieze, angular reeded handle and wide lip, egg-and-dart border, R & S Hennell, 1802. **$400**

JUG, milk, squat circular, leaf-capped handle, Britannia standard, 1937. **$100**

JUG, wine, tankard form, the ovoid body chased on the lower half with concentric flutes encircling a disk, chased with shells and leafage, the hinged lid with an urn finial, Solomon Hougham, London, 1817. **$500**

KETTLE ON STAND, Queen Anne style, pyriform with spherical finial, Ellis Jacob Greenberg, London, 1928. **$1,400**

MIRROR plateau, circular, silver-mounted, Birmingham, 1910. **$200**

MUG, christening, chased with two vignettes, one of a girl holding a garland of flowers, the other of a cloaked girl, Glasgow, 1862. **$550**

MUG, christening, pear shape, on applied floral-chased foot, body chased with a girl playing with a hoop, a barking dog at her side, London, 1848. **$450**

MUG, cylindrical, on circular foot, with leaf-capped scroll handle, body embossed and engraved with a scene of a goat and her young in a pen, Robert Hennell, 1858. **$600**

MUG, baluster form, with molded foot, the molded double-scroll handle issuing from a theatrical mask, Paul de Lamerie, London, 1738, height, 4 in. **$2,500**

MUSTARD POT, bellied circular, on scroll feet, sides chased with S-shape flutes and foliate borders, cover with flower finial and leaf-capped handle, 1835. **$1,350**

PAIL, cream, in the form of a hooped pail with gilt interior and openwork swing handle, waved rim, Walter Brind, London, 1755, height overall, 3³/₄ in. **$650**

PAIL, cream, swing handle, cylindrical, reeded, Ayme Videau, 1735. **$925**

PLATE, circular, reeded plain, Edinburgh, 1861, diameter, 9¹/₂ in. **$325**

PLATTER, meat, gadroon, foliate shell and anthemia rim, John Bridge, London, 1824, length, 15³/₈ in. **$1,400**

PLATTER, meat, shaped oval, with gardooned border, engraved with crest, John S. Hunt, London, 1846, length, 14 in. **$900**

English Victorian salver, London, 1854, with rocaille border, $1,400.
Courtesy of Christie's East, New York.

PORRINGER, part-fluted, two handles, decorated with a rope-twist body band and with stamped stylized foliate friezes, Benjamin Brewood, London, 1764. **$575**

SALVER, circular, with scrolling rocaille border, chased with band of scrolls, trelliswork, and flowers, William K. Reid, London, 1854, diameter, 18½ in. **$1,400**

SALVER, circular, 4 shaped panel feet decorated with rosettes and upright leaves, with beaded rims, Walter Tweedie, London, 1784. **$500**

SALVER, shaped circular, on 4 hoof feet with molded shell-and-scroll border, engraved with rocaille cartouche enclosing coat of arms, Robert Abercromby, London, 1739, diameter, 12½ in. **$1,600**

SALVER, small, circular, with open-cast fancy trellis rim, with trailing foliage decoration, 3 open cast feet, 1759. **$700**

SALVER, small gallery, circular, with trellis-pierced rim and beaded border, surface engraved with circular floral cartouches and leaves, on 3 cast festooned pierced feet, Stephen Smith, 1871. **$600**

SALVER, small, shaped circular, with molded and shell border, the surface engraved with rocaille armorials, on 3 cast feet, 1760. **$700**

SALVERS, pair, rectangular, with rounded angles, gadroon rims, raised on 4 panel supports, William Bennett, London, 1810, length, 11½ in. **$4,000/pr**

SAUCEBOATS, pair, George II, bombé oval form on 3 scroll-and-hoof feet, London, 1746. **$850/pr**

SKEP HONEY POT, of typical form, the detachable cover with ring finial, gilt interior, Richard Morton & Co., Sheffield, 1798, height, 4⅞ in. **$3,200**

TANKARD, tapered cylindrical form, with hooped sides and engraved vertical lines to simulate a barrel, James Scott and W. Hamy, Dublin, 1811, height, 7⅝ in. **$1,500**

TANKARD, pint, George III baluster style, with leaf-capped double-scroll handle and presentation inscription, height, 5 in. **$225**

TANKARD, baroque vessel with pyriform body, on a spreading threaded circular foot, leaf-capped double-reverse scrolling handle, Thomas Whipham, London, 1748. **$600**

English Charles II tankard, $9,500. Courtesy of William Doyle Galleries, New York.

English George III teapot, London, 1780, on matching American stand, $1,200. Courtesy of Christie's East, New York.

TAZZA, circular, on a rising foot, with a beaded compressed knop, chased with shells, foliage, and fruit, Sheffield, 1885.
$1,000

TEA AND COFFEE SERVICE, footed, with chased and repoussé floral and foliate designs, Martin, Hall & Co., London, hallmarks, 1875. $2,200/set

English George IV tea service, chased with flowers and scrolling foliage, $1,400. Courtesy of Christie's South Kensington, London.

English sterling Victorian tea service with fluted motif, c. 1886, $950.
Courtesy of Christie's South Kensington, London.

TEAPOT, plain drum form, with wood scroll handle and tapering spout, Alexander Field, London, 1799.   **$650**

TEAPOT, melon shape, on leafy scroll feet, embossed with
flowers and foliate scrolls against a matte background, with
bud finial, Robert Hennell, 1842.   **$1,000**

TEAPOT, argyle form, straight side, vertically lobed, raised
scalloped collar with bright-cut ornament, small covered spout
concealed inside, William Plummer, London, 1791.   **$3,300**

English George II sterling tea service with bright cut and reeded borders, c.
1805, $1,400. Courtesy of Christie's South Kensington, London.

TEAPOT, inverted pyriform, on spreading foot, with leaf-clad fluted spout, multiscroll wood handle and domed cover with knop finial, Robert Swanson, 1765.   **$550**

TEAPOT, modern globular, cover with knop finial, body chased with gadrooning and spiral flutes, Walker and Hall, Sheffield.

$275

TEAPOT, oval, with flared rim, bright-cut engraved with frieze of foliage and acorns, Urquhart and Hart, 1802.   **$600**

TEAPOT, spinster, small circular, with a reeded girdle on collet foot, stub spout and wood handle, Joseph Cradock & William K. Reid, 1818.   **$250**

TEA SERVICE, 3 pieces, bright-cut, on claw-and-ball feet, London, 1805.   **$1,400/set**

TEA SERVICE, 3 pieces, caldron shape, chased with animals, birds, and vines in the 18th-century taste, each on lion's-mask and paw feet, cover with swan finial, Dublin, 1900.

$1,000/set

TEA SET, 3 pieces, baluster form, the pleated bodies finely embossed with trailing lilies and leaves, scroll and floral feet, cast lily and foliate finial, John Edward Terry, 1830.   **$1,850/set**

English George III sterling tea kettle and stand, $900. Courtesy of Robert W. Skinner Gallery, Bolton, MA.

TEA SET, 3 pieces, of plain, bellied circular form, collet base, egg-and-dart borders, William Burwash and Richard Sibley I, 1809. **$1,500/set**

TEA SET, 3 pieces, squat circular form, matte bodies chased overall with stylized flowers and leaves, caryatid handles, 1835. **$1,400/set**

TEA URN, George III, urn form, beaded borders, loop handles, engraved coat of arms, Hennell, London, 1781. **$3,200**

TOASTED CHEESE DISH, rectangular, with gadrooned border, the hinged lid with bud finial, turned-wood handle, S.C. Young and Co., 1823. **$1,100**

TOAST RACK, novelty, body simulating bark and the bars each modeled as waterlily leaves, Yapp & Woodward, Birmingham, 1846. **$550**

TOAST RACK, oblong, 6-division wirework on scroll feet, with scrolling foliate handle, London, 1825. **$325**

TRAY, oval, 2 handles, with gadroon borders, raised on bracket feet, engraved with large armorials, Peter & William Bateman, 1812. **$8,000**

TRAY, shaped rim with repoussé and chased floral and shell motifs, engraved with coat of arms and trailing vines, length, 32 in. **$3,200**

TRAY, tea, 2 handles, reeded, bright-cut with a frieze of acorns, fruit, flowers, and foliage, John Hutson, London, 1795, length, 20 in. **$3,200**

TRAY, 2 handles, William and Mary style, plain rectangular form with shaped corners and reeded edges and handles, Crichton Bros., London, 1916. **$1,200**

TRAY, 2 handles, oval, with cast shell-and-scroll border, surface finely engraved with an arabesque-style foliate frieze, gadroon-and-shell handles, George Edward & Son, Sheffield, 1895. **$2,500**

TUREENS, sauce, and covers, pair, oval boat form with fluted lower bodies and covers, reeded rims, loop handles, and urn finials, Henry Chawner, London, 1788, length over handles, 9¾ in. **$1,900/pr**

VASE, Georgian reproduction, plain, urn shape with acanthus leaves and domed cover, surmounted by acorn finial, engraved, Carrington Bros., 1948. **$200**

VASE, trophy, banded and flared cylindrical form, chased with baroque flutes, ribbon-tied swags, masks, and formal foliage, Edinburgh, 1888.   **$2,100**

WAITER, George III, circular, on 3 hoof feet, scrolling border, maker JR, London, 1744, diameter, 7 in.   **$450**

WAITER, with beaded and foliate rim, the border pierced with swags of flowers, Lewis Herne & Francis Butty, London, 1762.
                                                                    $1,600

WINE COOLER, pail shape, with raised handles, removable liner and rim, maker's mark J.D. over W.D., Sheffield, 1929, height, 8½ in.   **$850**

French

BASKET, pseudo-hallmarks, 19th century, swing handle with foliate swag supported by 4 portrait busts of Directoire-style figures, diameter, 4 in.   **$125**

BEAKER, plain, tapering, on a gadrooned rising circular foot, with a molded rim, Paris, c. 1810.   **$225**

BEAKER, sterling silver, inverted bell shape, bowl applied with a shield-shape cartouche, 18th century.   **$325**

French amethyst glass night light with sterling surround, c. 1860. Courtesy of Alice and Derek Hamilton. Photo by J. Auslander.

BOTTLES, pair, silver-gilt mounted, vase shape, glass body overlaid with thistle leaves and flowers, with reeded loop handles, stoppers with thistle finials, early 19th century.

$1,100/pr

BOWL, covered, with ram's-mask and ring handles, pedestal foot with anthemia band, low domed cover with bud finial surrounded by spreading strapwork leaves, Paris, 1798–1809, diameter, 5⅝ in. **$1,500/2**

BOWL, serving, circular, with foliate scrolled handles, the domed cover with scrolling foliate rim with fruit-form finial, Paris, c. 1900. **$800/2**

CAFÉ-AU-LAIT POT, pair, plain, silverplated, coffeepot with tapering angular spout, hot milk jug with wood scroll handle, Christofle. **$110/pr**

CAFÉ-AU-LAIT SERVICE, 4 pieces, Art Deco, Puiforcat, Paris, c. 1920–40, coffeepot, milk pot, sugar bowl, and drinking mug, reeded rims, rosewood handles. **$6,500/set**

CANDELABRA, pair, 20th century, parcel-gilt, composed of 3 conjoined C-scrolls, applied in the center with a gilt triangle with D-form sconces, Jean E. Puiforcat, Paris, height, 3⅝ in.

$9,500/pr

CANDLESTICK, chamber, circular, applied with scroll-and-shell decoration, elongated handle with traces of an armorial, 19th century. **$450**

CANDLESTICKS, Directoire, pair, tapered faceted stems banded with Gothic foliage and rising from acanthus to campana-shape sconces, Jean-Pierre Bibron, Paris, c. 1800.

$1,700/pr

COFFEEPOT of ovoid form with waisted neck, lily leaf borders and scalloped spout terminating in a ram's head, Paris, c. 1825.

$1,300

COFFEEPOT, 19th century, silverplated, vase shape, on 3 leaf-capped paw feet with 2 friezes of foliage and berries, spout with bird's-head terminal, cover with artichoke finial. **$200**

COFFEEPOT, Directoire, pear shape with short fluted spout, stepped cover with bud finial, Joseph Gabriel Genu, Paris, 1798–1809. **$1,800**

COFFEE SET, Louis XV, 3 pieces, Robert Mognart, Paris, c. 1722–27, with vertical bands of arabesque tracery, resting on scrolling feet with grotesque-mask capitals. **$2,000/set**

Pair of French .950 silver standard covered vegetable dishes with artichoke and pomegranate finials. **Courtesy of Christie's East, New York.**

COFFEE SET, modern, 3 pieces in Louis XVI style.   **$850/set**

CUP with double-scroll handles, the shallow circular body applied with strapwork in alternating designs, molded foot, Louis XVI, 18th century.   **$1,200**

CUP AND SAUCER, chocolate, sterling silver, spiral-fluted, with applied cast rococo scroll handle.   **$325/2**

DESSERT STAND, silver-gilt, G. Keller, Paris, the reeded border with acanthus at intervals.   **$375**

DESSERT STANDS, pair, 4 scroll feet, cast, chased and applied with scalework and foliage panels (glass dishes missing), Odiot, Paris, c. 1850.   **$450/pr**

DISHES, 2 matching, each of shaped circular form with tongue-and-dart rim, the border pierced and engraved with shells, flutes, and flowers, on 4 scroll supports, Paris, 20th century, length, 9⅛ in.   **$800/2**

EWERS, pair, 19th century, silver-mounted, Puiforcat, Paris, pierced scroll and foliate frame, 12 in.   **$3,400/pr**

FLATWARE SET, silverplated, Old English style, with ribbon bound threaded border comprising 8 dinner forks, 8 salad/lunch forks, 8 knives, 8 teaspoons, 8 dessert/soup spoons, Christofle.   **$350/set**

JUG, claret, baluster form on silver base, leaf-clad handle, neck with pendant swags, hinged cover with grape-leaf finial, 12 in.   **$1,000**

JUGS, claret, pair, oval, spirally lobed glass bodies applied with chased rococo-style neck and base mounts, height, 11 in.

$1,800/pr

JUGS, claret, pair, spirally ribbed clear glass bodies mounted with silver acanthus leaf–decorated pedestal feet, scroll handles, neck bands and lids with fruit and foliage finial, Cardeilhac, Paris, c. 1900, height, 11¾ in. **$1,900/pr**

MUSTARD POT, cylindrical openwork form, sides with leaf straps and 2 classical lovers holding hands and kneeling before an altar of love, the cover with lily-leaf borders, pinecone finial, and bird's-head handle, Paris, c. 1825. **$400**

MUSTARD POT, openwork with fluted cover, the sides pierced with classical figures and fruit swags in panels, on 3 scroll feet, with glass liner, 19th century. **$175**

MUSTARD POT, vase shape, on a square base with claw-and-bun feet, foliate-decorated domed hinged cover with artichoke finial. **$385**

PLATE, early 20th century, silver-gilt in Empire style with leaf-tip rim, the border applied with female masks flanked by griffins, foliage, and urns on matte ground, on 3 winged-paw feet, diameter, 9½ in. **$1,500**

PLATES, dinner, set of 12, silver-gilt, Regency style, shaped guilloche-enameled rim, borders chased with foliate scrolled strapwork on a matted ground, A. Aucoc, Paris, c. 1900.

$4,500/set

PLATTER, fish, beaded and spot-hammered, shaped oblong.

$1,200

PLATTER, oval, border decorated with foliage, mid-19th century, 17½ in. **$775**

PLATTER, salmon, shaped oval with molded rim, applied with armorials and a coronet. **$900**

PRAYER BOOK, leather bound, printed in 1768, with a tortoise-shell and silver cover, with birds and foliage. **$1,200**

SALVER, 20th century, octagonal, on 4 scroll supports with plain surface, Puiforcat, length, 11 in. **$900**

SAUCEBOAT, Empire design, scrolling spout and handle with swan's-neck terminals and stand, Paris, 1809, length, 12 in.

$1,200

SLICE, fish, Antoine-Adrien Vautrin, Paris, scimitar shape, border of roses, engraved with fish, wood handle with join formed as conch shell issuing fish and eels. **$275**

TEA AND COFFEE SERVICE, 20th century, comprising coffeepot, teapot, creamer, and covered sugar bowl, each of paneled circular section on tiered circular foot, mounted wood handles and finials, Jean E. Puiforcat, Paris. **$3,500/set**

TEA AND COFFEE SET, comprising teapot, coffeepot, covered sugar bowl, creamer, and large coffeepot, Empire style, slender paw feet, animal-head spouts, leaf-tip borders, and bone handles, maker's mark E.E., Paris, late 19th century. **$2,850/set**

TEA AND COFFEE SET, 5 pieces, with matching condiments, in Art Deco taste, comprising teapot, coffee jug, hot water jug, creamer, covered sugar bowl, caster, pair of salt shakers, and pair of pepper shakers, paneled baluster form with vertical bands of beading, c. 1920. **$2,500/set**

TEA AND COFFEE SET, 4 pieces, comprising teapot, coffeepot, covered sugar bowl, creamer, quadrangular baluster form, lobed and fluted angles and panels of Regency-style strapwork, Puiforcat, Paris, late 19th century. **$3,500/set**

TEA SERVICE, small, French Odiot style with silver-gilt rams' heads and dragon motifs. **$7,500/set**

TEA SERVICE, traveling, in fitted box, comprising teapot, kettle on stand, tea caddy, milk flask, sugar tongs, 2 small trays, 2 teaspoons, and 2 china teacups. **$650/set**

TEA SET, small, 3 pieces, Puiforcat, Paris, Louis XVI style, paneled pear-shape bodies applied with festoons and decorated with rams' masks. **$2,500/set**

TRAY, circular, with stiff-leaf border, diameter, 13¾ in. **$500**

TUREEN, circular, fluted rim and matching tab handles, low domed cover with fluted ivory finial, Cardeilhac, Paris, c. 1930, length, 12 in. **$3,500/2**

TUREEN, silver and rosewood, cover with reeded rim and matching band, drum-shape rosewood finial, Jean Puiforcat, Paris, c. 1930–40. **$8,000/2**

TUREEN, soup, 20th century, parcel-gilt, hemispherical form, with gilt everted rim on pedestal foot with inverted gilt rim, cover with 2-tiered flaring knop finial, the top tier gilt, Jean E. Puiforcat, Paris, height, 10 in. **$5,500/2**

TUREEN, soup, cover and stand, of elongated octagonal form, the tureen with tapered sides and large faceted grip handles, slightly domed base and cover with faceted and cluster finial, G. Keller, Paris, c. 1930–40, length of stand, 18¾ in.

$8,500/set

TUREEN, 2 handles, circular, with reeded rims, the handles with foliate knops and shell terminals, the domed cover with cone finial centered by radiating flutes, Paris, 1819–38, length over handles, 11 in.

$1,900/2

VASE, cut glass, on a beaded spreading circular foot, beaded neck mount decorated with a frieze of lyres, birds, and swags, height, 7 in.

$110

Mexican

BOWL, serving, low, the scalloped lip with an incised line, marked M.R.M./Sterling, diameter, 9¾ in.

$150

CANDELABRA, pair, 5 lights, modern, each on stepped domed base with stylized border, the tapering stem with 4 scrolling branches surmounted by central socket on tapering cone support, Mexican, mid-20th century.

$950/pr

CIGAR BOX, oblong, cedar-lined, domed hinged cover with an applied foliate border, mid-20th century.

$350

DISH, relish, wavy scalloped-lobe sides, the dish divided into 4 compartments centering on a raised platform supporting the handle rising from a leafy calyx, marked ANFER/STERLING, length, 13½ in.

$250

Mexican Sanborns sterling bonbon dish, mid-20th century. Courtesy of Alice and Derek Hamilton. Photo by J. Auslander.

DISH, serving, on tripod base, wide at one end and narrowing at the other, with an applied lapover border, contemporary, marked AVA, length, 13 ⅛ in. **$200**

PITCHER, water, in Jensen style, diagonal mouth, harp-shape handle and tripod base, plain surface, marked CLS STERLING, height, 9 in. **$275**

PLATES, bread and butter, set of 12, each shaped circular, with molded borders. **$600/set**

SALVER, lobed, shaped circular, with applied scrolling foliate border, 8½ in. **$75**

SAUCE BOAT, traditional Georgian style, with flying-scroll handle and elongated spout, with applied scrolling border, marked A A, length, 8 in. **$125**

TABLE ORNAMENTS, pair, duck form, each realistically chased with feathers and inset with stone eyes, length, 10 in.
$1,300/pr

TEA AND COFFEE SERVICE, 6 pieces, comprising teapot, coffeepot, covered sugar bowl, covered creamer, waste bowl, hot water kettle on lampstand, and 2-handle oval tray with fluted rim, 20th century. **$7,500/set**

TEA AND COFFEE SET on tray, 4 pieces, comprising coffeepot, teapot, covered sugar and creamer, ovoid bodies on a shaped square ring foot, creamer with visor-shape mouth, the tray oval with scalloped border. **$2,000/set**

TRAY, relish, rectangular, the bowl with sloping sides and a scrolling edge with double border, marked CLS/Sterling, length, 13 in. **$250**

TRAY, tea, 2 handles, oval, with 4 foliate bracket feet with foliate scroll border, length, 27½ in. **$850**

Russian

BASKET, cake, with molded border, swing handle, interior gold-washed, Moscow, 1854. **$950**

BASKET, sweetmeat, oval, Moscow, 1886, basketweave panels. **$1,425**

CENTERPIECE, silver and cut glass, with cherub supporting glass, 1888, height, 18½ in. **$7,250**

CIGARETTE CASE, silver-gilt, agate base and lid, gem-set opening. **$700**

Russian sterling tazza, Moscow, 1886, $1,100. **Courtesy of Christie's East, New York.**

CUP, baroque, maker's mark IC, Moscow, c. 1773, repoussé, in the English manner. **$700**

CUP, vodka, on pedestal foot with beaded double-scroll handle, waisted body engraved with strapwork and foliage, 18th century. **$475**

CUPS, vodka, pair, nielloed, late 19th century. **$250/pr**

CUPS, vodka, set of 6 on matching waiter, unmarked, enameled bands. **$385/set**

DISH, bonbon, square, engraved with a basketweave design with a rope-twist handle, St. Petersburg, 1893. **$200**

KOVSH, engraved with geometric bands, by Antip Kuzmichev, Moscow, 1888. **$925**

LADLE, fiddle pattern, Moscow, 1889, length, 14 in. **$200**

SALVER, circular, on 3 knop supports with berried laurel and beaded rim, Fabergé, Moscow, c. 1900, diameter, 11 in.

$800

SUGAR BASIN, beaded, with swing handles on a rim foot.

$175

SUGAR BASIN, floral-engraved, caldron shape with 2 applied handles and a molded rim, detachable cover with compressed finial, 1883.   **$375**

TANKARD, cut glass, lidded, with applied scroll handle, hinged cover with presentation inscription, dated 1898.   **$475**

TAZZA, oval, with rope-twist handles on domed foot, chased to simulate basket with folded napkin, Moscow, 1886.

$1,100

TEA SET, 3 pieces, tapering frosted ground engraved with flowers, foliage, and berries in Art Nouveau style. **$1,000/set**

TEASPOONS, set of 9, spiral-twist handles.   **$200/set**

Russian three-piece tea set in Art Nouveau style, teapot illustrated, $1,000/ set. **Courtesy of Christie's South Kensington, London.**

Inkstands and Inkwells

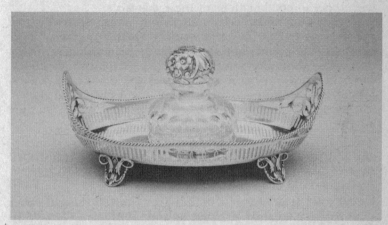

Gorham inkstand, 1888, $800. Courtesy of Christie's East, New York.

Before the middle of the 18th century in England, a writer used separate metal containers of ink and sand, each on its own tray, as well as a pen, wax, and penknife, also on a tray. Later, glass inkwells with sterling silver mounts were introduced. These proved easier to clean and led to the design of sterling silver stands with fittings to hold the bottles. Quite often the base had cast paw, ball-and-claw, or French scroll feet. The rectangular stands sometimes had hand-pierced gallery borders. These later examples were often made in boat shapes.

In the latter part of the 18th century, Matthew Boulton first used the term *inkstand*, referring to a sterling silver platform with glass pots. Most of these stands held ink pots and pounce or wafer boxes with a vase, bell, or taperstick in the center. The bell was used to summon a servant who dispatched the letter.

One of the well-known makers of early American silver inkstands was John Coney. The famous inkstand used at the signing of the Declaration of Independence was made by another recognized silversmith, Philip Syng, Jr.

Designs followed the styles of the English furniture makers. In the early 19th century the sphinx and other Egyptian symbols began to appear, with masks and ring handles. By the mid-19th century many inkstands were called inkwells and were made in pottery, glass, sterling silver, and other metals and sometimes in combinations of these materials.

Novelty designs depicting animals and human figures became the style, and by the late 19th century Tiffany, Gorham, Unger Brothers, and other American firms were producing highly decorative inkstands. Some were set with semiprecious stones, often in Art Nouveau form with designs of flowing waves, curves, sea creatures, nude women, and exaggerated florals. The designs were executed in silverplate as well as sterling silver.

INKSTAND, Art Nouveau, square, on bracket feet with shaped square inkwell stamped with stylized foliage, silverplated, Walker & Hall, Sheffield.   **$350**

INKSTAND, boat shape, with cut-glass inkwell, hinged cover with baluster finial, H.M., Birmingham, 1901.   **$350**

INKSTAND, Continental, 19th century, oval, surmounted by eagles' heads with outstretched wings, scroll and grotesque-mask decoration.   **$650**

INKSTAND, modeled as a cube with 2 pull-out drawers, 4 holes to hold pens, Phipps & Robinson, 1787.   **$4,500**

INKSTAND, oblong, on scroll feet, with 2 vase-shape inkwells and molded pen rest, applied with Celtic-style decoration.

$350

INKSTAND, rectangular, with 2 bottles, on hoof feet, with central taperstick, London, 1902.   **$1,800**

INKSTAND, shaped oblong on scroll legs, with applied scroll rim with 2 pen rests and 2 silver-mounted cut-glass inkwells, London, 1916.   **$550**

INKSTAND, silver-mounted, heart-shape tortoise shell with cut-glass inkwell, cover with spiral-twist finial, William Comyns, London, 1895.   **$550**

INKSTAND, silverplated, urn-form inkpot with baluster-shape platform. **$125**

INKSTAND, silverplated, urn-form inkpot within balustrated platform surmounted by urns and busts of children. **$150**

INKSTAND, Victorian, silver-mounted heart-shape tortoise shell fitted with a cut-glass inkwell, William Comyns, London, 4³/₄ in. **$750**

INKSTAND, with beaded oblong gallery, on rococo scrolling foliate feet, fitted with 2 inkwells, central taperstick with applied loop handle. **$200**

INKSTAND, with bust of a lady, crimped and gadrooned border, domed cover chased with rondel, Georg Gillet, London, 1882. **$900**

INKSTAND, George III style, sterling silver, oval on ball-and-claw feet, fitted with 2 silver-mounted inkwells and central taper holder, Mappin and Webb, London, 1898. **$300**

INKSTAND, openwork bracket supports with pierced gallery fitted with urn-form inkwell, pounce pot, and central candleholder, pierced and engraved with foliate scrolls, Dutch, 19th century. **$1,300**

Viennese silver inkwell, c. 1866, $7,000. **Courtesy of Robert W. Skinner Gallery, Bolton, MA.**

INKSTAND, rectangular, gadrooned borders, 2 oval inkpots, Crichton, London, 1913.   **$900**

INKWELL, capstan, molasses-glazed pottery with silver mounts, Walker and Hall, Sheffield, 1912.   **$175**

INKWELL, circular, capstan, cover inset with Goliath pocket watch, Sheffield, 1908.   **$775**

INKWELL, Continental, molded as knight's helmet.   **$500**

INKWELL, elaborately molded and applied with full-relief cherubs, swans, swags, lions' heads and paws, and borders, topped by royal crown and monogram, Austria, 1866.

$7,000

INKWELL, glass, silver-topped, tapering, with hobnail pattern– cut base and domed hinged cover, Birmingham, 1909.   **$225**

INKWELL, large, bell shape, with presentation inscription, Birmingham, 1919.   **$350**

INKWELL, large, silver-mounted cut-glass square well with domed hinged cover, Birmingham, 1910.   **$600**

INKWELL, on stand, oval, with pierced sides of pales and foliate scrolls, cut-glass inkwell with silver top, Gorham, 1888, length, 8¾ in.   **$800**

Georg Jensen inkwell on stand, $3,000. Courtesy of Christie's East, New York.

INKWELL, reeded and fluted circular capstan, London, 1903.
$375

INKWELL, Scottish, octagonal capstan, with hinged cover, Hamilton & Inches, Edinburgh, 1898. **$225**

INKWELL, silver-mounted horse hoof, mounts engraved with horsehair, lid hinged to reveal the inkpot, London, 1858.
$600

INKWELL, traveling, silver-mounted, stamped with rococo flowers and foliage, hinged cover engraved with a name, Birmingham, 1893. **$275**

INKWELLS, pair, modeled as port and starboard lanterns, London, 1900. **$1,350/pr**

TRAVELING, allover embossed, Gorham, late 19th century.
$275

TRAVELING, with screw-down top, engraved with a coronet, London, 1811. **$225**

Japanese sterling double perfume bottle, c. 1900, $150. Photo by J. Auslander.

*I*nterest in Oriental styles has spurred a rise in prices of Japanese silver from the 19th and early 20th centuries. The decoration is often highly embossed, depicting chrysanthemums, bamboo, and leafage against matte grounds. Other pieces bear extruded writhing dragon motifs.

Japanese silver of the mid-20th century has also excited renewed interest, especially in compacts, card cases, cigarette cases, and small decorative objects from this period.

BOWL, centerpiece, repoussé with peonies, diameter, 6½ in.
$150

BOWL, punch, body with modeled iris decoration amid scrolling waves, c. 1900.
$2,250

BOWL, punch, 12 cups and ladle, the plain circular bowl with octagonal, segmented applied lip on a vertical ring foot, the cups of similar form with smooth rims and C-handles, the ladle with a reeded handle, maker unmarked, .950 standard, post-1945. **$600/set**

BOX, cigarette, oblong, sterling silver–mounted, wood applied with a gilt stylized chrysanthemum. **$125**

BOX, rectangular, irises in high relief on stippled ground, length, 8¾ in. **$2,350**

CANDELABRA, pair, 3 lights, sterling, central shaft admitting a 3-light branch with removable central finial, weighted, maker unmarked, post-1945. **$250/pr**

COCKTAIL SHAKER and 12 goblets, .950 standard, the shaker and goblets with a peened surface, post-1945. **$325/set**

COCKTAIL SHAKER, chased with exotic birds and sprigs of cherry blossoms, on stippled ground, 11 in. **$700**

COCKTAIL STIRRER, with chrysanthemum handle, Arthur & Bond Yokohama, 9 in. **$135**

FLASK SET, traveling, second quarter 20th century, rectangular cylindrical form with hammered finish, top with 2 screw-on hinged caps engraved I and II for different alcohols, center with screw-on hinged cap opening to reveal a funnel and 6 nesting small tapered cylindrical beakers. **$1,000/set**

KNIFE, fruit, and fork set, Miyata, comprising 6 knives and forks in a fitted blue case, hollow handles. **$125/set**

TEA SERVICE, 3 pieces, compressed and chased with village scenes and with bamboo-style handles. **$500/set**

TEA SERVICE, 3 pieces, comprising teapot, cream pitcher, and covered sugar bowl, globular, with simulated bamboo handles and finials, applied with sprays of plum blossom and butterflies. **$1,300/set**

VASES, pair, surface engraved and pricked with a design of chrysanthemums and butterflies, height, 9 in. **$850/pr**

VASES, pair, with Fu dog mask and ring handles engraved with figures beneath trees, crossed flags, height, 8 in. **$250/pr**

Georg Jensen

Georg Jensen tea and coffee service, c. 1915–1930, estimate, $2,500–$3,500.
Courtesy of Butterfield & Butterfield, San Francisco.

Georg Jensen silver was created in Copenhagen, Denmark, in 1904, when Georg Jensen Silversmiths was established, and it was the inspiration for much of the Nordic influence on early-20th-century American silver. Jensen silver is noteworthy for its crisp, classical motifs with columnar supports and garlands. Many silversmiths worked for the firm under the Jensen trademark using their own names and designs.

Georg Jensen was famous for jewelry as well as for flatware and hollowware. The jewelry often featured moss agate, moonstones, malachite, amber, and other semiprecious stones. The firm is also noted for sterling silver with blossom decoration and hand-chased details or sculptured grape motifs. The Blossom pattern in flatware was introduced in 1919 and featured sterling silver with individually sculptured blossoms and leaf decoration. Other flatware patterns continue today; the Acorn pattern has been a best-seller since 1915. In 1927 the Pyramid pattern was created by Harold Nielsen. The Cactus pattern originated in 1930.

Collectors look for Georg Jensen articles marked Copenhagen rather than those with the U.S.A. mark.

All Jensen items listed in this guide are of Danish origin unless otherwise noted.

BASKET, sweetmeat, after 1945, an openwork leaf and tendril support, the handles with terminals formed as stylized flowers.
$200

BEAKER CUP, sterling, with Swedish import mark, plain design with flaring lip, Georg Jensen & Wendel A/S, design by Harald Nielsen.
$250

BEAKERS, set of 6, hammered surface applied with 3 dolphins, chased with girdle with shells centered by moonstones, numbered 118A.
$6,000/set

BOWL, centerpiece, flaring rim with 4 pendant rings bearing grape clusters, length, 14½ in.
$5,500

BOWL, centerpiece, covered, ribbed circular form, 4 pairs of pinecone feet attached, domed cover embossed and chased with overlapping foliage under a large cluster of foliage and bunches of beads, c. 1925, numbered 87, designed by Georg Jensen, height, 14 in.
$10,000

BOWL, centerpiece, Georg Jensen Silversmithy, c. 1934, numbered 296A, oval hammered bowl with 4 pendant grapevine handles, lobed knop above chased leafage applied with grapevine, STERLING/GEORG JENSEN in a crowned beaded oval 296A/GI/935/S, length, 14⅜ in.
$6,500

BOWL, deep circular, with hammered surface, on 8 foliate supports terminating and alternating with beads, 1930, numbered 584.
$1,600

BOX and stand, box of square sections, ribbed sides on bud supports, cover repoussé and chased with foliage centering a foliate-mounted amber bud finial, stand of shaped square sections, conforming decoration, 1939, numbered 30, length of stand, 6½ in.
$3,000/2

BOX, biscuit, cover with fluted borders and decorated with beads, ebony finial, numbered 530, height, 7½ in. **$6,000**

CANDELABRA, pair, 2 lights, after 1945, stem formed as stylized leaves with beads and scrolls surmounted by petals supporting scrolling reeded branches with octagonal sockets.

$8,500/pr

CANDLESTICKS, pair, each with circular sconce and drip-pan encircled with pendant grape bunches on a vine, on spiraling fluted stem with lobed knops, Georg Jensen Silversmithy, numbered 263A, designed by Georg Jensen, height, 6 in.

$4,200/pr

COCKTAIL SHAKER, hammered surface, the body chased with flutes, cover with grape tendrils, cap with pinecone finial, c. 1930, numbered 497A, height, 9½ in. **$1,400**

COFFEE SERVICE, Blossom pattern, comprising coffeepot, creamer, and sugar bowl, 3 foliate supports with carved ivory handles set at right angles to the body, berried bud finial, numbered 2A and 2H. **$3,100/set**

COFFEE SERVICE, comprising coffeepot, creamer, and covered sugar bowl, each with pear-form body and hammered surface, the wood handles and finials with beaded mounts, c. 1940, numbered 80A, designed by Georg Jensen. **$1,200/set**

COFFEE SET comprising coffeepot, creamer, and 2-handled sugar bowl, each with hammered surface, wood handles and finials with beaded mounts, c. 1930–40, numbered 80 B/C, designed by Georg Jensen. **$1,100/set**

COFFEE SET with matching tray in Cosmos pattern, comprising coffeepot, creamer, and covered sugar bowl, lower body decorated with upright lappets, ebonized wood handles, foliate terminals, oval tray with conforming decoration, number 45 and 45C, designed by Johan Rohde. **$4,000/set**

COFFEE SET, 3 pieces, Georg Jensen Silversmithy, 45C, designed by Johan Rohde in the Cosmos pattern. **$3,750/set**

COMPOTE, Georg Jensen Silversmithy, 451B designed by Johan Rohde, openwork stem decorated with scrolls, foliate, and beads. **$7,000**

COMPOTE, large flared bowl supported by openwork stem of scrolls and beaded foliage, circular tiered base with beadwork at intervals, c. 1934, numbered 250B, height, 12½ in.

$4,500

COMPOTE, large, Georg Jensen Silversmithy, c. 1930, numbered 196, designed by Johan Rohde, flared bowl with openwork stem of foliage and beads, stepped circular foot, hammered surface, 925S/DESSIN/JR in beaded oval, diameter, 11³/₈ inches. **$6,200**

COMPOTE, sterling silver, after 1945, flaring rims applied with border of scrolling grapevines, spiral fluted stem surmounted by lobes and beads, 7³/₄ in. **$1,500**

COMPOTE, flared circular bowl encircled at the base with berried fronds, with spiraling beaded baluster-shape stem, on circular foot, c. 1915–18, designed by Johan Rohde, height, 7¹/₄ in. **$3,000**

COMPOTE, flared circular bowl encircled at the base with pendant grapevine, with lobed twisted stem enhanced with beadwork, hammered surface, designed by Georg Jensen, height, 7³/₈ in. **$2,600**

COMPOTE, flared circular bowl encircled at the base with pendant grapevine with lobed twisted stem enhanced with grapes, designed by Georg Jensen, height, 12¹/₂ in. **$16,000**

CUP, covered, with beaded knopped stem, the base of the flared bowl supported by an openwork structure of scrolls and beadwork, the slightly domed cover with pear-shape finial, hammered surface, c. 1940, height, 6 in. **$1,600**

CUPS, 2 handles, set of 16, each of tapering cylindrical form with flared rim, hammered surface with double-scroll handles, Georg Jensen Silversmithy, c. 1930. **$1,000/set**

DINNER PLATES, set of 8, each circular with plain hammered surface, designed by Johan Rohde, diameter, 11 in.
$7,000/set

DISH, serving, and cover, large oval with hammered surface, rims of lozenges, the domed cover with detachable beaded foliate handle, numbered 63, length, 19¹/₈ in. **$5,000/2**

FLATWARE, Beaded pattern, comprising 6 each of dinner knives, salad forks, teaspoons, dinner forks, butter spreaders, dessert spoons. **$1,800/set**

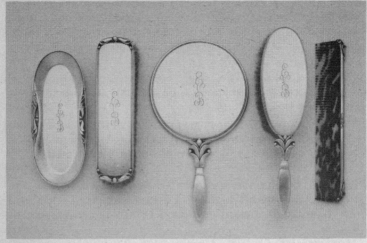

Georg Jensen Danish sterling dresser set with blossom motif, $650/set.
Courtesy of Christie's East, New York.

FLATWARE SERVICE, Pyramid pattern, comprising 12 each of
dinner knives, dinner forks, salad forks, coffee spoons, luncheon forks, dinner knives with serrated blades, dessert spoons,
cocktail forks, iced-tea spoons, teaspoons, pair of carvers, 3
fruit knives, and 5 serving pieces, designed by Harald Nielsen.
$7,000/set

FLATWARE SERVICE, Pyramid pattern, comprising 12 each of
dinner knives, butter knives, dinner forks, salad forks, dessert
spoons, teaspoons, and 6 fruit spoons.   **$4,000/set**

FLATWARE SERVICE, designed by Harald Nielsen, Old Danish
Regency pattern, comprising 12 each of dinner knives, dinner
forks, dinner spoons, coffee spoons, 11 teaspoons, and pair of
salad servers.   **$3,000/set**

FLATWARE SET, Acorn pattern, comprising 12 each of dinner
knives, fish knives, pastry forks, soup spoons, luncheon knives,
demitasse spoons, salad forks, dinner forks, dessert spoons,
teaspoons, luncheon forks, plus 10 serving pieces, designed by
Johan Rohde.   **$10,000/set**

GRAPEFRUIT SPOONS, set of 6, Acorn pattern.   **$200/set**

GRAVY BOAT, boat form with beaded foliate handle, the knop
chased with overlapping leaves, oval stand with openwork
beaded foliate ends, ladle with curling beaded foliate handle,
designed by Johan Rohde.   **$2,300/set**

INKWELL, circular, on circular stand with chased stylized egg-and-dart border, cover surmounted by openwork stylized leaf-and-ball finial, overall hammered surface. **$3,000**

LUNCHEON SERVICE, Acorn pattern, comprising 6 each of luncheon forks, salad forks, luncheon knives, teaspoons, cream soup spoons, and 2 iced-tea spoons. **$1,350/set**

PEPPER SHAKERS, salt cellars and spoons, Pyramid pattern. **$350/set**

PITCHER, baluster form with hammered surface, Georg Jensen Silversmithy, numbered 432A, designed by Johan Rohde, height, 9 in. **$1,900**

PITCHER, water, 1925–32, vase shape with applied scrolling grape clusters on floral-chased band, wood handle with grape cluster join, height, 9¼ in. **$3,000**

PITCHER, baluster body and lightly hammered surface, with bud finial, fluted bone handle, foot with openwork band of scrolls and beads, c. 1930, height, 8 in. **$1,100**

PLATTER with mazarin, for serving seafood, elongated oval form with partly fluted rim and shell terminals, hammered surface, the mazarin centered by an openwork chased lobster surrounded by trellis and with shell grips at each end, Georg Jensen Silversmithy, 1922, numbered 335, length, 30¼ in. **$20,000**

PLATTER, meat, Blossom pattern, numbered 2AA, length, 19¾ in. **$3,500**

SERVER, tomato, Pyramid pattern. **$225**

SERVERS, fish, pair, stems formed on both sides as 2 fish with beaded scallop shell in their mouths, acorn-shape blade and tines chased with a flowerhead surrounded by pierced and engraved tendrils, c. 1937, numbered 55. **$1,700/pr**

SET, fish, Continental pattern, 12 forks and 12 knives. **$700/set**

SPOON, serving, Acanthus pattern. **$250**

TABLESPOONS, set of 12, Cactus pattern. **$650/set**

TEA AND COFFEE SERVICE and a matching silver 2-handle tray, Blossom pattern, comprising coffeepot, teapot, creamer, covered sugar bowl, tea strainer and stand, with carved ivory handles, oval tray with openwork silver handles, c. 1935, numbered 2A/B/C/E and 77, designed by Georg Jensen. **$9,500/set**

TEA AND COFFEE SERVICE comprising coffeepot, teapot, water pitcher, creamer, covered 2-handle sugar bowl and small oval tray, each with ropework rims, hammered surface with ovolo knops, 1920–44, numbered 88 and 5A.   **$3,000/set**

TEA AND COFFEE SERVICE, Blossom pattern, 4 pieces, comprising coffeepot, teapot, creamer, and 2-handle sugar bowl, hammered surface, on 3 foliate supports, the pots and creamer with carved ivory handles.   **$7,000/set**

TEA SERVICE, 3 pieces, ivory-mounted silver.   **$2,000/set**

TEASPOONS, 12, Continental pattern, Denmark.   **$375/12**

TRAY, Georg Jensen Silversmithy, c. 1934, numbered 2D, Blossom pattern, rounded openwork corners of beaded blossoms, length, 22 in.   **$8,500**

TRAY, large oval with hammered surface, the border chased with lappets with molded rim, c. 1930, numbered 45, length, 23 in.   **$3,500**

TRAY, oval, 2 handles, with hammered surface, ropework rim, the cavetto with clusters of ovolos at intervals, c. 1936, numbered 239, length over handles, 22½ in.   **$3,200**

TRAY, small oval, with hammered surface, the openwork gallery composed of S-scrolls and beads, the handles capped with berries and foliage, numbered 377A.   **$4,500**

TRAY, small oval, with openwork ends of beaded foliage, hammered surface, numbered 2D, designed by Georg Jensen, length, 13³/₈ in.   **$3,500**

TRAY, 2 handles, 1925–32, oval, openwork handles with stylized buds and scrolls, length, 22 in.   **$2,750**

Judaica

Left. *Late 19th-century English silver filigree spice tower, $425.* **Right.** *Early 19th-century Austro-Hungarian filigree spice tower, $500.* **Courtesy of Christie's South Kensington, London.**

Through the years this area has been closely followed by some collectors, and many more have shown interest within the past year.

Collectors look for ritual objects used in the home or synagogue. Articles range from functional, everyday pieces to elaborate examples for special ceremonies. Many of the pieces were fashioned by Christian silversmiths because in many regions Jews were not allowed to practice the craft.

Styles of individual pieces range from Baroque, Rococo, and Neoclassical to the revival styles of the late 19th century, when Moorish and Oriental designs became popular. Items characteristically adopt the styles of the time, following furniture design elements.

Objects are also found with decorations of flowers and foliage but no "graven images." Hebrew inscriptions are another form of decoration. An inscription may bear the date and name of the person or group for whom the piece was made.

Objects collected include Sabbath lamps, candlesticks, textiles, menorahs, ceremonial cups, spice boxes, Torah ornaments, charity boxes, ethrog containers, and Purim and Passover pieces.

According to specialist dealer Peter Kassai, there are a number of things to remember when purchasing Judaica. Hanukkah menorahs made in the 17th, 18th, and 19th centuries should follow the design styles of the period. Menorahs are eight-branched candelabra with a helper or servant candle cup making a nine-branched holder. There are instances where an eight-branched light has been adapted with the addition of a single Sabbath candlestick into what appears to be a Menorah. Additional forgeries have been made by bending hallmarked sterling silver spoons into the eight shallow containers for oil used in an earlier period.

All types of cups are being called kiddush cups when, in actuality, many were simply wine cups. Beakers used as kiddush cups had to hold at least four ounces of wine, as proscribed in the Talmud. The few extant from the 17th century are most often in museum collections. In the mid-18th century in affluent Germany, kiddush cups with engraved biblical scenes or Hebrew inscriptions began to appear. Early examples from Spain or Portugal do not exist because the Jews were expelled from these countries. Forgeries on cups include Hebrew inscriptions that do not make sense and later engravings depicting biblical scenes or the Star of David.

Spice boxes and towers were not common in the 18th century, but many examples exist from 1870 to the present. In the 1900s a great many were produced in Poland, Germany, and Austria with hallmarks on all parts. Israeli reproductions of these abound today.

Torah pointers are rare because they were originally only for synagogue use and were not made in great quantities. The same applies to Torah breastplates, crowns, and bells.

Collectors often confuse sugar boxes with ethrog boxes. Many sugar boxes have been adapted by adding a casting of the

Lion of Judah as a finial. The best examples are in the shape of the ethrog, or fruit, with a period inscription.

Early Passover or Seder plates had six cups for the various condiments used during the order of the service. In the last fifty years very elaborate examples have been produced.

Just as in all other fields of collecting, one should check for contemporary inscriptions and forged marks. Proof of origin is generally found in stylization and workmanship.

CANDLESTICKS, Sabbath, pair, baluster form, decorated with flowers and fluting, with a presentation inscription in Hebrew, London, 1919. **$575/pr**

CANDLESTICKS, Sabbath, pair, baluster form, fluted and floral-stamped, on domed rising shaped-square bases, London, 1829. **$900/pr**

CANDLESTICKS, Sabbath, pair, baluster form, engine-turned and foliate-engraved, scrolling foliate feet, Austro-Hungarian. **$600/pr**

CANDLESTICKS, Sabbath, pair, baluster form, with flowers and fluting, each on 3 openwork rococo feet, presentation inscription in Hebrew, London, 1919, height, 11½ in. **$350/pr**

CHALLAH TRAY, Continental, border chased with a Hebrew inscription and design on matte ground. **$650**

Left. *Late 19th-century German silver charity box, modeled as a synagogue,* $900. Right. *Rare 18th-century German silver Hanukkah lamp, $11,500.* Courtesy of Phillips, London.

CHARITY BOX, late 19th century, German, parcel-gilt, hexagonal body modeled as a synagogue, chased with 6 doors and windows above with onion-domed roof forming hinged cover.
$900

HANUKKAH LAMP, rare, 18th century, German, rectangular body with foliate-chased cover opening to reveal 8 oil compartments raised on 4 rampant-lion feet, backplate embossed with a menorah flanked by 2 jugs and affixed with single rectangular oil jug, Rotger Herfurth, Frankfurt-on-Main, c. 1765.
$11,500

HANUKKAH LAMP, Continental, 8 scroll branches and removable servant light.
$350

KIDDUSH CUP, German, silver-gilt, with fruiting vines and Hebrew inscription relating to the "Day of the Holy Sabbath," Augsburg, 1763.
$5,100

KIDDUSH CUPS, Russian, group of 15, engraved thimble-form cups, one footed example.
$400/set

KIDDUSH CUPS, set of 6, gilt-lined, circular bases with waisted stems, engraved with wriggle-work decoration, Birmingham, 1913.
$300/set

LAMP, Sabbath, 18th century, Dutch, 7-sided star form, mask decoration, pierced drip pan below crown, pendant flame finial, Hendrik Griste (I), Amsterdam, 1768.
$55,000

MENORAH, cartouche-form back with peacock motif, surmounted by crown finial.
$300

PLAQUE, framed, depicting rabbi, after an engraving by Boris Schatz.
$125

PRAYER BOOK, with sterling silver Russian mount engraved with fruiting vines, inscribed Hebrew script, c. 1900.
$500

SPICE CONTAINER, flower form, marked, made in Palestine, Teppich.
$145

SPICE TOWER, 18th century, German, pierced with windows, small hinged door, with 2 of the original 5 pennants remaining, sides engraved with brickwork and later inscribed in England with the Royal Crown above "C&R" and "1666," maker's mark AR Frankfurt-on-Main, c. 1730.
$10,500

SPICE TOWER, sterling silver filigree, with baluster stem and pennant finial, London, 1896, height, 10 in.
$425

SPICE TOWER, sterling silver, with rope-twist decoration, applied with several pennants, interior fitted with a bell, Austro-Hungarian, 1819, height, 10¼ in.   **$500**

TORAH BREASTPLATE, Continental silver, rectangular with applied filigree border, surmounted by crown, 13½ in.   **$750**

TORAH FINIALS, pair, one stamped "sterling" only, other unmarked.   **$500/pr**

TORAH FINIALS, pair, with pierced flowers and scrolls, finials formed as birds with outstretched wings (bells replaced), height, 13¾ in.   **$800/pr**

Samuel Kirk

Left. *American sterling and cut glass, heart-shaped, rouge pot, $225.* Right.
American Kirk sterling, heart-shaped, watch holder, $275. Photo by J.
Auslander.

Samuel Kirk began his silversmithing firm in 1815 after he
had apprenticed in Philadelphia and moved to Baltimore. Still
in existence today, Samuel Kirk & Son, Inc., is one of the oldest makers of sterling silver in the United States.

Kirk's earliest work was in simple form, often with half-fluted
bodies and engraved decoration. In the early part of the 19th
century it was not unusual for families to send Kirk sketches
of their home to be incorporated into the designs of the pieces
of silver they had ordered. Many of the designs are castle-like
in appearance. It is not known whether these were depictions
of European styles or actual chateaus that were dismantled and
brought to this country to be reassembled.

From about 1820 to the present the firm has produced the
elaborate repoussé work for which they are famous, incorporating native American flowers and foliage. Kirk's production

included every type of hollowware as well as sets of flatware, napkin rings, and small items for the boudoir.

Today's collectors look for the earlier pieces, especially those with the eleven-ounce mark connoting coin silver.

BOWL, punch, baluster form with everted undulating rim, deeply chased with fruit and elaborate foliage and flowers, c. 1905, diameter at rim, 11 in. **$4,500**

BOWL, punch, repoussé, c. 1890, on pedestal foot, the bowl overall chased with flowers and foliage. **$2,800**

BOWL, sugar, covered, with vase-shape creamer chased with flowers, foliage, a butterfly and birds on a matte ground, pomegranate finial, both with angled handles headed by a ram's mask, 1828. **$1,500/pr**

CANDLE SNUFFER, embossed foliage. **$150**

COFFEEPOT, multiscroll handle, leaf-capped spout, floral sprig finial, the body overall repoussé with flowerheads and acanthus on stippled ground, 1840. **$1,300**

American S. Kirk & Son Co. repoussé water pitcher, $1,500. Courtesy of Christie's East, New York.

CREAMER and covered sugar bowl, vase shape, chased with flowers on matte ground, angular handles topped by rams' heads, 1880–90.   **$500/pr**

DISHES AND COVERS, vegetable, pair, shallow circular form chased with vertical lobes and flutes, gadroon rim, cover with bud finials surrounded by spreading chased shells and leaves.   **$2,300/pr**

JAR, biscuit, silver-mounted, barrel-form cut glass with removable repoussé cover.   **$500**

MONTEITH, body chased with scenes of castles amid flowerheads and scrolls, detachable rim chased with flowerheads and scrolls, crest, 1880–90.   **$3,000**

PITCHER, water, repoussé, curving rustic handle, body overall chased with flowerheads on stippled ground.   **$1,500**

PLATES, bread and butter, set of 8, repoussé border of flowerheads and foliage.   **$600/set**

PLATES, service, dozen, repoussé borders, central monograms.   **$9,950/12**

TEA AND COFFEE SERVICE, 6 pieces, 1880–90, teapot, coffeepot, cream pitcher, sugar bowl, waste bowl, and kettle on plated stand, squared handle applied with rams' heads, grape-cluster finials, bodies overall chased with flowerheads on stippled ground.   **$6,000/set**

TEA CADDY, allover repoussé floral decoration, flower finial, c. 1900.   **$375**

Pair of S. Kirk & Son repoussé sterling dessert stands, 1880–1890, $1,100/ pair. Courtesy of Christie's East, New York.

TEA SERVICE, 4 pieces, comprising teapot, covered sugar bowl, waste bowl, and cream pitcher, each compressed globular on spreading circular foot, overall repoussé with flowerheads on stippled ground, the squared handles with rams' heads, the covers with grape-cluster finials. **$3,500/set**

TEA URN, vase form, embossed and chased allover with buildings, a ruin, a boat, and fishermen among flowers and foliage, flower spray finial, 1846–61, height, 18 in. **$3,200**

TRAY, PIN, repoussé border, engraved cross-hatched center, c. 1840. **$150**

TUREEN, soup, covered, late 19th century, chased with flowers on stippled ground, leaf-clad handles, cover with flower-clad ring handle. **$3,800/2**

VASE, trumpet form on pedestal base, chased allover with flowers and foliage, matching applied borders, 1896–1925, height, 15³⁄₈ in. **$2,700**

WATCH HOLDER, heart shape, embossed floral decoration, c. 1900. **$250**

Matchsafes

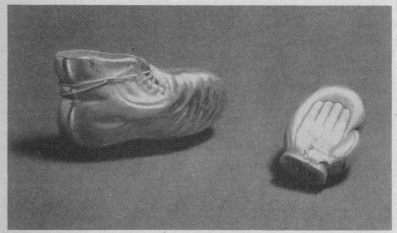

Left. *Silverplate matchsafe in form of shoe, $225.* **Right.** *Sterling matchsafe in form of boxing glove, $750.* Photo by J. Auslander.

Wooden matches were carried in pocket-size containers made of sterling silver, silverplate, brass, and other metals before the advent of pocket matches and lighters. Matchsafes were often suspended from a gentleman's watch fob. Most safes date from the late 19th century and were produced in England, the United States, and other countries until the early part of the 20th century.

American matchsafes were made with rococo scrollwork detailing, engraving, gadrooning, and Art Nouveau decorations. Many are embossed with what the prudish Victorians felt were scandalous scenes depicting nude or semidraped females. There were also safes with designs of horseback riding, cycling, football, baseball, and bowling, as well as gambling and card playing. Many also depicted dogs, cats, pigs, owls, and other animals. Souvenirs of fairs and conventions were also popular themes for manufacturers. Occasionally, an advertising matchsafe in figural sterling silver was made.

One of the symbols of the cultured Victorian gentleman was the wearing of articles that depicted famous artworks. These scenes indicated that the gentleman's scope of knowledge included the art world. Therefore, some safes displayed well-known paintings and sculptures in the style of Psyche and Love, The Storm, and Leda and the Swan as chased designs.

Gorham, Blackinton, Unger Bros., Kerr, and Webster are a few of the American manufacturers that produced matchsafes. Unusual designs with smokers, golfers, skulls, snakes, and grotesque faces were made by these manufacturers. The mark was generally struck in the inner lid. Many were also monogrammed by the jeweler who sold the safe.

In England matchsafes were called vestas and were often made in figural silverplate forms depicting animals and human figures. Sterling silver vestas with enameled yachting symbols, rugby motifs, creels of fish, and dance hall ladies are the most desirable. English matchsafes should be fully hallmarked.

Many enameled safes have been restored or recently enameled over earlier sterling cases. When in doubt about an expensive purchase, use a black light for verification.

ART NOUVEAU nude, American, late 19th century. **$75**

BOOK SHAPE, with engraved decoration, Hilliard & Thomason, Birmingham, 1880. **$300**

BRAZIL NUT, realistically modeled and inscribed, 1896.
$400

CASE, large, later enameled with a black-stockinged cancan girl, with wooded scene in background, London, 1888. **$1,000**

CIRCULAR, chased with a bowling match, American, 1907.
$250

CIRCULAR, embossed with scene of a football game, Birmingham, 1902. **$450**

COMBINATION sterling silver whistle and vesta case (matchsafe), T.J., London, 1881. **$300**

COMBINATION whistle and vesta case (matchsafe), engraved, Birmingham, 1892. **$275**

DOG AND QUAIL in relief, silverplated, American, early 20th century. **$22**

EDWARDIAN, circular, sterling silver, stamped with a billiard-room scene with players and onlookers, Birmingham, 1906.
$650

ELKS LODGE, with elk on each side in heavy relief, American, early 20th century.   **$40**

ENAMELED front, depicting a woman in theatrical dress seated on a balcony, silverplated.   **$200**

ENAMELED front, with scantily clad woman, Continental, early 20th century.   **$700**

ENAMELED with a mounted huntsman and his pack of hounds, Birmingham, 1893.   **$375**

ENAMELED with lady racegoer seated astride a large horse-shoe, Continental, early 20th century.   **$300**

ENAMELED, oblong, with 3 naval pennants, London, 1888.
                                                                $275

ENAMELED SILVER, Tiffany & Co., 1910, with stripes and stylized stars in black against forest green ground with mustard accents.   **$750**

ENGRAVED FRONT, depicting group of motorists, 1906, diameter, 1½ in.   **$500**

FISHERMAN'S CREEL, oval basketwork body with nameplate, interior with Essex crystal depicting two trout laid out on riverbank, Thomas Johnson, 1882.   **$3,400**

FLORAL DESIGN, chased, American, late 19th century.   **$65**

GUILLOCHE-ENAMELED in bright green, with white bead borders, Continental, late 19th century.   **$275**

MULE'S HEAD, cast electroplated, English, 1890.   **$160**

NOVELTY, man in the moon with gem-set eyes, silverplated, late 19th century.   **$200**

OBLONG, nielloed with a checkerboard pattern, Russian, early 20th century.   **$200**

PADLOCK FIGURAL, with patented opening action, Birmingham, 1890.   **$375**

PIG FIGURAL, Birmingham, 1907.   **$500**

RECTANGULAR, engine-turned, foliate border, American, late 19th century.   **$50**

SQUARE, nielloed with a checkerboard design, Continental, 1907.   **$100**

TABLE LIGHTER, novelty, modeled as a mid-18th-century rococo tea caddy, with shells, foliage, and musical trophies suspended from a ribbon, William Comyns, London, 1901.
                                                                $200

TABLE LIGHTER, silver-mounted horn modeled as the Dragon of Wantley, one of his feet resting on a flaming grenade, Walker & Hall, Sheffield, 1929. **$1,100**

TEXTURED PATTERN, American, early 20th century. **$35**

TOY WATER PUMP figural, Sheffield, 1907. **$350**

Medical

Left. *Italian sterling medicine spoon with case, $100.* **Right.** *American sterling dental mixing cup with stand, c. 1875, $150.* Courtesy of H & H Antiques. Photo by J. Auslander.

Silver and combinations of sterling silver and ivory were used for many medical instruments and cased sets of instruments. Lancets of tortoise, mother-of-pearl, or ivory often had sterling silver mounts; forceps of bronze or sterling silver were also common.

In the 18th century both male and female catheters were almost always made entirely of silver, but by the first quarter of the 19th century some were produced in silverplate. Almost all of the sterling examples were hallmarked.

Eighteenth-century sterling silver etuis, which contained lancets, scissors, tongue depressors, tweezers, and surgical scissors, were generally also made of silver. Dental instruments, including mirrors, are frequently found in sterling silver. Sterling silver or silverplate ear trumpets, often decorated with wonderful engravings, can also be found, along with spectacles and their cases and quizzing glasses.

In addition, in the 19th century syphons used to administer medicine to children without spilling the dosage were being made in sterling and silverplate; by the end of the century there were also covered medicine spoons used for the same purpose.

Silver nipple shields were circular with piercing to allow the child to suck. The best examples are English hallmarked and in excellent condition.

Baby feeders began to be used because of the many deaths of young mothers or because a mother was unable to nurse her baby. The early types were flattened, often resembling a Roman oil lamp. These were followed by spout cups of tankard form with a side spout.

Dating from the early 18th century, pap boats are boat-shape dishes used to offer "pap," a soft food, to an infant or invalid. The earliest examples are simple, but the ones produced at the end of the 19th century were often decorated with shells. Examples are found in Sheffield plate as well as silver.

BLEEDING BOWL, 18th century, gilt-lined, the pierced handles scratch-engraved with initials. **$225**

DENTAL MIRROR, folding, George IV, Mary Ann Holmes, 1828. **$300**

FEEDING SYPHON, sterling silver, plain, with pierced strainer and clips, 1875. **$375**

LANCET CASE, chased with flowers and scrolls on frosted background (complete with two lancets), Hilliard & Thomason, Birmingham, 1859. **$325**

MEDICAL SPOON, sterling silver, George Adams, 1865. **$150**

MEDICINE FUNNEL, George III, with reeded borders, George Ewings, 1806. **$175**

MEDICINE SPOON, silver gilt, by J. Aldwinkle & J. Slater, 1882. **$180**

MEDICINE SPOONS, folding, tablespoon and teaspoon, leather case, American, Blackinton, late 19th century. **$85**

NIPPLE SHIELD, George III, A.J. Strachan, 1803. **$275**

NIPPLE SHIELD, plain, T&I Phipps, George IV, 1821. **$500**

PAP BOAT, typical form, with everted rim, London, 1801. **$225**

PAP BOAT, engraved with a name, possibly Colonial, unmarked. **$75**

PAP BOAT, gadrooned, William IV, London, 1836.   **$100**

PAP BOAT, German, boat shape with gilt interior and coiled-serpent handle, Johann Bernhard Vormann, Munster, c. 1800.
$800

PAP BOAT, George III, plain, 1790.   **$575**

SPATULA-CUM-SPOON, bar shape, punched Egan Cork, 1922.
$175

SPATULA-CUM-SPOON, with wide stem, by T. Johnson, 1856.
$225

TOOTHBRUSH, tooth powder box, and tongue scraper, George III, in fitted red leather case, William Parkyns, 1792.
$500/set

TOOTHBRUSH, within container, Richard Lockwood & Jim Douglas, 1801.   **$250**

Miniatures

Pair of Continental silver miniature candlesticks, 18th century, $350/pair.
Photo by J. Auslander.

Miniature sterling silver pieces are widely collected today and have been made as children's toys since the 17th century. Often miniatures were copies of household items—
candlesticks and pots, tea sets, and other utensils. Pieces also
were made in the forms of furniture, figures, boats, and car-
riages. Most were produced in England and Holland and were
made in large quantities by the end of the 19th century. Dolls
were treated to sterling silver chatelaines and posey holders.
Although they do exist, they are now extremely rare. Few
American miniatures are extant. Hallmarked European miniatures are more readily available.

In the late 19th century, Birmingham, England, faced com-
petition from the Dutch factories for production of silver
miniatures and became a center for what were considered toys
in England. Dollhouse furnishings and accessories for dolls
were most often made. Some of the more unusual pieces included inkstands, scissor cases, etuis, and even filigree spinning
wheels and chandeliers.

At the turn of the 20th century in Russia, Fabergé produced a tiny silver-gilt birdcage complete with a bird of hardstone having diamond eyes and gold claws. It is now in the collection of Queen Elizabeth. Other Russian pieces include ewers, milk jugs, and chalices, often with Cyrillic lettering.

ARMOIRE with 3 drawers, hinged door, Dutch, c. 1900.
$350

ARMOIRE, bow-front, on ball feet, upper part with 2 hinged doors die-stamped with figures, lower part with 2 drawers die-stamped with scrolling foliage, Dutch, early 20th century.
$185

CANDLESTICKS, pair, acorn decoration, late 18th century, Continental. **$350/pr**

CARRIAGE drawn by 6 horses, with hinged top, Dutch, early 20th century. **$275**

CHANDELIER, 6 lights, Dutch, early 20th century. **$525**

COFFEEPOT, tapering form, on 3 feet, with double-scroll handle, Dutch, late 19th century. **$100**

MANTEL CLOCK, silver-mounted, Continental, 1912. **$100**

MERRY-GO-ROUND with cast figures on horses, Dutch, early 20th century. **$275**

MODEL OF A GIRL and her dog at a village pump, Dutch, early 20th century. **$110**

MODEL OF TWO GENTLEMEN engaged in a game of billiards, Dutch, early 20th century. **$125**

SOFA, embossed with cherubs, London, 1903. **$100**

SOFA, stamped with floral and ribbon-swag decoration, Continental, 1905. **$175**

TABLE, stamped with figures in a garden scene surrounded by foliate and scrollwork, Continental, early 20th century. **$110**

TABLE, stamped with putti within scrollwork decoration, on lion's-paw feet, Birmingham, 1902. **$75**

TANKARD, tapering, with scroll handle, James Rush. **$300**

TAPERSTICK, with baluster column and shaped circular base with shell ornament, late 18th century. **$250**

TEA AND COFFEE SERVICE, Queen Anne style, with rectangular tray, Birmingham, early 20th century. **$175/set**

TEA CADDY, toy, canted box shape with hinged, stepped, domed cover, probably Robert Holmes Senior, Dublin, c. 1750.
$600

TEA KETTLE, pear shape, with domed, hinged cover, stand and burner, sterling silver, early 20th century. **$125**

TRAY, silver-gilt, with pierced gallery sides, embossed with 2 foxes, William Capon, 1844. **$475**

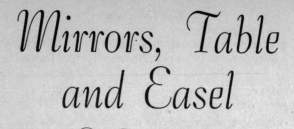

Mirrors, Table and Easel

French dressing table mirror in Louis XVI style. **Courtesy of Christie's East, New York.**

In the 18th century most table mirrors, or those with easel backs, were part of fitted toilet seats and were made of sterling silver, tortoise shell, or crocodile with sterling silver mounts.

By the 19th century, larger, more elaborate examples were made, with pierced and repoussé details depicting flowers, human figures, and foliage.

At the turn of the 20th century in England, William Comyns was one of the most prolific makers of easel-back mirrors. These were often produced to match vases or candlesticks. Matching mirrored plateaus to hold scent bottles were also made, with circular or rectangular bases detailed with rococo shellwork or cherubs.

English examples are hallmarked and most often made in Birmingham, Chester, or London. In the United States, Tiffany, Dominick & Haff, and Kerr made splendid examples.

DRESSING TABLE, Art Nouveau, shaped oblong, the mount stamped with scrolling flowers and foliage and with 14 vacant boss cartouches, fitted with a beveled glass, Birmingham, 1903, 20 in.   **$1,000**

DRESSING TABLE, heart-shape glass frame surrounded by silver pierced and embossed with putti, fauns, and masks, Dominick & Haff, New York, c. 1900.   **$1,300**

DRESSING TABLE, neoclassical style, shaped oblong with easel support, applied with ribbon and floral swag and beveled mirror.   **$500**

DRESSING TABLE, set of 3, each of cartouche shape with repoussé scrolls, easel supports, height, 12 in.   **$1,000/set**

DRESSING TABLE, silver-gilt, the frame with narrow wrigglework borders and applied engraved quatrefoil motifs at each corner, of arched shape with in-curved sides, probably German, first half of 18th century.   **$2,750**

DRESSING TABLE, silver-mounted, shield shape, tortoise-shell, London, 1897.   **$1,200**

DRESSING TABLE, mirror edged with a plain silver surround, marked G & S Co., Ltd., London, 1937.   **$350**

DRESSING TABLE, Victorian, silver-mounted, heart shape, with pierced mount of scrolling flowers, figures of courtier and knight at base, William Comyns, London, 1886, height, 13½ in.   **$750**

EASEL MIRROR, frame acid-etched in a scrolling ivy pattern, Tiffany & Co., c. 1910, height, 17¾ in.   **$1,500**

HEART SHAPE, Dominick & Haff, pierced border with doves, floral scrolls, and grotesque mask, height, 11¼ in.   **$400**

PIERCED BORDER with putti, trelliswork, and flowerheads, London, 1900, height, 26 in.   **$1,450**

Miscellaneous

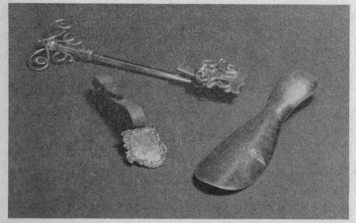

Fashion accessories, c. 1880. Top. Tiffany sterling libretto holder, $275. Left. Luggage tag, $50. Right. Shoe horn, $75.

The miscellaneous category contains some of the unusual items not covered in the major categories. Included are purses, muffs and hand warmers, a conductor's baton, and even a tiara.

Bottle Openers

Dating from the turn of the 20th century to the present time, bottle openers were made with silverplated, sterling silver, and horn handles with silver mounts. Silverplated examples advertised local companies, whereas sterling silver ones often matched flatware services. Tiffany, Cartier, and Jensen examples are among the most collectible.

Paste Pots (Mucilage or Glue)

Before there were throw-away plastic glue sticks and other containers, paste pots were in use. Most were made of pressed or cut glass with sterling silver or silverplate screw caps and a place to hold a brush. Many were made to match desk sets.

Soap Cases (Boxes)

Soap boxes made in the 17th and 18th centuries were ball shaped and footed, with pierced lids, and are quite difficult to locate.

Most soap boxes that are found date from the late 19th century. They are usually oval or rectangular with decorative motifs depicting flowers, cherubs, hearts, and Art Nouveau ladies. Those made for men have engine-turned or hand-hammered designs.

ASHTRAY, Art Nouveau, semidraped woman, curved border, stamped sterling only, late 19th century.   **$150**

ASHTRAY, embossed cherubs and clouds, Unger Brothers, late 19th century.   **$225**

BADGE, star shape, each point bright-cut with flowerheads, the center engraved with an initial, London, 1828.   **$200**

BATON, silver-mounted ebonized wood, the mount stamped with flowers and foliage, London, 1888.   **$125**

BELT, woven filigree, bead-decorated with shaped clasp, Turkish.   **$275**

BOOK COVER, Continental, unmarked silver-mounted tortoise shell with heart-shape mounts and shaped clips, 1820, Book of Common Prayer.   **$200**

BOTTLE OPENER, sterling handle, early 20th century, American.   **$25**

BOX, jewel, heart shape, embossed florals, velvet lined, lock and key, Gorham, late 19th century.   **$550**

BUCKLE, large, Victorian, cast and pierced with grotesque masks, flowers, and foliage, S.J., London, 1893.   **$110**

CANDLE SNUFFER, cone-shape ebonized wood handle.   **$35**

CARRIAGE LAMP, silver-gilt, folding, cylindrical, engraved with elaborate monogram, Frederick Purnell, London, 1886.
                                                                          $2,000

COMPASS SUNDIAL COMBINATION, French, late 18th century, allover engraved.   **$2,800**

CORN HOLDERS, pair, figural ears of corn, American, sterling silver.   **$25/pr**

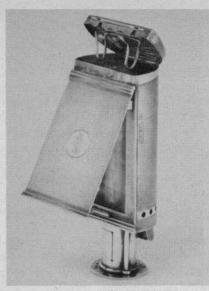

English sterling carriage lamp, c. 1864, $2,200. Courtesy of Christie's South Kensington, London.

Gorham sterling corn picks and butter spreaders, c. 1880, $825/set of 12. Sterling corn salt and pepper shakers, $175/2. Courtesy of H & H Antiques.

American coin silver knife rest. **Courtesy of Nancy and Bruce Thompson.**

EVENING BAG, the mount and handle both pierced and chased with putti and vines, wool workbag with varicolored embroidery. **$725**

GLOVE STRETCHER, allover engraved, American, late 19th century, Whiting. **$45**

GLOVE STRETCHER, embossed florals, Tiffany & Co., late 19th century. **$125**

HANDBAG, bright-cut with foliage and engraved with an initial, lined in silk and with chain and finger ring attached, Birmingham, 1910. **$325**

HAND WARMER, silver-mounted, oval, with safety chain, Barrett & Sons, London, 1913. **$175**

LORGNETTE, Art Nouveau, shaped handle, cast with a face of Medusa, her locks continuing into the elongated handle, c. 1900. **$1,500**

LUGGAGE TAG, floral-engraved border, American, late 19th century. **$35**

LUGGAGE TAG, suitcase shape, engraved border, early 20th century, American. **$45**

MEDALLION, large, with floral-chased border mount, one side engraved with a classical maiden leaning against a tomb with urn and weeping willow, in a landscape, the other side with memorial inscription, Charles Rawlings, London, 1825. **$625**

MUFF WARMER, stamped with friezes of floral and scrollwork decoration, with a shaped cartouche. **$65**

MUG, shaving, embossed sterling, wreath motifs, late 19th century.   **$125**

MUG, shaving, engraved florals surrounding cartouche, American, silverplated, late 19th century.   **$100**

MUSTACHE COMB, all silver, American, early 20th century.
                                                                                 $65

OSTRICH EGG, applied with 3 stylized paw feet, beaded and foliate-pierced and engraved mount applied with the stylized figure of an ostrich, with a body band pricked with scrollwork.
                                                                                 $275

PASTE POT, crystal, with embossed sterling lid, Gorham, late 19th century.   **$100**

PASTE POT, crystal, sterling lid inset with amethyst-colored stone, American, late 19th century.   **$125**

PLATES, Franklin Mint, 18, diameter, 8 in.   **$900/18**

POCKETKNIFE, silver handle in the form of a cast lion, steel blade, possibly English, c. 1700.   **$175**

POMANDER, oval, the pierced cover chased with an 18th century-style wedding carriage, figures, and church bells, William Comyns, London, 1905.   **$325**

PRESENTATION TRUMPET, 19th century, engraved, rocaille cartouches, one with royal cypher flanked by Stars and Stripes and the Red Ensign, other surmounted by an eagle, 1850.
                                                                                 $4,000

PURSE, enameled one side, with initials within a blue border, Birmingham, 1907.   **$160**

PURSE, enameled with a spray of flowers and initials, gem-set opening, Russian, late 19th century.   **$550**

PURSE, mesh, sterling silver, with attached change purse and compact, American, late 19th century.   **$125**

PURSE, oblong, engraved with strawberries and flowers, probably Russian, 2¼ in.   **$450**

SALT SPOON, Fiddle pattern, English, late 19th century. **$25**

SALT SPOON, shovel shape, American, early 20th century.
                                                                                 $5

SALT SPOON, Tiffany, Chrysanthemum pattern.   **$35**

SHOEHORN, embossed rose motifs, Gorham, late 19th century.
                                                                                 $100

Eighteenth-century sterling compass and sundial. **Private collection. Photo by J. Auslander.**

SHOEHORN, engine-turned motifs, Tiffany & Co. early 20th century.   **$100**

SHOEHORN, Irish, engraved with a monogram, Dublin, 1909.
                                                                                                 $225

SOAP CASE, embossed florals surrounding cartouche, American, late 19th century.   **$125**

SOAP CASE, engine-turned motifs, English, early 20th century.
                                                                                                 $100

SOVEREIGN CASE, triple, large, plain, circular, with suspension loop, C & C, Chester, 1908.   **$275**

STRING HOLDER, cut glass with sterling mounts, Gorham, late 19th century.   **$350**

STRING HOLDER, engraved sterling, Tiffany & Co.   **$350**

TALC SHAKER, embossed chrysanthemums and leafage against matte ground, Chinese Export, c. 1880.   **$325**

THERMOMETER, desk, silver-mounted tortoise shell, English, late 19th century.   **$150**

THERMOMETER, embossed florals, folding cover and suspension loop, American, late 19th century.   **$175**

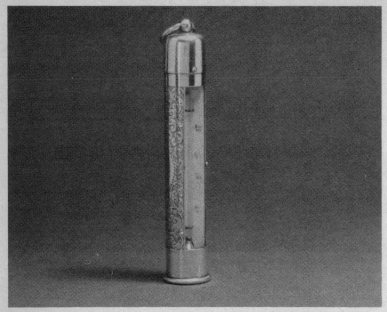

American sterling thermometer with door, c. 1885, $175. Photo by J. Auslander.

TIARA, silver, and matching chignon pin, with sprays of delicately wrought leaves with buds and flowers attached to a central wire, the pin of three sprays tied by a ribbon at the base, unmarked, probably Continental.   **$300/2**

TOOTHBRUSH JAR, crystal, with embossed sterling cover, early 20th century, American.   **$45**

TOOTHBRUSH JAR, crystal, with enameled sterling cover, English, early 20th century.   **$75**

TOOTHPICK, 14-karat gold, American, early 20th century.
$150

TOOTHPICK, early 20th century, American, sterling.   **$35**

TOOTHPICK HOLDER, Indian holding aloft a cornucopia of flowers on a foliate chased and reeded plinth and with a square base, claw-and-ball feet, Portuguese.   **$800**

WATCH HOLDER, silver-mounted, formed as an arched tower, front engraved with a 16th-century-style gentleman mounted on a horse, looking up at a lady gazing from a window, Birmingham, 1912.   **$550**

Napkin Rings

American sterling napkin rings. **Courtesy of Nancy and Bruce Thompson. Photo by J. Auslander.**

In the Victorian era it was the custom to reuse one's own linen napkin for several days when dining with family, and napkin rings were used to identify the various napkins. Most were made in sets of six or a dozen and often were engraved with name and date. If a name was not engraved on the ring, a number might have been used to distinguish the rings and ensure receiving the same linen napkin at each meal.

Rings are found in both sterling silver and silverplate, with engraved or embossed motifs. Wonderful examples in mixed metals were made by Tiffany, Gorham, and Shiebler in the late 19th century. Kerr and Unger Brothers produced elaborate floral rings, some with Art Nouveau ladies' heads. Children's napkin rings with embossed nursery scenes and rhymes were also popular in the late 19th and early 20th centuries. Very often napkin rings were given as christening gifts, together with a matching bowl, cup, and flatware. China and Japan produced sterling rings with bamboo and prunus designs for export to

America. Early-20th-century examples with Mickey and Minnie Mouse in brightly enameled colors are highly collectible today.

Silverplated napkin rings were more elaborate, with cast depictions of full-figure animals, Kate Greenaway children, and carts with movable wheels. Others featured flowers, leaves, animals, and even bud vases made as part of the napkin ring. Collectors also look for the combination of condiment set and napkin rings.

Glorious American silverplate examples were made by Wilcox, Meriden, Tufts, and Reed & Barton. Some have been recast, including the marks, so look for finely detailed, sharp examples. Check to see if an animal form has been added to a simple napkin band to make it more salable.

BARREL with cupid at each end, silverplated, Meriden, late 19th century.   **$225**

BEADING, engraved "Alice," width, 1 in.   **$18**

BIRD on top, figural, with spread wings, and barking dog, silverplated, Reed & Barton, late 19th century.   **$125**

BRIGHT-CUT FLORAL and foliate engraved, set of 6, molded ovals, in a fitted case, Mappin & Webb, Sheffield, 1903.
     $300/set

CHILD RIDING TURTLE, figural, American, silverplated late 19th century.   **$125**

CLIP, Lunt, in Mt. Vernon pattern, early 20th century, American.   **$85**

ELK with hornlike antlers, pulls ring on wheels, long trailing yokes, American, late 19th century, silverplated.   **$250**

ENGRAVED, numbered, set of 6, plain, circular, Messrs. Barnard, London, 1900.   **$350/set**

HAND-HAMMERED, American, early 20th century.   **$25**

KATE GREENAWAY FIGURAL, American, Derby, silverplated, late 19th century.   **$195**

KITTEN PULLING CART, figural with ring, wheels revolve, American, silverplated, late 19th century.   **$275**

LARGE SIZE, plain, reeded borders, American, early 20th century.   **$85**

LITTLE GOAT PULLING CART, figural, wheels revolve, American, silverplated, late 19th century.   **$275**

NUMBERED, set of 6, bright-cut with ivy leaves, in a fitted case. **$125/set**

PRANCING HORSE PULLING CART, American, silverplated, late 19th century. **$295**

REEDED, set of 6, engraved with a crest, Thomas Bradbury & Son, Sheffield, 1917. **$250/set**

RING ON SHEET OF MUSIC, violin leaning on ring, Wilcox, American, silverplated, late 19th century. **$300**

SAILORS, 2, figural, American, Rogers, silverplated, late 19th century. **$225**

WAISTED, pair, sterling silver applied with scrolling foliate borders, in a fitted case, London, 1909. **$125/pr**

Nutmeg Graters

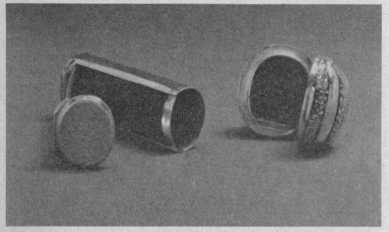

Left. *English nutmeg grater, c. 1788, $625.* Right. *American Tiffany sterling nutmeg grater, c. 1880, $750.* Courtesy of H & H Antiques. Photo by J. Auslander.

In Elizabethan days highly spiced foods were favored, and nutmegs were considered a fine condiment and gift. They were used to flavor ale and wine punches and also were thought to be a stimulant.

Pocket nutmeg graters were in great demand from the late 18th century to the middle of the 19th, the best being made in sterling silver. It became stylish to carry your own nutmeg with a grater in a small container. The earliest forms of graters were simple box types with a place to store the whole nutmeg. By 1750 graters began to have decorations of shellwork and rococo scrolls. Those in urn form with a split along one side date from the late 18th century. After that most were cylindrical. In England those made before 1790 were often unmarked and were unusually small to avoid assay and duty tax. At the close of the 18th century, newer forms included the egg, urn, and barrel shapes. Others resembled goblets, strawberries, walnuts, and shoes. These were further decorated with wriggle work and bright-cut engraving. Graters made at a later time had engine-turned engraving.

Butlers' graters are considered quite rare. They were usually four to six inches in length with an exposed grater and large handle. Originally, the grater hung from the butler's belt or chatelaine along with the keys to the wine cellar, a corkscrew, and a wine taster.

BUTLER'S, reeded, with loop handle, engraved with a crest, London, 1831. **$550**

DOUBLE-HINGED, lid bright-cut with a vignette of a bowl of fruit on a sunburst ground, Phipps & Robinson, London, 1828. **$600**

ENGINE-TURNED, cylindrical, of oval sections, Birmingham, 1831. **$450**

HEART SHAPE, sterling silver, the base and lid engraved with a heart, Continental. **$475**

KITCHEN, cylindrical, with loop handle, John Reily, 1805. **$700**

KITCHEN, usual form, with gadroon border, Thomas Phipps and Edward Robinson II, 1806. **$800**

OVAL, decorated with friezes of spotwork, lid similarly decorated, Joseph Taylor, Birmingham, 1800. **$225**

OVAL, box shape, with bright-cut frieze, center with monogram, Susanna Barker, 1792. **$400**

OVAL, double-hinged, lid engraved with an initial and bright-cut with laurel wreaths and a decorative border, William Stevenson, London, 1828. **$350**

OVOID, stamped with scrollwork, flowers, and foliage, maker's mark only, S.M. **$475**

RECTANGULAR, with cut corners, lid engraved with an armorial and initials, Phipps & Robinson, London, 1800. **$400**

RECTANGULAR, George III, base and lid engraved with foliage, Samuel Pemberton, Birmingham, 1809. **$325**

RECTANGULAR, gilt-lined, double-hinged, A.J.S., London, 1817. **$550**

RECTANGULAR, sides, base, and lid engine-turned, lid with presentation inscription in rectangular cartouche, J.L., London, 1819. **$625**

TEARDROP SHAPE, hinged cover engraved with a crest, probably c. 1740. **$225**

WALNUT FORM, with foliate and plain decoration, Victorian, sterling silver, Hilliard & Thomason, Birmingham, 1852.

$350

WALNUT SHAPE, with embossed flower banding, Tiffany & Co. **$750**

Overlay

Group of late 19th-century American sterling overlay bottles. Courtesy of Christie's East, New York.

Late Victorian and early-20th-century glass or crystal cologne bottles, decanters, flasks, and inkwells were overlaid with sterling silver tracery, which was, in turn, engraved with rococo swirls and florals. Many late-19th-century American styles of overlay featured floral and fruit forms, including roses, lilies, and thistles or grapes and leafage. Some rare examples have strawberry or blackberry motifs. Usually a cartouche of silver was designed for an engraved initial or monogram.

The overlay technique was also used for trivets, which were placed under wine or lemonade pitchers, teapots, or centerpiece bowls. Very small coasters in sets of twelve were made in the early 20th century.

The most desirable examples of overlay combine colorful glass with sterling silver tracery. Although cranberry, ruby, and vibrant green are the most highly prized colors, clear glass examples are also collected. Clear does not command as high a price as the colors.

American firms such as Kerr, Gorham, Alvin, Whiting, Mauser, and Black, Starr & Frost produced many pieces of overlay. It is sometimes difficult to find the maker's mark.

Silver overlay was also occasionally used on pottery, wood, and metal objects. Gorham decorated Rookwood pottery with sterling overlay.

When buying, check the objects carefully in good light to determine if there are interior cracks, bruises at the neck, or bits of overlay missing. Overlay should not be confused with silver deposit glass, which is simply silver painted onto glass and easily removed by washing.

BOWL, green glass, sterling silver overlay, Alvin, late 19th century, diameter, 12 in.   **$350**

COLOGNE BOTTLE, clear glass, cloudy, early 20th century, American.   **$100**

COLOGNE BOTTLE, cranberry glass with sterling silver overlay, 6 in.   **$375**

DECANTER, black glass, sterling overlay depicting golf figure, early 20th century, American.   **$325**

DECANTER, black glass, with 6 cups, sterling silver rooster motif.   **$300/set**

DECANTER, clear glass, tennis figures.   **$350**

DECANTER, bell shape, green glass overlaid with filigree decoration, conical cork attached by a chain.   **$125**

DECANTER, liquor, glass, bottle divided into 4 chambers with sterling pierced overlay of Japanese maple leaves, capped by silver tumbler, French, height, 13 in.   **$350**

INKWELL, ball shape, with overlay, Continental, late 19th century.   **$375**

JUG, claret, with scrolling thistle decoration, surrounding vacant cartouche, late 19th century.   **$850**

JUG, claret, vase shape, ruby glass overlaid with scrolling grapevines with leaves and clusters of grapes, late 19th century.   **$1,500**

PITCHER, claret, clear glass with sterling silver overlay, late 19th century.   **$450**

PITCHER, water, bulbous, clear glass, early 20th century.

$225

TRIVET, large, floral, American, early 20th century.   **$350**

TRIVET, teapot size, floral, early 20th century, American.
                                             $100

TRIVET, teapot size, rococo scrolls, early 20th century, American.   **$125**

Perfume Bottles

English sterling filigree perfume (scent) bottle, c. 1840, $350.

Eighteenth-century perfume bottles or boxes were often in bottle shapes, sometimes flattened in form and meant to be worn on a chatelaine. These were susperseded by bottles of glass with sterling silver or gold mounts. Many were beautifully faceted and by the mid-1800s were found in attractive shades of amber, ruby, cobalt, green, and cranberry. At the same time, double-ended cylindrical bottles were made with sterling silver mounts, one end for perfume, the other for smelling salts. Today these tend to be more popular in England than in the United States.

In the late 19th century in the United States, cut-crystal bottles with decorative sterling silver ornamentation in the form of cherubs, foliage, and women's heads were popular. In England and on the Continent there were many novelty porcelain bottles in the shapes of strawberries, acorns, nuts, birds, and eggs, all with sterling silver or silverplated caps and collars.

Art Nouveau examples are found entirely in sterling silver or silverplate, with lovely shellwork and foliate details, or in mixed metals.

Figural types include a series of sterling silver bottles depicting musical instruments, such as the lute, mandolin, violin, and cello; they were made in Holland and Germany in the late 19th and early 20th centuries. They are usually chased in 18th-century rococo style with court scenes and foliate details. Most have silver strings, and some have their own built-in stands.

Shells were another popular form for bottles and included several types of mollusks, clams, mussels, periwinkles, and scallops—all created in elaborately chased and embossed sterling silver and silverplate detail, some with parcel-gilt enrichment.

Swaddling baby forms were popular in Europe and England in the middle and late 19th century, and filigree-covered bottles exist from the 17th century. Eighteenth-century Chelsea porcelain and 19th-century French and English cameo glass bottles usually had engraved silver mounts.

Large glass bottles for cologne with sterling silver tops were generally found as part of elaborate dresser sets.

Double perfume flask, Tiffany, Persian style, 1875–1891, $1,300. **Courtesy of Christie's East, New York.**

BIRD'S-EGG SCENT BOTTLE, silver-mounted porcelain, Sampson Mordan, London, 1887.   **$175**

BOTTLE, STERLING, with funnel and fitted case, Mexican, mid-20th century.   **$75**

COLOGNE BOTTLE, flute-cut oblong glass, cut with swags of roses, tops with black and white guilloche enameling.   **$125**

COLOGNE BOTTLE, hobnail pattern, cut glass, square, hinged cover stamped with rococo flowers and foliage, Birmingham, 1910.   **$250**

COLOGNE BOTTLE, silver-gilt and tortoise-shell-mounted cut glass, London, 1920.   **$300**

COMBINATION HORN-SHAPE vinaigrette and scent flask, silver-gilt-mounted glass, T.J., London, 1874.   **$600**

COMBINATION NOVELTY SCENT BOTTLE and propelling pencil, with finger ring and chain attachment, Sampson Mordan, 1874.   **$325**

ETUI, EMBOSSED WITH FLOWERS and scrolls on a matte background, with chain attachment, containing a mounted glass scent bottle, Taylor & Perry, Birmingham, 1831.   **$400**

FISH, SCENT BOTTLE, large, cut glass, the silver-mounted screw top forming the fin, engraved with scalework, Sampson Mordan, London, 1884.   **$1,200**

JAR, SACHET, silver, hobnail pattern, heart shape, cut glass, cover stamped with a foliate border, Birmingham, 1907.
                                                            $225

LAY-DOWN, oval, yellow enamel overlaid with silver in the form of flowers, cased all around with silver, original screw closure, length, 2 in.   **$245**

PORCELAIN HORN, silver-gilt mounted, painted with birds in flight, one end formed as a vinaigrette, Sampson Mordan, London, 1871.   **$750**

SCENT BOTTLE, chased in a raffia pattern and applied with meandering sprays of flowering vine, with chased pink-gold flowers and buds and yellow-gold leaves, screw-on cap and chained finger ring, unmarked, 19th century.   **$750**

SCENT BOTTLE, modeled as a seashell, Birmingham, 1939.
                                                            $400

SCENT BOTTLE, 19th century, silver-mounted cut glass, novelty, fashioned as a chicken, the mount and the hinged head chased with plumage, with ruby glass eyes, 4½ in.   **$750**

Group of late 18th- and early 19th-century English scent bottles. **Top center.** *Scottish horseshoe shape with colored agate, $550.* **Courtesy of Phillips, London.**

SCENT BOTTLE, bright-cut engraved, depicting Little Bo Peep, London, 1894. **$275**

SCENT BOTTLE, cylindrical, double-ended, sterling silver, bright-cut with flowers, foliage, and birds, Sampson Mordan, London, 1882. **$385**

SCENT BOTTLE, cylindrical, bright-cut engraved with flowers, foliage, birds, and insects, Sampson Mordan, London, 1884. **$275**

SCENT BOTTLE, double-ended, cut glass, English, late 19th century. **$225**

SCENT BOTTLE, horseshoe shape, engraved and set with panels of colored agates, Scottish, 1880. **$550**

SCENT BOTTLE, late 19th century, Continental, with screw cap modeled as a baby in swaddling clothes and bonnet, unmarked, c. 1890. **$250**

SCENT BOTTLE, modeled as a flat fish with glass eye, Dutch, 1891. **$200**

SCENT BOTTLE, novelty, modeled as a lute stamped and chased with 17th-century style figures and arabesques, Continental, early 20th century.   **$250**

SCENT BOTTLE, novelty, modeled as a mandolin, stamped and chased with putti and arabesques, Continental, early 20th century.   **$250**

SCENT BOTTLE, oval, chased with scrollwork, flowers, and animals, the stopper formed as a swan.   **$275**

SCENT BOTTLE, seashell shape, decorated with mollusks and seaweed, London, 1888.   **$1,500**

SCENT BOTTLE, silver-mounted cut glass, flattened oval, mount bright-cut with flowers and foliage, Dutch, late 19th century.   **$225**

SCENT BOTTLE, silver-mounted cut glass, globular, engraved with initials, Birmingham, 1908.   **$125**

SCENT BOTTLE, tapering, part-fluted, with scrollwork, Birmingham, 1885.   **$250**

SCENT BOTTLE, Victorian pottery, in the form of an acorn with silver screw-top lid, Birmingham, 1888.   **$185**

SCENT BOTTLE HOLDER, unmarked, articulated fish, body engraved with scalework.   **$275**

Pincushions

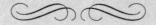

English sterling pincushions. **Top.** *Bull and carriage, $350.* **Left.** *Rabbit, $275.* **Right.** *Goat, $290.* **Courtesy of Phillips, London.**

In Victorian times the steel pin was a recent invention and costly to own. Pins were securely placed in pincushions and holders, which usually had a padded cushion containing powdered emery to keep the pins rust-free and sharp.

Embroidered pincushions were the first popular type. They were soon followed by novelty shapes depicting animals, birds, human figures, boats, hall racks, and cradles, with sterling silver frames or bases. The birds and animals vary in size from one-half inch to five or six inches. Among the animals, most of which were produced in Birmingham or Chester, England, in the late 19th and early 20th centuries, the bulldog and the articulated monkey are among the most desirable for today's collector. Many of the animals are being reproduced today. Check the hallmarks. Often the lack of crisp detailing will be a clue to dating the piece. Pincushions in every style of shoe or slipper form, from elaborate closed Louis heels to flat Turkish slippers in a great array of sizes, were made during the late

19th and early 20th centuries in Europe, England, and the
United States.

BULLDOG FIGURAL, medium size, English, late 19th century.
                                                     $650

BULL FIGURAL, pulling a mother-of-pearl carriage, Birmingham, c. 1900.   **$350**

CHICKEN FIGURAL, small, English, early 20th century. **$175**

DOLL FORM, with sterling half-body, medium size, English,
early 20th century.   **$350**

DUTCH, ARMOIRE, figural, Tiffany & Company, c. 1890.
                                                     $475

ELEPHANT FIGURAL, small, English, late 19th century. **$225**

FOX FIGURAL, medium size, English, late 19th century.
                                                     $350

GOAT FIGURAL, maker's mark, Birmingham, 1921.   **$290**

GOLF CLUBS CROSSED, silver surround, English, early 20th
century.   **$350**

HEART SHAPE, embossed florals, English, late 19th century.
                                                     $150

MILITARY HAT FORM, English, early 20th century.   **$150**

MUZZLED BEAR FIGURAL, articulated, Birmingham, 1909.
                                                     $600

RABBIT FIGURAL, crouching, Adie & Lovekin Ltd, Birmingham, 1907.   ·   **$275**

RED CROSS FORM, English, early 20th century.   **$75**

ROCKING CRADLE, American, late 19th century.   **$150**

ROLLER SKATE, silverplated, English, late 19th century.
                                                     $300

SPIDER FIGURAL, large, English, early 20th century. **$950**

SWAN FIGURAL, Birmingham, 1921.   **$175**

Place Card Holders

Set of English silver-gilt place card holders, $300/4. Photo by J. Auslander.

During the middle and late Victorian era, meal presentations were elaborate affairs with many courses. To indicate the number of the course being served, sterling silver menu holders were placed on the table. The place card holder, indicating seating at the table, replaced the menu holder. They held charming cards, often hand-decorated with watercolors by the ladies of the household. Menu and place card holders were made in the shapes of animals, flowers, birds, fences, and sporting motifs. They were also combined with tortoise shell or had hand-painted inset porcelain plaques. Many of the full-figure animal and bird forms had shoe-button glass eyes. In America sets were made by Gorham and Tiffany, and many of these were sold in England from the late 19th century until World War I. Tiffany produced sterling silver examples in cast seashell and pineapple forms. Collectors look for unusual examples and pay higher prices for original boxed sets.

CIRCULAR, SET OF 4, each inset with a picture of a game dog holding a bird in its mouth, in fitted case, English, late 19th century.   **$300/set**

CIRCULAR, 6, PLAIN, in a fitted case, Sampson Mordan & Co., Chester.   **$350/set**

CIRCULAR BASES, set of 12, with figure of cherub playing instrument, Continental, late 19th century.   **$800/set**

CREST, pair, each modeled as an eagle with outstretched wings, London, 1891.   **$150/pr**

ENAMELED GAME BIRDS, 4, English sterling silver, each with a different bird, Sampson Mordan, Chester, 1904. **$1,200/set**

MIRRORS, small, beveled, set of 8, each on scrollwork frame, American, early 20th century.   **$475/set**

MODELED as an elephant in front of a palm tree, set of 4, Goldsmiths & Silversmiths Company, 1913.   **$750/set**

OBLONG, pair, tortoise shell inlaid with paterae and swags in a fitted case, William Comyns, Birmingham, 1913.   **$150/pr**

PARCEL-GILT, set of 4, applied with cast and chased models of game birds on plinths, in a fitted case, English, late 19th century.   **$550/set**

WISHBONES, double, set of 4, George Unite, Birmingham, 1920.   **$300/set**

Pocketknives (Fruit)

Although commonly referred to as pocketknives, most of these pieces were actually used as folding fruit knives. Those found today usually date from the late 19th century through the early part of the 20th century.

Folding fruit knives were made in England and the United States with sterling silver blades, which were replaced by steel blades in the 20th century.

Engraved examples are particularly collectible. There are rare tiny knives with corkscrews, some small enough to hang from a watch fob and others about five inches in length.

FOLDING, with corkscrew and tweezers, engraved sterling, early 20th century, American. **$125**

FOLDING, engraved foliate borders, American, coin silver.
$100

FRUIT, allover-engraved sterling, American, late 19th century.
$75

FRUIT, silverplated, late 19th century. **$22**

Posey Holders

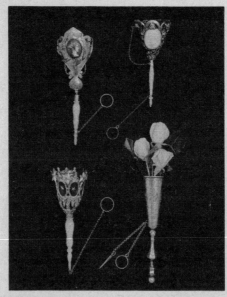

Group of mid-19th-century sterling and silverplate posey holders. **Collection of Marion and Robert Pape.**

*U*sually three to six inches in length, posey holders are cone- or cup-shaped. Filled with a nosegay, or bouquet, they were used to conceal street smells or were carried as part of a fashionable ensemble. Popular in the 18th century and extremely fashionable in the 19th century, posey holders usually have a slender handle (for ease of carrying), most often with a chain and finger ring and a pin to keep the flowers securely in place. Some posey holder handles open to reveal a tripod base. Pin-on, buttonhole, or lapel posey holders also were made, as well as some in child size. Decorations included engraving, embossing, enameling, and embellishing with pearls, agates, turquoise, garnets, semiprecious or precious stones, cameos, or mirrors. Examples in sterling silver and silverplate were made in the United States, China, England, France, India, and other countries.

In England those with makers' marks are coveted; in the United States, posey holders made by Kerr, Unger Brothers, or Tiffany are very desirable.

When buying, look for a posey holder with an *original* handle, and make sure the piece has no dents. Test for sterling silver content because very few are hallmarked. Note that very heavy silverplate in good repair often is mistaken for sterling silver. Filigree examples can be sterling silver or silverplate.

Prices range from quite low for a simple buttonhole posey holder to extremely high for rare examples containing vinaigrettes, mechanical types with petals that open and close, and oddities such as thermometers or aide-memoires incorporated into the cup.

BOSOM, MID-19TH CENTURY, French, blue opaline glass with sterling silver filigree flowers and bell. **$450**

BROOCH TYPE, sterling silver, flower holder applied with the head of a stag surrounded by a laurel wreath and ribbon swag. **$195**

BUTTONHOLE, gentleman's, mid-19th century, English, sterling silver, in original box. **$150**

BUTTONHOLE, late 19th century, sterling silver with applied fern. **$150**

CAST VICTORIAN PARCEL-GILT, the bowl formed from trailing foliage, the branch forming the handle. **$475**

CONE SHAPE, late 19th century, English, sterling silver, with openwork trellis motif and embossed fox and grapes, with shaped handle. **$475**

CONE SHAPE, late 19th century, French, sterling silver, with embossed and openwork butterfly and leaf-shape handle. **$450**

EMBOSSED, late 19th century, English, silverplate, with chased acorns and leaves and straight handle. **$325**

EMBOSSED, late 19th century, English, sterling silver, chased with thistles and leaves and straight sterling silver engraved handle. **$500**

EMBOSSED, late 19th century, English, sterling silver, with curved handle and top embossed with leafage vines and bunches of grapes. **$475**

EMBOSSED, with bulbous leaf and berry motif, c. 1870, silver-plated.   **$325**

EMBOSSED, STERLING SILVER, with heavily chased holly and leaves and shaped straight handle.   **$525**

EMBOSSED, STERLING SILVER, with open grape and leaf top, Scottish agate handle.   **$550**

EMBOSSED, STERLING SILVER, with pierced and heavily chased top with flowers and leafage, green-dyed ivory turned handle.   **$550**

EMBOSSED, STERLING SILVER, cup formed from vine leaves, grapes, and tendrils, with figure-8 tubular handle.   **$475**

EMBOSSED, VICTORIAN, sterling silver, bowl bright-cut with foliage and applied with birds collecting twigs, the straight tubular handle bright-cut, chain and finger loop attached. **$525**

ENGRAVED, FLORAL-DECORATED, late 19th century, French, sterling silver, with curved handle.   **$400**

FILIGREE, late 19th century, French, sterling silver, with leaf-shape top and curved handle.   **$425**

FILIGREE, late 19th century, Silesian, sterling silver, with top and self-wrapped handle.   **$450**

FILIGREE, VICTORIAN, sterling silver, widely flaring bowl and faceted handle formed from scrolled filigree work, with chain, pin, and finger loop attached.   **$500**

GILDED, late 19th century, English, silverplate, with turned mother-of-pearl handle and top pierced in ribbon and bowknot effect.   **$350**

GILT METAL, pierced and stamped with foliage, wood, grapes, birds, and birds' nests, handle stamped with foliage and scroll-work.   **$425**

GILT METAL, with 4 panels stamped and pierced with fuchias, foliage, and birds, mother-of-pearl turned handle.   **$375**

GILT METAL, ENGINE-TURNED, bowl applied with a floral and foliate rim, with tubular looped handle applied with foliate terminal, chain and finger loop attached.   **$375**

GILT METAL, PIERCED SCROLLWORK, acorns, and engraved handle with tripod base.   **$550**

PANELED, PETAL SHAPE, mid-19th century, English, sterling silver with pavé set garnets, carved and swirled mother-of-pearl handle, garnet-set finger ring and chain.   **$1,900**

PANELED, 4 SECTIONS, mid-19th century, French, sterling silver, terminating in points and straight handle, the entire piece allover engraved. **$450**

PANELED, 4 SIDES, extremely large, silverplate, with leafy top and leaf-capped handle. **$325**

PANELED, 4 SIDES, French, sterling silver, with flower-embossed center and scroll handle. **$425**

PANELED, 6 SIDES, Victorian, slender, bowl formed with shell terminals, chain and finger loop attached, Birmingham, 1899. **$450**

PIERCED AND STAMPED with shells and scrollwork, sterling silver, turned mother-of-pearl handle. **$450**

PIN-ON, mid-19th century, English, large, with shaped leaves and bird perched on leaf. **$350**

SECTIONED STERLING SILVER TOP, with engraved figure-8 handle, c. 1879. **$425**

SHELL FORM, with imitation pearls and leaves overpainted in green, handle of turned mother-of-pearl. **$650**

SIMPLE, LATE 19TH CENTURY, English, sterling silver, with straight engraved handle. **$425**

STRAIGHT FORM, STERLING SILVER, with chrysanthemums, blossoms, buds, and leaves in high relief, Unger Brothers, c. 1880. **$500**

TRIPOD, filigree, sterling silver, with tiny flowers at center and folding legs. **$750**

TRIPOD, late 19th century, French, sterling silver, with scalloped top monogrammed Edinburgh September 1891, legs with engraved motifs. **$775**

TRIPOD, mid-19th century, French, sterling silver, with amphora-shape cup having curved rim and engraved florals. **$750**

TRIPOD, Russian, sterling silver, with enameled Cyrillic lettering at top, dated 1881, in original case. **$2,200**

TRIPOD, sterling silver, engraved with reeding, with 3 hinged legs collapsing to form handle, London, 1882. **$750**

TRIPOD, tulip shape, the bowl engraved with flowers, foliage, and scrollwork, the handle with ball terminal unscrewing stand, with chain and ring attached, 8½ in. **$750**

Salts

Set of four English standing salt cellars in 17th-century style, c. 1873, $2,000/4. **Courtesy of Christie's South Kensington, London.**

*I*n medieval times in England it was common practice for a large and ornate master salt to grace the dining table; that was the origin of the salt cellar. During the late 1600s the individual trencher-style salt with a shallow center well began to be used. During Georgian times open salts with clipped or rounded corners appeared. This style continued through the late 18th century and had a revival in the early 19th century.

By the early 18th century legs began to be added to elevate the salt. Several types were used, often slender legs with mask or swag decoration on paw, ball-and-claw, or hoof feet. In the 19th century salts were cast or spun with rococo, shell, or swag designs. Cobalt blue glass liners used inside pierced salt cellars date from the mid-18th century. Some of these are intricately hand cut in rococo and chinoiserie styles.

Victorian salts were made in a great variety of shapes, usually with glass liners. In America the footed circular salt was produced in the early 19th century and was decorated with gadrooned borders, shellwork, or applied swags and bowknots. Others had pierced designs or beaded rims, Gothic motifs, and medallions. Boat-shape salts also became popular and were often bright-cut engraved with flowers and foliage. At the end of the 19th and the beginning of the 20th centuries, in both England and the United States, full-figure salt-and-peppers depicting barnyard animals and human figures became extremely popular.

Pepper casters originated in the 17th century in France. By the 18th century they had become more prevalent and were appearing in pear or octagonal forms. The early 20th century saw English pepperettes in the form of sailors, monkeys, cats, and birds. These fetch high prices at English auctions and shows today.

BEADED, PAIR, pierced and bright-cut oval on curved legs, each with glass liner, C.H., London, 1788. **$110/pr**

BOAT SHAPE, ON OVAL FOOT, set of 4, with reeded rim, engraved with crest, John Gold, London, 1800. **$750/set**

CALDRON SHAPE, pair, on lion's-mask and paw feet, with blue glass liner, Robert Hennell, London, 1871. **$225/pr**

CIRCULAR, GILT-LINED, STANDING, set of 4, in the 17th century taste, with masks and on cherub feet chased with flowers and applied with dragons. **$2,000/set**

CIRCULAR, SET OF 4, with key-pattern rims, raised on 3 ram's-head and hoof supports, Tiffany & Co., New York, c. 1865. **$2,600/set**

CIRCULAR, SET OF 6, modeled as quaiches, each with foliate-pierced handle, in a fitted case, London, 1912. **$400/set**

FIGURAL DOUBLE SALT, late 19th century, in form of a youth in 18th-century costume and tricorn hat, striding and holding a basket in both hands, another by his feet, Odiot, Paris, height, 6³⁄₈ in. **$2,500**

FIGURAL, PAIR, GORHAM, c. 1865, on shaped oval base with 2 realistically modeled foxes. **$750/pr**

FLORAL AND FOLIATE-CHASED, pair, on hoof feet, each engraved with a crest and with glass liner, London, 1856. **$150/pr**

English sterling shell salt cellar mounted on goat, c. 1849, $1,100. Courtesy of Christie's South Kensington, London.

GADROONED, pair, oval caldron on shell and hoof feet, Robert Hennell, London, 1790.   **$275/pr**

GEORGE II, pair, ornamented with engraved cartouches and cast lions' masks, ball-and-claw feet, George Wickes, 1742.
                                                                          $500/pr

GLASS, SILVER-MOUNTED, pair, and pair of salt spoons with ball terminals, in fitted case, Birmingham, 1906.   **$75/set**

GOTHIC REVIVAL OPEN SALTS, pair, circular, with crenelated border, triform base with 3 supports formed as lions bearing shields, Gorham, 1869.   **$450/pr**

NATURALISTIC, in the form of knobby shells, pair, raised on sprays of coral and conch shells, John S. Hunt, London, 1849, length, 4 in.   **$3,000/pr**

NAVETTE FORM, set of 4, with reeded band and reeded loop handles, engraved with band of rosettes and paterae, Robert Hennell, London, 1790.   **$1,400/set**

NORWEGIAN, longboat style, decorated with plique-à-jour enameling, with 2 stylized dragon-head terminals.   **$525**

OLD SHEFFIELD PLATE, pair, beaded, pierced, and bright-cut oval on claw-and-ball feet, each with glass liner.   **$100/pr**

OPEN, SET OF 4, each rectangular with dentilated border on shell feet with gold-washed interiors, glass liners, Dublin, 1809.
$600/set

PARTLY FLUTED, BOAT-SHAPE pedestal, set of 4, E.T., London, 1887.
$250/set

PEPPERETTE, MODELED AS A KITTEN, cast and chased sterling silver, Robert Hennell, London, 1875.
$1,200

PEPPERETTES, pair, modeled as owls, the detachable heads with paste-set eyes, silverplated.
$250/pr

PEPPERETTES, pair, octagonal, vase shape, on rising circular bases, each with a pointed finial, D.F., Birmingham, 1896.
$200/pr

PEPPERMILL, formed as a soda syphon, silverplated.
$65

PEPPERS, SILVER-GILT, modeled as poppy heads, set of 4, E.H. Stockwell, 1876–79.
$950/set

REGENCY, pair, molded oblong, on ball feet, each with an applied gadroon, shell and foliate border and glass liner.
$100/pr

ROCOCO SLEIGHS, set of 6, with swan's-head prows, each with seated cherub, Continental.
$700/set

RUSSIAN, PARCEL-GILT, throne salt engraved with Cyrillic inscriptions and stars, S. Ikonnikov, Moscow, 1880.
$400

SCALLOP SHELL form, pair, R. & W. Wilson, Philadelphia, c. 1865.
$650/pr

SHELLS, gilt-lined, pair, on dolphin feet, London, 1875.
$200/pr

SPIRAL-FLUTED, circular, on ball feet, set of 4, Heath and Middleton, London, 1888.
$225/set

SPIRAL-FLUTED, 4, pedestal, with 4 matching spoons with ball terminals, in a fitted case, Birmingham, 1892.
$250/set

TRENCHER, octagonal, on molded base, by James Seabrook, 1716.
$200

TRIANGULAR, pair, on scroll feet, borders with plique-à-jour mounts decorated with stylized shells and scrolls, with a pair of matching salt shovels, in fitted case, Norwegian. **$550/set**

TWO-HANDLE OVAL, pair, plain, reeded, on pedestal feet with blue-glass liners, looped handles, by Henry Chawner, 1787.
$375/pr

VEGETABLE, SET OF 4, in the form of a pumpkin and 3 different gourds, with textured gilt-metal bodies, with silver, copper, and enameled leaves, losses to enamel, c. 1880–90.
$850/set

Sewing Tools

Sterling needlework tools. Top. English sterling thread holder, c. 1880. Center. American Unger Bros. hem measure, c. 1880. Bottom. Dutch sterling scissor/sheath, late 18th century. **Courtesy of Nancy and Bruce Thompson.**

*N*eedle cases, pincushions, and thimble holders were all necessary to the fine art of needlework in the 18th, 19th, and early 20th centuries.

Needle cases were made in England, France, and China in the 19th century. They were also produced in the United States by Kerr, Unger Brothers, Gorham, Webster, and others. Figural needle cases made in France in the 18th and early 19th centuries often depicted human figures, including Napoleon, fishermen, and women.

Pincushions may be simple and circular with a sterling silver or silverplate border or of novelty animal designs with pincushion backs. These were often made in the late 19th and early 20th centuries in Birmingham and Chester, England. Also popular were basket forms, generally hung from a chatelaine.

Thimble holders in casket, acorn, or basket shapes were used to keep track of thimbles in the 18th and 19th centuries. They are found in silverplate and sterling silver and were made on the Continent, in England, and in other countries.

Scissor sheaths in sterling silver and silverplate were made in Holland, Germany, and England. They were used with matching scissors and often hung from a chatelaine.

Sewing clamps to hold the fabric taut while it was being worked were most often designed with a pincushion top and were generally silverplated. Most of the brass examples found in markets today originally had a plating of silver. The largest clamps originally were used in tailors' shops. The most collectible are in the forms of birds, butterflies, and dogs.

Bird clamps are being reproduced today in Japan with the original United States patent date embossed into the design. The detailing is not as sharp as on the originals.

Interesting novelties, such as sterling silver knitting needle covers in the forms of slippers, shoes, and dog's heads, were made in France and Holland in the mid-19th century, as were knitting needle sheaths and sets of tambour and crochet hooks.

BODKIN, figural owl with glass eyes, Birmingham, 1917. **$75**

BODKIN CASE, complete with thimble and cotton bobbin, engraved with flowers and bright-cut decoration.   **$600**

BODKIN CASE, incorporating a thimble, bobbin, and pin holder, with bright-cut decoration, late 18th century. **$1,300**

BODKINS, set of 3, boxed, American, early 20th century.

$50/set

BODKINS, SET, novelty, sports motifs depicting football, baseball, and boating, American, early 20th century.   **$225/set**

CLAMP, BIRD, red plush pincushion, silverplated.   **$175**

CLAMP, SEWING, butterfly at top, mid-19th century.   **$600**

CLAMP, SEWING, oversize, silverplated, dog at top.   **$950**

COMBINATION THIMBLE, bobbin, and pin holder on a pedestal foot, decorated with bright-cut decoration, mid-19th century.   **$450**

COMBINATION THIMBLE HOLDER pincushion, egg shape, embossed florals, Gorham, late 19th century.   **$400**

COMPENDIUM, MODELED as a walnut containing a hinged reel, tape measure, and thimble, unmarked, c. 1880.   **$700**

American darning egg with sterling handle, c. 1880, $75. Courtesy of H & H Antiques. Photo by J. Auslander.

DARNING EGG, ebonized with silver mounts. **$45**

ETUI, ivory egg with sterling silver sewing tools, late 18th century. **$750**

ETUI, leather case, 15-karat gold bodkin, scissor, thimble, and winders, late 19th century. **$900**

ETUI, opaline glass egg on gilded base, with silver-gilt tools, French, late 18th century. **$1,200**

GLOVE DARNER, with needle case. **$125**

GLOVE DARNER, Art Nouveau, embossed curves, American. **$75**

GLOVE DARNER, embossed floral motifs, late 19th century, American. **$75**

HEM MEASURE, Art Nouveau, cherubs, Kerr, late 19th century. **$175**

HEM MEASURE, sterling silver floral top, silverplated measure. **$50**

HUSSIF, containing bobbin and thimble holder, Dutch, late 18th century. **$900**

KNITTING NEEDLE ENDS, shoe shapes, French, mid-19th century. **$150/pr**

KNITTING NEEDLE ENDS, urn shapes, French, mid-19th century. **$135/pr**

Sterling needlework tools. Left. Eighteenth-century Dutch knitting needle sheath, $250. Right. French sterling knitting needle ends, c. 1870. Ball ends, $150/pair; engraved, $150/pair.

KNITTING NEEDLES, 14-karat gold, Tiffany & Co., early 20th century. **$750/pr**

KNITTING NEEDLES, enameled ends, American, early 20th century. **$250/pr**

KNITTING SHEATH, embossed florals, Dutch, 18th century. **$225**

NECESSAIRE, ivory, oblong, fitted with 6 sewing implements with bright-cut gilt mounts, French. **$375**

NEEDLE CASE, embossed floral, Gorham, American, late 19th century. **$75**

NEEDLE CASE, embossed stars, American, late 19th century. **$75**

NEEDLE CASE, figural, peasant woman, French, early 19th century. **$275**

NEEDLE CASE, filigree, Chinese, mid-19th century. **$100**

PINCUSHION, chatelaine type, embossed, circular, Kerr, late 19th century. **$125**

PINCUSHION, chatelaine type, fan shape, sterling silver mounts, American, late 19th century. **$125**

PINCUSHION, chatelaine type, woman's head, Unger Bros., late 19th century. **$175**

PINCUSHION, chick emerging from an eggshell, Chester, 1912. **$150**

PINCUSHION, crouching frog form, S. and Co., Birmingham, 1907.   **$250**

PINCUSHION, embossed scene of Windsor Castle, English, early 19th century.   **$450**

PINCUSHION, heart shape, sterling silver mounts, American, late 19th century.   **$150**

PINCUSHION, laced boot form, L and S., Birmingham, 1906.
                                                                   $200

PINCUSHION, modeled as an elephant, small, trunk raised, English, early 20th century.   **$150**

PINCUSHION, novelty, modeled as a pig, small, English, early 20th century.   **$150**

PINCUSHION, rabbit, small, English, early 20th century.
                                                                   $275

PINCUSHION, ring tree, novelty, formed as a parrot on perch, the parrot with a pincushion back, Birmingham, 1909. **$150**

REEL HOLDER, enamel and sterling silver, American, early 20th century.   **$150**

REEL HOLDER, simple design, English hallmarks, late 19th century.   **$225**

RIBBON THREADER, figural stork shape, baby inside, Dutch, late 19th century.   **$175**

RIBBON THREADERS, set of 4, American, early 20th century, boxed.   **$35/set**

RIBBON THREADERS, stork standing on turtle.   **$150**

SCISSORS, embroidery, sterling silver handles.   **$75**

SCISSORS/SHEATH, allover foliate engraved, late 18th century, Dutch.   **$275**

SEWING SET, thimble and scissors in original fitted box, sterling, c. 1910.   **$75/set**

SHUTTLE, TATTING, allover engraved with flowers and scrollwork, Gorham, late 19th century.   **$125**

SHUTTLE, TATTING, allover floral engraved, American, late 19th century.   **$75**

SHUTTLE, TATTING, enameled with floral motifs, Gorham, late 19th century.   **$200**

SHUTTLE, TATTING, plain engraved monogram, American, late 19th century.   **$50**

STRAWBERRY EMERY, sterling silver top, American, late 19th century. **$100**

STRAWBERRY WAXER, sterling silver top, Unger Brothers, late 19th century. **$125**

THIMBLE, BUCKET, embossed florals, English, mid-19th century. **$125**

THIMBLE HOLDER, acorn shape, American, late 19th century. **$150**

THIMBLE HOLDER, pierced and chased florals and cherubs' heads, American, late 19th century. **$200**

THIMBLE HOLDER, reticulated, allover floral decorated, American, late 19th century. **$75**

THREAD HOLDER, embossed florals and ladies' heads, American, late 19th century. **$200**

THREAD WINDER, allover engraved, Gorham, late 19th century. **$75**

THREAD WINDER, repoussé, Unger Brothers, late 19th century. **$100**

WOOL HOLDER, spherical, pierced and bright-cut with strapwork, flowers, and foliage and with suspension ring and chain, Glasgow, 1876. **$375**

Sheffield Plate

Sheffield plate dish ring, c. 1790, having unusual crest with woman's head.
Courtesy of Alice and Derek Hamilton.

Although it had been used before, the process of plating silver over copper became commercially profitable when it was introduced by Thomas Boulsover in England in the 1740s. Sterling silver had become very costly due to heavy taxation by the government, and that created a large market for the substitute, Sheffield plate. In the beginning most Sheffield plate was produced by cutlers, but later silversmiths began to work in the metal; and objects became more artistic, with a greater use of chasing, embossing, and engraving. Pieces were often heavily decorated to hide defects. Between 1785 and 1810 some of the finest pieces were created in simple or classical Adamesque styles.

One of the characteristics of Sheffield plate is an absence of plating on the underside. Most 18th century Sheffield plate has a heavy layer of silver, so the patina should resemble that of a solid silver piece of the same era. Also, most 18th-century pieces had inset cartouches of solid silver for a monogram or armorial. Snuffboxes, wine labels, wine coolers, candlesticks, coasters, épergnes, dish rings, and tureens were a few of the items produced.

Marks on Sheffield plate were erratic in England, but in France marking of Sheffield plate was compulsory. When new designs were created in sterling, they were soon followed in Sheffield plate. Many extremely fine objects were unmarked; therefore, one can often date a piece by the solid silver style. In 1784 the Sheffield plate makers were given permission to impress a maker's mark on the object.

BASKET, cake, beaded oval, wirework swing handles, c. 1780.
$135

BASKET, cake, with flower-decorated gadroon rim, chased with scrolls and berried foliage, interlaced ribbonwork handle rising from satyr masks, on 4 paw feet, c. 1820. **$1,200**

BASKETS, pair, early 19th century, length, 10½ in. **$150/pr**

BEER MUG, plain, tapering cylindrical, with reeded girdle and slightly spread base, wood underbase, scroll handle, and heart terminal, 1770. **$225**

BISCUIT BOX, novelty, book form, engraved "Biscuits" on spine. **$950**

BOX, circular, chased on cover with a cloaked figure holding a spear, flanked by roses and thistles, c. 1765. **$100**

BUTTER DISH, shell shape, on dolphin feet, c. 1775. **$175**

CANDELABRA, pair, 3 lights, the tapering circular stems partly lobed, fluted and curved branches with leaf motifs, center capitals with detached flame finials, base rims struck twice with the Soho double-sun mark, Matthew Boulton, 1810.
$2,400/pr

CANDELABRA, 3 lights, beaded borders, vase-shape stems, leaf-chased sconces, repairs. **$650**

CANDLESTICKS, pair, Neoclassical, on beaded and part-fluted rising shaped-square bases decorated with friezes, square columns applied with rams' masks and laurel swags, height, 12½ in. **$1,400/pr**

CANDLESTICKS, pair silverplated, 18th century, in the Neoclassical taste. **$800/pr**

CANDLESTICKS, pair, silverplated, bas-relief panels depicting figures—peace, war, Hercules—on a Neoclassical standard, late 18th century, height, 11 in. **$1,200/pr**

CANDLESTICKS, set of 4, plated, late 18th century, columnar form, draped Corinthian capitals, fluted shafts. **$2,500/set**

CENTERPIECE, plate, octagonal, on spiral-fluted and lion's-paw feet, 4 detachable scrolling branches with octagonal dish holder. **$375**

COASTERS, pair, circular, with applied open fruiting-vine borders. **$475/pr**

DISH, warming, covered, silverplated, silver finial in the form of a couchant lion, early 19th century, length, 13½ in. **$700**

DISH COVER, silverplated, oval, with gadroon handle, late 18th century, length, 12¼ in. **$400**

DISH CROSS, plain, the sliding supports and feet with shells, rope border, c. 1770. **$800**

EGG CRUET, with 6 gilt-lined egg cups with molded body bands and gadrooned circular salt cellar. **$150**

ENTRÉE DISH and cover on warming stand, gadroon rims with shells and foliage at intervals, the handles with lion-head terminals, on 4 lion-paw feet capped with foliage and shells, Matthew Boulton, c. 1815. **$700**

ÉPERGNE, gadrooned, on leaf-capped paw feet, with 4 detachable scrolling branches with oval dish holders, 16 in. **$500**

GOBLET ON TRUMPET FOOT, with beaded border, body half-fluted below, engraved Neoclassical cartouches and swags, c. 1790. **$175**

JUG, wine, plated, covered, Neoclassical form, height, 11½ in. **$125**

KETTLE, on warming stand, engraved foliate designs, on base with ornate feet, height, 16 in. **$300**

MAZARINE, oval, reeded border, pierced decorative motifs, tinned underbase, 1790. **$200**

MEAT DISH COVERS, pair, fluted oval, applied with friezes of flowers, foliage, and shells, each with a scrolling foliate handle. **$750/pr**

MEAT DOME, adorned with leaf and berry border, 2 coats of arms and elaborate handle, R. Gainsford, c. 1810. **$1,150**

MIRROR PLATEAU, circular, on lion's-paw feet, applied with a frieze of trailing vines, flowers, and scrolling foliage, length, 17½ in. **$1,150**

MIRROR PLATEAU, 3 sections, sides applied with running grapevine, rim with shells and leaves, shell supports. **$7,500**

SALVER, circular, with an applied scroll-and-shell border, the surface with let-in silver shield and flat-chased with fishscale and foliate shell decoration, on 3 scroll feet, J. Watson & Son, 1835. **$550**

SALVER, circular, shell and foliate supports, shell-and-scroll-molded border, engraved, scrolling foliage, Matthew Boulton, diameter, 19 in. **$800**

SALVER, oval, plain, the center engraved with a monogram on 4 shell feet, beaded border, 1790. **$800**

SALVER, shaped circular on gadroon, shell-and-scroll feet, border gadrooning, shells and scrolling foliage, cartouche engraved with an armorial crest and motto, Sheffield, c. 1800. **$150**

SAUCEBOATS, pair, small, plain, bellied oval on 3 shell-mounted feet, beaded borders, flying reeded scroll handles, c. 1775. **$1,400/pr**

SNUFFBOX, OVAL, silverplate, embossed with classical figures backed with spangled glass, c. 1765. **$250**

TANKARD, quart, wooden base and scroll handle with heart-shape terminal, Nathan Smith & Co., Sheffield, 1780. **$250**

TEA URN, c. 1810, floral finial. **$600**

TOAST RACK, wirework, boat-shape, 6 divisions. **$125**

TRAY, gallery, wooden, oblong, sides with an applied gadroon border, finely pierced with a leaf motif, on 4 ball feet, c. 1800. **$450**

TRAY, tea, shell flanked by leaves at each corner, handles with shell centers and leafy terminals, length, 24 in. **$850**

TRAY, tea, 2 handles, shaped oval, the gadroon rim with foliage at intervals, c. 1815. **$1,000**

TUREEN, sauce, and cover, pair, each of circular section, partly gadrooned, with leaf-capped reeded handles, Robert Gainsford, c. 1815, height, 7¼ in. **$950/pr**

Sheffield plate tea urn, estimate $400–$600. Courtesy of Butterfield & Butterfield, San Francisco.

TUREEN, soup, plated, lion's-paw feet, leaf handles, coat of arms, crest, and motto.   **$1,100**

TUREENS, sauce, and covers, set of 4, silverplated, c. 1815, chased and raised on lion legs, gadroon rims with shells and leaves, bud finials.   **$4,500/set**

WARMING DISH, plated, late 18th century, scrolling carry handles and angled shell-ornamented feet.   **$900**

WARMING STAND, oval, on ivory bun feet and with 2 turned-ivory handles, 24½ in.   **$350**

WINE COASTERS, pair, gadrooned, molded circular, turned-wood bases with vacant circular bosses.   **$100/pr**

WINE COASTERS, pair, silverplated, C-scrolls and cast grape leaves, early 19th century.   **$750/pr**

WINE COOLERS, pair, half-turned, frieze of leaves and flowers, lion-mask drop-ring side handles.   **$4,000/pr**

WINE COOLERS, pair, plated, c. 1810, of partly lobed campana form, pedestal foot, cornucopia handles, detachable rims and liners.   **$3,500/pr**

Silverplate—
American and
English

American silverplated (Meriden) jewel box with swing mechanism, $200.
Courtesy of Christie's South Kensington, London.

Interest in collecting American silverplate has intensified over the past few years.

From the middle part of the 19th century to the present almost all styles of pieces made in sterling silver were also made in silverplate. If you were not able to buy sterling silver, silverplate was available and affordable, and it looked like the more expensive silver.

Sheffield fused plate was followed in England in the 1830s by the development of plating by electrolysis, a process patented by the Elkington Company and later developed to a high degree in Birmingham and Sheffield. The object to be plated was bathed in a solution of various chemicals and sterling silver, and an electric current was passed through the dip to adhere the silver to the object. In this process edges were completely covered and could be replated as necessary. In the United States plated wares were made by electroplating over white metal, nickel silver, and copper.

Objects made reflected the designs that were popular during the time they were produced, often following furniture forms such as Gothic, Rococo, Egyptian, Oriental, Turkish, Colonial, and Assyrian Revival motifs. Naturalistic designs were evident on a great number of pieces of silverplate, many having cast branch and twig handles and nut or blossom finials. Entrée dishes with lifelike lobsters or crabs, nut dishes with crouching squirrels, and sardine boxes surmounted by full-figure sardines were considered the height of elegance for use on the table in the late 19th century. Many American pieces were produced in New England and New York by such makers as Rogers, Meriden, Reed & Barton, Wilcox, Derby, Gorham, Wallace, and Oneida.

For the dining room huge centerpieces, plateaus, condiment sets, figural napkin rings, place card holders, and knife rests were produced. Figural napkin rings with moving parts, such as carts with moving wheels, or elaborate forms incorporating a bud vase and other figural elements were often made by Simpson, Hall & Miller, and Tufts and are much sought after today. Butter dishes, spoon holders, nut dishes, and novelty salt and pepper shakers were made in great numbers. Today the most collectible of these depict cats, dogs, bears, birds, and human figures. It was de rigueur for the dining table to boast vast amounts of flatware, often with a dozen types of spoons—for tea, coffee, 5 o'clock tea, ice cream, oranges or other fruit, and at least fifteen other styles of spoons—at least eight different types of knives and forks, and elaborate serving pieces. Many of these had full-figure ornamentation. For the nursery one could buy complete boxed sets with porringer bowl, cup, spoon, and fork. Baby rattles and children's napkin rings also were made and are popular with collectors today.

For the boudoir, ladies enjoyed complete dresser sets with hand mirrors, brushes, jars, picture frames, and many types of jewel boxes, watch holders, and perfume bottles. Men were not forgotten: smoke sets were fashionable, along with match-safes, cigar cutters, cigarette boxes (often with sporting motifs), and humidors. Flasks and sporting trophies also were available. Again, novelty shapes command the highest prices.

Presentation pieces were quite popular; many were produced for yachting, golfing, and shooting events and for fire companies. Other collectible presentation pieces include those made for the Columbian Exposition in Chicago.

Desk items made in silverplate include figural inkwells, pen rests, rocking blotters, and stamp boxes.

At the beginning of the 20th century many companies produced souvenir or advertising items in silverplate; today these are another popular field of collecting.

In England from the mid-19th century to the present, a vast profusion of dining table and gentlemen's and ladies' fashion accessories were made by firms such as Dixon, Walker & Hall, and Elkington.

To identify the various types of plating combinations, many pieces manufactured were stamped with letters that indicated the base metal and plating process used. Pieces were marked as follows:

> EPNS—electroplate on nickel silver
> EPBM—electroplate on Britannia metal
> EPWM—electroplate on white metal
> EPC—electroplate on copper
> A.1—standard thickness of plating
> Double plate, triple plate, quadruple plate—these connote thickness of the plate

BASTING SPOON WARMER, engraved with a band of stylized foliage and with beaded rim, raised on 3 ball supports, Martin Hall & Co., England, c. 1880. **$150**

BISCUIT BARREL, engine-turned with ribbed body bands, circular stand with molded rim, Collis & Company, England. **$400**

BISCUIT BARREL, glass, decorated with stylized chrysanthemums, the mount with 2 rising scroll handles, the detachable cover with ball finial. **$145**

BISCUIT BOX, on winged and claw feet, engraved with foliage and laurel wreath, hinged lid with crouching artilleryman finial, and 2 lion's-mask handles, England. **$600**

BISCUIT BOX, Aesthetic movement, swing handles with twin fan-shape covers engraved with birds perched on flowering boughs, on pierced bamboo feet, England, 1880. **$800**

BISCUIT BOX, cut glass, silverplate-mounted, oval, on stand with 4 bracket and foliate supports, beaded border, England. **$600**

BISCUIT BOX, on rustic supports with twig handle, England. **$350**

BISCUIT WARMER, folding shell on scrolling foliate feet, with 2 swing laurel-wreath handles, England. **$600**

BOOKENDS, pair, formed as courtly figures, the gentleman bearing game, the lady with wine ewer and fruit, height, 9½ in. **$300/pr**

BOWL, NUT, shell with squirrel finial on a fluted pedestal foot, American, late 19th century. **$200**

BOX, collar button, ornately footed, American, diameter, 2½ in. **$20**

BOX, trinket, on stand decorated with foliage, hinged cover with a swing mechanism decorated with 3 birds perched on flowering branches, Meriden Britannia Plate Company, 1886. **$200**

BUCKET, cut glass, with silverplated rim and handle, American, height, 7 in. **$70**

BUN WARMER, rolltop, flutes and stamped border, English, late 19th century. **$400**

BUTTER DISH, covered, rolltop, engraved, late 19th century, American. **$50**

CANDELABRA, pair, 2 lights, in George II style, stems formed as a partly draped man supporting a nymph, who in turn holds the floral-decorated sconces, England, height, 17¼ in. **$3,200/pr**

CANDELABRA, 3 lights, pair, on stepped base with leaf tips at intervals, leaf-clad fluted knob stem supporting detachable scrolling leaf-clad branches, height, 23½ in. **$1,700/pr**

CANDLESTICKS, pair, neoclassical style, silverplated, Continental, 19th century. **$750/pr**

CANDLESTICKS, pair, Dutch style, silverplate, repoussé scenes and figures, American, c. 1920. **$145/pr**

CANDLESTICKS, pair, George III style, England. **$420/pr**

CANDLESTICKS, pair, silverplated, weighted bases, American, height, 9 in.   **$150/pr**

CANDLESTICKS, set of 4, fitted with candleholders and shades, on shaped-rectangular fluted bases, the fluted baluster-form stems surmounted by baluster-shape sockets, height, 10 in.
$850/set

CARD RECEIVER, leafy branches resting on 3 turtles, American, Rogers & Co., height, 7 in.   **$395**

CASTOR SET, 5 pieces, revolving, etched bottles, band with Japanese-style decoration, Gothic structured top and flowers.
$145/set

CENTERPIECE in neoclassical taste, with 2 cut-glass dishes centering a raised, partly draped figure holding cut-glass vase with extensions supporting 2 more bowls, all decorated with a border of cupids bearing swags, Elkington & Co., Birmingham, c. 1875, length, 28¼ in.   **$1,700**

CENTERPIECE, on 3 cast dolphin supports and with an engraved trefoil base with winged lion feet, fitted with a large cut-glass bowl.   **$225**

CENTERPIECE, Regency, 4-light candelabrum, bands of gadrooning and foliage, engraved with coat of arms, shell and gadrooned wax pans, Matthew Boulton, c. 1815, height, 23½ in.   **$300**

CENTERPIECE, shallow circular bowl raised on a short standard, surrounded by 4 large balls, domed circular foot, Christofle, mid-20th century, diameter, 13¾ in.   **$850**

CENTERPIECE, trefoil base decorated with shells, flowers, and foliage, fitted with a large trumpet-shape glass vase engraved with ferns and with a waved rim, 19½ in.   **$135**

CHARGER, circular, with wide chased band of fruit amid foliage and scrolls, with laurel border, Elkington, diameter, 16½ in.   **$160**

CHILD'S TRAY, engraved with tea being served to a girl in a cottage garden surrounded by flowering trellis, with vignettes of children at play, R.F.S. & Co., c. 1880, length, 16¼ in.
$800

COCKTAIL SHAKER, hand bell form, with polished wood handle, Kingsway Plate, English, 11 in.   **$150**

COCKTAIL SHAKER, novelty, formed as a bell, engraved with reeded bands, England. **$200**

COCKTAIL SHAKER, wood and silverplate, formed as a champagne bottle, with gilt simulated-cork stopper, Kingsway Plate Ltd., England. **$775**

CONDIMENT SET, Chippendale style, cut-glass bottles, silver worn. **$130/set**

DISHES, vegetable, pair, each of shaped oval fluted form with foliate scroll borders and detachable foliate ring handles, length, 11 in. **$320/pr**

EGG CRUET, Matthew Boulton, on 4 anthemion supports, with leaf-clad handle, fitted with 4 egg cups, height, 8 in. **$350**

EGG CRUET, 4 cups, circular, on scroll legs and with a gadrooned domed cover with wood button finial and 4 Hanoverian-pattern egg spoons. **$110**

ENTRÉE DISH, Victorian style, cover and handle applied with rococo scrolling foliage, Mappin & Webb, Princes plate.
$200

EWER, CELLINI STYLE, typical form, height, 12½ in. **$280**

FLAGON, in early Georgian taste, domed lid inset with simulated coins of George III, scrolling handles, and ring feet, Ellisbarker, English. **$100**

FLATWARE SERVICE, 1847 Rogers Bros., Heraldic pattern, 82 pieces, American. **$125/set**

GAME PLATTER AND COVER, oval, with gadrooned border, domed cover with dentilated border and detachable foliate-clad ring handles, engraved with crest, length, 24 in. **$650**

GRAPE BASKET AND SHEARS, silvered metal, handle formed as a grapevine. **$400**

HUMIDOR, GLASS with pipe finial, late 19th century, English.
$125

HUMIDOR, GLASS with silverplated lid, bulldog finial, late 19th century, English. **$325**

JEWELRY BOX, Tufts, paw feet, putti, shells, seaweed, putto finial, American. **$350**

LAMP BASE, trefoil, with fluted column and 3 scrolling foliate and lion's-paw supports, electrified. **$200**

LAMP SHADES, pair, pierced. **$40/pr**

MIRROR PLATEAU, T. and J. Cresswick, circular, on 3 lion's-head and paw foliate supports with egg-and-dart border, diameter, 18 in. **$1,000**

MIRROR PLATEAU, rectangular, gadrooned border on 4 ball feet, length, 26 in. **$1,100**

PICKLE CASTOR, Meriden, ornate insert with glass zipper-like panels, bulbous ribbed base, with pickle fork, American. **$95**

PICKLE CASTOR, cranberry insert, with matching fork. **$550/2**

PLAQUE, circular, decorated with a seminude classical maiden surrounded by handmaidens in a palace, mounted in green plush frame, Elkington and Co., 18 in. **$350**

PLATES, dinner, 18, shaped gadrooned rims, borders engraved with armorials, Thomas Bradbury & Sons, 1900. **$2,200/18**

PRESENTATION TROWEL, with ivory handle, in original case, English, 1896. **$50**

SALT AND PEPPER SHAKERS, depicting figural cats, American, late 19th century. **$225/pr**

SHAVING MUG, with engraved roses, late 19th century, American. **$125**

SIDEBOARD SERVING STAND, on 2 levels, with attached handles chased with a repeating segmented border of alternating panels of flowers, the face acid-etched with a central scene of children in a dog cart accompanied by a boy and maiden in rustic dress, Wilcox Silverplate Company, Meriden, CT, c. 1878. **$475**

SPOON HOLDER, Statue of Liberty, American, late 19th century. **$350**

SPOON WARMER, gilt, shell shape, on a naturalistic rockwork base decorated with shells, Archer Bros., England. **$150**

SPOON WARMER, novelty, formed as a pumpkin, tendril scroll handle with leaf thumbpiece. **$400**

SPOON WARMER, shell shape, on a naturalistic rockwork base, England. **$125**

SUGAR BOWL/SPOONHOLDER, bird lid, squirrel on handles, 12 spoon hooks, American. **$95**

TANTALUS SET, fitted with two glass decanters, height, 14½ in. **$70/set**

American silverplated spoon holder, c. 1885. Courtesy of Jeri Schwartz. Photo by J. Auslander.

American late 19th-century silverplated (Rogers, Smith & Co.) tea and coffee service, with tray, $1,210. Courtesy of Butterfield & Butterfield, San Francisco.

TEA AND COFFEE SERVICE, 6 pieces, with tray, Rogers, Smith & Co., c. 1870–75, lids surmounted by a rampant lion holding a shield, necks and tray border rolled with a frieze of putti enacting the rape of the Sabines, American.   **$1,100/set**

TEA AND COFFEE SERVICE on mask and bracket feet, engraved with friezes of stylized scrolling foliage and with angular handles and spouts, comprising coffeepot, teapot, cream jug, lidded sugar basin, and slop basin, Reed & Barton.

$350/set

TEA AND COFFEE SERVICE, Empire style, comprising coffeepot, teapot, cream pitcher, and covered sugar bowl, vase form on 3 paw supports with anthemion joins, the spouts formed as eagles' heads, covers with bud finials.   **$420/set**

TEA AND COFFEE SET, 4 pieces, Gorham, repoussé with flowers and blossoms.   **$200/set**

TEA AND COFFEE SET, 6 pieces, comprising teapot, coffeepot, covered sugar bowl, creamer, waste bowl, hot water kettle, rectangular tray, of square bombé form with gadroon rims and vertically lobed lower bodies.   **$2,700/set**

TEA KETTLE ON STAND, compressed globular, engraved with foliate scrolls, the cover with melon finial, height, 10 in.

$320

TEA KETTLE, PEAR SHAPE, with stylized flower-shape finial, on a stand with bun feet, with a burner, Christofle, Paris.

$275

TEAPOT, Royles patent, self-pouring, with shell-fluted terminals, James Dixon and Sons, Sheffield.   **$45**

TEA SERVICE comprising kettle on stand, teapot, coffeepot, cream pitcher, and sugar bowl, each pyriform, chased with foliage and scrolls, with bird finials, on two-handle tray.

$2,000/set

TEA SERVICE, George III style, comprising teapot, cream pitcher, sugar bowl, and kettle on stand, of part-fluted oval form with wood handles and knop finials.   **$180/set**

TEA SERVICE, traveling, stamped Marquet, comprising teapot, hot water kettle, tea caddy, milk flask, and sugar bowl, together with 2 teacups and a cake knife, in fitted case.

$400/set

TEA SET, 6 pieces, including covered butter with original insert, scroll and flower edging, Reed & Barton, American.

$200/set

American Gorham silverplated Classical Revival tea tray, $650. Courtesy of Christie's East, New York.

TEA URN, Reed & Barton, American, late 19th century. **$150**

TEA URN, Victorian, baluster form with scrolling handles on stepped base. **$600**

TOOTHPICK HOLDER, figural, Kate Greenaway type, boy holding art glass vase with colorful enameled sprays of flowers, James Tufts, late 19th century, American. **$350**

TRAY, gallery, oval, the pierced border with floral swags within gadrooned border, height, 24 in. **$320**

TRAY, tea, oval, with pierced vine and tendril handles and border, the ground engraved with stylized vines, length, 28 in. **$325**

TRAY, tea, rectangular, leaf handles, border with chased rondels of lions' heads, bellflower swags, molded grapevine border. **$385**

TRAY, tea, rectangular, with gadrooned and foliate border with 2 reeded handles, engraved with coat of arms, length, 28 in. **$1,000**

TRAY, tea, 2 handles, Classical Revival, oval, on 4 bracket feet with die-rolled geometric border, handles applied with maidens' heads (one foot missing), Gorham, length over handles, 33½ in. **$650**

TRAY, 2 handles, rectangular, with foliate and shell borders, length over handles, 30 in. **$380**

TUREEN, soup, 2 handles, oval, and cover, decorated with flowers and foliage with egg-and-dart rim and stag finial, American. **$350**

TUREENS, sauce, pair, oval, on scrolling shell and foliate supports, with gadrooned border, the handles with oak cluster joins, length, 8 in. **$1,000/pr**

URN, part-fluted, on shaped square base on ball feet, reeded supports, with lion's-mask and ring handles, height, 12 in. **$550**

URN, covered, fluted sides, on a domed circular foot resting on a square base, the fluted cover with tapering neck and covered urn finial, Creswick & Co., Sheffield. **$200**

URN, elongated, decorated with high-relief band of Pan and other classic musicians, German, height, 28 in. **$200**

WATCH HOLDER, figural child and dog, large, American, late 19th century. **$250**

WATCH HOLDER, figural knight in armor, American, late 19th century. **$225**

Pair of silverplated sauce tureens with oak cluster joins, $1,000/pair.
Courtesy of Christie's East, New York.

WATERING CAN, typical form, engraved with a monogram, applied scroll handle, 14 in. overall. **$575**

WINE COOLER, urn shape, with gadrooned borders, handle joins formed as pharaohs' heads, Egyptian Revival, late 19th century. **$600**

WINE COOLERS, pair, campana shape, bands of acanthus and flowerheads, reeded handles, engraved with crest. **$2,400/pr**

WINE COOLERS, pair, Regency, plated urn form on square base with lobed band, the rising handles with satyr's-mask joins, c. 1820. **$1,800/pr**

Souvenir Spoons

Collecting souvenir spoons began in the late 19th century, when it was the custom for well-to-do families to travel to Europe on the Grand Tour. Almost every city and town, regardless of size, boasted a jeweler or silversmith who sold sterling silver or silverplate teaspoons, fruit spoons, and coffee spoons with embossed or enameled local views. These could be further decorated by having them engraved with the date and the recipient's name. The spoons were keepsakes brought home as reminders of the wonderful trip.

Silver manufacturers in America joined the craze and began to produce quantities of souvenir spoons. Some were decorated with state seals and insignia, local libraries, public and private schools, colleges, and historic sites. Others were made for fraternal organizations to commemorate a particular lodge or meeting.

Towns like Salem, Massachusetts, had special spoons made by the Daniel Low Company in several variations. For example, the witch spoon was made in various sizes, including teaspoon, fruit spoon, sugar shell, and demitasse spoon. The witch motif also was used on tongs, a strawberry fork, a letter knife, and even a thimble.

Also in the souvenir category are novelty spoons: Mickey and Minnie Mouse, the Dionne quintuplets, Yogi Bear, Mary Poppins, and the Campbell's Soup Kids.

Spoons with figures and legends advertising watches, Log Cabin Syrup, Planters Peanuts, and various teas are also popular. Skyline or silhouette spoons of famous cities, including New York and Chicago, are still quite collectible. Tiffany spoons depicting the Brooklyn Bridge, St. Paul's Church, Grant's Tomb, and the Flatiron Building are available but more difficult to find.

Every fair and exposition had its share of spoons, particularly the 1893 Columbian Exposition in Chicago. Many sizes were produced, and there was even a spoon depicting Mrs.

Potter Palmer, a well-known collector herself, who was president of the Board of Lady Managers of the Fair.

Spoons with seals or depicting buildings were made to commemorate the 1933 New York World's Fair and the 1933 Chicago Century of Progress Exposition.

For the present-day collector, spoons made to commemorate the launchings of Apollo 12 and 13 will probably increase in value.

BROWNIES, enamel and sterling silver, American, early 20th century. **$35**

CHARLIE McCARTHY, teaspoon, silverplated, American, early 20th century. **$15**

CHICAGO, 1934 (Century of Progress, 2nd year), sterling with plain bowl. **$25**

CHRISTMAS SPOON, Michelsen, Danish, sterling. **$85**

COLUMBIAN EXPOSITION, extra-fancy teaspoon. **$35**

COWBOY, full figure, sterling silver, American, early 20th century. **$100**

DIONNE QUINTUPLETS, set of 5, silverplated, figural handles, American, early 20th century. **$95/set**

INDIAN, head, single feather, corn, crossed hatchets on handle, "Ladawga," American, early 20th century. **$35**

INDIAN, parcel-gilt, full figure, American, early 20th century. **$275**

INDIAN, relief of feathered head at end, "Chicago" on handle, Masonic Temple in bowl. **$40**

INDIAN, sterling, American, dated 1891, 4 in. **$30**

KEWPIE, sterling silver, full-figure cutout, American, early 20th century. **$125**

MINER, sterling silver, '49 with pickax, parcel-gilt, American, late 19th century. **$150**

PRESIDENT McKINLEY DEMITASSE SPOON, figural handle, American, late 19th century. **$28**

R.B. ACTOR'S FUND FAIR, May 1982, silver teaspoon, round bowl, Gorham. **$150**

STATUE OF LIBERTY, full figure, Shiebler, American, late 19th century. **$125**

TEDDY ROOSEVELT RIDING A HORSE, full figure, sterling, American, late 19th century. **$75**

YELLOWSTONE NATIONAL PARK, Old Faithful (cutout), ladle, American, early 20th century. **$49**

Sports

Left. *Chinese sterling cup with rifles at base, c. 1900, $150.* Right. *Sterling pill box with engraved boat and rope twist surround, c. 1900, $225.*

During the past two years there has been a tremendous surge in the collecting of sports-related sterling silver and silverplate objects. Specialist auctions, sales, and shows have encouraged an already rising area of collecting. There are tennis, billiards, boxing, boating, fishing, golf, bicycling, hunting, and automobile-related items.

Collectors search for flasks, card cases, and humidors with sports motifs. Many of these objects were made in England and Europe in the late 19th century through the first quarter of the 20th century. In the United States, Gorham, Kerr, and Unger Brothers produced many such sporting objects.

Matchsafes, as well as card cases, cigarette cases, purses, memo pads, desk sets, frames, and hollowware, were made with sporting motifs from Victorian times into the early 20th century. Trophies, bearing a full-figure sportsman in sterling silver and silverplate, sell extremely well. Watch fobs and watches boast sports symbols, as do place card holders, often with the addition of brightly colored enameling. Sports medals, in gold and sterling silver, sometimes with the Tiffany mark, are now found at major shows.

Early compasses, set in silver, bosun's whistles, golf tees, and canes housing billiard cues and fishing rods are often silver-mounted. Desk clocks and thermometers are often mounted with crossed golf clubs or riding crops.

Cocktail shakers engraved with "19th Hole," sets of golf spoons, and ladies' hat pins with golfing motifs are still available. Decanters with engraved hunting or golfing scenes and colored glass with sterling silver overlay are in demand.

Silverplate and sterling silver inkwells with full-figure early automobiles were made in Europe and may still be found in markets and auction rooms.

There are many marriages among sporting collectibles, including ashtrays and inkwells with cast golf clubs and riding crops added. With the increase of interest in this field, greed often takes over. Be aware. Silverplated toast racks with crossed golf clubs are also being recast, complete with original marks.

ADMISSION TICKET, sterling silver, Liverpool Race Course on one side, "Liverpool Race Course," on the other, "Proprietor's Ticket," c. 1815. **$600**

BOWL, Revere style, used as a racing trophy, engraved with a horse in a pasture, Dominick & Haff, American, late 19th century, diameter, 11 in. **$400**

CHATELAINE, golf motif, with suspended score card and pencil, silverplated. **$350**

COMPASS, silver-mounted, with ring and mother-of-pearl case, English, mid-19th century. **$350**

CUP, loving, sterling silver, 3 handles, with presentation inscription, Howard & Co., 1905, height, 8½ in. **$700**

EGG CRUET STAND, silverplated, crossed golf clubs and ball, English, early 20th century. **$300**

FLASK, chased scene depicting golfer and caddy, with Art Nouveau surround, American, late 19th century. **$850**

FLASK, engraved scene depicting fisherman in pond, American, silverplated, late 19th century. **$125**

Left. *American sterling, Unger Bros., three-handled cup, $950.* Right.
American sterling, Unger Bros., bonbon dish, $750. Courtesy of Richard W.
Oliver, Kennebunk, ME.

GAME MARKER, sterling silver, with indicators for up to 30
pheasant, grouse, hare, and rabbits, Walter and John Barnard,
London.   **$1,000**

HAT PIN HOLDER, with sterling silver golf bag and pincushion
base, English, early 20th century.   **$350**

HAT PIN STAND, with circular pincushion base, applied with
2 sterling silver golf clubs and two golf balls, Birmingham,
1910.   **$250**

HUNTING HORN, sterling silver, London, 1873.   **$475**

JUG, claret, silver-mounted cut glass, neck mount applied with
fox-hunting trophies in strapwork cartouches, cover chased
with a fox mask and hunting trophies, thumbpiece modeled as
a gilt hound with front paws resting on a 5-bar gate, maker's
mark I.F., London, 1856.   **$1,700**

MATCHSAFE, male golfer, sterling silver, American, early 20th
century.   **$250**

MATCHSAFE, sterling silver, stamped with a gentleman playing golf and several onlookers, Birmingham, 1907.   **$600**

MATCHSAFE, sterling silver, stamped with a lady playing golf,
Birmingham, 1906.   **$600**

MODEL, racing scull and pair of oars, in a fitted and lined case, c. 1890.   **$750**

PENCIL HOLDER, sterling silver, modeled as a golf bag with leather strap handle, engraved with simulated stitching, Birmingham, 1912.   **$220**

PINCUSHION, on circular base, modeled as a robin with a golf club beneath one wing, Birmingham, 1910.   **$500**

PRESENTATION CUP and cover decorated with foliage and with applied figures of runners, 2 handles, presentation inscription dated 1899, American, height, 22 in.   **$110**

RACE CARD BOOK, silver-mounted, green leather applied with a monogram and coronet, London, 1900.   **$175**

RING STAND formed from 3 crossed golf clubs on a rising circular base, London, 1931.   **$300**

SALT AND PEPPER SHAKERS, silverplated, modeled as golf balls, English, early 20th century.   **$125/pr**

SPOON, chased with female golfer swinging club, English, early 20th century.   **$55**

SPOON, chased with male golfer swing club, English, early 20th century.   **$55**

SPOON, enameled, presentation, golf club, Scottish, 20th century.   **$35**

SPOON, surmounted by golf ball, English, early 20th century.   **$35**

SPOON, terminal full-figure Devil and crossed golf clubs, English, early 20th century.   **$45**

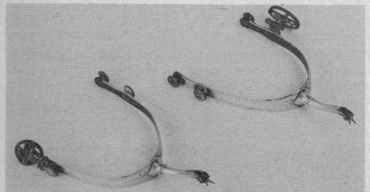

Pair of English Sheffield plate spurs, c. 1790, $400. **Courtesy of Phillips, London.**

SPURS, pair, George IV, buckle fastenings, James Collins, Birmingham, 1829. **$750/pr**

SPURS, pair, plain, with engraved feather-edged borders, Sheffield plate, early 19th century. **$400/pr**

SPURS, pair, silverplated, complete with buckles and leather strap, box, Gorham Mfg. Co., early 20th century. **$150/pr**

TEASPOONS, set of 6, the handles struck with crossed golf clubs and balls, English, early 20th century. **$125/set**

TROPHY, goblet shape, with beaded border on base, mid-stem, and underside of bowl, prize for Cambridge University Athletic Games, Trinity College, March 1863, Daniel Houle & Charles Houle, London, 1861, height, 8 in. **$225**

TROPHY, 2 handles, vase form, marked sterling, rustic border, handles formed as grapevines, body chased with grape leaves, engraved Riverton Gun Club, 1903, height, 16½ in. **$2,600**

TROPHY CUP, vase shape, beaded, 2 handles, part-fluted body chased with a vignette of a man on horseback surrounded by rococo scrolling foliage on a textured ground, inscription stating that trophy is "A Facsimile of the Malta Inter Regimental Polo Cup," cover with a finial in the form of a polo player, Gibson & Langman, London, 1889. **$1,300**

TROPHY CUP, 3 handles, etched with figure of golfer in plus-fours, engraved with presentation inscription, Tiffany & Company, 6 in. **$550**

Left. *Tiffany sterling vase, $325.* **Center.** *Silverplate clock with figure and clubs, $600.* **Right.** *Silverplate figure of golfer, $180.* **Courtesy of Richard W. Oliver, Kennebunk, ME.**

TROPHY CUP, 2 handles, Redlich, applied with golf clubs and laurel sprigs, engraved with presentation inscription, American, late 19th century, height, 6½ in. **$400**

VINAIGRETTE, silver-gilt, lid applied with 2 jockeys and horses, grill pierced and engraved with flowerheads and scrollwork, T.N., Birmingham, 1821. **$500**

WATCH, pocket, open face, Tiffany & Co. chased, golfer practicing swing. **$1,800**

Tea Caddies

Left. *George III sterling coffee urn.* Right. *George III sterling tea caddy.*
Courtesy of Christie's East, New York.

Tea caddies were used for airtight storage of tea, a precious
commodity in the 17th and 18th centuries. The name "caddy"
was derived from the old Malayan word *kati*, indicating a
weight of approximately 1¼ pounds, probably originally a
measure of the tea weight.

Sterling silver caddy forms were first used in England in the
18th century; although rare in the United States, they were
made in the late 18th century by Paul Revere and other silversmiths. Caddies often had their own spoons and were also
made to match tea services.

Designs used in England and France in the late 18th and early
19th centuries utilized neoclassical drapes and swags, shellwork, husks, and cartouche motifs. Caddies were almost always made with hinged lids and locks and keys. Often the

interior of the caddy was divided with two inner compartments and a bowl for mixing the various teas. Dutch and Chinese examples were often chased and embossed with foliage and human figures. In England tortoise-shell caddies quite often had sterling silver or silver-gilt mounts with elaborately engraved designs. The shapes of tea caddies have varied, the earliest examples generally being square. Oval and vase-shaped caddies often were decorated with engraved garlands and swags. Dutch and Chinese examples were chased and embossed with foliage and human figures.

APPLIED AND REPOUSSÉ decorated with prunus and tree bark, Chinese Export, late 19th century.   **$325**

CADDY, formed as an 18th-century knife box, tortoise shell, sterling silver mounted, bow front, applied with foliate-pierced mounts, swing handle and lock, Martin Hall, Sheffield, 1911.
$1,400

CHASED BOMBÉ SHAPE, with flowers and foliage, on bun feet, John Henry Rawlings, London, 1890.   **$525**

CHASED REEDING, with domed cover and rope-twist bands and a part-fluted oblong finial, fitted with a lock and steel key, Dutch, late 18th century.   **$550**

Continental, cased, tête-à-tête tea service w/tea caddy, $900. **Courtesy of Wolf's Auction Gallery, Cleveland, OH.**

Pair of English George III sterling tea caddies and mixing bowl in case, estimate, $7,500. Courtesy of Phillips, London.

EDWARDIAN, gadrooned, shaped, Birmingham, 1905. **$275**

GADROONED AND GILT-LINED QUATREFOIL, on paw feet, with hinged handle, Birmingham, 1907. **$275**

GADROONED OVAL, domed hinged cover with ivory finial, Chester. **$250**

NOVELTY, modeled as a sedan chair, openwork crown finial, Continental, 1895. **$1,000**

OBLONG, CUT GLASS, silver-mounted, with detachable cover, unmarked, Continental, late 18th century. **$100**

OVAL, fluted in 18th-century taste, flower finial, body and cover chased with rococo flowers and foliage, London, 1901. **$375**

OVAL, tapered form, engraved with a trellis pattern, Stephen Smith, London, 1868. **$1,100**

OVAL, beaded, with lift-off cover, engraved with 2 floral, foliate, and ribbon shield-shaped cartouches, Birmingham, 1913. **$275**

OVAL, engraved with bands of foliage and flowers, drapery, foliate swags and oval cartouches, lid with wood finial, with key, William Sumner, London, 1788, height, 5 in. **$1,900**

PAIR OF GEORGE III CADDIES and a blending bowl en suite, with flowers, scrolls, and fluting, floral finials and bases pierced with flowers and scrolls, Samuel Taylor, 1763, wood case with carved bead borders and silver mounts.   **$7,000/set**

QUEEN ANNE PERIOD, elongated form, stepped base, Edmund Pearce, c. 1710.   **$2,100**

RECTANGULAR, on molded base with canted corners, the sliding cover with domed lid, John Farnell, London.   **$950**

REEDED AND TIED BORDER, fitted with a lock, the rising cover with artichoke finial, Austrian, 1890.   **$425**

SQUARE, the sides chased with hunting scenes, Calcutta, height, 6 in.   **$600**

STAMPED, 18th-century style, having lift-off cover, with figures and putti within rococo scroll cartouches, Amsterdam, 1895.   **$450**

STAMPED WITH LAUREL SWAGS, floral and ribbon decorations, Birmingham, 1910.   **$275**

VASE SHAPE, stamped with Dutch rural scenes in scroll cartouches, Berthold Muller, Continental, 1907.   **$450**

WAISTED FORM, with two repoussé floral bands, Gorham, late 19th century, height, 4 in.   **$200**

Tea Caddy Spoons

Group of English sterling tea caddy spoons. Courtesy of Phillips, London.

During the mid-18th century, when tea was a scarce commodity, it was necessary to have a spoon to measure the amount of tea to be used. At first several styles of handles were used, usually in combination with a shell-form bowl. This form was so popular that the spoons were called tea caddy shells until the mid-19th century. The first types of handles were in the Onslow style. Then the shield-top form, referred to as Old English, became popular, followed by those with bright-cut engravings or in the Fiddle pattern. At the same time Birmingham silversmiths offered the jockey cup and other novelty forms. They also added leaf motifs, including tea, vine, oak and acanthus leaves, as decoration. Also at this time, the hand-form spoon became popular. The cast Chinese Mandarin spoon portrayed a Chinese holding a tea plant in his hand with a cast floral border. Filigree wirework spoons in leaf, shell, and scoop shapes were produced in England in the first quarter of the 19th century by Italians who had immigrated to England. Spoons also were made in thistle, acorn, and frying pan forms. Decorations consisted of engraving, chasing, and embossing. Look for hallmarked examples.

ACORN BOWL, with wide band of diaperwork beneath ribbed and reeded decoration, feather-edge handle, Joseph Taylor, Birmingham, 1802.   **$500**

CAST FRUITING-VINE HANDLE, the decoration extending into the silver-gilt bowl, Francis Higgins, 1854.   **$500**

CAST LEAF, parcel-gilt bowl, and matte looped, stalked handle, George Adams, 1869.   **$500**

CHINOISERIE, center with Chinaman flanked by a tree and part of a pagoda, attributed to William Wardell, Birmingham, 1807.   **$1,000**

CURVED VINE-LEAF BOWL, stamped with grapes and leaves, the ring handle with applied fruiting-vine decoration, George Unite, Birmingham, 1861.   **$300**

DOLPHIN HANDLE with matte scallop bowl, Henry Aston, Birmingham, 1861.   **$950**

FIDDLE PATTERN, ovoid bowl, engraved with acorns and leaf sprays, J. & H. Lias, 1821.   **$110**

FILIGREE, horseshoe-shape bowl, with wirework foliage, the handle flanked by 2 scrolls, unmarked, c. 1800.   **$350**

FILIGREE, oblong bowl, with "petal" edge decorated with wire scrolls, unmarked, c. 1800.   **$250**

FRYING PAN FORM, circular, engine-turned bowl with central rosette and border of foliage, Matthew Linwood, Birmingham, 1807.   **$400**

JOCKEY CAP design, with reeded surfaces, Joseph Taylor, Birmingham, 1798.   **$425**

JOCKEY CAP, unmarked, corrugated cap with wide filigree peak decorated with 2 crescents, c. 1800.   **$525**

KING'S PATTERN VARIATION, handle chased with a classical girl and her dog sitting beneath a tree and enclosed within a wreath of flowers, John Bettridge, Birmingham, 1818.   **$425**

LEAF FORM, matte bowl chased with veins and having a looped-stalk handle, Matthew Linwood, Birmingham, 1802.

$175

MODELED HANDLE, depicting an ancient Egyptian male head, stem with Greek key prick-dot engraving, Hilliard & Thomason, Birmingham, 1884. **$260**

NOVELTY, modeled as a broom with simulated wood handle, George Fox, 1867. **$1,300**

OVAL, cast bowl decorated in relief with a Chinese mandarin holding a tea plant, the handle profusely decorated with flowers, Edward Farrell, 1816. **$2,500**

PARCEL-GILT CAST BOWL, chased in relief with flowers and leafage, leafy scroll handle terminating in a rococo cartouche enclosing 3 game birds, George Adams, 1890. **$500**

PARCEL-GILT OVOID BOWL, chased in relief with leaves and berries, George Adams, 1848. **$325**

PLAIN, WAVY-EDGE BOWL, with scroll-engraved handle, Alfred Taylor, Birmingham, 1862. **$100**

PROVINCIAL fiddle-and-shell pattern, with scalloped bowl, Lister & Sons, Newcastle, 1841. **$125**

RIGHT-HAND FORM, with flat handle with curved top, bright-engraved with prick-dot zigzag decoration, Josiah Snatt, 1805.

$700

SCALLOPED BOWL, embossed with a flower flanked by leaves, the entwined leafy stalk handle with applied flower and bud, Hilliard & Thomason, Birmingham, 1852. **$350**

SCALLOPED, FROSTED BOWL, crescent loop handle embellished with fruiting vines, George Unite, Birmingham, 1860.

$225

SCUTTLE-SHAPE FORM, engraved with diaperwork, S-scroll handle, Cocks & Bettridge, Birmingham, 1804. **$400**

STRAWBERRY LEAF FORM, matte surface chased with veins, Joseph Taylor, Birmingham, 1809. **$375**

THISTLE-SHAPE FORM, engraved with flowers on a matte background, John Bettridge, Birmingham, 1822. **$275**

VOLUTE HANDLE, cast with shaped oval bowl resembling a stylized flower divided into matte panels engraved with flowers, John Figg, 1856. **$350**

Tea Infusers, Strainers, and Spout Strainers

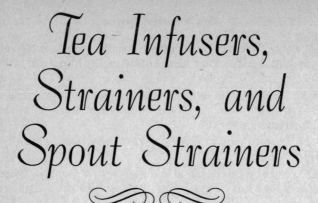

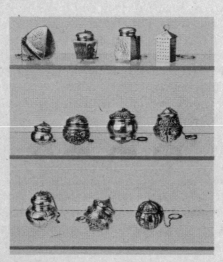

Group of late 19th-century American sterling tea balls. Courtesy of Wolf's Auction Gallery, Cleveland, OH.

Tea infusers, also known as tea dips or tea balls, were made in large quantities in the late 19th and early 20th centuries in the United States and England. Usually they were hinged oval or circular forms with a pierced body and chain.

Infusers were made in many shapes—teapots in many styles, the Liberty Bell, Chinese lanterns, and ball shapes—and are highly collectible. During the late Victorian era there were unique tea balls in the form of pumpkins, tomatoes, and full-blown flower heads. Unger Brothers and Gorham were among the firms making allover repoussé infusers that matched tea sets. The Chinese also made infusers with bamboo motifs for export to America. Collectors boast that at least two hundred different styles were produced.

On American pieces, check the inner lid for sterling silver marks. In England marks were usually placed on the body of the infuser. When buying, make sure the hinge and pin are original and working properly.

Recently, a tea infuser in the form of a bunch of grapes was listed as one of the most expensive, ranging in price from $500 to $600 if in pristine condition.

Strainers designed to fit across a teacup began to appear in the latter part of the 19th century. By the early part of the 20th century they were being produced in great quantity in Holland for export to other countries. They were usually chased with 18th-century-style court scenes, windmills, farms, and Baroque-style fruit designs. In the United States many strainers were made in the Art Nouveau style, with curved flower forms and Japonesque designs. Some had embossed sterling silver floral borders and ebonized handles. Smaller versions often sat in their own matching glass dish with sterling silver banding.

Spout strainers for teapots seem to have become popular in America in the middle part of the 19th century. Two long prongs in V-shape, with a strainer basket at one end, were suspended into the spout of the teapot. These were intended to carefully strain the tea leaves, but instead most dripped the tea on the tea cloth. Those most often collected today are in flower-basket or bucket forms. Also sought are those deeply embossed in the shapes of poppies, wild roses, and other recognizable floral forms. Strainers were marked sterling, and most had makers' marks as well. They were made in America, on the Continent, and in Russia.

Tea Infusers

ACORN-FORM FIGURAL, American, early 20th century.   **$50**
BALL FORM, with allover repoussé rose and leaf motifs, American, late 19th century.   **$100**

BALL FORM, large, pierced and stamped florals, Whiting, late 19th century. **$75**

BUNCH OF GRAPES, full figure, American, late 19th century. **$550**

CHESTNUT FORM, with its cover, leaf-form chain, handmade by Cathleen Bunt, 1976. **$350**

DRUM WITH FLUTED ENDS, American, early 20th century. **$100**

EGG FORM, allover pierced star and floral motifs, Whiting, late 19th century. **$50**

EGG SHAPE, with delicate fern piercings, John Harris, London, 1855. **$675**

EGG SHAPE, large, repoussé foliate rococo motifs, American, late 19th century. **$190**

FIGURAL, allover embossed floral motifs, German, .800 standard, early 20th century. **$175**

FLORAL REPOUSSÉ decorations allover, Gorham, late 19th century. **$100**

HINGED OVOID FORM, Atkin Brothers, Sheffield, 1909. **$190**

KETTLE FORM, stamped, American, early 20th century, with chain. **$50**

LANTERN, with repoussé swirl decoration, with chain, American, late 19th century. **$100**

LANTERN FORM, stamped, American, late 19th century, Whiting, with chain. **$100**

LIBERTY BELL FORM, American, late 19th century. **$225**

MELON SHAPE, with embossed floral bands, American, late 19th century. **$100**

NUT FORM, with pierced and floral decorations, Gorham, late 19th century. **$125**

PUMPKIN FORM, full figure, English, Birmingham, 1902. **$225**

REPOUSSÉ, with engraved fern scrolls, large, Whiting, late 19th century. **$175**

RETICULATED DESIGN, large, Gorham, late 19th century. **$120**

STRAWBERRY FORM, with embossed decoration and chain, Whiting, late 19th century. **$150**

Group of late 19th-century sterling tea caddies, tea strainers, and teapot.
Courtesy of Wolf's Auction Gallery, Cleveland, OH.

TOMATO FORM, stamped decoration, Gorham, late 19th century. **$225**

WALNUT FORM, stamped decoration with chain, Howard & Co., New York, late 19th century. **$200**

WALNUT FORM, pierced decoration, Whiting, late 19th century. **$150**

Strainers and Spout Strainers

CUP STRAINER, decorated with figure of boy with water buckets and windmill scenes, Dutch, second standard silver, maker HH. **$80**

CUP STRAINER, lozenge form with spoon handle, set on conforming cut-crystal and sterling drip base, Whiting, early 20th century. **$140**

CUP STRAINER, Neoclassical garland motif, base with ram's-head and hoof feet, pierced vase and garland apron, on stand, length, 5 in. **$155**

CUP STRAINER, Norwegian, gold-washed silver and pink guilloche enamel, circular bowl, spoon handle, fitted case, length, 4½ in. **$230**

CUP STRAINER, pierced bowl suspended above the open mouth of a dragon. **$140**

CUP STRAINER, wide fluted form with hinged cover, ivory handle and finial, Gorham, late 19th century, length, 7½ in. **$190**

DELICATELY PIERCED BOWL, French, first standard silver, length, 8 in. **$55**

LONG HANDLE, scrolls and beading, repoussé rim, American, early 20th century. **$45**

PIERCED BOWL, with 2 openwork handles, large, length, 9½ in. **$90**

SPOUT STRAINER, basket form, American, late 19th century. **$100**

SPOUT STRAINER, basket of fruit form, American, late 19th century. **$150**

SPOUT STRAINER, basketweave, Austrian, c. 1890. **$125**

SPOUT STRAINER, boat form, with lion-head ends, Gorham, late 19th century. **$80**

SPOUT STRAINER, bucket form, Russian, late 19th century. **$125**

Group of late 19th-century American and Continental tea spout strainers. Courtesy of Wolf's Auction Gallery, Cleveland, OH.

SPOUT STRAINER, cap form, Russian, late 19th century.
$125

SPOUT STRAINER, classical shell form, American, late 19th century. **$150**

SPOUT STRAINER, embossed poppy form, Gorham, late 19th century. **$125**

SPOUT STRAINER, fluted oval with flowers, Gorham, late 19th century. **$100**

SPOUT STRAINER, French, repoussé fluted basket style, late 19th century. **$100**

SPOUT STRAINER, in form of silk purse, Gorham, late 19th century. **$150**

SPOUT STRAINER, kettle form, repoussé flowers, Kirk, late 19th century. **$125**

SPOUT STRAINER, kettle form, Wallace, early 20th century.
$125

SPOUT STRAINER, oval basket form, Gorham, late 19th century. **$150**

SPOUT STRAINER, oval helmet with lion masks, English, late 19th century. **$125**

SPOUT STRAINER, scallop shell form, American, late 19th century. **$175**

SPOUT STRAINER, walnut form with embossed motifs, American, late 19th century. **$175**

STRAINER AND DRIP CUP, mounted in loop frame, height, 6½ in. **$70**

Thimbles

American sterling thimble with gilt band having embossed wild roses, $150.
Photo by J. Auslander.

Thimbles have been made almost since the beginning of time in all materials, including sterling silver, silverplate, and ivory or tortoise with sterling silver or gold mounts. Most often those in simple, undecorated forms are used for everyday work and are not eagerly sought.

During the late 18th and early 19th centuries sterling silver English filigree thimbles were made with their own threaded holders and an enclosed scent bottle. The scent was used to dry the natural oils in the fingertips before touching delicate fabrics. The advanced collector covets these thimbles.

At the same period in Holland ridged sterling silver finger guards were made to wear on the opposite hand from that on which the thimble was used. These were almost always hallmarked and made in a range of sizes. Thimble collectors generally also like to have a finger guard in their collection.

Coin silver examples are readily available in the United States, usually engraved with scenes depicting villages, boats, and farms. Even though they are beautifully wrought, they do not command high prices. Sterling silver thimbles depicting American and English fairs, stately homes, and souvenirs of exhibitions fetch extraordinarily high prices. Beginning collectors can still find many available at nominal prices, made in the late 19th and early 20th centuries in the United States by Simons, Ketchum McDougall, and Webster, with bands depicting flowers, grapes, anchors, cupids, and houses.

American scenes commemorating the gold rush, the expansion of the railroads, the St. Louis Fair, Salem witches, and the "Stitch in Time" are on the most wanted list. In England commemorative thimbles from the coronations, Westminster Abbey, Brighton Pavilion, and Windsor Castle are tops in collecting. From France 19th-century thimbles depicting Aesop's Fables are the most collectible. Check them for crispness of detail because they have recently been reproduced. Nineteenth-century English thimbles with town or spa names, bought as trifles or souvenirs of a holiday, are another category of thimble collecting. Collectors also hunt for thimbles with friendship and love motifs. Advertising thimbles, many with an elaborate verse and logo, were popular giveaways in the early 20th century. Child-size thimbles were often embossed "For A Good Girl" or "A Token For A Good Child," and these are also collected today.

Collectors should check for holes and solder repairs because they rapidly reduce a thimble's value.

ABALONE BAND, on sterling silver, early 20th century.   **$35**

ANCHOR BAND, engraved, American, late 19th century.
$125

BAMBOO LEAVES, chased and engraved, Chinese Export, c. 1860.   **$150**

BRIGHTON PAVILION, engraved design, English, early 19th century.   **$450**

COLUMBIAN EXPOSITION, American, late 19th century.
$325

CORAL BEADS inset on sterling silver, Continental, late 19th century.   **$125**

CUPID-EMBOSSED BAND, Simons Brothers, Philadelphia, late 19th century. **$225**

DAISY PATTERN, embossed and engraved, English, Charles Horner, early 20th century. **$50**

DORCAS, steel-lined, English, late 19th century. **$75**

ENAMEL, on sterling silver snow scene, Norwegian, early 20th century. **$150**

FABLES DE LA FONTAINE (old), French, late 19th century. **$450**

FILIGREE, English, mid-18th century. **$325**

FILIGREE WITH SCENT BOTTLE, English, mid-18th century. **$900**

FINGER GUARD, ridged bands, Dutch, early 19th century. **$175**

GOLDEN SPIKE, railroad commemorative, American, late 19th century. **$650**

GOOD GIRL, child size, engraved border, English, late 19th century. **$30**

GRAPE BORDER, heavily embossed leaves and vine, American, late 19th century. **$150**

KNURLED BORDER, American, early 20th century. **$35**

OSTRICH RACE, chased and engraved, Continental, late 19th century. **$250**

PANEL BAND, engraved border, American, early 20th century. **$35**

PATENT, ENGLISH, late 19th century. **$300**

PETITE FLOWERS, American, early 20th century. **$13**

ROYAL SPA, English, late 19th century. **$75**

SALEM WITCH, Daniel Low, American, late 19th century. **$650**

SCENIC BAND, engraved houses and lake, coin silver, American. **$45**

STITCH IN TIME, American, late 19th century. **$350**

STONE TOP, inset sterling silver, Continental, late 19th century. **$75**

WASHINGTON, DC, chased and engraved, American, late 19th century. **$150**

WILD ROSE, sterling silver with gilt band, heavily embossed, American, late 19th century.   **$125**

WINDMILLS, enamel band, on sterling silver, Continental, early 20th century.   **$45**

WINDSOR CASTLE, engraved, English, c. 1840.   **$550**

The Tiffany Charisma

Pair of American Tiffany sterling covered tureens, $12,000/pair. **Courtesy of William Doyle Galleries, New York.**

*U*sually, silver is collected for decorative value, for a particular design or maker's mark, but all manner of silver made by Tiffany & Company always manages to encompass universal collecting appeal. From its beginning in 1837 as Tiffany & Young to the present day, Tiffany has had its own following in each era.

Styles have changed over the years, but except for special commissions, Tiffany's design elements have always been fairly conservative in approach. One of the major designers working in this tradition from 1854 until 1870 was Edward C. Moore. In the mid-19th century Classical Revival motifs featured the Greek key, beaded borders, and acanthus leaves. Other motifs were rococo scrollwork and cast deer- and boar's-head finials and handles on hollowware pieces.

By the last quarter of the 19th century Persian motifs were popular. The Japanese style began with flatware in the Japanese pattern in 1871 and Vine in 1872. This was followed by hollowware made with hand-hammered grounds. Many of these pieces had applied leaves, insects, and birds in copper and gold. Also during this period the still-popular Chrysanthemum pattern was introduced for flatware and was followed by a similar design for tea sets, vases, candlesticks, bowls, pitchers, trays, and salts. Allover repoussé floral designs depicting wild roses, ferns, and violets were used for dresser sets.

In the early part of the 20th century Colonial Revival silver was popular, and Tiffany made some reproductions of Revere and Brasher silver. This was followed by the stylized form of the 1920s and 1930s, when Art Deco, or Art Moderne, with its geometric motifs and engraved lines, became a major influence.

Unique and ornately decorated pieces of Tiffany silver are currently breaking all previous auction records.

BASKET, bread, 1902–07, Georgian taste.   **$600**
BOWL, with applied fern and flower rim, the body chased with a variety of flowers above vertical palm leaves, on leaf-headed paw feet, c. 1880, diameter, 9⅝ in.   **$2,000**

Tiffany sterling hammered cream pitcher and sugar bowl, c. 1880. **Courtesy of Christie's East, New York.**

BOWL, centerpiece, silver-gilt, oval, with overhanging grape-vine rim, the sides pierced with a band of scrolling foliage above a band of chased-scrolling foliate-centering flowerheads, c. 1880–90, length, 14¼ in. **$2,500**

BOWL, small, 2 handles, "Japanese style," applied with a fish swallowing an insect and engraved with reeds and waterplants, hammered ground, c. 1880, diameter, 3¾ in. **$2,200**

BOWL, sugar, niello Persian style, small, etched, applied and chased with ogee cartouches enclosing strapwork and flower-heads, raised spade-shape handles, 1875–91, length over handles, 5½ in. **$800**

BOWL, 2 handles, bombé oval form on 4 scrolling feet with applied scroll border, chased with flowers and fruit on stippled ground, 1875–91, length over handles, 13⅓ in. **$1,900**

BOWLS, finger, set of 12, each of tapering cylindrical form, with plain surface and molded rim, 1907–47, diameter, 5 in. **$1,500/set**

BOX, cigar, rectangular, with hammered monogrammed sur-face and cedar lining, 1907–47, length, 9½ in. **$1,100**

CANDELABRA, pair, 5 lights, each with beaded and lobed bases on 4 paw feet headed by shells and foliage, reeded tapered stem with a central knop, c. 1900, height, 16¾ in. **$11,000/pr**

CANDLESTICKS, chamber, figural, pair, Moore for Tiffany, c. 1865, the handles formed as figures of Hercules with out-stretched arms pulling rope. **$1,400/pr**

CANDLESTICKS, set of 4, fluted, tapering form on spreading fluted oval bases, weighted, height, 10 in. **$2,600/set**

CANDLESTICKS, set of 4, George III style, after originals by Ebenezer Coker, London, 1765, octagonal baluster stems and gadroon borders, 20th century, height, 11 in. **$4,750/set**

CASTORS, PAIR, in Chrysanthemum pattern, baluster shape, pierced detachable covers with flower finials. **$1,200/pr**

CENTERPIECE, shallow circular form, undulating rim pierced and chased with diaper panels between bunches of flowers, pedestal foot, c. 1895, diameter, 11¾ in. **$1,600**

CENTERPIECE, Neoclassical style, triform base, vase-shape stem buttressed by slender scroll supports with paw terminals and anthemion tops mounted with flowerheads, 1854–65, height, 12½ in. **$1,200**

CENTERPIECE, fluted fan shape, pierced with formal foliage above a cast band of chrysanthemum flowers and leaves, 1902–07, length, 13¾ in. **$1,800**

CENTERPIECE, shallow circular form, with domed rim pierced with diaper and chased with flowers, applied with a border of grapevine, ferns, shells, and scrolls, 1891–1902, diameter, 15 in. **$2,500**

CENTERPIECE, oval, sides centered by classical female heads in cartouches, strap handles rising from female masks, pedestal base with claw feet, 1870–75, length, 17¾ in. **$4,000**

CENTERPIECE, parcel-gilt, in Chrysanthemum pattern, 1891–1902, with everted fluted scalloped rim applied with chrysanthemums, diameter, 15 in. **$5,000**

COCKTAIL SHAKER and 12 silver goblets, the shaker of tapering cylindrical form, with molded rims, strapwork handle, goblets each with tapering cylindrical bowl, baluster stem, circular foot, 1907–47. **$1,500/set**

COFFEE SERVICE, Persian style, 4 pieces, comprising coffeepot, creamer, 2-handle covered sugar bowl, and oval tray, etched with arabesques and scrolling foliage, the pot of elongated pear form with hinged onion-domed cover, 1907–47.
$2,800/set

COLD MEAT FORK, Canterbury pattern. **$165**

COMPOTE, Chrysanthemum pattern, on domed base applied with chrysanthemums, scalloped everted rim applied with chrysanthemums. **$2,000**

COMPOTE, die-rolled bands of interlaced ribbonwork enclosing flowerheads on stem and border of bowl, in full relief, 1870–75, height, 7¾ in. **$1,700**

COMPOTE, shallow circular bowl, decorated with embossed and chased flowerheads, handles capped by songbirds perched on nests, pedestal foot, frosted finish, c. 1865–70, height, 9 in.
$1,450

COMPOTES, pair, Chrysanthemum pattern, scalloped rims with scrolling chrysanthemum border. **$3,500/pr**

COMPOTES, pair, circular, with scalloped rim with shells at intervals, pierced and engraved with foliate scrolls, trumpet feet, 20th century, diameter, 9 in. **$1,500/pr**

CREAMER, "Japanese style," gourd form, with hammered surface, applied with 2 crawfish and engraved with reeds, c. 1880–90.   **$2,500**

CREAMER AND SUGAR BOWL, Japanese style, ear-form handles, cast and pierced with foliage, flowers, navettes, and ovolos.   **$900/pr**

DEMITASSE POT, Chrysanthemum pattern, c. 1890.   **$1,800**

DESSERT STANDS, pair, circular, on domed bases, the bold paw feet with acanthus joins, chased with flowers, surmounted by knop chased with flowers, the scalloped everted border chased with shells, scrolls, and flowers, 1902–07.
$3,000/pr

DESSERT STANDS, pair, molded square bases, wave-sided square tops with chased borders and monogrammed centers, c. 1880–90, width, 7 1/2 in.   ·   **$2,500/pr**

DESSERT STANDS, 2, repoussé on domed circular bases with paw and foliate supports, oval parcel-gilt dish with wide, everted, scalloped border, chased with flowerheads, ferns, and rocaille, height, 9 in.   **$6,500/2**

DISH, asparagus, and liner, rectangular, with undulating rim, applied with shells, scrolls, and flowers, matching pierced and engraved liner, 1902–07, length, 14 1/4 in.   **$2,100**

DISH, asparagus, rectangular, on ball-and-paw supports with rocaille scrolls, flowers, and trelliswork, liner pierced with bellflowers and scrolls, length, 12 1/2 in.   **$2,200**

DISH, asparagus, with cover, rectangular, with undulating sides, ends formed as pierced cartouches topped by flower sprays, removable liner, 1891–1902, length, 13 3/4 in.
$1,700/2

DISH, shell form, fluted pierced border chased with rocaille scrolls and flowerheads on stippled ground, c. 1890. **$1,250**

DISH, sweetmeat, pair, oval, with waved, reeded rims and gilt interior, chased with borders of flowers on matte ground, c. 1880, length, 6 3/4 in.   · **$700/pr**

DISHES, pair, covered, circular, chased with spiral flutes, dentilated border, domed covers with leaf-clad ring handle, 1875–91, length over handles, 10 1/2 in.   **$4,200/pr**

DISHES, pair, serving, oval, Chrysanthemum pattern, with slightly scalloped rims, 1891–1902, length, 10 in. **$2,000/pr**

DISHES, 2, shaped oval form, rims widening and applied with songbirds perched on sprays of leaves, c. 1870. **$1,100/2**

DRESSING MIRROR, rectangular, with bands of Florentine scrolls, 12½ in. **$700**

DRESSING SET, comprising hand mirror, hairbrush, 2 clothes brushes, shoehorn, comb, buffer and stand, buttonhook, nail file, pillbox, rouge pot, trinket box; relief decorations of stylized buds in trelliswork and stylized acanthus leaves. **$1,200/set**

ÉPERGNE, stem formed as a classical woman holding in her hands a hoop fitted with 4 bowls with bud terminals, her head supporting a larger matching bowl, all with frosted surface, 1865–70, height, 16 in. **$7,000**

FLASK, 1875–91, chased and applied with crowing rooster in tree with chick below, engraved on reverse "Drink to me only." **$1,600**

FLATWARE SERVICE, partial, English King pattern, in mahogany fitted case, consisting of 12 each of dinner knives, luncheon knives, tablespoons, luncheon forks, butter spreaders, demitasse spoons, bouillon spoons, cream soup spoons, dinner forks, fish forks, cocktail forks, citrus spoons, 11 teaspoons, 4 serving pieces, 4 serving forks. **$10,000/set**

HOT WATER KETTLE on lampstand, in English Regency taste, chased with rococo ornament, 1891–1902. **$1,800**

ICE PAIL, "Japanese style," hemispherical, applied with sprays of leaves and flowers on hammered ground, c. 1873–91, diameter, 7 in. **$3,600**

KNIFE, cake, Japanese pattern, silver and silver-gilt engraved with vines, bamboo, and cucumber, c. 1871. **$550**

LADLE, ice cream, Lap Over-Edge pattern. **$575**

LADLE, punch, Persian pattern. **$625**

LADLE, soup, Chrysanthemum pattern, swirl oval bowl, the stem decorated in relief with chrysanthemum leaves and topped by a chrysanthemum bud, c. 1880. **$800**

LADLE, soup, Tomato Vine pattern. **$650**

PITCHER, small, "Japanese style," with bulbous body applied on one side with a fish turning through applied and chased reeds, on hammered ground, matching circular tray, c. 1886, height of pitcher, 4¼ in. **$7,200/2**

PITCHER, covered, pear shape, the front boldly embossed with a frowning mask with flowing beard spreading around the neck, bands of flowers and spiral beaded flutes, c. 1885, height, 11¾ in.   **$4,000**

PITCHER, covered, vase shape, on pedestal foot, beaded and Greek key borders, chased with acanthus, handle topped by a female head, cover with finial formed as a seated putto blowing a horn, c. 1860, height, 12 in.   **$2,000**

PITCHER, sterling silver, c. 1887, bulbous C-scroll handle, the body chased with foliage, rocaille on stippled ground, 7 in.   **$3,450**

PITCHER, water, circular body chased with a band of winged lions, stylized foliate handle rising from a nymph's head wearing a leafy headdress, c. 1865–70, height, 9 in.   **$4,500**

PITCHER, water, baluster form with hammered surface, etched with a sinuous monogram, c. 1880–90, height, 7½ in.   **$2,000**

PITCHER, water, baluster form, etched with a band of husks and strapwork on matte grounds, c. 1915–20.   **$800**

Tiffany sterling water pitcher, 1891–1902, with shells and bell flowers, $2,200. **Courtesy of Christie's East, New York.**

PITCHER, water, shaped rectangular, on spreading base with fluting at corners, applied with shells, scrolls, and trailing bell-flowers, 1891–1902, height, 9½ in. **$2,200**

PITCHER, water, vasiform with harp-shape handle, the lower body decorated with upright overlapping leaves, the shoulder with band of laurel wreaths enclosing rosettes, with rims of lozenges, 1907–47. **$850**

PITCHER, water, bombé body chased with a band of oak and palm leaves, lip with spreading oak leaves and chased with profuse flowers on matte ground, c. 1885, height, 7 in. **$2,100**

PLATES, dessert, set of 12, undulating gadroon rims, the borders pierced and chased with scrolling acanthus, c. 1885, diameter, 8½ in. **$3,500/set**

PLATES, service, set of 12, molded rim, monogrammed. **$5,000/set**

PLATES, service, set of 12, the rims decorated with sloping leaves alternating with lobes, inner band of small leaves, 1907–47, diameter, 11 in. **$8,500/set**

PLATES, soup, set of 12, each circular with plain surface, molded rim, the border engraved with crest, 1947–56. **$3,200/set**

PLATTER, meat, Chrysanthemum pattern with undulating border, 1902–07, length, 19¾ in. **$4,200**

PLATTER, meat, Chrysanthemum pattern, oval, applied with border of chrysanthemums, length, 18 in. **$3,200**

PLATTER, meat, shaped oval, molded and gadrooned borders, c. 1907–47, length, 20½ in. **$1,600**

PLATTER, shaped circular, with molded rim and plain surface, 1907–47. **$550**

SALVER, circular, with Greek key and bead border, by Moore for Tiffany, 1855, diameter, 12 in. **$700**

SALVER, circular, on 3 beaded strapwork supports with Greek key and bead border, by Moore for Tiffany, c. 1860, diameter, 9 in. **$750**

SALVER, engraved with anthemion banding, on scrolled supports, c. 1870, diameter, 13 in. **$1,200**

SALVER, "Japanese style," triangular form on 3 foliate supports, the honeycombed surface etched with undulating monogram, c. 1880, length, 10 in. **$700**

SALVER, square, "Japanese style," hammered surface applied with an underwater scene of applied copper fish, a suspended double lure in brass, silver, and copper and a brass crab, c. 1880–90, width, 9½ in.   **$11,000**

SALVERS, pair, plain shaped circular form, in George II style, raised Chippendale borders, trifid terminals, 20th century, diameter, 12¼ in.   **$1,700/pr**

SERVER, fish, Antique Ivy pattern.   **$275**

SERVER, pie, Olympian pattern, silver and silver-gilt, c. 1878.
                    $375

SERVICE PLATES, set of 12, plain circular form with molded rim, c. 1915.   **$6,500/set**

SERVING FORK, tines gold-washed, San Lorenzo pattern.
                    $125

TANKARD, tapered square form, upper body modeled in the form of a stylized bird head, chased with spirals, scrolls, and graduated beads of hammered ground, c. 1880, height, 9¾ in.
                    $11,000

TAZZA, shallow circular form, flower and scroll rim, body and pedestal base profusely chased with flowers on matte ground, shell-and-scroll handles, rising from leaves, c. 1880, width, 12⅝ in.   **$1,750**

TAZZA, circular, on spreading circular foot chased with foliage, with shell border, 1873–91.   **$650**

TAZZA, shallow circular form with trumpet-shape foot, openwork borders of clover leaves and flowers, c. 1890, diameter, 11⅝ in.   **$900**

TAZZA, shallow circular form, rim applied with 2 spread-winged exotic birds, 1873–91, diameter at rim, 12½ in.
                    $1,300

TEA AND COFFEE SERVICE, comprising teapot, coffeepot, covered sugar bowl, cream pitcher, and waste bowl, compressed globular, with applied beads at neck, engraved with panels of ivy, the covers with leaf and bud finials, by Moore for Tiffany, 1865–70.   **$4,200/set**

TEA AND COFFEE SERVICE, c. 1870–74, Ivy Chased pattern.
                    $19,000/set

Tiffany sterling tea and coffee service with bird finials, $19,000. **Courtesy of William Doyle Galleries, New York.**

TEA AND COFFEE SET and 2-handle tray, comprising teapot, coffeepot, covered sugar bowl, creamer, and waste bowl, quadrangular form, molded borders, faceted swan-neck spouts and harp-shape handles, 1907–48, length of tray over handles, 23¾ in. **$4,500/set**

TEA AND COFFEE SET, comprising teapot, coffeepot, creamer, covered milk jug, covered sugar bowl, waste bowl, and kettle on lampstand, pear shape on spreading bases, partly chased with scrolling foliage and flowers, c. 1854. **$6,000/set**

TEAPOT, Moorish style, globular, chased, etched, and oxidized with strapwork, scrolling foliage, and rosettes, domed hinged cover with scalloped rim and ball finial, c. 1880, height, 5⅜ in. **$3,300**

TEA SET, comprising covered sugar bowl, creamer, waste bowl, teapot, and hot water kettle on lampstand, engraved with Indian-style foliage and stamped girdles of mogul strapwork, 2-handle tray with matching borders, c. 1875. **$4,000/set**

TEA SET, 3 pieces, small, comprising teapot, creamer, and covered sugar bowl, baluster form, chased with stiff palm leaves, flowers, and ferns, basketweave spout and handles, c. 1880. **$1,000/set**

TEA SET AND TRAY, comprising teapot, covered sugar bowl, and creamer with bombé circular bodies, embossed in Kirk style with flowers on matte grounds, similar square tray engraved with trellis pattern enclosing flowerheads, c. 1880, width of tray, 11 in. **$2,500/set**

TRAY, circular, Chrysanthemum pattern, with applied chrysanthemum and garland border, 1891–1902, diameter, 11 in.
$1,200

TRAY, circular, with molded Chippendale border, diameter, 12¼ in.
$800

TRAY, circular, with stylized wave border, 1891–1902, diameter, 13 in.
$800

TRAY, small, parcel-gilt, Japanese style, shaped rectangular form on 4 supports, the border applied with bleeding hearts, foliage, and a beetle, c. 1880, length, 7⅛ in.
$1,000

TRAY, smoking, oval form with cut-out handles, cord rims, with matching cigar lighter and cutter, 1907–47.
$1,200/set

TRAY, tea, oval, with scrolling acanthus and rosette border and rising reeded acanthus and rosette-clad handles, 1891–1902, length, 29¼ in.
$8,000

TRAY, 2 handles, rectangular, with rounded angles, the raised border decorated with scrolling foliage centering flowerheads above a band of flutes, c. 1880–90, length over handles, 26¼ in.
$6,000

TRAYS, pair, 2 handles, Chrysanthemum pattern, oval, with borders and handles decorated with flowers and foliage, reeded rim foot decorated with leaves at intervals, 1891–1902, length over handles, 16⅛ in.
$6,000/pr

TUREEN, soup, with cover, oval vase shape on a pedestal foot, forked loop handles rising and terminating with foliage, domed cover with bud finial, 1894, length over handles, 15 in.
$2,300/2

TUREEN, soup, and cover, boat shape, forked scroll handles rising from stiff leaves and spreading into sprays of buds, c. 1880, length over handles, 16½ in.
$4,000/2

TUREEN, soup, with cover, boat shape, the rim with a die-rolled border of mogul-style strapwork and flowers, lightly chased with an Indian-style band of foliage, 1875–91, length, 16⅛ in.
$3,800/2

TUREENS, pair, covered, repoussé with floral motifs.
$12,000/pr

VASE, Moorish-style, silver and copper, baluster form, lobed sides, flared neck, etched with scrolling foliage on copper ground, reeded rim with leaves at intervals, 1902–07.
$2,000

VASE, tall trumpet form, partly engraved with stylized buds and leaves, molded foot, 1907–08, height, 20 in.   **$1,500**

VASE, 3 handles, 1873–91, 3 paw feet, joins wide repoussé band of mythological figures amid scrolling foliage, leaf-clad reeded handles, height, 9 in.   **$6,000**

VASES, Art Nouveau, pair, body encircled with anemones and foliage, 1891–1902, height, 15³/₈ in.   **$5,500/pr**

VASES, pair, tapered cylindrical form, base rim of leaf tips, shoulder chased with a band of anthemia on matte ground, c. 1920–30, height, 15¼ in.   **$2,200/pr**

WINE COOLER, large, vase shape with cast collar of ovolos and foliage, double swing handles rising from pairs of classical female heads, on 3 winged and horned lion monopad feet, 1865–70, height to rim, 13⅛ in.   **$9,000**

Vinaigrettes

Rare Swedish silver vinaigrette with music box, c. 1840, $5,000. Courtesy of Tom Bisceglia. Photo by J. Auslander.

Used to ward off disease or unpleasant odors, tiny boxes with vinegar-soaked sponges, known as vinaigrettes, became popular in the 15th century during Henry VII's reign. They were crafted of sterling silver or gold with beautifully perforated lids. Later they were fitted with a tightly fitting outer lid to preserve the vinegar and often were referred to as sponge boxes.

Until the early part of the 19th century, most were carried in the pocket. After that they were most often suspended on a watch fob.

In the late 18th and early 19th centuries, when vinaigrettes appeared in the greatest quantities, Birmingham, England, became the center of sterling silver vinaigrette production. The shapes varied: circular, rectangular, square, purse and book shapes, shell, heart, and even pocket watch forms. The flexible fish form, as well as cornucopia, acorn, and walnut shapes, also were made.

Most late-18th- and early-19th-century vinaigrettes were heavy compared with the later lightweight, rolled silverplate boxes. Interior lids were pierced and highly engraved in the early examples, with designs that included flowers, leaves, birds, and scrolls. Later ones were plainer in design, and most were gilded to prevent discoloration from the acid in the vinegar.

In the early and mid-19th century lids were often cast and heavily embossed with scenes of English national interest, such as Windsor Castle, York Minster, and St. Paul's Cathedral. The vinaigrette reached a great height of popularity in the mid-19th century, when they were often exchanged as love tokens. Afterward the vinaigrette was replaced by brightly colored glass scent bottles.

Most vinaigrettes were hallmarked with a full set of marks on their bases, and the grill was struck with the makers' marks. These included the initials of Matthew Linwood, John Shaw, Samuel Pemberton, Joseph Taylor, Nathaniel Mills, and Peter and Ann Bateman.

Recently, an extremely rare vinaigrette, enclosing a music box in its base, has appeared on the market.

Many tiny boxes have appeared in the marketplace with newly pierced interior lids, changing the box to a much more costly vinaigrette. These generally are unmarked on the grills.

BOOK, engraved with "tartan" decoration, Gervase Wheeler, Birmingham, 1838. **$300**

BOOK, silver-gilt, William IV, with engine-turned decoration, maker's mark T.D., 1835. **$600**

BOOK FORM, William IV, lid with engraved rectangular cartouche, Taylor & Perry, Birmingham, 1833. **$350**

CASTLE TOP, chased in low relief with a view of Newstead Abbey, Nathaniel Mills, Birmingham, 1838. **$600**

CASTLE TOP, view of Westminster Abbey, silver-gilt, Nathaniel Mills, 1842. **$1,000**

CASTLE TOP, cover chased in relief with a view of Windsor Castle, Francis Clarke, Birmingham, 1838. **$450**

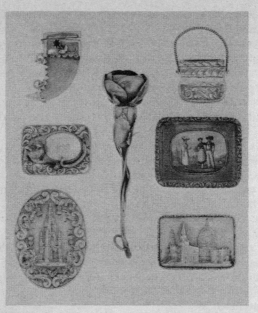

Group of English sterling vinaigrettes including rare cat, second row, left, **$5,000. Rose form, center, $1,500. Courtesy of Phillips, London.**

CAT, silver-gilt, body engraved with peacocks and foliate scrolls, cover applied with a cat, curled up and set with a "blister-pearl," James Beebe, 1837.   **$5,000**

ENGRAVED, with fishscale decoration, grill engraved with leafage, John Bettridge, Birmingham, 1817.   **$275**

FISH, articulated, Regency, realistically engraved body, hinged to reveal a simply pierced grill, Birmingham, 1818.   **$1,000**

FISH, articulated, sterling silver, Samuel Pemberton, Birmingham, 1817.   **$600**

FOB WATCH FORM, George IV, silver-gilt, T.N., Birmingham, 1821.   **$225**

GEORGE III, engine-turned decoration, Samuel Pemberton.   **$110**

HANDBAG, upright form, engraved with scrollwork, Gervase Wheeler, Birmingham.   **$325**

HORN SHAPE, chased with birds, flowers, and scrollwork, the grill pierced and engraved with flowerheads, T.J., London, 1873.   **$600**

Group of English sterling vinaigrettes in box form, Gorham horn-shape vinaigrette, and George III baby rattle. **Courtesy of Christie's East, New York.**

NOVELTY, modeled as a walnut, inscribed "S. Mordan & Co., London," c. 1880. **$550**

OBLONG, silver-gilt, engine-turned, with raised border of fruiting vines, the pull-out grill pierced with a bird amid fruiting vines, William Edwards, 1812. **$475**

OBLONG, silver-gilt, engine-turned, with raised borders of flowers, Birmingham, 1826, Nathaniel Mills. **$400**

OBLONG, with beveled sides chased with guilloche and reeded bands, the grill pierced and engraved with a bird amid flowers, Samuel Pemberton, Birmingham, 1816. **$225**

OVAL, reeded form, with working music box in base, Swedish, c. 1840. **$5,000**

OYSTER SHELL FORM, George III, silver-gilt, Matthew Linwood, Birmingham, 1805. **$375**

POCKET WATCH FORM, bright-cut, grill finely pierced and engraved with flowers and foliage, Augustus George Piesse, London, 1862. **$450**

PURSE FORM, GEORGE III, with prick-dot wavy decoration, John Shaw, Birmingham, 1818. **$300**

RAILWAYMAN'S LANTERN FORM, silver-gilt, hinged cover with swivel glass reflector, red on one side, green on the other, Henry William Dee, 1870. **$950**

ROSE FORM, silver-gilt, Henry William Dee, 1868. **$1,500**

SILVER-GILT, cover set with Swiss enamel panel depicting a man and two women wearing national costume, Thomas Edwards, 1832. **$2,500**

SKULL POMANDER, back of the head divided into 6 compartments, probably German, 17th century. **$600**

STRAWBERRY FORM, embossed design, Birmingham, 1883.
$300

WHISTLE AND VINAIGRETTE COMBINATION, stamped with flowers and scrollwork, George Unite, Birmingham, 1875.
$600

WILLIAM IV, engine-turned motifs, Thomas Shaw, 1830.
$165

Wiener Werkstätte (Vienna Workshop)

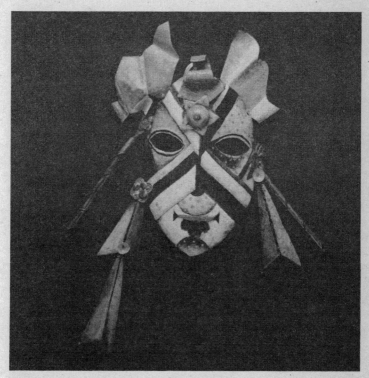

Mask enameled by Fritzi Low, Wiener Werkstätte, $8,800. Length, 13".
Courtesy of Christie's Park Ave., New York.

*A*t the turn of the 20th century some of the artists and crafts-men in Europe, who called themselves Secessionists, joined into groups and they exhibited and critiqued their own artworks. One of the most important, the Wiener Werkstätte, was almost wholly composed of artists from the Vienna Secessionist group, nearly one hundred in all. They created what they referred to as the "modern" Vienna style, a counterpart to the English Arts and Crafts movement.

Vienna Workshop pieces were produced in sterling silver, silverplate, and chrome. Some had enamel decoration, inlaid woods, or inset malachite or other stones. Hand-hammered grounds were commonly used, and most were created in geometric or Cubist forms. Clocks, boxes, candlesticks, purses, and jewelry were produced at this time and were stamped Wiener-Werkstätte (WW entwined) and also had the names of some of the most famous designers, Josef Hoffmann, Kolomon Moser, and Dagobert Peche.

BASKET, rectangular, with angular integral handle, the sides pierced with geometric gridwork, designed by Josef Hoffmann, c. 1904–06.   **$3,000**

INKSTAND, silvered metal, rectangular top with beaded edge set with 3 horizontally molded pyramidal hinged covers repoussé with blossoms and lozenges and set with octagonal ivory finials, opening to a central inkwell and two square cavities, designed by Otto Prutscher, c. 1910.   **$8,500**

PIANO LAMP, silverplated, the square domed base supporting an attentuated S-scroll arm with circular ring hung with black and white patterned cloth shade, designed by Josef Hoffmann, c. 1908.   **$9,500**

PIN, oval, decorated with a small songbird with a black enamel eye, designed by Koloman Moser, c. 1910.   **$1,000**

PIN, rectangular, decorated in brilliant blue enamel with a nude female seated on a striped chaise longue, attributed to Dagobert Peche, c. 1920.   **$1,500**

Whistles

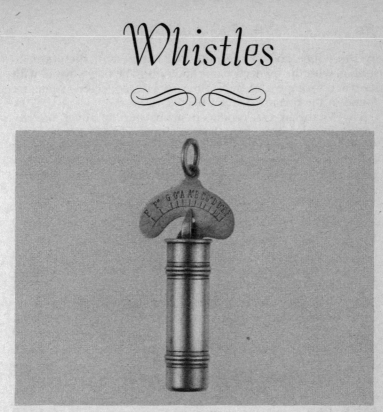

English sterling tuning whistle, c. 1902, $800. Courtesy of Phillips, London.

*U*sed for necessity or carried for whimsy, whistles, also known as calls, have become highly collectible. There are an extraordinary number of styles and a great variety of materials employed in their manufacture.

Georgian and Victorian baby whistles were often made in combination with bells, rattles, and mother-of-pearl or coral teething sticks. They were also found in silver-gilt with coral. A very small number in miniature or doll size were made. Bells and the coral or mother-of-pearl stick should be original and unbroken.

Collectors look for sterling silver bosuns' whistles, made from the 17th century to the present and used to pipe sailors aboard a ship and issue signals on board. The best examples have allover engraving. Sterling silver whistles also were used

by the police and in the military. The best of these are inscribed with the owner's name and rank. The dog whistle, with
its narrow shape and high pitch, is also collected. Some are
found in the form of a dog's head.

The Victorian era produced many sterling silver novelty
whistles in the shape of a shoe, pig, or owl and often in combination with a matchsafe. Some were inlaid with Scottish agate or ivory. Ladies' or military chatelaines often held a tiny
whistle. Tuning pitch whistles, produced in the 19th century,
are quite rare.

BOOT FORM, miniature size, Birmingham, 1893.   **$400**

BOSUN'S CALL, bright-cut with thistles and foliage, Birmingham, 1872.   **$400**

BOSUN'S CALL, engraved with leafage, Hilliard & Thomason,
Birmingham, 1877.   **$325**

BOSUN'S CALL, handle spot-engraved, bowl applied with anchors surmounted by crowns, George Unite, Birmingham,
1879.   **$350**

BOSUN'S CALL, miniature, Birmingham, 1883.   **$585**

COMBINATION WHISTLE and vesta case, cylindrical, engraved with birds, foliage, and initials, A.H. & J.G., London,
1883.   **$425**

ENGRAVED, small, Birmingham, 1903.   **$170**

HORN, silver-mounted, carved with a crocodile, 1870.   **$150**

PROPELLING PENCIL and whistle combination, contained
within a flat fish, whistle forming the tail, Hubert Thornhill,
1888.   **$400**

REPOUSSÉ floral design, with loop, 1½ in.   **$50**

TUNING, with graduated scale of notes, English.   **$800**

Wine Labels

Group of English sterling wine labels together with Tiffany label, with swan's head terminal. **Courtesy of Phillips, London.**

By the latter part of the 18th century wine labels were being made in Sheffield plate as well as in sterling silver. In addition, they were fully hallmarked, and some examples had bright-cut engraved decoration.

Sterling silver wine labels were originally used to identify the contents of wine bottles rather than as decoration. During the 18th and 19th centuries labels were referred to as bottle tickets or tags, even though they did not have the chains associated with later labels. Bottle tickets were generally smaller and curved to hang around the neck of the bottle. They bore unusual names such as Nig, Shrub, and Rhenish (wines). Design shapes included crescents, ovals, and escutcheons, often with pierced or embossed details.

In the 19th century, bottle labels were generally larger and had decorations of vines, leaves, flowers, shellwork, and

419

grapes. One can also find depictions of Bacchus and satyrs. Labels have been found in both England and France, indicating that they were exported to the Continent.

In England wine labels went out of style after 1860 because bottles of wines themselves had to be labeled to be sold.

ARMORIAL, modeled as a rampant-lion crest, one foot raised above a ball, upon a rectangular title scroll incised "Claret," James Hyde, 1799.   **$900**

BOAT SHAPE, set of 3, pierced and bright-cut later engraved "Port," "Sherry," and "Marsala," London, c. 1800.

$250/set

BOAT SHAPE, terminating at either end in swan's head, grapes, and vine leaves above swags of flowers and pierced in pseudo-Oriental style, "Chartreuse," Tiffany & Co., late 19th century.   **$475**

BOTTLE RING LABELS, set of 4, large plain rectangular form incised "Hock," "Lisbon," "Vin-De-Grave," and "Champagne," James Fray, Dublin, c. 1815.   **$350/set**

CRESCENT SHAPE, stamped out with bead and laurel borders and Neoclassical urn flanked by swags, incised "Claret," Benjamin Tait, Dublin, c. 1785.   **$250**

CURVED RECTANGULAR FORM, pair, bright-engraved borders, base applied with cut-out band of leafage and central floral motif, incised "Claret" and "Sherry," probably Samuel Teare, Dublin, c. 1790.   **$350/pr**

FRUITING VINE and leafy scroll design, the title scroll flanked by two seated dogs and pierced "Convent," c. 1840.   **$225**

GOBLET SHAPE, with bright-engraved zigzag borders, incised "Champagne," Susanna Barker, c. 1790.   **$475**

MARQUIS'S CORONET FORM, incised "Port," Thomas Edwards, 1822.   **$700**

NAVETTE SHAPE, set of 3, with double-scroll surmount incised "Claret," "Sherry," "Madeira," Phipps & Robinson, 1794.   **$350/set**

OBLONG, with gadroon borders and projecting lips, incised "Lisbon," Benjamin Bickerton, c. 1765.   **$275**

OBLONG, with in-curved sides, reverse bead-punched border incised "Rum," Susanna Barker, c. 1790.   **$175**

OBLONG, with slightly domed top and in-curved sides, gadroon borders, incised "Shrub," William Scott, Dundee, c. 1775. **$275**

OBLONG SHAPE, pair, with gadroon and foliate borders, engraved "Sherry" and "Whiskey." **$85/pr**

OPENWORK OF FLOWER and S-scroll design, incised "Sherry," Susanna Barker, 1784–85. **$325**

OVAL, thread edge incised "Rum," by Peter & Jonathan Bateman, 1790. **$325**

OVAL, thread edge with double-scroll surmount capped by an oval monogrammed cartouche incised "Sherry," Phipps & Robinson, c. 1790. **$225**

OVAL, with shell, foliate, and fruiting-vine borders, pierced "Claret" and "Port," Emes & Barnard, 1819. **$225/2**

OVAL, border pierced with floral motifs and with bright-engraved zigzag border, incised "Lisbon," John Teare, Dublin, c. 1827. **$300**

OVAL, center engraved with crest, within a cut-out wreath and ribbon, all above a curved scroll pierced "Madeira," William Eaton, 1842. **$625**

RECTANGULAR, with prick-dot borders, clipped corners, and cut-out "umbrella" surmount, incised "Rum," W. P. Cunningham, Edinburgh, c. 1795. **$250**

RECTANGULAR, engraved surround, "Scotch," American. **$35**

RECTANGULAR, silver gilt, with 6 pendent "tassels," incised "Port," John Reily, 1804. **$250**

RECTANGULAR, Provincial, with zigzag borders, surmounted by an initialed shield flanked by scrolls and incised "Sherry," Cattle & Barber, York, c. 1810. **$475**

RECTANGULAR, thread-edge form with cut-out scroll surmount, incised "St. Peray," Laurence Nolan, Dublin, 1825. **$600**

RECTANGULAR, with bright-engraved borders and domed pierced floral surmount, incised "Vidonia," Samuel Meriton II, c. 1775. **$225**

RECTANGULAR, with gadroon border and inner thread edges, stylized flower motif in each corner, incised "Champagne," Margaret Binley, c. 1765. **$175**

SAUCE LABEL, crescent shape with zigzag borders, surmounted by an ovoid urn flanked by swags, incised "Elder," c. 1790.   **$90**

SCROLL, with bright-engraved zigzag border and stylized triple-leaf surmount, incised "Port," Thomas Watson, c. 1790.

$275

SHELL AND FRUITING-VINE DESIGN, title scroll surmounted by a putto astride a barrel, each incised "Currant" and "Grape," Richard Turner, 1819.   **$450/2**

SHELL FORM, set of 4, with raised nameplates enameled in black with the words "Claret," "Port," "Sherry," and "Burgundy," Benjamin Smith, London, 1807.   **$525/set**

SHIELD SHAPE, stamped borders, "Rye," American, early 20th century.   **$35**

SINGLE VINE LEAF, pierced, set of 4, "Madeira," "Claret," "Sherry," and "Port," London, 1845.   **$750/set**

S-SCROLL, incised and nielloed "Rum," by Hester Bateman, c. 1775.   **$160**

STAMPED-OUT HUNTING HORN, with coiled rope attachment, incised "Port," George Unite, Birmingham, 1857.

$600

VINE LEAF, set of 4 single, die-stamped with veins and pierced "Claret," "Sherry," "Port," and "Madeira," Rebecca Emes and Edward Barnard, London, 1826.   **$400/set**

Wine-Related Articles

Left. *Nineteenth-century silverplated wine funnel.* Right. *Irish wine coaster, c. 1792.* Courtesy of Alice and Derek Hamilton. Photo by J. Auslander.

Wine funnels came into use in the early 18th century because wine was sold by the barrel and had to be decanted at home. Silver funnels were most often made in two parts, the upper part having punched holes to filter out impurities. Many had detachable rims so that a piece of muslin could be inserted to filter the wine. Spigots with curved spouts appeared, and a clip was also attached to the funnel. By the late 18th century stands were available for use with the funnels. Decoration on them was simple—beading and gadrooning was used in most instances; fluting appeared later. A full set of hallmarks should be found on the bowl. The detachable spout should have the maker's mark and the lion passant. If of later manufacture, the piece should bear the sovereign's head and the date letter.

Sterling silver wine tasters, especially 18th- and early-19th-century examples made in France, are quite desirable. Most often these have fluted or lobed motifs with beaded or snake-entwined borders. Baroque-type decoration generally indicates a late-19th-century Dutch or German example. Very few English wine tasters exist, although in Scotland quaiches, or marriage cups, similar in form to wine tasters, were made throughout the 19th century. Vintners' wine tasters are extremely collectible and can be recognized by the design style: one half is fluted, and the other has a crimped edge. This configuration allowed them to be used by two people when trying new wines.

Wine coasters made their first appearance in England in the mid-18th century. Most had turned wooden bases with central sterling silver bosses, usually used for engraving a monogram or crest. Designs varied from pierced florals and flutes to engraved swags and bowknots. Generally, they were made in pairs. Single coasters have little value in comparison to pairs. Most coasters are hallmarked around the base. American coasters were made by Gorham and Tiffany with embossed swags, flowers, and cherub motifs.

Wine coolers, made in sterling silver, old Sheffield plate, and later in silverplate, were used in most homes by the late 18th century. They usually have a detachable liner and rim. Several forms were made, including pail and campana shapes, both with handles. Lobed designs are often combined with lions' masks and ring handles. Intertwined serpent handles and mask and vine-covered handles also were used. If the cooler is sterling silver, both the body and the liner should be hallmarked.

Flagons or jugs were used for serving wine and beer. Silver was a popular medium in the 18th century. By the 19th century glass jugs with sterling silver mounts were fashionable. Many were elaborately embossed and pierced, depicting grapevines, leaves, and fruit and having branch-form handles. Finials often had full figures depicting Bacchus. Caryatid handles were mostly used in the 18th century, and novelty claret jugs in the form of animals and birds were popular in the late 19th century.

BARREL SPIGOT, with reeded borders and removable key-form handle, Thomas Watson & Co., Sheffield, 1806, length, 6¼ in.
$1,200

BRANDY BOWL, crimped oval, chased with fruit and foliage, the center with a bust portrait of a man with a globe, Dutch, 17th-century style.   **$150**

BRANDY SAUCEPAN, on a skirted foot, with turned-wood handle, London, 1729.   **$200**

BRANDY SAUCEPAN, 18th-century style, plain, tapering, turned-wood side handle with heart-shape mounts, London, 1912, 7½ in.   **$500**

BRANDY SAUCEPAN, large, plain, compressed vase shape, turned-wood side handle with heart-shape mount, Thomas Jones, Dublin, 1789, 11 in. overall.   **$1,750**

CHAMPAGNE TAP, English, nickel-plated, with curved spout.
$35

COASTER, floral repoussé band, everted rim with flowerheads and leaves, Sheffield, 1817.   **$425**

COASTER, fluted circular, with applied trailing-vine border, ground inset with a shaped circular boss stamped with vines, William Bateman, London, 1833.   **$550**

COASTER, pierced, bright-cut and beaded with vacant square cartouche and polished wood base, London, probably 1782.
$150

COASTERS, pair, Old Sheffield plate, circular with applied scrolling foliate rims, turned-wood bases with vacant circular bosses.   **$225/pr**

COASTERS, pair, reeded, pierced, and bright-cut, circular, decorated with acanthus leaves and floral and foliate swags, probably London, c. 1780.   **$1,600/pr**

COASTERS, pair, Sheffield plate, circular, with applied gadroon, shell and foliate borders.   **$175/pr**

COASTERS, pair, silverplated, circular, the lower part of sides with raised Neo-Gothic style festooning, turned-wood bases with center electroplated bosses, English, c. 1870.   **$400/pr**

COASTERS, pair, silverplated, with pierced and embossed sides.   **$450/pr**

COASTERS, pair, small, silverplated, foliate-pierced and engraved, circular, with molded rims, Italian.   **$90/pr**

COASTERS, 2 matching, Dutch, sides pierced with linked double ovals, beaded and reel rims, Rotterdam, 1803.   **$900/2**

Pair of Regency vase-form wine coolers with grapevine motifs. **Courtesy of Christie's East, New York.**

COCKTAIL SET, comprising flagon-form cocktail shaker, 6 stemmed cups, and circular tray, Tiffany & Co., New York, 1943–45. **$2,300/set**

COOLERS, pair, campana form with molded borders and square pedestal bases, Tiffany & Co., New York, 1947–55, height, 10¾ in. **$3,500/pr**

CRADLE, pierced, on scroll supports with scroll handle, London, 1910. **$700**

DECANTER, glass, silver-mounted, spiral-fluted vase shape, London, 1889, 8¼ in. **$500**

DECANTER, liqueur, glass cut with arabesques and with open-work mount stamped with putti, harvesting vines, finial formed as a satyr holding aloft a cornucopia. **$525**

DECANTER, silver-mounted cut glass with fluted mushroom stopper, 11½ in. **$275**

DECANTERS, pair, silver-mounted, hobnail-pattern cut glass, shaped square, oblong mahogany tantalus. **$350/pr**

DECANTER STAND, Old Sheffield plate, trefoil form, on foliate and shell feet, with rococo decoration and fitted with 3 cut-glass decanters. **$185/set**

DECANTER STAND, square base with gadroon border, the reeded frame with stiff leaf supports, on fern-cast and scroll feet, with center-decorated handle, holding 4 contemporary cut-glass decanters, Rebecca Emes and Edward Barnard, 1817. **$1,800/set**

EWER, covered, baluster form on spreading foot with caryatid handle, chased with acanthus leaves, tied laurel wreaths, and flutes, shell thumbpiece, Continental, height, 11½ in. **$800**

EWER, gourd form, cast neck of scrolling leaves, spout with horse head terminal, the handle of pierced and cast leaves, London, c. 1869. **$1,200**

FLASK, flattened egg shape, the base with removable cup, screw-on cap reversible to form a bung and measure, Taylor & Hamilton, Glasgow, c. 1770–80, length, 7¼ in. **$1,800**

FRUIT STRAINER, with pierced circular bowl applied with 2 pierced, shaped handles, London, 1728. **$750**

FRUIT STRAINER, molded, circular, with 2 applied scroll handles and with a molded rim and shaped clip, Edinburgh, 1778. **$180**

FUNNEL, beaded, with curved spigot and shaped clip, Joseph Bradley, London, 1787. **$675**

FUNNEL, campana shape, narrow ropework girdle, Solomon Hougham, 1816. **$950**

FUNNEL, part spiral-fluted with curved spigot, bowl with an applied gadroon and shell border and shaped clip, Philip Rundell, London, 1819. **$3,200**

FUNNEL, plain design, engraved with crest, Robert Hennell, 1787. **$750**

FUNNEL, reeded, with curved spigot and plain clip. **$775**

FUNNEL, reeded, with shaped clip and curved spigot, engraved with a crest, London, 1792. **$550**

FUNNEL, typical form, Hester Bateman, London, c. 1780. **$400**

FUNNEL, with reeded border and keyhole-shape thumbpiece, Peter & William Bateman, 1808. **$750**

JUG, claret, glass, spiral-fluted, scroll handle and flat hinged cover, Birmingham, 1891, 10¾ in. **$225**

English wine jug, 1840, cranberry glass with cast cage in vintage design,
$4,800. **Courtesy of Wolf's Auction Gallery, Cleveland, OH.**

JUG, claret, plated, cylindrical glass body with baluster base
etched with clusters of vine leaves, the plated rim engraved
with fruiting vines, the spout cast in the form of a smiling mask
with vine supports, 1870.   **$600**

JUG, claret, silver-mounted, plain baluster glass body with
raised fruiting-vine frieze with masks, the spout cast as a satyr's
mask, cover surmounted by cast lion supporting a shield, Henry
Wilkinson & Co., 1896.   **$950**

JUG, claret, tapering, chased with waterlilies and bulrushes,
satyr's mask spout and domed hinged cover with griffin finial,
Birmingham, 1872, 12 in.   **$1,200**

PITCHER, tapering, molded with rib decoration and applied
scroll handle, London, 1878, 12¼ in.   **$1,200**

QUAICH, silver-gilt, octagonal, plain with pierced cast lug handles either side, on collet foot, Thomas Bradbury, Sheffield,
1925.   **$275**

Silver, mounted, cut glass English claret jug, London, 1889, $1,600.
Courtesy of Christie's East, New York.

QUAICH, spot-hammered, the 2 shaped handles with Celtic knot decoration, border engraved with a motto in Gaelic, London, 1916. **$225**

STIRRUP CUP, fashioned as the head of an Irish wolfhound, Continental, unmarked, late 19th century. **$2,000**

STOPPER, bottle cork, cast, modeled as a hound's head with open mouth and slavering tongue, E. H. Stockwell, c. 1880. **$250**

French sterling wine tasters, early 19th century. Courtesy of Alice and Derek Hamilton. Photo by J. Auslander.

TASTER, with serpent handle, bowl inset with coin, 19th century, French. **$575**

TASTER, with serpent handle, late 18th century, French.

$850

TASTER, circular, decorated with stylized floral and foliate swags and inset with a coin dated 1790, French, 19th century.

$350

TASTER, circular, inset with a religious medallion, bowl engraved with a name and with various trophies, shaped thumbpiece with a scene of the Crucifixion, French. **$500**

TASTER, French Provincial, saucer shape, Gabriel Tillet, Bordeaux, 1730–32. **$3,000**

TASTER, French, with ring-and-serpent handle, half-fluted body with prick-dot decoration, possibly Paris, 1738. **$500**

TASTER, punch-beaded, circular, with applied serpent handle, bowl chased with a frieze of stylized flowers and vines and engraved with initials, French. **$175**

TASTER, spot-hammered, circular, with molded rim and applied scroll handle, the bowl inset with a coin, Continental.

$110

TASTER, 2 handles, shaped circular form with lobed sides, wavy edge and S-scroll handles, Sicily, 1700. **$1,400**

TROLLEY for 2 bottles, base with 4 wheels, with handle terminating in bone grip, mounted with 2 wine coasters cast and pierced with infant bacchanals and leopards in the shade of grapevines, ribbon-tied, silver-gilt base plates, London, 1863, length overall, 12³/₄ in. **$3,200**

Writing Accessories

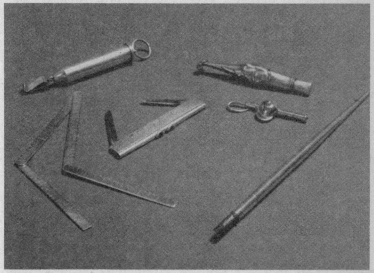

Group of late 19th-century writing tools. Tiffany sterling letter scale, $150.
Folding sterling ruler, $100. Double pencil and knife, English sterling,
$225. Elephant silverplated pencil, $75. Jockey hat silverplated pencil, $50.
Silver dip pen, $75.

During the 19th century the social custom of letter writing developed into a high art form. Schools taught penmanship, and manufacturers sold wares to cater to this new fashion.

Writing accessories included pen wipes in the form of pigs or dogs in sterling silver or silverplate, their backs inset with bristles. Others were simple box shapes with sterling surrounds. A popular Victorian style was a pen wipe composed of several circular layers of felt or velvet sewn together with a sterling silver human or animal figure in the center.

Straightedge and folding rulers were made in many sizes, in all sterling silver or ivory with sterling silver mounts.

In 1822 in England, Sampson Mordan invented the propelling, or mechanical, pencil. It became exceptionally popular, especially when produced in the form of dogs' or horses' heads, Egyptian mummies, owls, guns, tennis racquets, fish, or hunting horns.

Desk paper clips in sterling silver and silverplate, embossed with full-blown roses, lilies, or ladies' heads, were made to match elaborate desk sets. There also were novelty clips, sometimes quite large, with elaborate motifs including hands, horseshoes, dogs' heads, and wishbones.

Dip pens with sterling silver handles were made in quantities in the Victorian era with allover embossed florals, spiral-twist handles, or engine-turned engraving in combination with tortoise shell, ivory, mother-of-pearl, or coral. A few sterling silver examples had peeps or Stanhopes on the top of the handle. (Peeps or Stanhopes are photographic images that have been reduced in size.) Sometimes the pens are found with their original silk-lined leather cases. In both England and France a novelty sterling silver pen was produced in the shape of a quill pen, with its engraving simulating feathers.

Writing or stationery boxes were popular in England and the United States in the late 1800s. They were elaborately decorated with stamped, pierced, and engraved sterling silver or silver-gilt mounts on papier-mâché or tortoise-shell grounds. Often they were part of large desk sets, including blotter ends, inkstand, letter rack, and other accessories.

William Comyns was one of the most prolific makers of writing accessories in England, using rococo motifs and cherubs. In the United States, Dominick & Haff and Gorham produced fine examples.

Letter Openers (Knives)

Large numbers of letter openers, or letter knives, were produced in the late 19th and early 20th centuries in sterling silver, silverplate, and combinations of ivory, tortoise, agate, and jade with sterling silver mounts. Blades generally were made of silver, silverplate, tortoise shell, mother-of-pearl, wood, or ivory. Novelty letter knives with cast figures depicting owls, foxes, dogs, cats, and Kate Greenaway figures are very collectible. Others were produced with sporting motifs. American firms produced letter knives in sterling silver and silverplate as advertising giveaways or commemorative tokens. Page cutters, which are, in actuality, extremely large letter knives, were very popular in the 1890s.

Steven Helliwell, in his excellent book *Collecting Small Silverware*, cautions the reader to be aware that letter knives can be easily converted from English sterling silver meat skewers.

Seals

In the 18th and 19th centuries a writer sealed a letter by dripping sealing wax on it, then impressing his or her personal cypher on the hot wax with a hand seal. This was done to ensure that the letter arrived unread and intact. Seals were made in many mediums, including sterling silver, silverplate, gilt metal, hardstone, and even crystal. They were also made in combination with jade, quartz, and coral. Initials, crests, and designs in intaglio were cut into the seal.

Seals were made in several sizes. By the 19th century desk seals were often quite elaborate, with full-figure sterling silver or silverplated handles that often matched a desk set. These are eagerly collected today. Seals were made with ribbed or embossed metal handles and depicted owls, Punch, classical figures, or famous personalities. Boxed sets containing seals with glass or semiprecious stones were intaglio-engraved with flowers, days of the week, or mottoes. All of these screwed into sterling silver handles. Seals in wheel form were useful in offices because they could be engraved with days of the week and other legends. There were also sterling silver seals in cylindrical form that contained their own stick of sealing wax. There was even a seal containing a music box that played a popular tune.

Fob seals, which hung from a watch fob, are highly collectible. They are quite small, usually with a ring for hanging and a quartz, amethyst, bloodstone, or glass base that has been intaglio-cut and mounted with silver.

Stamp Boxes

When penny stamps first appeared in 1840 in England, a need for stamp boxes arose. During the late 19th century both sterling silver and silverplate stamp boxes in single and double sizes were produced to fit into a pocket or hang from a watch fob or chatelaine. Designs in the shape of envelopes, often with engraved names or dates or enameled stamps, command a high price today. A few desk examples made in Japan at the end of the 19th century have exquisite Satsuma plaques depicting bunches of wisteria blooms inset into the sterling silver tops against gilt-enriched grounds.

Larger sterling silver desk boxes were made to match desk sets. Novelty forms in the shapes of dogs, bears, owls, and horses were made in both sterling silver and silverplate with places for several stamps inside.

The variety of small stamp boxes is almost endless. Some have hidden slides to hold the stamps; others have slanted depressions or, if double-sided, a center wall.

Circular sterling silver boxes for rolls of stamps were often made in the mid-20th century by Tiffany and Cartier. These are not fast sellers unless they have unusual enamel decoration.

String Holders

String holders were popular in the late 19th and early 20th centuries. Most were oval or spherical in shape and made in silverplate, sterling silver, or a combination of cut glass and sterling silver. String holders were made in two halves that opened to insert a ball of string. One end of the string was then pulled through an opening, thus avoiding tangles.

AIDE-MEMOIRE, leather, silver-mounted, with a retractable pencil, London, 1895.   **$350**

BALUSTER-FORM SANDER, with traces of gilding, detachable cover pierced with quatrefoils and scrolls, Paul de Lamerie, London, 1732.   **$800**

BLOTTER, oblong, mount stamped with rococo flowers, foliage, and trelliswork, engraved with a coronet, William Comyns, London, 1891.   **$375**

CHATELAINE NOTEPAD, applied with vacant oval cartouche within a border of Prince of Wales plumes, London, 1872.   **$125**

COMBINATION DESK RULER and paperweight, engraved in both inch and centimeter measurements, London, 1912, 12 in.   **$375**

DESK BLOTTER, oblong, green leather and moiré silk, the mount pierced and stamped with arabesques of putti and flowers, William Comyns, London, 1908.   **$475**

DESK BLOTTER, oblong, leather and moiré, mount pierced and stamped with flowers, rococo scrolling foliage, and trelliswork and with a scroll cartouche, American.   **$385**

DESK BLOTTER, silver-mounted, green leather, pierced and stamped with rococo flowers and scrolling foliage, London, 1897. **$500**

DESK BLOTTER, silver-mounted, oblong, leather stamped with cherub and arabesque corners with a central vignette of a newlywed couple leaving the church in a coach and horses, with 4 church bells, cherubs' masks, and arabesques, William Comyns, London, 1904. **$600**

DESK CALENDAR, revolving, body enameled in bright blue and applied with crowns, Continental. **$225**

DESK NOTE CLIP, applied with a horseshoe, the mount engraved, London, 1922. **$400**

DESK RULER, sterling silver, engraved in both centimeters and inches, Chester. **$275**

DESK SEAL, formed as a statue of Mercury, sterling silver, Continental, late 19th century. **$175**

DESK SEAL, sealing wax case and vesta combination, engine-turned cylindrical, French, Bointabure, Paris. **$150**

DESK SEAL, white metal, the wooden handle carved with a dog with rabbit. **$275**

DESK SET, 3 pieces, French "Japanese style" parcel gilt, comprising letter opener, seal, and pen handle, decorated in relief with insects and flowers, in lined box, Paris, c. 1880. **$450/set**

ETUI, traveling, tapering shape, bright-engraved with bands of guilloche decoration and zigzag lines, cover opening to reveal an ink compartment with screw-on cover and detachable pen, Joseph Willmore, Birmingham, c. 1800. **$475**

LETTER BOX, leather-and-silver-covered, overlaid with a pierced silver cover of cherubs in clouds with roses, Mauser Mfg. Co., 1877. **$750**

LETTER CLIP, modeled as a seesaw on an oblong tortoise-shell-mounted base, engraved with simulated planks and balanced on a simulated log. **$275**

LETTER CLIP, silver-mounted, heart-shape tortoise shell, London, 1907. **$350**

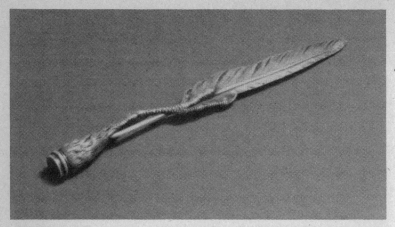

American sterling combination letter knife and table seal, $250. Photo by J. Auslander.

LETTER KNIFE, in the form of a sword, parcel-gilt sheath engraved with scrolls and with chain and loop attached, hilt of sword cast with a lion's head, H.W.D., London, 1873.   **$750**

LETTER KNIFE, with tortoise-shell blade, handle fashioned in the form of a kitten's head, London, 1880.   **$750**

LETTER KNIFE, with tortoise-shell blade, silver handle stamped with 18th-century-style figures, foliage, William Comyns, London, 1892.   **$400**

LETTER KNIFE, Aesthetic Movement, carved ivory handle depicting pair of owls, parcel-gilt scimitar blade engraved with birds, foliage, insects, and sun rising over mountains, all in Japanese taste, 1883.   **$1,200**

LETTER KNIFE, green-stained ivory handle with sterling silver ferrule and mounts stamped with laurel leaves and berries.   **$190**

LETTER KNIFE, Scottish, sterling silver, formed as a saber with openwork cage shield, polished wood handle, steel blade, Edinburgh, 1906.   **$125**

LETTER KNIFE, silver-mounted, with scimitar-shape ebony blade and boar's-tusk handle, mount pierced and chased with rococo flowers, London, 1892, 15½ in.   **$200**

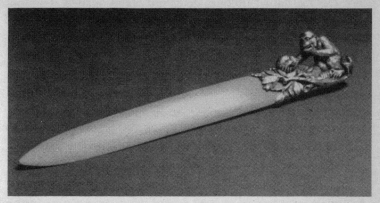

Russian sterling and ivory letter knife, depicting monkey contemplating skull of man, c. 1908, $595. Courtesy of H & H Antiques. Photo by J. Auslander.

LETTER OPENER, novelty, in the form of a saw, London, 1894. **$300**

MAGNIFYING GLASS, desk, sterling silver, the mount pierced and chased with masks and arabesques, Japanese ivory handle carved with 3 apes, William Leuchars, London, 1889. **$1,000**

MAGNIFYING GLASS, large, spiral-fluted pistol handle stamped with foliage and flowers, Birmingham, 1892. **$325**

MAGNIFYING GLASS, silver-gilt, supported by an eagle with outstretched wings, engine-turned handle with beaded and bud terminal, Continental, late 19th century. **$575**

PAPER KNIFE, ivory, with spiral-fluted waisted handle, in a fitted case, London, 1891. **$275**

PAPER KNIFE, sterling silver, the handle and blade engraved with foliate scrolls and set with different-color agates, Mackay & Chisholm, Edinburgh, 1898. **$1,200**

PAPER KNIFE, silver handle stamped with birds and scrolling foliage on a textured ground, London, 1891, 16 in. **$250**

PENCIL, mummy pendant, sterling, Continental, 1930. **$75**

PENCIL, retractable, in the form of a cannon, Sampson Mordan, English, mid-19th century. **$450**

PEN TRAY, crimped oblong, stamped and chased with putti, flowers, and scrolling foliage, London, 1889. **$300**

PEN TRAY, shaped oblong, gadrooned and beaded, London, 1898.   **$225**

PORTFOLIO, silver-mounted leather, having silver plaque repoussé with scrolling flowers amid trelliswork and rocaille scrolls, William Comyns, London, 1898.   **$500**

RULER, sterling silver, folding, 1 foot, engraved in calibrated inches.   **$100**

RULER, sterling silver, folding, 12 in., in sheath with loop attached.   **$250**

SEAL, silver, matrix engraved with initials, Hester Bateman, 1780.   **$110**

SEAL, swivel, with silver-gilt mount chased with scrolls and acanthus leaves and having a faceted citrine handle, 1835.   **$800**

SEAL, William IV, modeled as a man's bare leg, 1833.   **$900**

SEALING WAX SET, pocket size, in oblong box with cover, engine-turned raised goldlike monogram, a baluster form silver-gilt seal, socket (folding) and division for taperstick, sealing wax compartment with striker for matches, Goldsmiths & Silversmiths Co., 1912.   **$775/set**

STAMP BOX, formed as a postcard engraved with a name and postmark, English, late 19th century.   **$250**

STAMP BOX, cylindrical, American, early 20th century.   **$75**

American sterling stamp boxes, c. 1880. **Left. Collection of Nancy and Bruce Thompson. Center. *$125.* Right. *$125.* Photo by J. Auslander.**

English sterling string holder with cutter at top, Birmingham, 1874.
Courtesy of Nancy and Bruce Thompson. Photo by J. Auslander.

STAMP BOX, cylindrical, enameled decoration, Gorham, late 19th century. **$125**

STAMP BOX, full-figure bear, opening to reveal compartments, silverplated, late 19th century. **$350**

STAMP BOX, table size, American, silverplate, with embossed geishas, late 19th century. **$125**

STAMP BOX, table size, Japanese sterling silver with enameled floral sprays. **$375**

STAMP CASE, double-sided, Art Nouveau, embossed flowers, American. **$150**

STAMP CASE, double-sided, engraved "STAMPS," American, late 19th century. **$150**

STAMP CASE, double, oblong envelope shape, engine-turned, English, late 19th century. **$150**

STAMP CASE, envelope form, ribbed, with stone-set clasp, Continental. **$125**

STAMP CASE, envelope form, enameled postage stamps, American, late 19th century. **$150**

STAMP CASE, lid enameled with a 1-penny postage stamp, London, 1890. **$550**

STATIONERY BOX, Art Nouveau, silver-and-red-leather-mounted, oblong, mounts pierced and stamped with flowers and scrolling foliage, Birmingham, 1905. **$625**

STATIONERY BOX, silver-and-leather-mounted, matching desk blotter, each applied with shaped corner mounts and central monogram, William Comyns, London, 1902. **$550/2**

STATIONERY BOX, silver-and-red-leather-mounted oblong, the mounts stamped with cherubs' heads amid clouds surrounded by scrolling foliage, in the style of Angelica Kaufmann, William Comyns, London, 1897. **$800**

STATIONERY BOX, silver-mounted brown leather, matching oblong blotter, mounts stamped with cherubs' heads amid clouds in the style of Angelica Kaufmann, shells and scrolling foliage, William Comyns, London, 1896. **$1,200/2**

STATIONERY FOLDER, silver-mounted red leather, mount pierced and stamped with rococo flowers, foliage, trelliswork, putti, and birds, London, 1905. **$450**

STRING HOLDER, spherical, on ball feet, chased with masks, birds, flowers, and scrolling foliage, William Comyns, London, 1900. **$350**

Resources

Auction Houses

Richard A. Bourne Co.
P.O. Box 141
Hyannis Port, Massachusetts
02647

Butterfield & Butterfield
220 San Bruno Avenue
San Francisco, California
94103

Christie's
502 Park Avenue
New York, New York 10022

Christie's East
219 East 67th Street
New York, New York 10021

Christie's South Kensington
85 Old Brompton Road
SW 7–3LD
London, England

William Doyle Galleries
175 E. 87th Street
New York, New York 10128

Richard Oliver
Plaza 1, U.S. Route 1
P.O. Box 337
Kennebunk, Maine 04043

Phillips
Blenstock House
7 Blenheim Street
New Bond Street
W1Y 0AS
London, England

Robert Skinner, Inc.
Route 117
Bolton, Massachusetts 01740

Wolff's Auction House
1239 West 6th Street
Cleveland, Ohio 44113

Museums

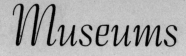

California

Los Angeles City Museum of Art
Los Angeles, California

M. H. deYoung Memorial
Museum
San Francisco, California

Connecticut

Silver Museum
Meriden, Connecticut

Wadsworth Atheneum
Hartford, Connecticut

Yale University Art Gallery
Garvan Collection
New Haven, Connecticut

District of Columbia

Smithsonian Institution
Washington, DC

Delaware

Henry Francis du Pont
Winterthur Museum
Winterthur, Delaware

Georgia

High Museum of Art
Atlanta, Georgia

Illinois

Art Institute of Chicago
Chicago, Illinois

Maryland

Samuel Kirk Museum
Baltimore, Maryland

Massachusetts

Museum of Fine Arts
Boston, Massachusetts

New Jersey

Newark Museum
Newark, New Jersey

New York

Brooklyn Museum
Brooklyn, New York

Cooper-Hewitt Museum
New York, New York

Metropolitan
Museum of Art
New York, New York

Museum of the
City of New York
New York, New York

New York Historical Society
New York, New York

North Carolina

Mint Museum of Art
Charlotte, North Carolina

Pennsylvania

Philadelphia Museum of Art
Philadelphia, Pennsylvania

Rhode Island

Museum of Art
Rhode Island School of Design
Providence, Rhode Island

Texas

Museum of Fine Arts
Houston, Texas

Vermont

Bennington Museum
Bennington, Vermont

Virginia

Chrysler Museum
Norfolk, Virginia

England

Brighton Museum
and Art Gallery
Brighton, England

British Museum
London, England

City of Birmingham Museum
Birmingham, England

Victoria and Albert Museum
London, England

Wallace Collection
London, England

Shows

Brimfield Flea Markets
Brimfield, Massachusetts

Hillsboro Antiques Show
Hillsboro, California

Houston Antique Dealers
Association Show
Houston, Texas

Miami Beach Convention
Center
Miami, Florida

Miami Expo Center
Miami, Florida

New Haven Coliseum
New Haven, Connecticut

New York Annex
26th Street and Sixth
Avenue
New York, New York

Papabello Shows
Cleveland, Ohio

SHA-DOR Baltimore Show
Baltimore Convention
Center
Baltimore, Maryland

SHA-DOR Washington
Armory
Washington, DC

Sideli Boston Antiques
Show
Boston, Massachusetts

Sideli One Day Shows
Boxborough, Massachusetts
Greenwich, Connecticut

Stella New York Pier Shows
New York, New York

The University Hospital
Antiques Show
Philadelphia, Pennsylvania

Westchester Enterprises
Park Avenue Armory
New York, New York

Westchester Enterprises
Shoreham Hotel
Washington, DC

Westchester Enterprises
White Plains Show
White Plains, New York

Winter Antiques Show
New York, New York

Clubs

Cats

Cat Collectors Club
31311 Blair Drive
Warren, Michigan 48092

Compacts

Compact Collectors Club
P.O. Box Letter S
Lynbrook, New York 11563

Inkwells and Inkstands

Society of Inkwell Collectors
5136 Thomas Avenue South
Minneapolis, Minnesota 55410

Pens

Pen Fanciers Club
1169 Overcash Drive
Dunedin, Florida 33528

Trade Publications

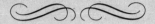

ANTIQUARIAN
Box 798
Huntington, New York
11743

THE ANTIQUE COLLECTOR
National Magazine House
72 Broadwick Street
London, W1V2BP
England

THE ANTIQUE DEALER AND
COLLECTORS GUIDE
Tower House,
Subscription Mgr.
Southampton Street
London WC2E7LS
England

ANTIQUE GAZETTE
929 Davidson Drive
Nashville, Tennessee 37205

ANTIQUE MARKET REPORT
P.O. Box 12830
Wichita, Kansas 67277

ANTIQUE MARKET TABLOID
10822 Child's Court
Silver Spring, Maryland 20901

ANTIQUE MONTHLY
Drawer 2
Tuscaloosa, Alabama 35402

ANTIQUE REVIEW
P.O. Box 538
Worthington, Ohio 43085

ANTIQUE TRADER WEEKLY
P.O. Box 1050
Dubuque, Iowa 52001

ANTIQUES AND AUCTIONS
NEWS
P.O. Box 500
Mt. Joy, Pennsylvania 17552

ANTIQUES AND FINE ART
434 South First Street
San Jose, California 95113

ANTIQUES WEST
P.O. Box 2828
San Anselmo, California
94960

ART AND ANTIQUES
89 Fifth Avenue
New York, New York 10003

ART AND ANTIQUES
WEEKLY
The Newtown Bee
Newtown, Connecticut
06470

ART AND AUCTION
250 West 57th Street
Suite 215
New York, New York

THE BUCKEYE MARKETEER
2256½ Main Street
Columbus, Ohio 43209

CAPE COD ANTIQUES
AND ARTS
P.O. Box 400
Yarmouth Port, Massachusetts
02675

CAPE COD
ANTIQUES MONTHLY
P.O. Box 340
East Sandwich, Massachusetts
02537

COLLECTORS NEWS
Box 156
Grundy Center, Iowa 50638

HOBBIES
1006 South Michigan Avenue
Chicago, Illinois 60605

THE MAGAZINE ANTIQUES
980 Madison Avenue
New York, New York 10021

MAINE ANTIQUES DIGEST
Box 358
Waldoboro, Maine 04572

MASSACHUSETTS
BAY ANTIQUES
9 Page Street
P.O. Box 293
Danvers, Massachusetts 01925

NEW ENGLAND ANTIQUES
JOURNAL
4 Church Street
Ware, Massachusetts 01082

NEW HAMPSHIRE–VERMONT
ANTIQUES GAZETTE
P.O. Box 40
Exeter, New Hampshire 03833

NEW YORK ANTIQUES
ALMANAC
Box 335
Lawrence, New York 11558

THE NEW YORK–
PENNSYLVANIA COLLECTOR
Drawer C
Fishers, New York 14453

RENNINGER'S
ANTIQUE GUIDE
P.O. Box 49
Lafayette Hill, Pennsylvania
19444

SILVER MAGAZINE
P.O. Box 1243
Whittier, California 90609

SOUTHERN ANTIQUES
P.O. Box 1550
Lake City, Florida 32055

SOUTHWEST ANTIQUES
NEWS
P.O. Box 66402
Houston, Texas 77006

TRI-STATE TRADER
Box 90
Knightstown, Indiana 46148

Glossary

Acanthus	Design ornamentation taken from acanthus leaf.
Aesthetic style	A style that became extremely popular in the United States and England in the 1870s and 1880s in Japanese style, which featured fan motifs with parcel-gilt and frosted effects, bright-cut engraving of flowers, foliage, insects, and birds.
Alloy	Two or more metals mixed in molten state.
Alpaca	Name occasionally found on German silver.
Anthemion	Honeysuckle motif used extensively on sterling silver and Sheffield plate during the late 18th and early 19th centuries.
Applied work	Cast decorations that have been soldered to a piece.
Arabesques	Interlocking or woven design of flowers and leafage.
Armorial	Depiction of a coat of arms.
Art Deco (Art Moderne)	Style popular in 1920s and 1930s based on geometric designs.
Art Nouveau	Late-19th-century style based on curvilinear, naturalistic motifs.

Assembled	Manufactured or made by more than one person, as in the case of some sets of flatware; also used to describe one piece composed from two different parts of other pieces.
Bakelite	A plastic form very popular in the 1920s and 1930s.
Baluster	Elongated pear-shaped form taken from the style of supports of stair rails.
Beading	Cast beads, usually in bands, that were applied to rims of trays, compotes, and napkin rings.
Bleeding	Term applied to silverplate or Old Sheffield plate when silverplate is worn through in some areas to the copper.
Bright-cut decoration	An extremely popular form of engraving executed with a shaped graver, used in England and America from 1770 until 1806 and again from 1870 until 1890; flowers, swags, and leafage are gouged to leave a crisp stroke that reflects light.
Brittania standard silver	Refers to .958 quality standard; introduced in England in 1697; compulsory use of this standard was abolished in 1719.
Butler's finish	Surface produced by revolving wire wheel, which makes tiny scratches, giving the object a satiny, dull appearance.
Cable design	Based on twisted-rope motif.

Cartouche	A form to enclose engraving of initials, crest, or armorials, sometimes enhanced with border of shells, leaves, ribbons, or masks.
Caryatid	Figure of woman used as base of object.
Cast	Formed in mold.
Casting	Parts that are produced in molds, such as handles, spouts, finials, and feet, and then applied by soldering.
Chasing	Decoration achieved by moving surface metal into low relief with a punch, whereby no metal is removed; design usually depicts flowers and leafage.
Chinoiserie	Decoration based on Oriental design motifs used on English silver, depicting birds, human figures, and flowers.
Coin silver	900 points silver, 100 points copper; used in the United States prior to the 1861 sterling standard.
Cut card work	Decoration formed by having pieces of silver cut into shape and soldered onto object.
Cutler	Maker of knives and utensils.
Diaperwork	A geometric motif often of diamond shapes filled with patterns.
Die stamping	Raising of decorative elements on sterling silver, often achieved by stamping or rolling designs on sheet silver.
Enameling	Technique used to cover a metal surface with a layer of colored glass.

Engine turning	Decoration achieved by machine, usually a pattern of lines in geometric form.
Engraving	Metal is removed in pattern by means of a sharp pointed tool or graver.
Etching	Surface decoration achieved with acid.
Feather-cut engraving	Bright-cut engraving used on flatware with feather-like motifs at borders.
Festoon	A curved garland of leaves or flowers.
Filigree	Metal wire drawn into ornate designs.
Filled (weighted, loaded)	Pieces made from thin sheets of metal and then filled with pitch, plaster, or cement to add stability; generally used on candlesticks, tall vases, and flatware handles.
Finial	Generally, a cast urn-, flower-, or fruit-shaped object affixed to top of piece.
Flatware	Term used for knives, forks, spoons.
Fluting	Straight or shaped ridges on part or all of piece.
Gadroon	Border decoration of reeds and flutes.
German silver	Also called nickel silver and not really silver but an alloy of nickel, copper, and zinc, often used as base metal for silverplating.

Gilding Coating of a silver object with a thin wash of gold; also known as silver gilt or vermeil.

Gothic A medieval style with arched motifs and strapwork, also an important revival period in the 19th century.

Greek key Classical design used for border decoration.

Grotesque Relief decoration depicting human and animal forms with foliage and scrollwork.

Guilloche enameling Object is first decorated with engine-turned motifs, then enameled so that engine turning shows through the glass.

Hallmark Mark used for English sterling to indicate silver or gold.

Hollow handle Handles made of two halves, with filler, and then soldered together.

Hollowware Hollow objects such as cups, vases, bowls, or centerpieces.

Makers' marks Symbol of individual silversmiths; early American marks are generally initials.

Matting Surface of object is textured by hand-hammering.

Navette Boat shape in outline.

Niello Engraving on silver, which is filled with black enamel or other substances, used in Russia and the Middle East.

Oxidizing Ornamentation emphasized by the application of an oxide, which creates deep shadows by darkening metal.

Parcel gilt	Parts of objects are gilded.
Patina	Lovely gloss or sheen achieved naturally or through years of tarnish and hand-polishing.
Provenance	Origin or derivation of object.
Repoussé	A form of decoration whereby the silver is raised by hammering from the back to form a design in high relief; after shaping, the front is detailed with other tools, and the result referred to as embossing.
Reticulation	Pierced or openwork on hollowware.
Rococo	Ornate curvilinear decoration using scrollwork, shells, and foliage, popular in the reign of Louis XV.
Shagreen	Untanned leather with granular surface from the hides of seals and sharks, used for etuis, lancet cases, and dressing table sets.
Sheffield (fused plate)	Process invented by Thomas Boulsover in 1743, consisting of a thin sheet of silver formed onto one or both sides of a piece of copper so that it appears to be solid silver; first used in Sheffield about 1760; later less expensive electroplating became more popular.
Silverplate (electroplate)	Technique of covering base metal, copper, nickel, or white metal with a layer of silver by electrolysis.
Sterling standard	.925 sterling silver out of 1,000 parts silver with 75 parts copper.

Trademark	Symbol or name of manufacturer on silver.
Trifid	Style in which handles are designed with three points.
White metal (base metal)	Alloy of tin with copper, lead, antimony, or bismuth used as base metal for silverplating.

Bibliography

American Art: 1750–1800, Towards Independence. Catalog of an exhibition, Yale University Art Gallery and Victoria and Albert Museum. Edited by Charles F. Montgomery and Patricia E. Kane. Boston: New York Graphic Society for the Yale University Art Gallery and the Victoria and Albert Museum, 1976.

Banister, Judith. *Old English Silver.* New York: G. P. Putnam's Sons, 1965.

Barr, Lockwood. "Kentucky Silver and Its Makers." *Antiques* 43 (1945): 25–27.

Beckman, Elizabeth D. *Cincinnati Silversmiths, Jewelers, Watchmakers and Clockmakers.* Cincinnati, OH: B. & B. Co., 1975.

Belden, Louise Conway. *Marks of American Silversmiths in the Ineson–Bissell Collection.* The University Press of Virginia, 1980.

Bohan, Peter, and Philip Hammerslough. *Early Connecticut Silver, 1700–1840.* Middletown, CT: Wesleyan University Press, 1970.

Brandon, Sue. *Buttonhooks and Shoehorns.* Shire Publications Ltd., 1984.

Buhler, Kathryn C. *American Silver, 1655–1825, in the Museum of Fine Arts, Boston.* 2 vols. Greenwich, CT: New York Graphic Society for the Museum of Fine Arts, Boston, 1972.

Buhler, Kathryn C., and Graham Hood. *American Silver: Garvan and Other Collections in the Yale University Art Gallery.* 2 vols. New Haven, CT: Yale University Press, 1970.

Burgess, Frederick William. *Silver, Pewter, Sheffield Plate.* New York: Tudor Publishing Co., 1937.

Carpenter, Charles H., Jr. *Gorham Silver, 1831–1981.* New York: Dodd, Mead and Company, 1982.

Carpenter, Charles H., Jr., and Mary Grace Carpenter. *Tiffany Silver*. New York: Dodd, Mead and Company, 1978.

Clarke, Hermann Frederick. *John Coney, Silversmith, 1655–1722*. Introduction by Hollis French. Boston: Houghton Mifflin, 1932.

Clarke, Hermann Frederick, and Henry Wilder Foote. *Jeremiah Dummer, Colonial Craftsman and Merchant, 1645–1718*. Foreword by E. Alfred Jones. Boston: Houghton Mifflin, 1935.

Colman Collection of Mustard Pots. Exhibition catalog. London: Victoria and Albert Museum, 1979.

le Corbeiller, Charles. *European and American Snuff Boxes*. Chancellor Press, 1983.

Currier, Ernest M. *Early American Silversmiths: The Newbury Spoonmakers*. New York: 1929.

———. *Marks of Early American Silversmiths: List of New York City Silversmiths 1815–1841*. Portland, ME: The Southworth-Athoensen Press, 1938; reprinted by Robert Alan Green, 1970.

Darling, Sharon S., and Gail Farr Casterline. *Chicago Metalsmiths*. Chicago: Chicago Historical Society, 1977.

Delieb, Eric. *Investing in Silver*. Corgi, 1970.

———. *Silver Boxes*. Ferndale Editions, 1979.

Delieb, Eric, and Michael Roberts. *Matthew Boulton, Master Silversmith*.

Durbin, Louise. "Samuel Kirk, Nineteenth-Century Silversmith." *Antiques* 94 (1968): 868–73.

Early Connecticut Silver, 1700–1830. Catalog of an exhibition held in conjunction with the Connecticut Tercentenary, 1635–1935. New Haven, CT: Yale University, Gallery of Fine Arts, 1935.

Ensko, Robert. *Makers of Early American Silver*. New York: Author, 1915.

Ensko, Stephen G. C. *American Silversmiths and Their Marks*. New York: 1927.

———. *American Silversmiths and Their Marks II*. New York: Robert Ensko, 1937.

———. *American Silversmiths and Their Marks III* New York: Robert Ensko, 1948.

Fales, Martha Gandy. *American Silver in the Henry Francis du Pont Winterthur Museum*. Winterthur, DE: The Henry Francis du Pont Winterthur Museum, 1958.

―――. *Early American Silver.* New York: E. P. Dutton and Co. Inc., 1973.

Forbes, H. A., John Crosby, Kernan Devereux, and Ruth S. Wilkins. *Chinese Export Silver, 1785–1885.* Milton, MA: Museum of the American China Trade, 1975.

Fredyma, James P. *A Directory of Maine Silversmiths and Watch and Clock Makers.* Hanover, NH: 1972.

Fredyma, John J. *A Directory of Connecticut Silversmiths and Watch and Clock Makers.* Hanover, NH: 1973.

Fredyma, Paul J., and Marie-Louise Fredyma. *A Directory of Boston Silversmiths and Watch and Clock Makers.* Hanover, NH: 1975.

Green, Robert Alan. *Marks of American Silversmiths.* Harrison, NY: Author, 1977.

Grimwade, Arthur G. *London Goldsmiths 1697–1837: Their Marks and Lives.* London: Faber and Faber, 1976; reprinted 1982.

Hammerslough, Philip. *American Silver Collected by Philip H. Hammerslough.* 3 vols. Hartford, CT: Author, 1958.

Holland, Margaret. *Silver: An Illustrated Guide to Collecting Silver.* Cathay Books, 1978.

Hood, Graham. *American Silver: A History of Style, 1650–1900.* New York: Praeger, 1971.

Houart, Victor. *Miniature Silver Toys.* Alpine Fine Arts Collection Ltd., 1981.

Hughes, G. Bernard. *Small Antique Silver.* New York: Bramhall House, 1957.

Hughes, Graham. *Modern Silver.* New York: Crown Publishers, Inc., 1967.

Jackson, Charles. *English Goldsmiths and Their Marks.* Reprint. New York: Dover Publications, 1964.

Jackson, Charles James. *English Goldsmiths and Their Marks: A History of the Goldsmiths and Plate Workers of England, Scotland and Ireland.* 2d ed., rev. London: Macmillan, 1921. Reprint, London: B. T. Batsford, 1949.

―――. *Illustrated History of English Plate.* 2 vols. London: B. T. Batsford, 1911.

Johnson, Eleanor. *Fashion Accessories.* Shire Publications, Ltd., 1980.

―――. *Thimbles.* Shire Publications, Ltd., 1982.

Kirk Sterling—A Complete Catalogue of America's Finest Sterling by America's Oldest Silversmiths. Baltimore: 1956.

Knittle, Rhea Mansfield. *Early Ohio Silversmiths and Pewterers, 1787–1847.* Cleveland, OH: Calvert-Hatch Co., 1943.

Kovel, Ralph M., and Terry H. Kovel. *A Directory of American Silver, Pewter, and Silver Plate.* New York: Crown Publishers, 1961.

Lichten, Frances. *Decorative Art of Victoria's Era.* New York: Bonanza Books, 1950.

Mackey, James. *An Encyclopedia of Small Antiques.* New York: Harper & Row, 1975.

McClinton, Katharine Morrison. *Collecting American Nineteenth Century Silver.* New York: Charles Scribner's Sons, 1968.

Rainwater, Dorothy T. *American Silver Manufacturers.* Hanover, PA: Everybody's Press, 1966.

———. *Encyclopedia of American Silver Manufacturers.* New York: Crown Publishers, 1975.

———. *Encyclopedia of American Silver Manufacture.* 3d ed., rev. Schiffer Publishing Co., 1986.

———, ed. *Sterling Silver Holloware: Gorham Manufacturing Company, 1888; Gorham Martelé, 1900; Unger Brothers, 1904.* American Historical Catalogue Collection. Princeton, NJ: Pyne Press, 1973.

Rainwater, Dorothy T., and Donna H. Felger. *American Spoons: Souvenir and Historical.* Camden, NJ: Thomas Nelson & Sons; Hanover, PA: Everybody's Press, 1968.

Rainwater, Dorothy T., and H. Ivan Rainwater. *American Silverplate.* Nashville, TN: Thomas Nelson; Hanover, PA: Everybody's Press, 1968.

Schwartz, Jeri. *Tussie Mussies: Victorian Posey Holders.* Author, 1987.

Snell, Doris Jean. *Art Nouveau and Art Deco Silverplated Flatware.* Des Moines, IA: Wallace-Homestead Book Company, 1976.

Stutzenberger, Albert. *American Historical Spoons.* Charles E. Tuttle Company, 1971.

Thorn, C. Jordan. *Handbook of American Silver and Pewter Marks.* Preface by John Meredith Graham II. New York: Tudor, 1949.

Turner, Noel D. *American Silver Flatware, 1837–1910.* New York: Barnes, 1972.

Utica Silver. Catalog of an exhibition. Utica, NY: Fountain Elms, Munson-Williams-Proctor Institute, 1973.

Waldron, Peter. *The Price Guide to Antique Silver.* Antique Collectors' Club, 1982.

Watney, Bernard M., and Homer D. Babbidge. *Corkscrews for Collectors.* Sotheby, Parke, Bernet, 1981.

Wyler, Seymour B. *The Book of Old Silver.* New York: Crown Publishers, 1937.

Index